AGENDAS AND INSTABILITY IN AMERICAN POLITICS

Chicago Studies in American Politics
A series edited by Benjamin I. Page, Susan Herbst,
Lawrence R. Jacobs, and James Druckman

AGENDAS AND INSTABILITY IN AMERICAN POLITICS

SECOND EDITION

Frank R. Baumgartner
and Bryan D. Jones

The University of Chicago Press
Chicago and London

BRYAN D. JONES holds the J. J. Pickle Chair in Congressional Studies in the Department of Government at the University of Texas at Austin. FRANK R. BAUMGARTNER is the Bruce R. Miller and Dean D. LaVigne Professor of Political Science at the Pennsylvania State University.

The University of Chicago Press, Chicago 60637
The University of Chicago Press, Ltd., London
© 1993, 2009 by The University of Chicago
All rights reserved. Published 2009
Printed in the United States of America

18 17 16 15 14 13 12 11 10 09   1 2 3 4 5

ISBN-13: 978-0-226-03947-3 (cloth)
ISBN-13: 978-0-226-03949-7 (paper)
ISBN-10: 0-226-03947-1 (cloth)
ISBN-10: 0-226-03949-8 (paper)

Library of Congress Cataloging-in-Publication Data

Baumgartner, Frank R., 1958–
   Agendas and instability in American politics / Frank R. Baumgartner and Bryan D. Jones.—2nd ed.
       p.   cm.—(Chicago studies in American politics)
   Includes bibliographical references and index.
   ISBN-13: 978-0-226-03947-3 (cloth : alk. paper)
   ISBN-13: 978-0-226-03949-7 (pbk. : alk. paper)
   ISBN-10: 0-226-03947-1 (cloth : alk. paper)
   ISBN-10: 0-226-03949-8 (pbk. : alk. paper)   1. Political planning—United States.
2. Policy sciences.   3. United States—Politics and government.   I. Jones, Bryan D.
II. Title.   III. Series.
   JK468.P64B38 2009
   320.60973—dc22

                                                                        2008041084

Contents

List of Illustrations   vii
Preface to the Second Edition   xi
Preface to the First Edition   xiii
Introduction   xvii

Part One: Theoretical Beginnings   1
1   Punctuated Equilibria in Politics   3
2   Policy Images and Institutional Venues   25
3   Studying Agenda Change   39

Part Two: Tracing Policy Change in America   57
4   The Construction and Collapse of a Policy Monopoly   59
5   Two Models of Issue Expansion   83
6   The Dynamics of Media Attention   103
7   Cities as a National Political Problem   126
8   Connecting Solutions to Problems: Three Valence Issues   150

Part Three: Structural and Contextual Change in Politics   173
9   Interest Groups and Agenda-Setting   175
10 Congress as a Jurisdictional Battlefield   193
11 Federalism as a System of Policy Venues   216
12 Governing through Institutional Disruption   235

Part Four: Agendas and Instability, Fifteen Years Later   253
13 Policy Subsystems, Puncuated Equilibrium, and Theories of Policy
    Change   255

Contents

14   Punctuated Equilibrium and Disruptive Dynamics   285

Appendix A: Data Sources   291
Appendix B: Regression Analysis of Agenda Dynamics   307
References   315
Index   331

Illustrations

Figures

4.1 Annual number of articles on civilian nuclear power and percentage of articles coded positive, 1900–1986   65

4.2 Increasing regulatory activities of the AEC/NRC   71

4.3 Increasingly negative tone of congressional hearings on nuclear power   75

4.4 Stock market performances of nuclear utilities versus other indices, 1962–1988   78

5.1 Annual coverage of smoking in the *Readers' Guide* and tobacco consumption, 1900–1986   91

5.2 Congressional hearings on smoking   94

5.3 Annual coverage of pesticides in the *Readers' Guide*   95

5.4 Congressional hearings on pesticides   99

6.1 Shifting topics of pesticide coverage in the *Readers' Guide*, 1900–1987   113

6.2 Changing topics of smoking and tobacco coverage in the *New York Times Index*, 1946–1988   116

6.3 Changing tone of government actions reported in the *New York Times Index* coverage of smoking, 1946–1988   116

6.4 Coverage of automobile safety in the *Readers' Guide* and traffic fatalities, 1900–1986   123

7.1 Articles in the *Readers' Guide* and congressional hearings on urban affairs   130

7.2 Congressional hearings on urban affairs and total federal grants to states and localities   133

7.3 Congressional hearings on urban affairs and federal grants to states and localities, by category   135

7.4   Responses to Gallup Poll question on America's most important
      domestic problems   145
8.1   Congressional and media attention to drug use   154
8.2   Congressional hearings on drug abuse   159
8.3   Congressional and media attention to alcohol abuse   162
8.4   Media attention to child abuse   165
8.5   Four categories of coverage of child abuse in the *New York Times
      Index*, 1900–1988   166
8.6   Congressional hearings on child abuse and *New York Times Index*
      coverage of government action   167
9.1   Trade associations in the United States   178
9.2   Ratio of profit to citizens' groups over time   181
10.1 Congressional hearings on pesticides by type of committee or
      subcommittee holding them, 1950–1988   206
10.2 Congressional hearings on air transportation, 1944–1989   212
11.1 Congressional hearings on intergovernmental relations   220
11.2 Impact of federal grants on state and local spending priorities   224
13.1 Congressional hearings on nuclear power, 1946–2005   258
13.2 *Reader's Guide* stories on civilian nuclear power   263
      A. Number of stories per year
      B. Percent of stories coded pronuclear
13.3 Annual coverage of smoking in the *Reader's Guide*, 1900–2001   267
13.4 Threshold effects in media images   267
13.5 Changing topics of smoking and tobacco coverage in the *New
      York Times Index*, 1946–2001   269
13.6 Government actions against tobacco   273
13.7 Media attention, surgeons' general reports, and government
      actions against tobacco   275
13.8 Congressional attention to urban issues given media attention and
      congressional ideology for Democratic and Republican presidents   282
13.9 Inflation-adjusted budgent authority for income security,
      1947–2007   283
A.1   Coverage of smoking in the *Readers' Guide* and the *New York
      Times Index*   297
B.1   Regression residuals for grants predicted by hearings on urban
      affairs   309

Tables

4.1   Public reactions to nuclear power plants in Texas   62
4.2   Expansion of congressional attention to nuclear power,
      1944–1986   75
4.3   Tracing the demise of a policy subsystem: Venue succession
      for nuclear power   81

6.1   Topic and tone of pesticide coverage in the *Readers' Guide to Periodical Literature*, 1900–1988   112

6.2   Topic and tone of smoking and tobacco coverage in the *New York Times Index*, 1946–1987   115

9.1   Percentages of profit, nonprofit, and citizens' sector groups very interested in different subject areas   183

9.2   Creation dates of environmental groups   187

9.3   Environmental group staff sizes, 1961–1990   187

9.4   Growth in staff size for selected groups and for all groups created before and after 1960   189

10.1   Growth of congressional staff, 1950–1985   198

10.2   Distribution of witnesses on pesticide hearings in Congress, 1900–1983   205

10.3   Venue and tone of congressional hearings on pesticides, 1900–1988   207

10.4   Venue and tone of congressional hearings on drug abuse, 1945–1986   208

10.5   Congressional hearings on drug abuse in two venues before and after 1968   208

10.6   Venue and tone of congressional hearings on smoking and tobacco, 1945–1986   211

13.1   Presidents' comments on nuclear power in their State of the Union addresses, 1946–2005   260

13.2   Topic and tone of tobacco coverage in the *New York Times Index*, 1946–2001   268

A.1   Summary of coding media coverage   293

A.2   Summary of coding congressional hearings   298

A.3   Summary of organization of *Readers' Guide* and *New York Times Index*   302

B. 1   *Readers' Guide* coverage and congressional hearings on urban affairs   310

B.2   Federal grants to states and localities predicted by number of congressional hearings, various categories of urban affairs, 1959–1989   311

B.3   Determinants of congressional hearings on drug abuse, 1945–1986   312

B.4   State investment ratios and the impact of consumption-based federal grants, 1955–1989   313

Preface to the Second Edition

We would like to express our gratitude for the contributions of scores of students to the ongoing research projects that we have conducted since this book was originally published. This ranges from the undergraduate students at Texas A&M, the University of Washington, and Penn State who worked on often tedious tasks of constructing the large databases we have developed to the graduate students (some now tenured professors), many of whom have become our collaborators over the years: Jeff Talbert, Jim True, Mike MacLeod, Tracy Sulkin, Sam Workman, Heather Larsen-Price, Ashley Watson, Michelle Wolfe, Josh Sapotichne, Lars Beer Neilson, and Shaun Bevan. Similarly, many colleagues at our home universities and elsewhere have helped tremendously in discussing ideas, contesting them, or in other ways: Jim Stimson, John Padgett, Jeff Berry, Donley Studlar, Beth Leech, John McCarthy, Peter May, and John Wilkerson. In recent years, we have forged a set of collaborations with colleagues in European universities who have extended and enriched our initial insights developed in pluralistic America to other western democracies. In particular Christoffer Green-Pedersen of Aarhus University in Denmark first saw the benefits of extending our perspectives and measurement strategies to other nations. Finally, we would like to acknowledge the support of Frank Scioli and the Political Science Program of the National Science Foundation, and to our University of Chicago editor over the years, John Trynseki.

Preface to the First Edition

From the beginning of this project in 1988, our ambition has been to write a theoretically based book that would discuss a range of issues quantitatively and comparatively over far longer periods of time than is current practice in political science. Nevertheless, the necessity of serial processing dictated that we began with one issue. In 1988, Texas A&M's Center for Energy and Mineral Resources funded our analysis of the nuclear power industry. That was a sobering experience. We were quickly reminded of the old adage "Fools rush in where angels fear to tread." For us, it was extraordinarily difficult to understand the major issues in the policies we chose and to compare those issues on the indicators we developed. For over two years, we gathered and coded data, simultaneously trying to comprehend the particulars of the policies we had chosen to study and to find ways to compare across issues and over time. We read books and stacks of articles on nuclear power, pesticides, smoking, child abuse, and all the other issues discussed here. Each of us knows many more details and factoids concerning these issues than any normal person would probably be willing to admit. During this time, we also supervised the creation of some very large data files. Readers of appendix A will appreciate our fears during that time that we might simply drown under the weight of it all.

We have been fortunate to have a number of able graduate assistants, however, who have kept the project running smoothly so that we could focus more on the analysis and on refining the intellectual framework. These research assistants include Steven Babalola, Doug Jones, Susanne Marrs, Charles McLemore, William Mitchell, Billy Hall, and Jeff Talbert. Billy Hall and Jeff Talbert remained on to the end and merit particular mention for herculean tasks well performed. Talbert did more than code and collect data, but helped supervise the others and helped develop the methods we report here. His own master's thesis also pushed the approach we developed a bit further.

Since 1989 we have presented papers at a number of conferences based on initial findings from this project. We have benefited from numerous comments from a variety of scholars, most of which, we are happy to report, were helpful, encouraging, and constructive. This was particularly useful, given the strange formulations some of our earlier drafts included. At one conference in Italy, our ideas seem to have been met with something approaching bewilderment, but we like to think that was due to the Alabama accent particular to one of us and the penchant for mumbling that characterizes the other. Less helpful was the rejection of one of our papers after being solicited for an edited volume. That was when we knew we had something important to say. The only trick was to say it in a way that others could understand.

Among those who have provided helpful comments based on those preliminary papers are Jim Anderson, Jeff Berry, Jon Bond, Chris Bosso, Bob Boynton, Roger Cobb, Charles Elder, Jeff Henig, Luigi Graziano, Dave King, Laury King, John Nelson, Jeremy Richardson, Bert Rockman, Bob Salisbury, Mark Schneider, and the late Jack Walker. Each of these people read parts of the book, discussed it with us, and helped us improve it. As is usual in our profession, these people took a lot of time for no reward except intellectual curiosity and these words; we greatly appreciate it. Chapter 4 is a revised version of our "Agenda Dynamics and Policy Subsystems," published in the *Journal of Politics* in 1991. Several anonymous reviewers also gave useful comments.

Three individuals read the entire manuscript very carefully and provided the best set of reviews either of us has ever seen. They focused clearly on the intellectual questions, pushing us to take our ideas about the American political system to a higher plane. These reviews were not only professional and conscientious, but they provided real intellectual challenges. We hope our last revisions and improvements to the manuscript meet at least some of the challenges offered us by Charles O. Jones, John Kingdon, and Clarence Stone.

The Department of Political Science and the College of Liberal Arts of Texas A&M University provided material assistance for which we are grateful. Marcia Bastian provided her usual high level of technical support in producing the tables and figures reported here. We also thank Edna Guillot for assistance throughout the project.

Finally, this has been a collaboration in the closest sense between the two authors. We came to the project with different professional backgrounds: Baumgartner in comparative politics, agenda-setting, policymaking, and interest groups; Jones in American policymaking, urban politics, and political leadership. Baumgartner saw rhetoric and issue definition as important; Jones insisted that the role of institutions had been virtually ignored in agenda studies. What we shared was a distaste for deterministic approaches to the policymaking process. In every aspect of the project, including each chapter of this book, no word has been left that has not been read, revised, and (on occasion) argued over about sixteen times. We did not have a strict division of labor, though on occasion one would take the lead in drafting one chapter while the other drafted another. However, after trading back and forth so many times, we think the final product is truly a joint effort. We of course had to decide a number of technical questions in organizing the data collection effort, and we did that jointly. However, a great part of this collaboration has been sitting with our feet up in one of our offices arguing about the nature of America's political system. Readers will see our joint conclusions in these pages. Listing our names in alphabetical order on the title page is meant to reflect not only an equal division of labor, but a truly joint enterprise.

John Tryneski of the University of Chicago Press has been both an extraordinarily supportive editor and a fine critic, as he commented on both the presentation and the substance of this book.

Introduction

O ver fifteen years have passed since *Agendas and Instability* was published in 1993. We have been very pleased at the reception the book has received in the scholarly and applied policy communities. We also applaud a new vitality in the study of public policy processes, resulting in an outpouring of research in the United States and Europe. An interest in the dynamics of policy characterizes these studies, and *Agendas and Instability* was part of this movement.

In this new edition, we have added a brief introductory chapter that highlights some changes in our thinking about policy dynamics in light of the vigor of the field, a new chapter updating selected subsystems that we traced in the original volume, and a new concluding chapter. We think the reader will find the study of tobacco and smoking particularly instructive, because it illustrates how great policy changes can occur that are easy to interpret within the framework sketched in this book, but that they must overcome great resistance to do so.

The Principal Claims

Our principal claim in this book is that the course of public policy in the United States is not gradual and incremental, but rather is disjoint and episodic. Long periods of stability are interrupted by bursts of frenetic policy activity. These bursts can happen through the mechanism of electoral change, most obviously in so-called mandate elections. Grossback, Peterson, and Stimson (2006) show the profound policy consequences of the mandate elections of 1964, 1980, and 1994.

But this is not what we emphasize here. We stress policy-by-policy change that happens through a very different dynamic. Policymaking at equilibrium occurs in more or less independent subsystems, in which policies are determined by specialists located in federal agencies and interested parties and groups. These interests reach policy equilibrium, adjusting among themselves and incrementally changing policy. But this can be profoundly undemocratic, as McConnell (1967) and Lowi (1979) among others argued, because the public is excluded from the discussion. Lowi's solution was "juridical democracy," basically the imposition of policies from the elected branches of government, which a hierarchical civil service faithfully carries out. All policy change in such a system mostly must happen through elections, and that is how citizens enforce democratic accountability.

Emmette Redford (1969) called this model "overhead democracy." He thought that it was not a sound empirical description of policymaking in America and, moreover, he thought that it was folly to try to impose such a top-down model. He saw an important place for the role of policy experts in the bureaucracy, and he thought that many policy disputes could be adjusted in subsystems in which affected interests got their say.

But Redford also saw that diffuse and newly emergent interests would be underrepresented in such arrangements. These interests, he claimed, "will find their greatest opportunity to challenge existing equilibriums of interest in the macropolitical system" (110). That is, they would "expand the conflict" to draw the attention of the president, the leaders of Congress, and the political parties. These macropolitical actors could act to incorporate these new or underrepresented interests in the policymaking process.

Until we set out to examine subsystem politics over time, the dynamic implications of Redford's theory lay unrecognized, with the sterling exception of the work of Charles O. Jones and his students. At first we did not set out to examine Redford's dynamic; it just leaped out of our studies of the policy subsystems analyzed in this book. Our accomplishment is not in recognizing the macropolitical-subsystem dynamic. Rather we were able to unify the Redford dynamic with the studies of agenda setting and conflict expansion work of Schchattsneider, Cobb and Elder, and Kingdon, thereby tying more traditional studies of public policy and public administration to them. We argued that no model of policy change was complete without an appreciation of the multiple venues of policy activity outside of the confines of the Washington establishment—the states and localities were fundamental parts of the policymaking dynamic. Finally, we saw the implications of the vigorous debate in formal political theory over whether political equilibria could exist. Our answer is yes, but they are partial (that is, they do not incorporate any sort of macropolitical balance), and they are temporary (because newly activated interests could upset them).

Perhaps most importantly, we argued that the Redford dynamic invariably leads to periods of stability and incremental drift punctuated by large-scale policy changes. The simple act of expanding the conflict by involving multiple venues had to destroy equilibria and shift policies dramatically. One did not need to wait for electoral realignments or "mandate elections" to observe punctuated change; it could happen in a single policy arena even when other areas were at stasis. A kind of rolling set of policy-by-policy punctuations could allow for more adaptability and adjustment than would be possible if the system had to rely solely on macrolevel, top-down change.

Of the seven policy subsystems we studied—nuclear power, pesticides, drug and alcohol abuse, smoking and tobacco, automobile safety, urban policy, and child abuse—only one, urban policy, could be clearly and unambiguously tied to partisan politics, although several more were influenced by the macropolitical dynamics swirling around them. Mandate politics and overhead democracy are critical for appreciating policy change, but they are not enough.

The Practical Implications of Policy Punctuations

We wrote this book as an exercise in political science, and were surprised and delighted that it received such a warm welcome among policy practitioners. Among policy activists, our emphasis on temporary equilibria, positive feedback effects, and the potential for rapid change was seen as providing a more optimistic role for individual citizens than the traditional models of impersonal historical trends based on the deep structure of society or large-scale organizations generally impervious to individual effort. James Gustave Speth, dean of the School of Forestry and Environmental Studies at Yale University, used our notion of policy punctuation to inject some analytically based optimism into the gloom that had descended on the environmental community in recent years (at least pre-Gore). In his environmental call to arms, *Red Sky at Morning*, after describing the dynamic explained in this book, he writes, "When the perception of an issue is systematically altered to engage a new and broader audience, perhaps by a crisis or major event, far-reaching change is possible" (Speth 2004, 200). He continues in a separate essay, "If Baumgartner and Jones were right, their thesis offered hope that today's bleak political prospects for global environmental threats might rapidly change, giving way to the sea change of progress on global challenges that we saw on domestic environmental issues in the 1970s" (Speth 2006, vii).

Such optimism in the possibility of change is indeed one implication of our work—so long as one remembers that reversals are not only possible, but are to be expected. Further, all punctuations may not go in the policy direction sought by any particular analyst or activist; some will likely be unwelcome indeed. Our story is evolutionary, and evolution has no sense of purpose. There is no punctuated equilibrium route to inevitable progress.

Recent Advances in the Study of Punctuated Equilibrium

There are two parts to the punctuated equilibrium story, and we have focused in the years since publication of our 1993 book on explaining the forces of stability as well as the causes of change. While the possibility of disruptive change engages many readers and can give hope to policy activists, stability is the rule for most issues most of the time. Our explanation for the stability has been much broader in its focus, much more *psychological* and *sociological*, than the more limited focus on institutional rules that has dominated much of political science in recent years. Institutions matter, but the institutions are embedded in broad social and political environments, and they operate within the limits induced by human cognitive capacity. These factors provide a greater explanation for the stability that structures politics most of the time than any particular institutional arrangement.

Our earlier analysis highlighted the linkages between *institutional* change and *policy* change, a point that escapes any approach that starts with the institutional design of government as a given. Rather than think of governmental institutions as fixed, altered only through some change in formal rules as neo-institutionalists in political science do, we saw them as evolutionary. We had, and still have, little patience with the approach to institutional analysis that misses the complex and exciting evolutionary dynamic that alters institutional structure as well as policy content.

If, however, policy processes were so dynamic, we would need better ways to trace these movements. We began the Policy Agendas Project (http://www. policyagendas.org/) soon after the completion of the first edition of *Agendas and Instability* in order to assemble comprehensive and reliable databases for the study of the evolution of American public policy since the Second World War. In fact, our first (and unsuccessful) proposal for a large-scale data collection project was submitted to NSF in 1993, the same year this book appeared. After an initial rejection based on the grounds that what we were proposing was impossible, we succeeded the following year and since then we have been busy constructing a series of databases about government activities across the entire post-1946 period. This project continues to expand, but its intellectual base is here in these pages, and it has not changed. But we invite students of public policy to make use of these datasets, examining the thesis we put forth here, challenging its premises and outcomes with sound data. Only by challenging and perhaps even destroying knowledge premises does scientific inquiry advance.

In this book, we trace the trajectories of a number of public policies over time, noting how they occasionally were but usually were not the object of much system-level attention. While we have been heartened to see that our findings had some impact on the study of public policy, we and others have wondered whether the particular cases we studied were an appropriate base from which to generalize to the entire political system. After all, we chose them partly because they were widely recognized examples of policy subsystems and because there was a strong secondary literature already existing: good historical studies on which we could rely. In any case, no matter how we had chosen them, *no* group of seven or nine or twenty-nine public policies could reasonably be thought of as a good basis for generalization. For example, we didn't cover defense and foreign policy, and if we had, a single case or two would hardly have covered those areas completely.

Indeed, some researchers in some policy arenas have not found evidence of punctuations (Cashore and Howlett 2007; Givel 2006a; Wood 2006b). We find this gratifying, since some policy areas could be resistant to major change for a very, very long time. If every researcher found major punctuations, then we would lose confidence in the ability of the theory to distinguish large changes from more modest changes in the case material. We have not argued that punctuations are everywhere; we have argued that policies alternate between stability and punctuation. We would be surprised if either stability or drift could last indefinitely, but we cannot say at this stage how often to expect a punctuation. This part of the theory is best tested not by case studies, though these help us understand the processes involved; rather, to know whether the system alternates, one should look at entire distributions of policies as we have done in later work. Since the punctuations are driven by many unrelated factors, their occurrence in a single policy field may not be predicted. Across all fields combined, however, there should be a combination of stability and radical change, not a set of smooth adjustments.

In the years since 1993, we have employed several approaches to the study of policy dynamics, each one different from the more traditional single-case historical treatment that we used in this book. Some of our new findings have addressed issues that could not have been considered with our earlier approach, but none have contradicted the central elements of this book.

Most importantly, the outpouring of studies from scholars in the United States and elsewhere, as well as our own work using the Policy Agendas Project datasets, has convinced us that punctuated dynamics is a very general feature of policymaking. It is not confined to the pluralistic arrangements of American democracy, nor is it confined to subsystem politics. Large-scale policy changes can be associated with electoral changes, or with the subsystem-based dynamics we explore here, or with a general sense of urgency that overwhelms the political system and causes political actors to unite and act in concert to solve a problem that has become extraordinarily salient. It is also the case that such major change is very rare, and most policymaking is stable and incremental most of the time. In the future, we are optimistic that a fuller theory of how these different aspects of policy punctuations operate, and how they interact with one another, will be possible.

Some Notes on a General Theory of Policy Punctuations

The most general test of the punctuated equilibrium theory is one we developed in *The Politics of Attention* (2005). Armed with a comprehensive database of sixty-two categories of spending covering fifty years of history, we simply constructed a frequency distribution of annual changes in the budget, for con-

sistently defined spending categories, over these three thousand plus observations. The result, presented in figure 4.14 of that book, showed a distinctive
shape: a huge bulge of very small changes in spending based on the previous
year's base, relatively few moderate shifts, and a considerable number of tremendous decreases and very large increases.

This distribution is consistent with punctuated equilibrium, but it also could
be generated by other types of processes that involve policy punctuations.
Statistically, the distribution of policy changes reflected in these budgetary
figures is a *power-law*, the same distribution that scientists have observed in
many natural phenomena including the sizes of earthquakes compared to their
frequency, avalanches, forest fires, casualties in wars, the number of links between Web sites, and in other areas (see Barabasi 2005). Power-laws are also
known as Pareto distributions after the sociologist/economist Wilfred Pareto.
Pareto noted that incomes are often distributed in this highly unequal manner,
with a small proportion of individuals' earnings controlling a large proportion
of the total income available.

In our study of budget changes one could similarly state that a small proportion of the budget categories accounted for a tremendous proportion of
the aggregate policy change, with most categories accounting for very small
amounts of change indeed. Similarly, most earthquakes are tiny, but a few account for a tremendous proportion of the overall energy released. Most wars
are small but occasionally tens of millions are killed, hence accounting for
most of the deaths.

All of these distributions have in common some process by which "the rich
get richer" or "one thing leads to another" or an "escalation of conflict"—
concepts of momentum that are so common in everyday speech that all are
familiar with them. Such everyday occurrences are evidence of positive feedback processes that we described in 1993 to be at the heart of the punctuated
equilibrium model.

Our evidence about the prevalence of punctuated equilibrium processes
across all the categories of the entire federal budget in the entire postwar period certainly cannot be criticized for small scope or questionable generalizability. Moreover, these distributions also characterize the budgets of many
other countries and political systems (Jones et al. 2007). On the other hand,
by putting all categories of spending and all years into a single frequency distribution, we gain in comprehensiveness, but we lose in attention to historical
content, the specifics of each policy area, and familiarity to political scientists.
Moreover, we cannot distinguish between general punctuated dynamics and
the particular dynamic of punctuated equilibrium.

The distributional approach, we believe, has great potential to elucidate important characteristics of political systems and we expect to follow-up with
more such studies. However, it is unusual in political science and strikes many
readers as highly abstract. Plus it is *no substitute* for the kinds of careful case

studies that we undertook in this book, and which other scholars have used to show the generality of the specific dynamic of punctuated equilibrium (see True, Jones, and Baumgartner 2007 for a review).

A major technique we introduced in the cases presented in this book was a careful attention to quantitative measurement of policy change. We claim here, and we continue to believe strongly, that the best case studies incorporate both qualitative and quantitative information in their development. We offer our updating of selected cases in chapter 13 as evidence of the potential when quantitative assessment with good data is merged with an appreciation of history and context.

Bounded Rationality as the Underpinning of our Approach

Underlying our work in this book is an understanding of political decision making that is firmly based in *bounded rationality*. That is a term that refers to the failure of people to tally up costs and benefits from a potential decision and then to choose the best course of action (which technically is called "maximizing the potential returns"). Instead, their decision-making procedures are incomplete and driven by severe limits on their attention spans. Political systems, like people, can focus intensely only on a limited number of public policies, which is one major reason that policymaking is invariably assigned to policy subsystems, in the United States as well as across the world.

Over time bounded rationality has become an ever more fundamental component in our thinking. We focus in this book on the incomplete nature of public discussion of the policy issues we studied. Political actors shifted in surprisingly rapid succession from overwhelming enthusiasm for a given technology, industry, or public policy to equally universal criticism. Where was the middle ground? Where is an effort at comprehensive rationality in weighing costs and benefits? In subsequent work we have explored the reasons for this in some detail. Bryan Jones in particular went on a foray into cognitive psychology in his *Reconceiving Decision-Making in Democratic Politics* (1994) and *Politics and the Architecture of Choice* (2001), and the ideas about cognitive limitations on human and institutional decision making that he developed there formed the foundation of the work we have done together since then.

We argue in *The Politics of Attention* that policy stability is a function of two distinct sources. The first is "friction" in the "rules of the game" that make it difficult for any action to take place in a political system. The formal rules that govern policy action require a great deal of energy to overcome—by electing a new party with fresh ideas, for example. Unequal resources among actors can be mobilized to reinforce the strong resistance to change built into the American policymaking system, but these resources are less useful in overcoming friction (Baumgartner et al., 2009). The second source of stability may be found in the cognitive and emotional constraints of political actors—the bounds on their rationality. Because policymaking organizations are composed of human beings, the cognitive and emotional limits on their rational analytical abilities are reflected in these organizations.

The strong force of bounded rationality was emphasized in early work on public policy and budgeting (Wildavsky 1964; Fenno 1966), and these scholars recognized the role of bounded rationality in imposing stability on a potentially chaotic process. What they missed are the implications for longer-run change: these systems were too stable, and were not capable of responding to changing social and economic realities by admitting emergent interests into the process.

This does not deny the role of formal rules, but it does suggest that the neoinstitutional focus on formal rules is quite incomplete. The neoinstitutional perspective is completely based on the analysis of formal rules. Policy change within a set of rules can occur only when the actors within the system change—through elections. To the contrary, we argue that both formal rules and bounded rationality contribute to stability. Both must be overcome to generate policy changes, but political actors can change their minds even absent an election. We show in this book that policy punctuations are possible even without the replacement of recalcitrant policymakers through elections. So paradoxically enough, bounded rationality is responsible both for stability and change. Stability because the rules and routines studied in the early budget studies act to "fix" understandings and ways of operating; change because people occasionally feel an intense sense of urgency that something must be done and proceed accordingly.

Bounded Rationality and the Success of Reframing

The sense of urgency and the consequent political mobilization are often associated with new information or new interpretations and issue definitions of available information, and this is what can lead to major policy changes. One of the reasons why *Agendas* attracted a large audience among policy activists and scholars, we think, is that it explains, in a relatively optimistic tone, that American government is not all gridlock all the time. Occasionally major breakthroughs do take place. Along with two colleagues, Baumgartner followed up on this idea recently in a book-length study of one of the most striking, yet least expected, policy changes in recent history: the decline of capital punishment. In spite of the War on Terror, the Bush presidency, and continued importance of evangelical perspectives on religion, between 1993 and 2007 there was more than a 60 percent decline in the number of death sentences in America, reversing a generation-long trend toward increasing use of the ultimate punishment. Baumgartner, De Boef, and Boydstun (2008) explained this trend as the result of a positive feedback mechanism similar to what was explained in these pages with regard to other remarkable policy reversals. By shifting attention away from the previously dominant frame of morality (where more Americans, by a substantial margin, support an eye for an eye rather than a forgiveness perspective) to one focused on the possibility of bureaucratic error, inefficiency, cost overruns, and the possibility of executing the wrong person, a broad network of advocates upended the debate.

The Decline of the Death Penalty and the Discovery of Innocence tells a remarkable story of the impact of positive feedback and framing on a major, and unexpected, policy reversal. One of the most striking elements of this story is how the positive feedback process propelled a group of marginalized citizens into some substantial policy success. Who is more marginalized than death row inmates, after all?

Before one concludes on an overly optimistic assessment about the possibility of policy change no matter what the odds, a reality check is in order. The reemphasis on the death penalty as a mechanism of both the expression of moral outrage and crime control in the 1970s was itself a reversal of a long-term trend from the 1930s, and a relatively abrupt one at that. The current increasing disfavor of the approach is itself a "reversal of a reversal," reinforcing what we said earlier: there is no punctuated equilibrium process leading toward inevitable progress. That holds whatever side of the death penalty debate one comes down on.

Occasionally, as the study of the death penalty shows, the stars can align so that surprising policy shifts can come about, and when they do come about the momentum associated with these changes can be so powerful that dramatic policy reversals result, just as we described in 1993. But is this very common? Baumgartner was involved in another project to try to assess that, along with colleagues Jeff Berry, Marie Hojnacki, Beth Leech, and David Kimball. They interviewed 315 lobbyists, advocates, and policymakers in Washington, DC, asking them about their activities on a randomly selected group of ninety-eight policy issues. With a large number of policy issues covering all areas of American government, and with personal interviews focusing on how the advocates were attempting to frame the issue, this team was able to assess just how often efforts to reframe debates were successful. Not very often. They found that lobbyists were constantly *trying* to spin the issues, but that they were usually held in check by some powerful forces including: (1) the scarcity of attention; (2) the activities of their rivals, who countermobilized in the face of serious threats; and (3) the shared and highly complex understandings of the public policy consequences of any proposed changes. If the *public* discussion of most policy issues is highly simplified most of the time, the *professional* understanding of Washington-based public policies is sophisticated indeed. Across the ninety-eight cases they studied, the status quo policy remained in place over 60 percent of the time, even four years later. The number of cases where one would say a significant redefinition occurred was about 5 percent (see Berry et al. 2007).

Looking over long periods of time, we observe that many issues show periods of stability interspersed with occasional large shifts in public understandings and public policy directions. Looking at a cross section of many issues over a shorter period of time, we observe that most issues see little or no policy change. However, even in the cross-sectional study Baumgartner and colleagues conducted, they found that when policy did change, it tended to change dramatically. Further, if about 5 percent of the cases on which lobbyists are active are reframed within a four-year period, this corresponds with much higher levels of reframing, and policy punctuations, when the analysis covers several decades.

In any case, the more recent study puts the emphasis on the causes of stability in politics, not so much the causes of change. Stability comes from many sources. Two of the most important are the crush of other issues that are constantly competing for space on the public agenda and the shared understandings of the complexity of public policy that characterize the professional communities of policy experts that surround virtually all public policies in America. These insights correspond with what we wrote in these pages in 1993 but give greater weight and empirical evidence to them.

Comparative Public Policy

Our various strategies for investigating the ideas we developed in these pages from different approaches are not limited to what we describe above. We both are actively collaborating with a large (and growing) network of scholars in many countries to recreate the databases of the policy agendas project so that we can conduct the same types of analyses elsewhere as we have been able to do for the U.S. federal system. Results from Britain, Canada, Denmark, France, Spain, Italy, Switzerland, Belgium, the Netherlands, plus the European Union and the State of Pennsylvania, are of course not all yet available. However, initial findings from many different countries and political systems suggest that many of the characteristics we have observed in the United States are not peculiar to that system by any means. Budgetary allocations follow a power-law wherever we have explored the question. Governmental activities have become ever-more complex. Jurisdictional boundaries have grown heavier with overlap and complication. Issues have surged onto the public agenda unexpectedly. Policy framing matters everywhere. Comprehensive rationality in the context of modern parliamentary government is as impossible as it is in pluralist, federated ones. We look forward to a series of studies that will explore these and similar questions in great empirical and historical detail. For the first time, a truly comparative approach to the study of policy development, across all policy activities of western democracies, will be possible.

We started this discussion over fifteen years ago with a review of the historical development of a number of public policies in the United States in the period following World War II. It has been gratifying to see how far we have come in exploring the implications of these ideas in the years since then. Extensions have been built from the methodological approach we developed in these pages; for example, in establishing comprehensive databases of *all* government activities rather than those surrounding any single policy issue, the basis of the analysis in *Agendas and Instability*. Research methods, computer technology, and research opportunities have developed at a rapid pace.

Consider, for example, that when we started looking at the creation of our databases in 1993 we worked from written paper copies of human-coded abstracts. Comprehensive electronic archives of government activities are now the rule, vastly increasing the scope of feasible research projects. These are exciting developments and promise to continue to build a better theoretical understanding of how policies change. These new techniques have led to modifications, elaborations, and extensions of the arguments presented in this book, but we believe that they provide considerable evidence for the book's fundamental arguments. Policy evolution is disjoint and episodic; much major policy change occurs outside the course of electoral politics; resistance to change is not solely a function of conservative rules of the game and the resources of the actors; it has its roots in the cognitive and emotional architectures of people. While it was not possible to revisit all the subsystems we examined, we have written a new chapter updating a number of our empirical studies on nuclear power, smoking, and urban affairs and reviewing some of the theoretical issues we have raised here, reflecting recent scholarship. We look forward to seeing how much further the next fifteen years will push the literature down the road of studying policy dynamics.

PART ONE

Theoretical Beginnings

We propose a punctuated equilibrium model of policy change in American politics, based on the emergence and the recession of policy issues from the public agenda. During periods when issues emerge, new institutional structures are often created that remain in place for decades, structuring participation and creating the illusion of equilibrium. Later agenda access can destroy these institutions, however, replacing them with others. In our first three chapters, we outline the theoretical focus that drives the research. First, chapter 1 discusses agendas and instability in politics. Chapter 2 discusses the importance of how issues are portrayed and which institutions have jurisdiction over them. The interaction of these two forces drives the punctuated equilibrium mechanism we describe. Finally, chapter 3 describes our quantitative and empirical approach to the study of policy change in America, comparing our approach with those of others.

1

Punctuated Equilibria in Politics

Does the American political system provide safe haven for privileged economic interests, or does it ensure competition among political ideas, constantly providing opportunities for those on the losing side of the political debate to reverse their fortunes? Is it conservative, resisting change through the complex institutions of separated powers and federalism, or does it provide numerous opportunities for policy entrepreneurs to try out new ideas? Do mass publics influence elite behavior, or do elites govern with little democratic accountability?

These are among the great questions of democratic theory endlessly debated by political scientists. In this book we show why both sides of each of these rhetorical questions have merit, but not at the same time and in the same place. We develop a model to account both for long periods of stability and domination of important policy areas by privileged groups of elites, and for rapid change in political outcomes, where apparently entrenched economic interests find themselves on the losing side of the political battle.

Many areas of the American political and economic system appear to provide continuing benefits to the same group of privileged elites, with few signs of change. Such arrangements have carried many different labels: policy subsystems; islands of functional power; systems of limited participation; iron triangles; power elites. Each of these terms suggests a structural arrangement that benefits elites. But these descriptions have been incomplete. Two things have been missing from descriptions of elite privilege. First, the manner in which ideas undergird these arrangements is seldom analyzed. Second, the longer-run fragility of these arrangements has often escaped students of the policy process.

In this book, we describe the conditions that often lead to the creation of policy monopolies—structural arrangements that are supported by powerful ideas.]This subject has received much attention in political science. We also discuss the dynamics of decay in such systems, a topic that has received scant attention. Finally we address the conditions under which policy monopolies fail to form, that is, when other patterns of politics emerge. This is particularly common in large-scale policy problems where the political parties and major social groups disagree on potential solutions. We argue that all of these processes can be understood with reference to a single model of the political process, the agenda-setting model.

We show how the agenda-setting process implies that no single equilibrium could be possible in politics, and how the generation of new ideas makes many policy monopolies unstable in the long run. As disadvantaged policy entrepreneurs are successful in convincing others that their view of an issue is more accurate than the views of their opponents, they may achieve rapid success in altering public policy arrangements, even if these arrangements have been in place for decades. They need not alter the opinions of their adversaries; as new ways of understanding old political problems take hold, different policymakers and governmental institutions suddenly begin to claim jurisdiction over issues that previously had not interested them. The old policymaking institutions find themselves replaced or in competition with new bodies that favor different policy proposals. So agenda-setting has important policy consequences, and these are expected often to be dramatic reversals rather than only marginal revisions to the status quo. In the end, we depict a political system that displays considerable stability with regard to the manner in which it processes issues, but the stability is punctuated with periods of volatile change. Hence any study of the dynamics of American political institutions must be able to account for both long periods of stability and short, violent periods of change—again, with respect to the processing of issues, not in the basic constitutional framework.

In this book, we adopt an empirical focus, studying a number of important public policies over long periods of time. We compare the development of issues both over time and across areas, and we demonstrate the forces that create both incrementalism in many circumstances and rapid changes in others. We gather a broad range of both quantitative and qualitative information in order to demonstrate the validity of a single model of the policy process and of agenda-setting that can explain both stability and rapid change, since we believe that both of these features are important characteristics of how policies are made in the United States.

Governance and Agendas

Pluralist works such as those by Truman, or even Madison, have tended to assume that the mobilization of one group will lead to the countermobilization of another. In this book, we note some important instances where countermobilizations have occurred. As a description of the entire system of policymaking, however, this view is misleading. Major political decisions affecting the political system for decades to come are often made in the absence of countermobilization. Rather, waves of enthusiasm sweep through the political system as political actors become convinced of the value of some new policy. They create the institutions to pursue the policy, often in the absence of serious opposing voices. The political system may later settle into a period of incrementalism surrounding a new point, but we should not mistake this incrementalism for evidence of a true political equilibrium. Rather, it may be a structure-induced equilibrium, that is, one that relies on the continued power of certain political institutions (see Shepsle 1979). In the agenda-setting process, however, these institutional jurisdictions may be manipulated by strategic entrepreneurs (see Riker 1980). Thus, the same processes that create incrementalism in many areas of the economy may also create the opportunities for dramatic change.

One strong critique of the countermobilization thesis has been voiced by Grant McConnell (1967) and Theodore Lowi. Lowi (1979) decries the tendency of modern American pluralism to degenerate into "islands of functional power" (Sayre and Kaufman 1965) seemingly immune from popular control. Many political scientists have focused on the problem of differential intensities of preference in society and the consequent likelihood of preferential treatment for intense minorities over the public interest. This has particularly been a theme in studies of the policy process, where studies focusing on iron triangles, policy subsystems, and policy networks have long dominated. Such "policy monopolies" are indeed powerful. But they are also fundamentally unstable, as we argue in the coming pages.

To date, the study of policy subsystems has not been integrated with agenda-setting models. John Kingdon (1984) has developed an approach to the study of agendas that separates problems, solutions or policies, and opportunities, and analyzes the conditions under which all three "streams" come into phase. Kingdon provides a "close-up" view of the infusion of new ideas into the policy process and is convincing in his arguments that problems and solutions ought be analyzed separately in order to understand governmental decision-making. At the systems level, however, agenda-setting is part of the same process of policymaking that produces stability in other cases. New policies are not continually adopted because many are simply variants on a theme that has been pursued in the past. When a general principle of policy action is in place, policymaking tends to assume an incremental character. When new principles are under consideration, the policymaking process tends to be volatile, and Kingdon's model is most relevant.

The American governmental structure is highly disaggregated. American public policy is primarily the sum of many actors in numerous "decision-making systems organized around discrete programs and issues" (Thurber 1991, 319). Each of these decisional systems may be characterized by domination by a single interest, by competition among interests, or by disintegration (Meier 1985). But each characterization is a snapshot of a dynamic process. Moreover, this process may be affected by either positive or negative-feedback at any of these points in time. When a system is subject to negative feedback, an initial disturbance becomes smaller as it works its way through time. In positive feedback, small disturbances become amplified, causing major disruptions as they operate across time. As Meier (1985) notes, these systems can be linked in complex networks, with events in one affecting events in another.

Policy subsystems are continually being created and destroyed in American politics. When they are strong, they may be able to enforce a conservative and incremental process. As they are being created or destroyed, however, changes can be dramatic and self-reinforcing. In sum, the American political system is a mosaic of continually reshaping systems of limited participation. Some are strong, others are weak; some are being created, and others are being destroyed at any given moment. These processes ride a longer wave of secular change that favors some ideas at some particular times, and therefore some policy monopolies, over others. Indeed, it has been assumed by some that the more open modern era of American politics, inaugurated by the 1960s, is inhospitable to policy monopolies. Yet a closer look suggests that many groups find niches within the governmental structure (Browne 1990). Nonetheless, it is not enough just to look at the "creative destruction" of policy monopolies; we must also examine the historical factors that make them possible at some times and infeasible at others.

Policy Monopolies

Every interest, every group, every policy entrepreneur has a primary interest in establishing a monopoly—a monopoly on political understandings concerning the policy of interest, and an institutional arrangement that reinforces that understanding. Nobody likes protracted conflict and continual competition. Much preferable to a system of constant conflict is one where each side retreats into a given area where its influence is uncontested. Obviously, convincing others that one group should be granted such a monopoly of influence may not be easy. However, policy monopolies abound in every political system. Experts in all areas spend much of their time convincing others that "outsiders" are not qualified to make decisions in a given area. This is usually accomplished by arguing that the questions to be decided are highly complex technical matters, that the decisions being made have few social impacts, or that those social impacts are neutral or unavoidable. So bankers claim their lending practices are based on neutral rules, doctors argue that accepted medical practices give them a clear guide on complex issues of life and death, and the military argues that it can be the best judge of the nation's defense needs. Of course any "outsider" who dared question the judgments of the profession-als in any of these areas would meet the hostility, indignation, and resentment of the experts who feel that they are the only ones knowledgeable enough to decide such things. Clearly, everyone wants a policy monopoly. Equally clearly, many groups have them, or have had them in the past.

[Policy monopolies have two important characteristics. First, a definable institutional structure is responsible for policymaking, and that structure lim-its access to the policy process. Second, a powerful supporting idea is asso-ciated with the institution.] These buttressing policy ideas are generally con-nected to core political values which can be communicated directly and simply through image and rhetoric. The best are such things as progress, par-ticipation, patriotism, independence from foreign domination, fairness, eco-nomic growth—things no one taken seriously in the political system can con-test. If a group can convince others that their activities serve such lofty goals, then it may be able to create a policy monopoly. Once such positive under-standings of public policy questions come to be accepted, government offi-cials move to foster the development of the industry or practice involved. Of course the government is interested in fostering economic growth, in indepen-dence from foreigners, in high-quality education, in bringing "drug kingpins" to justice, and in a host of other things. The trick for policymakers is to con-vince others that their policy, program, or industry represents the solution to one of these long-standing policy problems (see Kingdon 1984).

Political scientists have studied what we have termed policy monopolies in a variety of settings and have used several different terms for the phenomenon, including *iron triangles, policy whirlpools,* and *subsystem politics* (Griffith 1939; Redford 1969). All have stressed the lack of interference by broader political forces in subsystems, and deference to the judgments of experts. None, however, has stressed the importance of positive images in supporting the system of deference and noninterference.

Constructing a positive image, then, is closely related to the creation of a policy monopoly, as government institutions are created or redesigned to pro-mote the activity. Those most closely involved in promoting the industry nat-urally come to play a key role in establishing government policy. Participation in a policy monopoly is structured by two things: the formal or informal rules of access discourage the participation of "outsiders," and the prevalent under-standings of the policy are so positive that they evoke only support or indiffer-ence by those not involved (thereby insuring their continued noninvolve-ment).

The dilemma of differential intensities of preference is that those with a vested interest in a given policy area will always be more active than those with nothing to gain. Agenda-setting is concerned with the question of whether those with only a single vested interest are able to dominate policy-making in their area, or whether a broader range of actors becomes involved; it is therefore a fundamental question in a democracy. A policy monopoly is a system where intensities of preference work as Madison feared they might. Behind a wall of institutional arrangements designed with their help, and with a public or an official image also created by their own efforts, some policy experts enjoy tremendous freedom of action, seldom being called upon to justify their actions in terms of broad public accountability.

While concerned policymakers often strive toward the establishment of policy monopolies, such a state of affairs is remarkably difficult to sustain in the open American political system. As a consequence, many policy subsystems are incomplete policy monopolies. The classic tight subsystem was described by Maass (1951) in his study of river projects in 1949. Maass reports unity of interests in the subsystem, with the Army Corps of Engineers, congressional committees, local political actors, and major interest groups all collaborating toward the end of developing local river projects. However, Redford reports a far less tidy subsystem for civil air regulation in the late 1950s, even though participants were generally unified in their outlook on the role of government in maintaining and promoting the nation's air transportation system (1969, 99–102; see also 1960). By the mid–1970s, Heclo discerned a tendency for subsystems to broaden into "issue networks," loose collections of interested parties that often disagreed about the development of policies (1978).

This discussion makes clear that there must be a dynamic associated with the various attempts to construct and undermine policy monopolies. Destruction of policy monopolies is almost always associated with a change in intensities of interest. People, political leaders, government agencies, and private institutions which had once shown no interest in a particular question become involved for some reason. That reason is typically a new understanding of the nature of the policies involved. Where proponents claim that a practice serves only to promote equality and fairness, two widely shared goals in America, opponents may argue that in fact it harms the environment, leads to profits for foreign investors, is a waste of taxpayer resources, or something else. Any given policy usually could be associated with many contending images, so logically these may change over time, and in fact the dominant public understandings of many public issues have often changed in the past. In the wake of crumbling public images, policy monopolies that were constructed behind their shield have often weakened or even disintegrated.

Simply because a disadvantaged interest proposes a new interpretation of events and attempts to attract the attention of allies in other areas of the political system does not mean that those challengers will be successful. The advantaged fight back, attempting to reinforce their original view of the situation. And there is no reason to assume that those originally favored by the political system will not be able to use their superior resources and political connections to their advantage. On the other hand, all disadvantaged actors are not small and defenseless. Often monopolies are broken up by the intrusion of powerful groups from other areas of the economy. As the economy grows ever more complex, interactions among previously distinct groups become more common. Increasingly, these lead to jurisdictional battles between powerful groups on both sides. Even where a political battle pits economically powerful Goliaths against much poorer Davids, the victory of Goliath is not to be taken for granted. The skills and resources useful in private negotiations may not be the same as those useful in public debates. Technical expertise, inside contacts, and legal skills may prove to be of no value where an emotional public media campaign is waged. So if a challenging group is able to choose an arena where its special skills are reinforced and where the skills and resources of its opponents are rendered useless, then it may win. It is possible in some cases, therefore, for the weak to upend the strong. These reversals in fortune are by no means to be taken for granted, but they do occur from time to time.

When looked at during a particular time, a political system may appear to offer many havens to favored economic interests, safe in their well-insulated monopolies. Fifteen years later, however, many of those interests may have been replaced, even though the system as a whole may still feature many monopolies. The destruction or creation of policy monopolies may be much faster than people realize, so the cumulative impact of the continual, but sporadic, creation and destruction of policy monopolies may be that a competitive and pluralistic political system is much less conservative than it sometimes appears.

Agenda-Setting and Equilibrium

Models of policymaking are generally based on the twin principles of incrementalism and negative feedback. Incrementalism can be the result of a deliberate decisional style as decision makers make limited, reversible changes in the status quo because of bounds on their abilities to predict the impact of their decisions (Lindblom 1959; Hayes 1992). For example, new budgets for agencies are generally based on the previous year's allocation (Wildavsky 1984). Incremental changes in political systems can also be the result of countermobilization. As one group gains political advantage, others mobilize to protect themselves. In such situations, mobilizations are subject to a negative-feedback process in which changes from the current state of the system are not large.

Both forms of change, one deliberate and the other inadvertent, result in a self-correcting system. If deliberate incremental decisions characterize policymaking, then decisions that lead to undesirable consequences can be reversed. Hence deliberate incrementalism allows a system to maintain a dynamic equilibrium with its environment. Similarly, a democratic system that allows groups to mobilize and countermobilize will display dynamic equilibrium. When the system veers away from balance, it corrects itself, always tending toward an equilibrium between the demands of democratically organized interests and the policy outputs of government. This view of a political system at balance is quite conservative, since it implies that dramatic changes from the status quo are unlikely.

Even a casual observer of the public agenda can easily note that public attention to social problems is anything but incremental. Rather, issues have a way of grabbing headlines and dominating the schedules of public officials when they were virtually ignored only weeks or months before. Policy action may or may not follow attention, but when it does, it will not flow incrementally. In the scholarly literature on agenda-setting, incrementalism plays little role. Rather, focusing events, chance occurances, public-opinion campaigns by organized interests, and speeches by public officials are seen to cause issues to shoot high onto the agenda in a short period.

Herbert Simon has noted that such intermittent performance characterizes certain classes of social systems. In such cases, "the environment makes parallel demands on the system, but the system can respond only serially" (Simon 1977, 157). That is, the system is grappling with a great number of real, tangible, problems, but its leaders can attend to them only one at a time. In such situations, just how problems capture the attention of policymakers is critical. The intermittent nature of high-level attention to a given problem builds into our system of government the possibility not only of incrementalism, but also of periodic punctuations to these temporary periods of equilibrium.

Why have students of the policy process so often ignored the nonincremental nature of the allocation of attention to problems in political systems? There are two reasons. First is the traditional division of labor among scholars. Those who have studied policy implementation typically have not emphasized the dramatic changes that often occur in the public agenda, and those who focus on the agenda often discount the strong elements of stability or incrementalism present in other parts of the policy cycle. Second is a tendency among some to view the disruptive acts of agenda access as political penumbra, either symbolic events designed to reassure the mass public (Edelman 1964) or as furious activity that fails to solve problems (Downs 1972). Taking a broader view of the policy process forces us to consider seriously both the politics of negative feedback and the processes of agenda-setting that lead to dramatic change. In this book, we show that both of these processes are at work simultaneously in American politics, and that they interact to produce long periods of relative stability or incrementalism interrupted by short bursts of dramatic change. Far from being penumbra, these bursts alter forever the prevailing arrangements in a policy system.

In the pluralist model of countervailing forces in the political system, "potential groups" mobilize when their interests are threatened (Truman 1951, 30). In the absence of artificial or legal barriers to organization and lobbying, social and professional groups can be expected to protect themselves, as the invisible hand of action and reaction produces a sort of equilibrium in politics just as the invisible hand of the marketplace does in economics. While few accept these notions of unfettered organization these days, especially after Olson's (1965) discussion of the inherent advantages of certain kinds of groups over others in generating the support needed to mobilize effectively, perceived threats do indeed produce increased mobilization in many cases (see Hansen 1985).

The most significant criticisms of the pluralist approach have focused on bias in the mobilization of interests. As E. E. Schattschneider wrote over thirty years ago, "The flaw in the pluralist heaven is that the heavenly chorus sings with a strong upper-class accent" (1960, 35). He noted that the essence of political conflict is the scope of participation. Because in any given issue there are always more people disinterested than those involved, competition between winners and losers in the original policy dispute gives incentives for the losers to enlarge the scope of conflict. For Schattschneider, enlargement of the scope of political conflict was essential to the democratic process. This insight remains central to all studies of agenda-setting, since it raises the question of the motivations of those seeking to put something on the public agenda or to keep something from reaching it. Roger Cobb and Charles Elder (1983) continued this line of inquiry by noting the mechanisms by which policymakers attempt to expand the sphere of participation in a given policy dispute.

Much of recent agenda research has centered on the question of where policy ideas come from. John Kingdon (1984) reinvigorated agenda research with his study of the genesis of policy ideas and the exploitation of "windows of opportunity" by policy entrepreneurs. Milward and Laird (1990), reviewing five cases of agenda-setting, found that issue definition, policy knowledge, and opportunity interacted to yield agenda success.

The question "Where does policy come from?" is interesting but misleading. There is generally a surfeit of policy ideas in society. However, alternatives are structured out of politics by the existing "winners" in the policy process, who fuse their policy to strong symbols: progress, national identity, economic growth, and so forth. New alternatives often reach the decision making stage through fresh definitions of old issues (Baumgartner 1989; Stone 1989). "Losers" can often redefine the basic dimension of conflict to their advantage, thereby attracting previously uninvolved citizens. The issue-definition perspective, then, ties the role of Schattschneider's notion of conflict expansion to the content of the ideas coming into the political system.

Neglected in this line of thought are the policy consequences of agenda-setting. What happens when new ideas become the prevailing wisdom in a policy community? Understandings of important public policy issues have clearly changed over time. As these understandings have been altered, so policy processes and policy outcomes have changed as well. We focus here on these links, tracing the effects of change in policy understandings when these occur. We also note that agenda status changes over time. Some issues are high on the governmental or public agenda at one time, then recede from it later. Issue definition and agenda-setting are related, because changes in issue definition often lead to the appearance of an issue on the public agenda. We take these studies as our starting point and focus here not on the reasons for these changes, but on their consequences.

Focusing on consequences directs our attention to institutional structures. All political institutions channel conflict in a particular way; all are related to the mobilization of bias. Noting the structure of bias inherent in any set of political institutions not only shows who is advantaged, however; it also shows what changes might come about from destruction or alteration of an existing arrangement. Those left out of the original system may not be heard there, but if the structures are changed, then dramatic changes in the mobilization of bias may result. Institutional structures in American politics are generally not easy to change, but when they do change, these changes often lead to dramatic and long-lasting changes in policy outcomes. So institutions play an important role in this analysis, since they make possible a system of periods of relative stability, where the mobilization of bias is structured by a set of institutions that remain stable for some period. However, these periods of stability may be linked by periods of rapid change during which the institutional framework is challenged. Because of this, incremental changes are less important than the dramatic alterations in the mobilization of bias during these critical periods. The result is that the American political system lurches from one point of apparent equilibrium to another, as policymakers establish new institutions to support the policies they favor or alter existing ones to give themselves greater advantage.

Searching for Equilibrium

Political science is the study of how political preferences are formed and aggregated into policy outputs by governments. Obviously the institutions of government are complex, so how preferences are aggregated by these institutions is not easy to determine. It would be nice if we could isolate the great forces acting on democratic policymaking and show that these forces reach equilibrium at some point. That is the way classical physics worked. That is the model economics has followed. Indeed, the search for equilibria and partial equilibria has been touted as the cornerstone of the scientific approach, because systems at or near equilibrium are well behaved and amenable to causal analysis (Riker 1980; see also Bentley 1908).

At equilibrium, a system of democratic policymaking would be stable in two senses. First, its essential features would not change significantly, and, second, should a force push the system away from equilibrium, it would move back toward equilibrium over time. A system can remain relatively unchanging over an extended period of time and not be at equilibrium if external forces are sufficiently weak, so one should not equate stability with equilibrium under all circumstances. If a system is not at equilibrium, even minor shifts in inputs may lead to dramatic changes in outputs. Since the behavior of systems at equilibrium is much easier to understand and to predict than systems without equilibrium, scholars have been drawn to them. However, equilibria may be less common in politics than is often thought. Systems that are not at equilibrium show greatly ranging behaviors that are not easily predictable. However, if we hope to understand them we must grapple with the causes and the consequences of their inherent instability.

Political scientists have undertaken two grand initiatives that attempt to establish the existence of equilibria in politics. These are, first, social choice theory and, second, group theory and pluralism. Social choice theory takes individual preferences as fixed and examines how they are combined to yield collective choices. In *Liberalism against Populism,* William Riker (1982) provides a survey and critique of the social choice approach. Riker's critical point is that social choice theorists have demonstrated conclusively that equilibria are rare in politics; indeed, they may not exist at all. Most fundamentally, any voting scheme is unstable with three or more voters in two or more dimensions of conflict. This is the well-known paradox of voting, first analyzed by the French mathematician Concordet in the late eighteenth century and rediscovered by Duncan Black in the 1950s. In the three-voter, two-dimension situation, there is no policy (made up of levels from the two dimensions of conflict) that guarantees equilibrium. That is, there is always another point which can attract more support than the status quo. After reviewing much of the literature in social choice, Riker concludes: "And what we have learned is simply this: Disequilibrium, or the potential that the status quo be upset, is the characteristic feature of politics" (1980, 443).

Considering that equilibrium outcomes could not be assumed even for small groups making decisions, models of how the complex institutions of government collectively generate public policies could not possibly be at equilibrium. In any situation where voting matters, stability is dependent on the dimensions of conflict present, on the order in which decisions are made, on the number of alternatives considered at the same time, on how alternatives are paired if choices are made in sequence, on the number of voters taking part in the decision, and on a variety of other characteristics that are not related to or affected by the distribution of the preferences of those making the decision. In such a situation, strategic entrepreneurs can manipulate the voting situation to achieve their objectives, even if they cannot change the preferences of those making the decision. Most importantly, any time political actors can introduce new dimensions of conflict, they can destabilize a previously stable situation. Since this often can be done, any stability is not necessarily indicative of equilibrium (Riker 1982; see also 1980, 1983, 1984, and 1986).

Since political stability is contingent on the actions of political entrepreneurs, any hope of establishing conditions of political equilibrium must be found at the institutional level (see Shepsle 1979). But even here, equilibrium is not guaranteed, since institutions can be changed. "Institutions are no more than rules and rules are themselves the product of social decisions. . . . One can expect that losers on a series of decisions under a particular set of rules will attempt (often successfully) to change institutions and hence the kind of decisions produced under them. . . . Thus the only difference between values and institutions is that the revelation of institutional disequilibrium is probably a longer process than the revelation of disequilibria of taste" (Riker 1980, 444–45). In the chapters to come, we will see numerous examples of efforts to change institutional structures in order better to reflect the preferences of those affected by the decisions they generate. Riker argues that institutions may be seen as "congealed tastes," changing more slowly than preferences, but changing nonetheless (1980, 445).

Institutional rules inevitably have policy consequences, which is why seemingly arcane decisions, concerning rules changes in Congress, for example, so often become the subject of intense debate. Changing the procedures of decision making often has unintended consequences, however; policymakers are therefore generally conservative in altering them. So institutions, procedures, and rules play a key role in determining outcomes, since they inevitably favor some groups more than others, but change in institutions may come about only slowly or during periods of crisis (see, for example, Krehbiel 1991).

Another area where theorists have grappled with these questions of equilibria is in group theory and pluralism. In the purest form of group theory, interest associations interacted as vectors in Euclidean space, and public policy was the net result of the struggle. In this approach, voting was less important than freedom of association, and policy was conditioned more by group action in inter-election periods than in elections. It was easy to show that this early version of group theory did not comport with reality; too many interests failed to participate or were excluded by those who did. Most sought out niches in the governmental structure where they could dominate, but where other groups would not be able (or interested) in struggling with them. The system of American governance looked more like mutual noninterference than group struggle. Political stability, then, could not be found in the balancing of interests, although it might be found in a system of noninterfering policy monopolies.

European scholars never adopted these American ideas of group politics because they attributed much greater independent powers to the state. In fact, the organization of governmental institutions plays an important role in structuring political participation, forcing some groups out while allowing other groups into the process. So institutional forces can push the system away from whatever equilibrium it might have reached if the competition among groups were the only thing that mattered.

Pluralist theorists suggested a more complex alternative: elected political leaders brokered coalitions that differed by issue areas, and democratic accountability was maintained because of the electoral sensitivities of the elected leader (Dahl 1961). But some elements of any electoral coalition seemed "more equal" than others. Political economists argued powerfully that business interests were so predominant in capitalist democracies that they could always upset democratic policymaking. Charles Lindblom (1977) has aptly termed this the "privileged position of business." Stability could well stem from the overwhelming dominance of business interests. Yet business interests themselves seem variable in their power across time, seemingly unable to establish an equilibrium point (Jones 1986; Vogel 1989). Moreover, different elements of the business community were often at odds on public policy issues.

In a democracy, an equilibrium would balance citizen preferences and public policies through a combination of elections and the open struggle of interest groups. This doesn't happen. Instead, stability is enforced through a complex system of mutually noninterfering policy monopolies buttressed by powerful supporting images. It would seem, then, that no particular arrangement in a democracy can succeed in establishing a point of equilibrium. Our models of politics are so unsatisfactory because we have insufficiently appreciated this point. In the words of Riker, this has led to great discomfort among those seeking to build general theories of politics.

Yet the realization that the search for equilibria in politics may be fruitless can liberate. While it is not often articulated by them, political scientists with a strong focus on case histories have always harbored the deep suspicion that politics was too complex, too contingent on ill-understood details, and too dependent on strategic action at the proper time to be bound by general theory. On the other hand, the general theorists are right in feeling that a better understanding of the political cannot be had through description and induction alone. It is not theory that is misplaced; it is the search for equilibria that is. An approach to the study of politics that rejects a faith in equilibria has the potential of unifying the theoretical and the descriptive.

We begin with the supposition that political systems are never in general equilibrium. But this does not imply that political systems are in continual chaos. Stability may be maintained over long periods of time by two major devices: the existing structure of political institutions and the definition of the issues processed by those institutions. Schattschneider's famous dictum that "organization is the mobilization of bias" (1960, 71) symbolizes the strong tendency of institutions to favor some interests over others. This advantage can be maintained over extended periods of time. Associated with such institutional arrangements is invariably a supporting definition of relevant policy issues. In particular, issues may be defined to include only a single dimension of conflict. The tight connection between institution and idea provides powerful support for the prevailing distribution of political advantage. But this stability cannot provide general equilibrium, because a change in issue definition can lead to destabilization and rapid change away from the old point of stability. This happens when issues are redefined to bring in new participants. Similarly a change in institutional rules of standing or of jurisdiction can rupture an old equilibrium. If a social equilibrium is induced only by the structures that determine participation in its choice, then altering the structures (or changing the rules) can cause the equilibrium quickly to disappear.

Issue definition, then, is the driving force in both stability and instability, primarily because issue definition has the potential for mobilizing the previously disinterested. The structure of political institutions offers more or fewer arenas for raising new issues or redefining old ones—opportunities to change understandings of political conflict. Issue definition and institutional control combine to make possible the alternation between stability and rapid change that characterizes political systems.

Positive Feedback in Politics

We generally think of politics as governed by laws characterized by negative feedback. As political actors invest more and more political resources into the political fray, they achieve a smaller marginal effect for their efforts. As opponents to a given policy mobilize, they may be able to make some incremental improvements in their station, but sooner or later they reach a limit. The privileged groups give up a small degree of power when attacked, but they retain their essential superiority. More and more resources must be brought to bear by the disadvantaged to gain the same degree of improvement. The system maintains relative stability, changing only slowly, and not usually by large amounts even over long periods. An entire political system based on such a model is very conservative. When shocks are introduced into a system dominated by negative feedback, the system moves away from its equilibrium for a time, but then returns to the status quo ante.

At times, however, political actions are subject to positive feedback. Small inputs can cascade into major effects as they work their ways through a complex system (Arthur 1988, 1989, 1990). Political science has developed terms to describe such situations: escalation, bandwagons, slippery slopes, and waves. New political movements take shape, gain momentum, and become irreversible. Rather than finding diminishing marginal change, each change is greater than the last one. Political ideas become popular quickly and diffuse throughout large areas of the political system until they have replaced many old ones. Political bandwagons build up power, as politicians and interest-group leaders become active in a new cause as it gains popularity. Ideas diffuse from one policy arena to another, often coming as a surprise to those who had previously operated independently from other areas. This process is not incremental; rather, changes come quickly and dramatically.

Any political phenomenon characterized even over a short range as exponential, or as a power function in which the exponent is greater than unity, displays positive feedback over that range. One important instance of such positive feedback occurs in the growth of government organizations. Kaufman (1976) and Casstevens (1980) show that the ages of government organizations follow an exponential form. This is growth without limits; Casstevens comments that the pattern suggests "no predators and no shortage of sustenance for governmental organizations" (1980, 164).

A second example of positive feedback occurs in the diffusion of policies across political systems. Many new initiatives by, for example, state governments in the United States are not emulated by other states (Walker 1969). Some innovations, however, "catch on" and become the thing to do. In the late 1970s and early 1980s, state governments became far more aggressive in pursuing private firms with incentive programs in order to promote economic growth. New programs were justified in terms of the tools available to competing states, and ideas were shared in national meetings of economic development directors. The result was rapid diffusion of new policy ideas. In this situation, a saturation point can be reached: most or all states adopt a particular set of economic development programs, so the positive-feedback does not last forever.

Such policy diffusion can be described by a logistic growth curve, or an S-shaped curve. Policy adoption is slow at first, then very rapid, then slow again as the saturation point is reached. During the first phase, adoption may be very slow as ideas are tried out and discarded. Then a positive-feedback phase takes place for some programs, as they rapidly diffuse. Finally, negative feedback is reestablished as the saturation point is reached. We argue that a number of policy innovations follow patterns of growth more like this than like incrementalism, with its decreasing marginal returns. Increasing marginal change is common in politics. Of course not all policy changes or innovations catch on; by noting the possibility of positive marginal returns, we certainly do not imply that such returns are inevitable. Policy diffusion, with its S-shaped curve, is remarkably like a punctuated equilibrium model in which the system shifts rapidly from one stable point to another (Eldredge and Gould 1972; Eldredge 1985; Gould 1989).

Political scientists have used the term *issue expansion* to discuss positive-feedback effects that cause issues to move quickly among many decision-making units. This causes various parts of the political system to direct attention at the issue which is in the process of expansion. Charles O. Jones describes the expansion of conflict over energy policy in the wake of the Arab oil emgargo this way: "Expansion is up, out, and over—up in public and institutional hierarchies . . . ; out to groups that declared an interest in energy policies . . . ; and over to decision making processes in other nations or groups of nations. . . . [This has the effect of] forcing resource-based subsystem participants into considering each other" (1979, 105).

The points at which a political system or subsystem changes from negative to positive feedback are critical, but they have generally not been studied systematically by political scientists. Rather, political scientists have written of them in particular cases, describing windows of opportunity, interaction effects, and swings in the national mood or noting how important it is to take advantage of trends. However, the different logics of positive and negative feedback are fundamental to understanding a single system, like the American policy process, that sometimes produces incrementalism and sometimes radical change.

The politics of positive feedback follow a different logic from those of negative feedback. When shocks or changes are introduced in this system, they may lead not just to a momentary deviation from normal, with a more or less rapid return to the status quo, but rather to new points of stability, as the system settles down at a point radically different from the original. If politics and policymaking can be said to follow such a dynamic, then we can expect stability during certain periods, but with the possibility of rapid, dramatic, and nonincremental change. In many cases, dramatic change has inviolable limits. The logistic diffusion curve implies such a limit; under such circumstances positive feedback has a definite end. Periods of stability, characterized by negative feedback often follow such periods of rapid change. So, many systems are characterized by long periods of negative feedback and short bursts of positive feedback.

Attention, Apathy, and Punctuated Equilibrium

The lack of a general equilibrium in politics does not rule out partial equilibria, especially where those partial equilibria are enforced through institutional structures such as policy subsystems. Such partial equilibria are not maintained through a balance between policy preferences of the mass public and the policy outputs of government. Rather, such arrangements are maintained through the allocation of attention of governmental elites and the apathy of those not keenly interested in the particular issue handled by the policy subsystem.[1]

---

1. The precise definition of an equilibrium is less important for the purposes of this book than are questions of stability and change. We have adopted the terminology of punctuated equilibrium because it evokes the images of stability interrupted by major alterations to a system. However, systems may be stable without necessarily being in equilibrium, so we do not wish to assert that

A major source of stability in political systems is the distribution of intensities of preferences. At any single time, a political system may feature many areas of privileged access to decision making, allowing powerful economic interests to secure advantageous treatment from the policymaking system. Because of the system of incentives created by differential intensities of preference, the self-interested typically have an inherent advantage, since most citizens are not concerned about the policy. Specialists, experts, and others with an economic interest in the nature of public policy in a particular area are the dominant makers of public policy in that area. Because the interested share preferences, or at least share understandings concerning the basic dimension of conflict, the paradox of voting does not arise. The policy system is stable because those participating share values.

Some political scientists have conjectured that such decision-making arrangements can result in institutionally induced equilibria (Riker 1982, 189; Shepsle 1979). For example, a congressional committee may be structured to include a majority of members having favorable preferences toward the policy that the committee has jurisdiction over, excluding both the indifferent and the opposition. More critically, controversy would involve only one dimension, say farm subsidy benefits versus budgetary costs. Other dimensions of conflict, say environmental consequences of maintaining marginal farms through subsidy, would not intrude. Voting would generally be at equilibrium, because the issue is limited to one dimension.

Similarly, policy subsystems can be viewed as such institutionally induced equilibria. Redford writes that "subsystems provide stability for existing equilibriums among interests" (1969, 102). Yet in a democracy a primary source of instability is the citizen indifference upon which policy subsystems are based. So long as the possibility exists of mobilizing the previously indifferent through the redefinition of issues, no system based on the shared preferences of the interested is safe. If people outside the policy system can be convinced that the policy in question has impacts beyond the existing set of participants, they can be brought into the conflict. Preferences are no longer uniform, and the system is not guaranteed to be stable over the long term, even though it may be as long as interest is not expanded to the previously uninterested.

Disaggregated decision systems thrive on what Simon has called the serial processing capacity of legislative bodies: "When questions are important and controversial . . . they have to be settled by democratic procedures that require the formation of majorities in legislative bodies or in the electorate as a whole. Consequently, the voters or the legislators must for periods of time

---

all periods of stability are signs of equilibrium; they could simply be due to a lack of outside disturbances (see Prigogine and Stengers 1984). The term *punctuated equilibrium* was proposed by palentologists Niles Eldredge and Stephen Jay Gould to describe gaps in the evolutionary record (Eldredge and Gould 1972).

attend simultaneously to more or less the same thing" (1983, 81). Because so many issues must be decided by government, parallel processing is accomplished by policy subsystems in an environment of low attention by the legislature or broader political elites. Hence the job of losers in a policy subsystem is to move the issue from the realm of parallel processing to the realm of serial processing by reallocating attention. The inability of Congress to oversee policy subsystems continuously leads to a system of "fire alarm oversight" in which Congress pays attention to an issue only when citizens or groups challenge administrative decision making (McCubbins and Schwartz 1984). Delegation except when the alarm is raised is seen as rational—presumably a response to the limits of serial processing.

Most issue change occurs during periods of heightened general attention to the policy. In the process of agenda-setting, the degree of public indifference to given problems changes dramatically. Since this is the structure on which policy subsystems are based, it should not be surprising if periods of agenda access are followed by dramatic changes in policy outputs. Indeed, this is precisely why policy entrepreneurs fight so doggedly either to push their issue toward the public agenda or to ensure that it not arrive there. Through the mechanisms of agenda access and issue definition, the broader forces of political control may intervene from time to time, changing policies from what the self-interested might prefer. Policy monopolies are highly favorable policy-making structures for those who participate in them, and they produce seeming equilibria that may be far from what another group of participants might prefer. Agenda-setting is a process that has the potential of disturbing these partial equilibria in politics. The strategic incentives for policymakers to understand the importance of agendas have long been clear; the policy consequences of agenda access can be dramatic. Further, including agenda-setting and differential intensities of preference and of attention into our models of policymaking has the possibility of making them account both for stability and change.

In the United States, media attention to public policy issues tends to follow a pattern of either feast or famine. Important political questions are often ignored for years, but during certain periods almost every general media outlet features similar stories prominently. Because individual media outlets tend to base their coverage partly on what other media outlets are covering, this mimicking behavior offers further reinforcement to the lurching behavior of agendas. Issues are low on the public and media agenda during certain periods, but during others a huge proportion of the general media outlets in the United States may feature coverage. No wonder policy experts often view the media with disdain or even outright hostility. Each time there is a surge of media interest in a given topic, we can expect some degree of policy change.

As a consequence of the dynamics of the allocation of attention, the partial equilibria of policy monopolies tend to be temporary. Moreover, they tend to be disrupted turbulently rather than gradually. Charles O. Jones and Randall Strahan (1985) describe exactly this kind of subsystem destabilization in the case of energy policies. External shocks (in their case the Arab oil embargo) affect all relevant policymaking institutions simultaneously, causing change in each one of them rather than in only one or a few. In another work, Jones discussed "speculative augmentation" (1975). In both cases, existing policy subsystems are overwhelmed by a flood of new participants or by dramatic new policy proposals. Over the long run, open, democratic political systems are characterized both by policy monopolies, as the political system struggles with its limited capacity to process numerous issues simultaneously, and by turbulent disruptions, as attention is directed at the issue again. That is, democratic systems are composed of punctuated partial equilibria.

The mobilization of the apathetic provides the key to linking the partial equilibria of policy subsystems in American politics to the broader forces of governance. As different groups become active on a given issue, partial equilibria of preferences are altered quickly from one point to another. Apathy is the key variable in politics. Some seek to promote it, others to fight it. Depending on the degree of apathy that prevails, different groups will see their views adopted as the majority view. As the level of apathy changes, so do majority opinions.

The Structure of Political Conflict

Disaggregated decision systems are not the sum of American politics. Public policymaking also responds to the great cleavages of society, and these cleavages have been traditionally organized by political parties. Political conflict over each program in each subsystem recapitulates in one form or another the great policy issue of the twentieth century—How much government? But the major intrusions of governmental power—and the major attempts to roll it back—have been organized not by interest groups linked to government in policy subsystems, but by political parties. This does not mean that such issues emerge in the partisan arena. Indeed, they often emerge elsewhere and are drawn into partisan conflict when one party sees an advantage in doing so. When an issue is drawn into this cleavage, it becomes a partisan issue. The issue is not left to the experts in policy subsystems; it occupies the major energies of the president and congressional leaders. This level of attention has been termed "macropolitics" to distinguish it from "subsystem politics" and "micropolitics" or individual political behavior (Redford 1969).

There is good reason to conceive of "macropolitics" as simply an extension of the process of creation, destruction, and failure of policy monopolies. Political parties, after all, are implicated in the construction of policy subsystems (Lowi 1979). Subsystems tend to be disrupted when the macropolitical institutions intervene, generally modifying their operating rules (Redford

1969, 105). When an issue receives sufficient attention, it often can no longer be confined to subsystems. Then parties may be drawn to it because it has the potential of conveying electoral advantage.

When an issue is defined electorally, it normally gets articulated to fit past frames of reference that the parties convey to the voters. As a consequence, partisan conflict is often stable and repetitive. Democrats, after all, generally stand for more government and in favor of the less-favored classes, while Republicans preach less government and draw their sustenance from the better-off. The policy images underpinning a subsystem are influenced by the configuration of partisan forces at its birth, as are the operating principles of the subsystem.

Partisan politics are also occasionally subject to major agenda shifts and positive feedback. Students of elections recognize this and have searched for so-called critical or realigning elections—periods when parties adopt new issues to appeal to new constituencies, resulting in a fundamental shift in the social bases of support for the parties. But William Riker has noted that this search is misplaced: "the fundamental and underlying change is not in election results but in political agendas" (Riker 1982, 288). Agendas can change without realignments occurring—a point brought home by the work of Carmines and Stimson (1989) concerning changes in the partisan bases of support for civil rights issues.

Politics are different when organized along partisan lines, because maintenance of policy monopolies is normally not possible. There is too much general attention, and there are too few disinterested citizens. Nevertheless, the struggle over issue definition continues unabated. There is great advantage to the proponents of more government if government activity is viewed as a collective endeavor to improve society. Conversely, conservatives are benefited if the general image of government is an organization that limits freedom for all to benefit specific interests. So partisan conflict is about ideas as much as it is about clashing interests of social groups. The great "transforming" leaders of James MacGregor Burns (1978) are those political leaders who can modify the terms of the macropolitical debate. While policy monopolies may be impossible at the macropolitical level, general understandings about the limits of public power are indeed possible.

The Approach of this Book

We have argued that much of the political world is never at equilibrium, but that points of stability are created and destroyed at critical junctures throughout the process of issue development. Moreover, political conflict occurs in the United States in two great arenas: within the partisan organization of conflict and within smaller policymaking systems. Each domain is characterized by the strategic struggle over the definition of issues. Because the definition of issues is so central to political processes in disequilibrium, this book is devoted to the understanding of the issue definition process. We are particularly interested in the consequences of issue definition. Issue definition is a purposive process, that is, it is accomplished by political leaders who want to achieve something. That may be either the construction of a policy monopoly or the destruction of someone else's policy monopoly. Because policy entrepreneurs want government to do something (or to refrain from doing something), issue definition is intimately related to agenda processes. So any study of issue definition must also be a study of agenda control and access.

Our approach to the study of issues may be termed comparative issue dynamics. We study a number of issues over a relatively long time span, and we do so quantitatively to the extent possible. The issues we have chosen to study represent both the process of monopoly construction, which is characterized in the policy literature as subsystem politics, and the partisan realm. We were guided in our choice of policy areas by the availability of good, careful case studies, because our desire to discuss several issues over long times would make it impossible to be sensitive to the many details of policy development that good case studies can illuminate. The whole idea of disequilibrium and critical points suggests that such details can be extremely important in policy development. However, we show that too frequently the monumental events that many take as critical points in policy development are chimeras; they are events that symbolize policy change but happen well after the issue has been redefined. For these reasons, our quantitative approach is necessary to separate out real critical points from reconstructed ones.

In chapter 2 we explain our approach to the study of policy agendas, an approach linked to the definition of policy images and the structure of political institutions. Chapter 3 details the specifics of comparative issue dynamics and compares it to other approaches to the study of policy agendas. In chapter 4 we examine in detail the rise and fall of a policy monopoly—that surrounding the use of civilian nuclear power—and illustrate the power of our approach by following a single issue over a long time span. Chapter 5 shows that the processes observed for nuclear power are more general: they apply to pesticides and to tobacco policy. There we study empirically the dual mobilization thesis, which states that the consequences of increased attention (that is, agenda access) depend on the tone of that attention. In chapter 6 we look at the issue development process in the mass media, with data from the three policy areas already studied plus transportation safety. Chapter 7 introduces an issue that crosses the partisan dimension of politics—urban affairs—and it ties the agenda process to empirical indicators of policy outputs. Chapter 8 focuses on three valence issues, in which only one side of an issue is legitimate; we use the examples of drug abuse, alcohol abuse, and child abuse. Important agenda questions remain even in cases where all agree on the nature of the problem, because there remain many possible solutions.

Chapters 9, 10, and 11 turn to more institutional features of the American system, showing secular trends and changes that have affected the entire political system, not only one issue at a time. Chapter 9 relates changes in the interest-group system to the construction and destruction of policy subsystems. Chapter 10 shows how Congress, and in particular its committee system, can serve as an important policy venue in the mobilization process. It discusses both secular trends within Congress and some particular cases: pesticides, smoking, drugs, and air transportation. Chapter 11 depicts federalism as a system of linked policy venues and notes that no description of policy-making in the United States can be complete without attention to the federal structure. Finally, chapter 12 shows how the comparative issue approach buttresses the notion of politics as a process in disequilibrium.

The interactions of changing understandings of issues within a policy community and changing degrees of interest from different institutions within the governmental structure make it clear that few privileged groups should be confident that they will remain so forever. Those who dominate the process at one time may be only minor players as the issue comes to be understood in a different manner, and as a different group of governmental institutions begins to exert control. As issues emerge and recede from the public and from different governmental agendas, different groups are helped and hurt. So the allocation of political and economic resources in the American political system is closely tied to the allocation of attention by its government and private elites.

2

Policy Images and Institutional Venues

In chapter 1 we focused on the ideas of positive and negative feedback, on the differences between stability and equilibrium, and on the importance of punctuated equilibria in politics. The key to understanding this alteration between stability and change lies in the process by which issues get defined for policy action. In this chapter we show how policy images, or public understandings of policy problems, affect policy development. But they do not do so singlehandedly. The institutional structure within which policymaking occurs is related to these images, since different institutions may be more or less favorable toward a particular image of a policy. So the receptivity of an institutional venue is also critical in policy development. The interaction between changing images and venues of public policies leads precisely to the type of positive feedback described in chapter 1 as the cause of disequilibrium politics. A system of punctuated equilibrium, with its characteristic shifts from one point of stability to another, can be produced by the interaction of these two important components of the policy process. In this chapter we describe this process in detail.

Policy Images

How a policy is understood and discussed is its *policy image*. Policy images play a critical role in the expansion of issues to the previously apathetic. Because all people cannot be equally interested or knowledgeable about all issues facing society, specialists in any particular area have an advantage over all others. Since they know the issue better, they are sometimes able to portray the issue in simplified and favorable terms to nonspecialists. Specialists spend most of their time communicating with each other, of course, but from time to time they must explain their policies to the broader public or to elites with only a passing interest in the area. This type of communication requires some simplified ways of explaining the issues and justifying public policy approaches to them. As a result, every public policy problem is usually understood, even by the politically sophisticated, in simplified and symbolic terms.

Because a single policy or program may have many implications, or may affect different groups of people in different ways, different people can hold different images of the same policy. Policies will differ in the degree to which a single image is well accepted by all. In some cases, there is virtually no disagreement about the social or political implications of a given policy, while in other cases there may be considerable conflict over the proper way to describe or understand it. Often, proponents of a policy focus on one set of images, while opponents refer more often to another set of images.

The creation and maintenance of a policy monopoly is intimately linked with the creation and maintenance of a supporting policy image. In those cases where monopolies of control have been established, there tends to be a single understanding of the underlying policy question. So policy monopolies are often supported by the acceptance of a positive policy image and the rejection of possible competing images. Consider the case of entrance into the professions. Where members of a profession control the entry of others into it, this is usually done in the name of ensuring quality. But of course limiting the number of entrants into a profession affects the supply of those offering the same or similar services, and therefore the salaries and the prestige of the entire profession. So the same policy may have two opposite, and competing, images: ensuring high quality, and economic self-interest and the creation of a cartel. For different professions, the relative strengths of these two competing images vary greatly, but in general the members of a profession would certainly prefer to have attention focus on the first image rather than the second.

Policy images are always a mixture of empirical information and emotive appeals. These appeals can be subtle or strong, but they are invariably present. Hence every policy image has two components: an empirical and an evaluative. We refer to the evaluative component of a policy image as its *tone*. The issue of civilian nuclear power brings forth images that are rooted in both empirical observation and evaluation. Once the image of civilian nuclear power was positively associated with economic progress. Today it is more likely associated with danger and environmental degradation. Tone is critical to issue development because rapid changes in the tone of a policy image held by key social actors (such as the mass media) often presage changes in patterns of mobilization. That is, as the tone of stories in the mass media changes, say, from positive to negative, opponents of the policy have an opportunity to attack the existing policy arrangement. Christopher Plein has described the emergence of the biotechnology industry as it first had to overcome a public image dominated by fears of mutant organisms gone wild. The industry has been successful so far, he argues, in part because of its ability to foster a more controlled, serious, and optimistic image (1991).

Social Conditions and Public Problems

Social conditions do not automatically generate policy actions. Arguments must be made and accepted that a given problem can be solved by government action before a social condition becomes a public policy problem. So before a problem is likely to attract the attention of government officials, there must be an image, or an understanding, that links the problem with a possible governmental solution. Deborah Stone calls this problem definition: "Problem definition is centrally concerned with attributing bad conditions to human conditions instead of fate, or nature" (1989, 299). When bad conditions are attributed to nature, government need not intervene; where the same conditions are argued to stem from human or government sources, or at least to be amenable to such solutions, then government action is much more likely. An earthquake is not a public policy problem, since it cannot be prevented or avoided by government action. Building code violations that make the damage from an earthquake more severe than necessary are public policy problems, however, since government actions can solve them, at least theoretically.

Related to this question of attributing problems to causes within human control is that of taking a private or public perspective on the issue. Many problems may be seen as private misfortunes for those who undergo them or as public policy failures that the government should address. When a student drops out of school before learning to read or write, for example, that is a private misfortune. When businessmen complain that the collective lack of training in the work force is making the United States less able to compete in the international marketplace, that is a public problem that calls out for a governmental response. From a private misfortune that implies no necessary governmental intervention, the issue of educational attainment is translated into one of economic growth and the competitiveness of the American economy—certainly something that should interest and preoccupy Washington policymakers. Private problems need to be linked to public causes in order to demand governmental attention. Argumentation, and the construction of policy images, plays a key role in this process.

Giandomenico Majone writes that

> Objective conditions are seldom so compelling and so unambiguous that they set the policy agenda or dictate the appropriate conceptualization. In the 1950s the issue of poverty was a minor one in American public consciousness. In the 1960s, with little

change in the distribution of income, it became a significant part of public policies. What had changed were attitudes and views on poverty, and beliefs in the capacity of government to find solutions to social problems. A particularly important new element was the emergence of an intellectual consensus about the 'structural' causes of poverty. (1989, 24)

In other words, as the image of the issue changed from that of a private misfortune to a public problem amenable to government solutions, the issue rose high on the government agenda.

Competing images may emerge from a given set of conditions, especially when policymakers believe that different policy outcomes will follow from different understandings of what the facts mean. So images, or popular and elite understandings of public policies, are an integral part of the political battle. Competing participants attempt to manipulate them to suit their needs. Since a given policy typically has many different implications, it can be linked with many competing images. Deborah Stone sees this manipulation as inherently part of politics: "Problem definition is the active manipulation of images of conditions by competing political actors. Conditions come to be defined as problems through the strategic portrayal of causal stories" (1989, 299). Political struggle, then, involves conflict over the definition of policy images.

Policymakers obviously have incentives to portray issues in different ways, depending on what they might gain from different understandings, but no single policymaker is often in a position of determining alone what understanding will come to dominate. The process by which whole communities of experts come to accept one causal story over another is an important part of the policy process, since it determines what governmental responses will be on and off the national agenda. Even if individual policymakers may realize their interests in seeing one policy image being accepted over another, no single policymaker is in a position to determine the success or failure of any particular image. This is a much more complex process, one on which we focus in the pages to come.

Problems and Solutions

Raising a problem to the public agenda does not imply any particular solution. For example, let us say that the problem of poor educational attainments is raised to the national agenda, as in 1991. There remain a number of public policy solutions that government may adopt in order to solve this problem. These include increasing teachers' salaries, altering the ways teachers are trained, giving vouchers to send children to private schools, guaranteeing more equitable financing of public schools across rich and poor communities, paying greater attention to the health and nutrition needs of the poorest students, and enacting a great variety of other possible solutions. Obviously, different interests are affected as much by the mix of available solutions that policymakers choose as they are by the choice of problems that dominate the agenda. The trick for a policy entrepreneur is to ensure that the solution he or she favors is adopted once a given problem has emerged on the national agenda. John Kingdon describes how policy entrepreneurs did this in the area of urban mass transit systems in the 1970s and 1980s. They argued first that their programs were the solution to the problems of traffic congestion when these problems were on the national agenda in the 1960s. Later, as such environmental problems as air pollution from private cars rose on the agenda, they showed how the same programs were the obvious solution. After that problem ebbed from the agenda and issue of energy conservation rose in reaction to the 1973 oil embargo, they argued that these programs should be part of the national solution to that problem (Kingdon 1984, 181).

Kingdon argues that much of the policy process is determined by the artful connection of solutions to problems. As governmental leaders shift their attention from one problem to the next, policy entrepreneurs responsible for administering programs argue that their program represents the best solution to the new problem, even though originally it may have had no relationship to that problem. Again, argumentation and creation of a new understanding of an issue are at the heart of the political process. So policymaking is strongly influenced not only by changing definitions of what social conditions are subject to government response, as Deborah Stone (1989) alerts us, but also and at the same time by changing definitions of what would be the most effective solution to a given public problem. Policymakers have powerful incentives, therefore, to manipulate both aspects of the public debate. However, just like no single policymaker can ensure that his or her version of a causal story will be accepted by the entire political system, no single entrepreneur is in a position to guarantee that his or her solution will be adopted even if the government does focus on solving the problem. Individual incentives to manipulate the definition of issues are strong, but no individual alone has the power to determine these definitions. Rather, that definition is at the heart of the political battle.

New Dimensions of Conflict

William Riker argues that policy entrepreneurs use argumentation as a formidable political weapon in their efforts to manipulate political debates. He writes that the political leader who is able to define the symbols associated with two sides of a debate will easily be able to dominate the outcome. He describes the case of a senator opposing Defense Department plans to dispose of nerve gas in his state. As long as the debate was understood as a question of which state would get the gas, of course the vote could be expected to be ninety-eight to two, with the vast majority of the senators breathing a sigh of relief that a state other than their own had been chosen and only the two unlucky senators from the chosen state opposing the measure. Of course those responsible for finding a site would want the issue understood in those terms. For those two senators from the losing state, on the other hand, their only route to victory involves a change in understanding: they introduced a new dimension of conflict. In Riker's example, this was accomplished by arguing that the removal of the gas from an overseas base implied a change in the nature of the treaty relationship between the United States and that country, and that the Senate had not been adequately consulted about these changes. Since senators are never happy about voting to allow the executive branch to usurp the Senate's power to play a role in treaty negotiations, many opposed the bill (see Riker 1986, 110). From a position of almost guaranteed victory, this rhetorical turnaround led the Defense Department and the Nixon administration to an embarrassing defeat in the Senate.

If a given debate has a number of different implications, then one may be able to alter other people's views by shifting the focus of their attention from one set of implications to another. This may occur, as in Riker's example, even without any changes in the facts, or new evidence surrounding the issue. Since attention typically does not focus simultaneously on all the important points of a complicated debate, manipulating the allocation of attention can be a powerful strategy in policymaking.

There are many ways of understanding most public policy questions. While Riker and Kingdon describe some dramatic examples of success, we should not jump to the conclusion that altering the nature of public debates is necessarily simple or to be taken for granted. Single policymakers rarely have the opportunity to exert such influence. Still, they try, and clearly some understandings of complex public policies do come to predominate. Baumgartner showed in the case of French educational policy that policymakers differed systematically in the ways in which they described the same policy questions, depending on their positions. Those who stood to gain if the issue were considered as narrow and technical overwhelmingly emphasized these aspects of the question, while those who stood to lose if the issue were relegated to the civil service argued consistently that issue concerned such broad political questions that Parliament should be involved (1989, 129–86). Similarly, Cobb and Elder describe the different types of oratory necessary to mobilize different constituencies (1983). So the same issue is described in different ways, depending on one's target. Those wishing to mobilize broad groups attempt to focus attention on highly emotional symbols or easily understood themes, while those with an interest in restricting the debate explain the same issues in other, more arcane and complicated, ways.

Policy Venues

Policies must be understood and discussed in some ways. We have termed this the *policy image*. Similarly, some institutions or groups in society must have the authority to make decisions concerning the issue. We term this the *policy venue*. Policy venues may be monopolistic or shared, that is, a single issue may simultaneously be subject to the jurisdiction of several institutions, or it may be within the domain only of one set of institutions.

David Kirp has argued that there are five ways in which many policy issues can be defined, each with strong implications for what groups will be considered legitimate to make the decision, and therefore what the decision will be: "A given policy question may be regarded as best settled by recourse to *professional* expertise, and in that event, expert say prevails. Alternatively, the question may be resolved by relying on *political* judgment . . . ; by stressing *legal* norms . . . ; or by depending on *bureaucratic* standards. Lurking in the background is a fifth possibility, the determination to let the *market* . . . fix policy outcomes" (1982, 137–38).

Kirp argues that the education of handicapped students had long been subject to bureaucratic and professional norms in the United States and Great Britain, but that the 1960s saw a transformation toward a political model of decision making for these issues in the United States. In any case, he writes that "the way a policy problem gets defined says a great deal about how it will be resolved" (1982, 137). Professional and personal power is closely linked with the maintenance or the change of issue definition over time. We will see that such changes in issue definition over time are not as rare as is sometimes imagined.

Policy images are generally better received among one group of people than another. An agriculture committee in Congress is more likely to view pesticides as a way of increasing farmers' profits, while an environmental group is more likely to focus on the negative health effects of the same issue. So images may be accepted or rejected depending on the institutional arena in which they are raised. If decisions are made concerning a given issue across a variety of institutions, there is no reason why each institution may not have a different understanding of the issue. Tobacco policy in the agriculture arena is seen as an important source of jobs; in health policy circles it evokes images of disease; in insurance and business cost-containment circles it is seen as a source of increased health insurance premiums; in foreign trade circles it is seen as an important source of U.S. export earnings. Each institutional venue is home to a different image of the same question.

There are no immutable rules that spell out which institutions in society must be charged with making which decisions. Depending on the issue and on the way it is understood by those potentially involved, it may be assigned to an agency of the federal government, to private market mechanisms, to state or local authorities, to the family, or to any of a number of institutions. History, constitutional arrangements, cultural understandings, and the performance of institutions on similar issues in the past all affect the current assignment of issues to institutions. In the United States, some decisions are made in Congress, some by executive branch officials, some in the courts, some at local levels of government, some by private investors through the stock and bond markets, some by businessmen, some by consumers. Issues assigned to the market in one country may be controlled by the state in another, for example, health care policy, air travel, railroads, and telephones. These differences in issue assignment create differences in policy, as different groups are favored or disadvantaged by different institutional arrangements.

Policy venues are the institutional locations where authoritative decisions are made concerning a given issue. Policymaking authority is not automatically assigned to particular venues. On the contrary, how an issue gets assigned to a particular arena of policymaking is just as much a puzzle as how an issue comes to be associated with one set of images rather than another. Just as images may change over time, so may venues. Further, just as an issue may at times have multiple images, so may it fall within the jurisdictions of several venues.

Some types of image may be well accepted in one venue, but considered inappropriate when raised in another institutional arena. Norms of compromise, fair shares, and reciprocity common in the legislative arena have little legitimacy in the courts, for example. Similarly, electoral politics may offer opportunities for activists to change images, as the control over the portrayal of issues shifts away from executive agencies and technocratic elites. Associated with the public campaigns of elections is often an emotionally charged set of policy images, where issues previously discussed within closed groups of elites in wholly technical terms might lead to massive public debates and high-sounding rhetoric. Because cities and states organize different constituencies than do national political institutions, they may be receptive to different policy images. Indeed, because of variations in culture and economic circumstances, cities and states differ significantly among one another in their receptivity to particular policy images. So images are linked with venues. The variety of venues of policymaking in American politics can allow many contrasting images of the same issues to flourish at once. When we consider images of public policies, therefore, we must also consider the question of venue.

Just as some policy problems are firmly associated with one set of images while other problems are associated with a number of competing images, some policies are firmly within the jurisdiction of a single institution, while others face the competing influences of a number of jurisdictions. As a result of this competition among venues, institutional assignments may change over time. Education policy in the United States is mostly a state and local government function, but the federal government has played an increasingly important role over time. Similarly, many of the greatest changes in the civil rights policies in the United States have come from changes in the relative powers of states and the federal government to enforce policies. Dramatic changes in policy outcomes are often the result of changes in the institutions that exert control.

Although the issue assignments apparent at any one point in time may seem permanent, changes in institutional jurisdictions are common over time. For example, the U.S. federal government has increasingly become involved in a number of policy areas that were previously reserved to the states, with the result that many policies were reversed over time. The New Federalism of the Reagan years was a clear effort to achieve policy goals through a shift in issue assignment, from the federal level to the states. Shifts from executive agencies to congressional control within the federal government are commonplace, as are shifts from one agency to another. All of these movements, whether they be from the government to the market, from the states to the federal government, from the executive branch to the courts, from one committee to another in Congress (see King 1991), or from any other set of institutions to another, represent the potential for shifts in policy outcomes and therefore are of interest to policymakers.

Some policy problems become so closely associated with particular levels of government or institutional venues that change is unlikely. National defense and monetary policy are obviously within the domain of the federal government, and no local authorities are likely to encroach on these policymaking domains. Since the creation of NASA, space policy has been firmly under its control with only occasional disputes with the Pentagon and the private sector. Police protection in the United States is clearly associated with local levels of government, and a national system of police would be unthinkable here. There is no iron-clad logic that requires police forces to be mostly local affairs, only historical tradition. Powerful local police departments would be just as unthinkable in France as a powerful national police force would be in the United States. Just as with images, then, we may distinguish among those venues where jurisdictional authority is firmly established and those where change is more likely. These links may come from logic or from tradition; they may be codified in the constitution, or they may emerge from common practice.

While some issues are firmly a part of a particular policy jurisdiction, the institutional authorities in charge of other policy problems are not so clearly defined. This may be because the problems are new and societal responses to them have not become routinized, because there are many possible solutions but no clearly superior ones, or because problems are extremely complex and pose many contradictory or unrelated questions, each of which may interest different groups of people. Drug prevention policy in the United States is the object of efforts by a number of competing institutions, none of which has a clear jurisdictional monopoly. Police departments, customs officials, immigration officers, the military, the IRS, the FBI, local schools and hospitals, and many other government and private authorities are all involved, each playing a slightly different role. Large public policy problems often involve a wide range of institutions, each of which focuses on a different aspect of the broad question.

Secure policy subgovernments can and do build up around particular issues, thus creating policy niches. The generation or the avoidance of controversy surrounding a policy is closely related to the venue within which it is considered. Where there is no controversy, niches can become very secure. Where controversy increases, the venue of decision-making authority is more likely to change. Similarly, where jurisdictional boundaries are changed, previously secure policy niches can be destroyed, and issues which had once been consensual may suddenly become the objects of increased controversy and public scrutiny. Venue changes, in short, are influenced by, and influence in their turn, the generation or the containment of controversy.

One broad implication of the notions of venue and niche is that levels of government may specialize in different policy options. This has occurred in the United States, where the national government has been the center of consumption policies designed to satisfy the demands of constituents for policies unrelated to economic growth, while the states and localities have pursued investment policies designed to promote economic progress (Peterson and Wong 1986; Jones 1989). In Great Britain, the policy specialization between governmental tiers was so strong that the term *dual state* was coined to capture its dynamics (Saunders 1979). The specialization of policy venues in the two cases was reversed, which indicates how images and venues may interact in a number of different ways. We note in some detail in chapter 11 how, as a whole, the U.S. states and localities have focused on different policies than the federal government. These policy specializations have changed over the decades, however, so there is nothing fixed about them. And we can easily see that in other countries, contrasting specializations have been developed. So the existence of multiple venues in the federal system ensures that there may be a variety of contrasting policies being followed at once. However, it does not ensure which venues will be home to which policies.

Losers always have the option of trying to change the policy venue from, say, the national government to subnational units, or from so-called iron triangles to election politics, and such efforts are a constant part of the policy process. Redford (1969, 110) argues that "interests that fail to gain influence in the subsystems may obtain it through the macropolitical system." Clarence Stone (1976) has shown that, at the local level, community groups are more successful in affecting community development projects in the open, public, forums used in the policy adoption stage, but that business-oriented elites are more effective in the quieter, more technical and bureaucratic, implementation stages. Conversely, in a study of nuclear power policy in the United States, Campbell (1988) argues that business elites enjoyed privileged access in the policy adoption stage, while citizen groups were more powerful in the implementation stage. While particular venues may confer general advantage on business or other specific groups, the simple existence of alternate policy venues is more important than the distribution of advantage conferred by a particular venue. Many venues with only vague or ambiguous constraints on their jurisdictional boundaries create opportunities for strategically minded policy entrepreneurs to shop for the most favorable locus for their policies. Fewer venues with tighter or more explicitly defined boundaries limit the opportunities for venue shopping and discourage entrepreneurial behavior.

Sometimes issues change over time, becoming rooted in a new issue area. A number of issues that were once in the exclusive domain of states and localities in the United States have shifted toward the federal level. Civil rights policy may be the most prominent example where such a shift has been both dramatic and productive of striking policy results. Other issues, such as education, health, and transportation, have also seen the gradual encroachment of the federal government into areas which were once out of its control. Chapter 11 shows important changes in the policy specializations of the national, state, and local governments in the United States over the postwar period. Chapter 7 also shows an increasing involvement of the federal government in certain local policies during the 1960s and 1970s, followed by a decline in the 1980s. So changes in the venues where particular policies are made can occur over time, and issues can become stable in their association with a new arena of policymaking.

Images and venues are closely associated with each other. Policymakers attempt both to manipulate the dominant understanding of the issues with which they deal and to influence the institutions that exert jurisdiction over them. Those hoping to have a given image accepted may find their arguments unsuccessful when raised in one venue, but successful in another. Similarly, those seeking the attention of a given group of actors may find that arguments successful with another group have no success there. So the searches for favorable venues and reinforcing images are related. We consider the implications of these interactions next.

Interactions

Schattschneider's (1960) conception of conflict expansion forms the basis of our notion of institutional venue and points to the importance of image as well. Schattschneider argued that losers in a policy debate have the motive to change the roster of participants by appealing to those not currently involved in the debate. If they can appeal to the right group of potential participants, they may be able to change their losing position into the winning one, as more and more people become involved in the debate on their side. In any debate, he argued, the current list of participants is by no means to be taken for granted. In fact, the most powerful strategy of politics is to enlarge or limit the scope of the debate to include or exclude those groups whom one can predict will be for or against one's position. So political debates take place in an atmosphere where the losing side seeks the attention of potential allies not currently involved in the issue, while the winning side attempts to restrict participation in order to preserve its advantageous position.

Cobb and Elder (1983) build on Schattschneider's work, describing the rhetorical strategies used by policymakers in explaining issues in broader and broader terms, as they attempt to mobilize larger and larger constituencies on their behalf. The authors view the process as the successive mobilization of larger and larger groups, as in a series of concentric circles (1983, 104–29). Issues reach the public agenda, and policy monopolies are often destroyed, they argue, as conflict expands from specialists, to attention publics, to the informed public, and finally to the general public.

Yet there is a second manner in which issues may gain agenda entrance: venue shopping by strategically minded political actors. This strategy relies less on mass mobilization and more on the dual strategy of the presentation of image and the search for a more receptive political venue. Both Schattschneider and Cobb and Elder are correct in their essential insights: those on the losing side of a debate will have the incentive to look for allies elsewhere. These conflict expanders are not limited only to appealing to wider and wider groups; rather, their strategies may be much more complex and specific. They may identify particular venues, such as congressional committees, state government organizations, courts, private businesses, or any other relevant institution in their search for allies. In this process of searching for a more favorable venue for consideration of an issue, image manipulation is a key element. As issue expanders attempt to attract the attention of a new group of policymakers, they must explain why the issue is appropriate for consideration within that venue (see also Majone 1989, 41). So changes in image are used purposefully, in an effort to attract the attention of the members of a particular new venue.

In this view, the mass public represents but one of many potential venues for a policy debate, and strategic policymakers can often be successful in changing policymaking systems without any direct appeals to the broad public. The agenda-setting process is much more complicated than the comparison of issues that are "on" and "off" the public agenda would imply. Rather, there are many possible institutional agendas, and for the policymakers who seek that institutional niche where decisions would likely go in their favor, none is inherently better than any other. Policymakers use manipulation of the understandings of policies as purposive tools in their search for the policy venue that will be most favorable to their interests.

Just as changes in how issues are understood can lead to changes in issue assignment, institutional reorganizations and jurisdictional changes can produce changes in policy, as the same issue is considered by a different group of policymakers with different views than in the previous venue. Changes in jurisdiction may come from institutional reorganizations through jurisdictional aggrandizement by policymakers hoping to enlarge their sphere of influence (see King 1991), through a process of diffusion of innovations, as governmental institutions follow each other rapidly in enacting similar changes (see Walker 1969; Eyestone 1978), or through a more direct influence of one institution on another. These changes are likely to have a continuing effect. A single change in venue may lead to later changes in image, leading to further changes in venue, and still further changes in images and policy outcomes. If institutions can induce equilibria as Shepsle argues, then changes in institutions can induce different equilibria; the period of change from one to the other may be dramatic.

Image-Venue Interaction and Punctuated Equilibria

Any model of the policy process which seeks to explain both incrementalism on the one hand and rapid change on the other must appreciate the interaction between issue assignment and political rhetoric. Where the rhetoric begins to change, venue changes become more likely. Where venue changes occur, rhetorical changes are facilitated. With each change in venue comes an increased attention to a new image, leading to further changes in venue, as more and more groups within the political system become aware of the question. Thus a slight change in either can build on itself, amplifying over time and leading eventually to important changes in policy outcomes. The interactions of image and venue may produce a self-reinforcing system characterized by positive feedback. Such systems can produce long periods of no change or dramatic reversals in outcomes in relatively short periods of time—exactly the type of thing described in chapter 1.

As an example of how image and venue changes may reinforce themselves, consider a case where an environmental group is continually on the losing side of regulatory decisions made within the executive branch of the federal government. Let us assume that the environmental group achieves some initial success by appealing to a previously uninvolved group in Congress. The group's understanding of the issue, disregarded or considered marginal in the original jurisdiction, may receive a more favorable hearing here. Then Congress may pass legislation that allows protagonists greater access to the courts or the regulatory process, thereby allowing the environmental group greater powers even in those venues where previously it had been weak. Further, the laws passed by Congress may explicitly make legitimate certain rhetorical symbols, so the venue change may lead to changes in image as well. From one strategic appeal, a whole series of self-reinforcing changes in image and venue may potentially follow. Such a scenario is not purely hypothetical. When Congress passed the National Environmental Protection Act (NEPA) in 1969, calling for environmental impact statements and allowing for much greater access to the courts, this one piece of legislation changed the nature of participation both in the courts and the regulatory process, and forced these other institutions to give greater consideration to certain aspects of environmental policy that had been ignored in the past. When the Environmental Protection Agency was created shortly after the passage of NEPA, it created a new institutional venue where a variety of issues could be discussed. So strategic appeals from one venue to another may lead to dramatic changes over time. In other words, there may be a snowball effect, as image and venue changes continue to reinforce each other over time.

The degree to which problems are tightly linked to images is related to the degree to which a single arena of policymaking exerts monopolistic control over a policy. Where images are in flux, one may also expect changes in institutional jurisdictions. Conversely, where venues change, the terms of the debate may be altered still further. Where venues are tightly controlled, on the other hand, changes in image are less likely; where changes in image are ruled out, the odds of effecting changes in venue are correspondingly lower. So image and venue can combine to produce rapid change, or they may interact to reinforce the current assignment of authority. Both stability and rapid change in policy outcomes can come from the same process.

We have argued thus far that the existence of numerous independent decision-making subsystems in American politics provides stability in the policymaking process. But the exclusion of the apathetic also provides a potential destabilizing force as policy entrepreneurs try to redefine issues to appeal to them. If these new groups enter the political fray, existing policy monopolies can be upset. Hence the system of disaggregated decision-making, which serves to channel political conflict, is in effect a network of what social choice theorists have called structure-induced equilibria. In this chapter, we have detailed the mechanisms by which such structure-induced equilibria can be destabilized: the interaction between policy image and existing institutional venues. In the next several chapters, we examine several cases of such interactions. First, we turn to a discussion of our methods.

3

Studying Agenda Change

Over the long term, policymaking is characterized by change in public understandings of policy problems and in the institutions that vie for policy control. In pluralist political systems, the interaction of image and venue allows for rapid changes in policy outputs during some periods and for prolonged stability during others. If we look at policy dynamics in the short term, however, we can be misled. Policies can look chaotic and conflictual or stable and consensual at a single time point, whereas longer-run policy development may incorporate both features. In order to appreciate these complexities, we must be able to observe a number of public policy problems over extended periods of time. Further, we need indicators of how the issues are understood and of their institutional assignment over time. This chapter dicusses our approach and compares it to other ways scholars have addressed similar questions in the past.

Studies of public policy are legion, but questions of agenda-setting have been addressed by relatively few large-scale studies. One major reason for the limited number of studies of agenda-setting has been its intractability. The lack of general, as opposed to case-specific, indicators of agenda status has operated against theoretical progress. Associated with the dearth of systematic measures is a methodological tradition of intensive case studies, an approach that has been made necessary by the inability of researchers to develop methods to allow more extensive comparisons of agenda status for a range of issues. So methods, indicators, and research traditions have all limited the development of more general theories of agenda-setting.

The lack of justifiable indicators of important aspects of the policy process has been a common indictment. Greenberg et al. were already complaining fifteen years ago about the "growing disjuncture between theory and research," noting that empirical tests of important theories of public policy were made virtually impossible because of a lack of indicators. Concepts, variables, and theories that appear straightforward at first blush often prove intractable when researchers attempt to use them systematically (1977, 1532).

Our approach to this problem of indicators can be summarized quickly. We take advantage of everything we can find in the published literature, in official records, and in media accounts of public policy controversies in order to gather comparable data over long periods of time and across a range of issues. By using publicly available quantitative indicators of agenda status, we gather comparable information for a larger number of issues than are typically studied, and we track those issues for periods of forty to a hundred years. This allows us to make both cross-sectional comparisons of different issues at a single time and longitudinal comparisons of a single issue over time. These data allow the study of changes in venue and changes in image, but they cannot elucidate the actions of policy activists and groups that drive the process of change. We have assembled the rich case study material that has been published in each of the areas of study, in order to note the actions of particular groups and individuals. Finally, we elaborate a more complex idea of agendas. Instead of conceiving only of issues being "on the agenda" or "off the agenda," we consider the multitude of institutional arenas for policymaking within the federal system. Hence we have assembled information on agenda access in as many of these venues as practicable.

The Research Design Problem

The first difficulty of studying the agenda-setting process is methodological. Political scientists have conducted two basic kinds of studies of issue dynamics: cross-sectional studies of several issues at one point in time, and longitudinal case studies of single issues. Cross-sectional, or policy typology, studies of policymaking have tended to emphasize how different types of issues generate different levels of conflict and controversy in the political system; for example, *redistributive* issues are supposed to be different from *regulatory* issues. In the language of agenda theorists, some issues are treated as high agenda items, with great media coverage, while others remain part of specialized policy subsystems, with little public attention. Typically, this is explained with some reference to the content of the policies themselves.

Those studies that have taken a longitudinal approach have not always reached the same conclusions. Studies tracing an issue over time show that the same issue has emerged or receded from the public agenda, with little change in its substantive contents. These studies are not in direct contradiction with each other, since the policy typology literature does not deny that issues can change over time. Still, the changes observed in the longitudinal studies are often very rapid and cannot be explained by the slow change in policy content that the typology literature admits may occur. In sum, political scientists studying similar questions tend systematically to emphasize different aspects of it, depending on their approach.

We seek to develop a system of analysis that would allow us to combine the best of each of these approaches. Our emphasis on the changing policy images leads us to agree with the longitudinal studies that stress temporal variation in policy visibility, mobilization, and support. We also note, however, how this change is more common in certain areas than in others, suggesting that issue content does have an effect, as the policy typologies stress. Most importantly, our methodology allows us to combine the extensive coverage of the cross-sectional approach, looking at a range of issues, with the emphasis on policy dynamics more common in case studies of single issues over time.

Cross-sectional Comparisons

The policy typology literature is based on cross-sectional comparisons of public policy issues, asking why some are politically controversial while others are consensual. These studies are more closely associated with the agenda-setting literature than many realize, since the typologies purport to explain why some issues are more likely to be the topics of public debate and controversy than others. The content of an issue is said to affect the mobilization of constituencies, which in turn determines whether the issue becomes politicized or not (see Lowi 1964; Wilson 1973; Ripley and Franklin 1987). Some issues (e.g., redistributive) mobilize broad constituencies; others (e.g., self-regulatory) interest only narrow groups. Because they mobilize broader or narrower constituencies, different types of issues are more or less likely to be the stuff of public debate. Without using the terms, these scholars are studying agenda access.

James Q. Wilson (1973), for example, proposes a typology of issues which distinguishes between those issues with concentrated versus dispersed costs and benefits, thus creating a fourfold classification. William Gormley distinguishes between issues on the basis of conflict and technical complexity, also creating a fourfold classification (1983, 159). Such classifications are typical of a broad range of studies based on cross sectional comparisons of issues. Certainly, highly complex issues around which there is no important conflict are likely to remain far from the public agenda, as Gormley rightly asserts. Similarly, issues that distribute costs widely (such as slightly higher consumer prices or taxes) but that allocate benefits narrowly (say, to farmers, military contractors, or other recipients of government grants or contracts) are likely to remain within the realm of pork-barrel politics, as Wilson writes. Intensities of preference certainly matter, and differential participation in the policy process is likely to lead to different types of policymaking systems surrounding different issues. This, in sum, is the lesson of the literature on typologies.

Because most studies that have proposed typologies have been based on cross-sectional comparisons of many issues at a single time, they have not dealt with the question of dynamics. It is clear, however, that issues change over time, and that some issues once considered consensual now are associated with much greater conflict, just as once conflictual issues now are accepted by all. One way to make the typology literature fit with this notion of dynamics is to note that it is not the issue itself that matters so much as the public or elite understanding of the issue. With an emphasis on changing perceptions of issues, the key element of usefulness of the typology literature hinges on our understanding of how perceptions, or understandings, may change. But this change in focus is fundamental. Where images are at the center of the analytical framework, as they are for us, one must address the efforts of policy entrepreneurs in attempting to alter other people's understandings of the issues with which they deal.

As perceptions of issues change, new groups of policymakers are drawn to them and old groups fade away, shifting their attentions to something else. These changes in the institutional loci of decision making, related to changing images of the policies themselves, prove decisive in determining policy outcomes. Policy entrepreneurs attempting to alter other people's understandings of a given public policy issue face many constraints, of course. Still, so many issues have changed in their public perception over the last century that it is clear our theories must not take for granted how we generate and maintain our images of public policy problems. This must be an integral part of our theories of agenda-setting; it tends not to be an important part of most typologies presented in the literature. For example, Hank Jenkins-Smith and colleagues (1991) traced participation among federal agencies, interest groups, and others in the debates concerning off-shore oil and gas leasing, finding a core of regular participants as well as others whose participation was intermittent. A snapshot of the process taken at any given time would have given a misleading picture of a dynamic process.

The policy typology literature is related to another large body of studies that documents how large sectors of the economy can be effectively taken out of the political world of mass interest, party platforms, and interest-group conflict. Studies of "systems of limited participation" (Cobb and Elder 1983) have rivaled election studies in the volume of literature they have generated. At least since Bentley (1908), political scientists and commentators have been fascinated by the power of experts to dominate the policy process in their areas (see Baumgartner 1989 or Walker 1991 for a partial list of such studies). If policy communities are "autonomous" from broader political forces, they have been known variously in the literature as "policy whirlpools," "iron triangles," "policy networks," "subsystems," or "subgovernments." More generally, political scientists studying interest-group behavior have focused on the development of diffuse "issue networks" or "policy communities" as these have replaced the more structured "iron triangles" and "subgovernments" of the past (see Griffith 1961; Redford 1969; Heclo 1978; Hamm 1983, Gais, Peterson, and Walker 1984; Walker 1983, 1991; Ripley and Franklin 1987; McFarland 1987; Berry 1989a, 1989b; Fritschler 1989).

Considerable debate has raged in the literature concerning the relative abilities of communities of experts to control the policy process in their areas and to remain insulated from broader partisan debate. Scholars have noted that descriptions of tightly controlled and stable subgovernments marked by consensus may be increasingly difficult to maintain in the modern political system (see Berry 1989b; Browne 1990). More common may be issues marked by considerable conflict from within a vaguely defined issue network (see also Sabatier 1987, 1988). As the economy and the political system grow more complex, greater numbers of interest groups, institutions, and advocacy organizations are formed, increasing the links of interdependence tying together different areas of the economy. So it may be more difficult in the 1990s to maintain a subsystem independent of outside political influences than it was in the past (or these subsystems may become smaller and more specialized: see Browne 1990). In any case, political scientists are concerned with the relative ability of policy specialists to build and maintain a policy monopoly, to insulate themselves from the political system, to be granted powers within the area of their jurisdictional control.

Studies of policy subsystems are closely related to studies of agenda-setting because of the impact of the nature of the policy community on the policy process. Issues previously understood in consensual terms have emerged as the objects of considerable controversy among experts, as policy communities have become more diverse. Simply put, there are more experts now than there used to be, and communities of experts are more likely to house significant internal conflicts. Faced with disagreement among those who should be qualified to decide, political leaders must make decisions where once they needed only to ratify those decisions already made by experts. Where the nature of a policy community changes from small, consensual, and homogeneous to large, conflictual, and heterogeneous, the likelihood increases that a given issue will rise higher on the national political agenda.

Compared to those areas marked by limited participation and consensual views, loosely defined issue networks dominated by intense conflicts from within are much more likely to see their members appealing to political leaders for support, pushing their issues high onto the public agenda. Issues are less likely to emerge on the public agenda where specialists have developed a powerful subgovernment and where they all agree on the best direction of government policy. So studies of issue networks, policy communities, subgovernments, and the like are also closely related to the agenda literature. Just as Molière's Monsieur Jourdain had to be informed that he had been speaking prose for many years, the authors of these studies may not realize that they are analyzing the agenda problem, even though they have been doing so for a long time. Their findings are central to questions of agenda-setting because of the importance of context in determining the dynamics of policy-making.

Another group of studies based on a cross-sectional design has focused on the power of elites in dominating agendas. A group of studies in the 1960s and 1970s in particular documented the remarkable ability of elites to keep their issues "off the agenda" (see, for examples, Bachrach and Baratz 1962; Edelman 1964, 1989; Crenson 1971). These scholars saw the ability to use symbols and rhetoric as an important mechanism by which elites manipulate masses (see also Gamson 1990). Rhetoric and symbols present important strategic tools for all those involved in the policy struggle, not only for dominant elites. When we consider a number of issues over long periods of time, we note again and again that the same issue has come to be associated with different symbols, or understandings, at different periods of time. Sometimes these understandings reinforce the positions of the already powerful. In other cases they break up powerful subsystems. The same tools can be used by both sides.

So discussions of issue typologies and of interest group or policy community behavior, generally based on cross-sectional observations, tend to argue that issue content affects the mobilization of constituencies, which, in turn, determines the level of politicization, or agenda access. Certain types of issues are naturally likely to mobilize constituencies of different sizes and biases, according to these studies. These conclusions are correct as far as they go, but they do not go far enough. The mobilization of constituencies does not flow naturally from the content of public policy issues, because mobilization can be affected by different understandings of the same issues. The "contents" of complex public policy issues are subject to varying interpretations. Often the same issue can be viewed either from a social or technical point of view; often, single policies have multiple implications, each of interest to a different constituency (see Greenberg et al. 1977; Wilson 1973).

Cross-sectional studies are subject to two problems concerning the link between issue content and political mobilization. First is that just mentioned: the same issue can be understood in different ways, and these understandings may change over time. Second, and equally important, there may be secular changes over time in the relative mobilization or organization for political action of different sectors of the population. Increasing reliance on television and electronic means of communication may have a differential impact on the mobilization of potential constituencies. Those who were once difficult to contact may become more easily mobilized. Those who once could be counted upon to respond to partisan appeals may no longer be interested in the party organization (see Walker 1991). In short, the social institutions that channel the mobilization of constituencies change over time, so any link between issue content and social mobilization should not be expected to be permanent. Finally, national changes in receptivity to political ideas can alter the prevailing advantage for mobilization. The deregulation movement of the late 1970s and early 1980s affected many subsystems and made it more difficult to contemplate regulation when financial markets were hit by speculative excesses in the 1980s. The importance of secular shifts, affecting many issues simultaneously, may easily be demonstrated by the simple fact that certain periods of recent political history have seen the destruction of many systems of limited participation. During other periods, many have been created.

The mid–1970s saw many subsystems destroyed or weakened: those relating to tobacco, pesticides, air and water pollution, airlines, trucking, telecommunications, and nuclear power were all destroyed or radically altered (Jones 1975; Derthick and Quirk 1985; Bosso 1987; Campbell 1988; Fritschler 1989). Academic metaphors describing policy subcommunities also suggest the changing nature of subgovernments—from iron triangles through issue networks to advocacy coalitions—from tightly structured systems of limited participation through more fluid boundaries and easier access to the incorporation of conflict within the subsystem. Reforms in congressional procedures in the 1970s played an important role in altering the policy processes surrounding many issues during that time (see Dodd and Schott 1979). The 1970s were not simply an aberration, but the breakup of systems of limited participation, like their creation, can be explained in a systematic way. These large changes sweeping through the political system cannot be discussed sensibly with a cross-sectional model.

Just as there have been notable periods of destruction of policy subsystems, there have been periods during which large numbers of them were set up. Many subsystems grew in tandem with the postwar economy and can be traced through the development of the interest-group environment active in Washington and elsewhere. Hansen (1985) shows a rapid increase in membership for farm groups in the years following World War Two, stimulating the development of the modern agriculture subsystem. Aldrich and Staber reported increases in the number of active trade associations in the United States from fewer than 200 at the turn of the century to about 1,400 in 1950, and to about 2,300 in 1980 (1986). While the 1940s and 1950s were periods of growth for trade associations, the 1960s and 1970s saw a flowering of citizens' and consumers' groups, according to Walker (1983, 1991). These changes in the nature of the interest-group environment in national politics created important changes in the ways in which policies were made. Many previously well-insulated policy communities found themselves affected by policy conflicts that once had not affected them, while others were able to maintain considerable autonomy. For example, the 1980s saw the rapid growth of financial consultants, pension-fund managers, and others exploiting the growth and technological innovation in the financial markets. Subsystems responsible for regulating financial markets were able to assert autonomy even in the face of the 1987 stock market collapse (perhaps because of its subsequent recovery).

Of course authors of cross-sectional studies do not claim that their findings will remain valid for all time, and we do not mean to imply that they have. Issue content and political mobilization are clearly associated with each other, but only in a complicated way. Cross-sectional approaches to the study of this relationship have sometimes reached overly simplified conclusions, but the problem is not solved simply by adopting a longitudinal design. Let us consider the findings of a range of longitudinal studies.

Longitudinal Studies

Where scholars have been interested particularly in questions of agenda status, they have most often followed a longitudinal design. Nelson's (1984) study of child abuse is an excellent example: a single case is followed over many years in order to show how the same issue, once considered outside the realm of government action, later came to achieve high status on the national political agenda. In all likelihood, the content of the issue had not changed dramatically over time. However, the development of a large professional community of social workers, state welfare officials, and other professionals provided a constituency that could be mobilized to press for increased government attention to an issue that had long been ignored. So in the absence of any change in the facts about child abuse, changes in the level of mobilization of important constituents could, and did, occur. This mobilization, in turn, led to the emergence of the issue on the nation's public agenda. Apparently the link between issue contents, mobilization of groups, and agenda access is not iron clad, this longitudinal study showed.

Many studies have noted cases where a given issue was first treated as part of a specialized community of experts, but later emerged on the national political agenda. Downs (1972) described the general process of surges and declines in public interest for environmental issues. Walker (1977) traced specialized elite attention, public attention, congressional attention, and the severity of the problem for a number of public policy issues in the 1960s and 1970s. He found that elite and mass attention could shift dramatically even in the absence of changes in the substance of the problem. Focusing events, new statistical reports, spillovers from other areas of policy, and other factors affected the agenda of the U.S. Senate, he found. The link between issue content, mobilization of constituencies, and official attention is complicated, to say the least.

Bosso's (1987) study of pesticides is an excellent example of the longitudinal approach. He found great differences over time in how the same issues were considered: once as part of a tightly knit subgovernment in favor of the development of increased pesticide use, then later as part of an extremely conflictual issue network composed of environmentalists and critics of government policy as well as agricultural supporters of the programs. In a very different policy area, Derthick (1979) showed dramatic changes in the nature of policymaking for Social Security, as the program changed from its early period of consensual nurturing to the more adversarial politics of the 1970s.

In short, longitudinal studies of single issues have often shown considerable changes in policy styles and agenda status that cannot easily be reconciled with the findings of the cross-sectional studies. If issue typologies focus on the difference between regulatory and redistributive issues, for example, arguing that important political debates are more likely to occur surrounding redistributive issues than surrounding other types of issues, then the redistributive issues should constantly be in the public eye, and the regulatory ones should be chronically underscrutinized by the broad political system. Virtually every study of agenda-setting has found, however, that issues emerge and recede from the public agenda without important changes in the nature of the issues themselves.

The longitudinal approach may be best suited to studying the rise and fall of individual issues from the public agenda, but it has serious drawbacks in the areas of generalizability and comparability. The best longitudinal studies have usually been limited only to a single issue (Downs 1972; Campbell 1979; Derthick 1979; Nelson 1984; Carmines and Stimson 1986, 1989; Bosso 1987; Jacob 1988; Weart 1988). No matter how well done or how theoretically informed many of these studies may be, their applicability to other areas or to other issues is easily questioned. In addition, the various agenda studies in the literature often are not directly comparable to each other, since each author adopts a slightly different theoretical approach to guide the research; all this makes efforts to compare across the extant body of literature hazardous at best.

Comparative Case Analysis

A few studies of agenda-setting have not relied on the intensive analysis of a single case. While none of these studies makes systematic use of longitudinal data, they all explicitly compare processes across diverse issues. Studies by Riker (1986), Polsby (1984), and Kingdon (1984) further emphasize the importance of individual strategies of manipulation. Riker's heresthetic artists convince others that issues concern those questions of principle that are especially likely to motivate them to act, and Kingdon's policy entrepreneurs skillfully attach their solution to whatever problem happens to be making political headway. Polsby attempts to "tease out . . . a few general propositions about the process of innovation in American politics" (1984, 146) in his study of eight cases of new political programs. There can be no guarantee of representivity of the eight case studies, but there is some effort to theorize on a greater basis than a single case.

Riker's (1986) study of political manipulation adds to our understanding of issue change in two ways. First, his cases are drawn from an impressive range of human affairs, so there is no doubt that political manipulation occurs often and in a great variety of circumstances. Second, Riker's study is the most theoretically focused of the studies of manipulation. Riker identified three broad types of manipulation: (1) agenda control; (2) strategic voting; and (3) dimensionality (147ff.). The first two types of manipulation have to do with control of the formal rules and strategies of voting in social choice situations; the third, with rhetorical arguments that are used to change the nature of the debate. Both types of heresthetic are important for agenda studies: policy entrepreneurs attempt to manipulate both the rules and the institutions of policymaking, and the understandings that others develop of the issue. They know that both sets of factors may serve their interests.

Kingdon (1984) presents the broadest study to date of agenda-setting, again because of an impressive combination of evidence across a range of issues and explicit attention to theory building. Riker's rhetorical manipulation is clear in many of the examples Kingdon describes. Kingdon's evidence, based on a number of case studies coded from secondary sources, and interviews with 247 policymakers in Washington over four years of fieldwork, is particularly impressive. Kingdon was able to observe the rise and fall of many issues from the public agenda even over the relatively short time period covered by his study. Issue content, or at least official understandings of it, must change quickly if agenda status changes so quickly as Kingdon describes.

Theories of agenda-setting and political manipulation are often based on the actions of individual policy entrepreneurs. From Schattschneider to Cobb and Elder and to Riker and to Kingdon, we know that certain individuals are likely to attempt to push issues either toward or away from the public agenda. Finding support for these theories has typically called for detailed case studies of instances where manipulation has occurred or where the treatment of a public policy question has changed over time. For example, Baumgartner (1989) studied thirty cases of French education policy in order to compare those few that emerged as a part of the national political agenda with those many that did not. Gathering sufficient information to document strategic behaviors associated with agenda access has usually limited researchers to only a few cases, thereby reducing potential generalizability. The detailed study necessary to show individual strategies of policymaking in action has generally precluded large-scale studies of agenda-setting behavior.

Developing a New Approach

This book is based on our attempts to develop an alternative approach to the study of agenda-setting, one that would allow a synthesis of the best elements of the longitudinal and cross-sectional approaches. This involves some compromises. In order to maximize our ability to observe and compare across cases, we have sought indicators that could be gathered from the public record for many issues, covering many decades (often the entire twentieth century). Such indicators are not available for all issues, or for all times, and their quality can vary. On the other hand, we believe that the development of the field has been severely hindered by lack of an explicit comparative approach, so we have plowed ahead rather than returning to the carefully constructed case studies characteristic of the field.

Our focus on publicly available records, in particular media coverage of policy debates, differs from several important studies and so deserves some attention. Kingdon noted that media coverage and congressional hearings often did not correspond to those issues that his informants within the Washington community described as high on the governmental agenda. Some issues discussed in the media or in congressional hearings were not important agenda items, according to his research, and others that were important were rarely discussed (1984, esp. 231–32). Similarly, Baumgartner found in his study of thirty cases of education policymaking in France that significant media coverage occurred in only three cases: reliance only on media coverage to describe the important agenda items would have covered only the tip of the iceberg, according to that research (1989, esp. 46–47). Both Kingdon and Baumgartner covered issues in much greater detail than we do in this book. Their research was based on intensive interviews with officials involved in making policy, either during a period of four years, in Kingdon's case, or in a single year, in Baumgartner's. In this book, we give up the detailed discussion of the state of a particular agenda during a relatively short period, but focus instead on the long-term trends in interest and discussion for much larger policy questions. For purposes of describing the state of official and public concern with nuclear power, pesticides, smoking, and the other broad issue areas we discuss in this book, we find that media coverage does indeed correspond to official concerns.

Our approach focuses on a different level of detail and uses a much longer time frame than other research on this topic. We are careful to avoid overinterpretation from our quantitative indicators, however. It is of course possible that minor variations could occur in the number of hearings on a given topic, or number of articles published in the newspapers on a given issue, without that issue truly moving up or down on the governmental or public agenda. We therefore avoid placing too much importance on minor annual changes in these indicators; rather, we emphasize large-scale changes that show relatively long-lasting change (often the type of thing that informants inside of government overlook as obvious and therefore fail to mention in interviews). Further, we find in virtually every case that the periods we pinpoint as those of issue emergence also correspond to those described in other published sources.

We can trace the development of public policy issues through a variety of sources. In almost every case, we are interested in two related concepts: whether the issue is on the agenda of a given governmental or other institution, and whether the tone of activity is positive or negative. We use media indicators to note the degree to which an issue is on the broad public agenda and to assess the tone of elite understanding at a given time. We use a variety of governmental and other sources to trace the rise and fall of the same issue on the agendas of a number of institutional venues of policymaking. In this way, we can trace an issue as it moves from one venue to another (if it does) and track how public or elite understandings of the issue change (if they do).

Below we discuss the types of data we have collected and explain what they represent. Individual indicators are explained in the substantive chapters where they are used, and appendix A gives more detailed information about intercoder reliability tests, data sources, and the like.

Media Coverage

Studies of the role of the mass media in setting the national agenda have commonly used intensity of coverage as an indicator (see Waste 1990 for a summary of studies). In one variant, Spencer Weart (1988) analyzed media images of nuclear power in the United States. Among other things, Weart coded every article appearing in the *Readers' Guide to Periodical Literature* for selected years from 1900 to 1986—over three thousand articles in all. First, he was interested in documenting levels of attention, which he did simply by comparing the number of articles on nuclear power to the total number of articles in each year. While there is some variation in the number of articles included in each year's *Readers' Guide* volume, these percentages generally compare closely with the simple number of articles on the topic. We have compared levels of attention in a variety of media outlets, including the *Readers' Guide,* the *New York Times Index,* and a variety of indices of electronic media. Generally, levels of coverage may differ slightly from one to another, but the trends of emergence or recession from the public agenda can be clearly ascertained from any of them (see Patterson and Caldiera 1990; Mazur 1981a, 1981b). One sophisticated quantitative study of AIDS coverage found that six media outlets all focused on the issue simultaneously. Everett Rogers and his colleagues studied three major newspapers and the three network news programs and found very high correlations among all six outlets. In their words, "When one medium carried a relatively large number of news stories about AIDS, so did the other media" (Rogers, Dearing, and Chang 1991, 9). As issues become news, virtually all media outlets focus on them; as they become old news, almost all show a drop in attention. When we want to know whether an issue is news, therefore, it is not difficult; we simply count the number of articles published in an index of media attention for a given year. We focus mostly on the *Readers' Guide* and on the *New York Times Index* in this book.

We are interested not only in levels of attention, but also in the nature of that attention. Here Weart made a significant innovation: he coded each title "on civilian uses of nuclear energy with clearly positive (hopeful) or negative (fearful) implications" (1988, 387). His coding of the *Guide* proved remarkably easy to replicate for other issues. After all, an article on pesticides entitled "New Double Duty Insecticide" (which appeared in the May 1969 issue of *Farm* magazine) is different from one entitled "Nerve Gas in the Orchards" (appearing in *The Nation,* 22 June 1970). In fact, for many of the issues we studied, we found that virtually every article appearing in the *Readers' Guide* or the *New York Times Index* could be coded in terms of a simple rule: if you were an industry leader, would you be pleased or unhappy to see such a title? For nuclear power, positive items typically are those focusing on the promise of cheap fuel, on the ways technological progress will transform society for the better, on advances in safety mechanisms, and the like. For pesticides, positive articles focus on such things as plans for the eradication of disease or on increased agricultural outputs; for smoking, export earnings, profits for U.S. companies, or increasing sales of cigarettes. Interestingly, even on so-called valence issues, such a simple rule works: would the hallucinogenic drug industry want a story to appear on addiction?

The assessment of tone is important because it sets the context for agenda access. Enthusiasm and criticism have opposite effects when they come to dominate media coverage of, and public discourse surrounding, a particular issue. Tone also provides a clue to the critical points in an issue's development. When the tone is changing rapidly, systems are likely to undergo change. When attention increases following a change in tone, rapid change is almost certain.

Using the general approach developed by Weart, we created a more refined coding scheme, used for most of the issues discussed in this book. In addition to noting the general tone of the article as evidenced by its title, we noted whether the title indicated concern with economic or financial implications; with government actions (new laws being discussed, agency activities at the local, state, or federal level, or court activities); with the severity of the problem itself; or with other elements. So each general tone (positive or negative) could be subdivided into a more complex scheme, indicating concern with the problem, its economic implications, or the actions government should or should not be taking. In some cases, we further divided the government activities to identify court cases separately, since in a few cases (such as child abuse and tobacco) these represented a large proportion of the total government activities reported in the media. This coding scheme allows us to note whether an issue is being discussed as part of the governmental agenda or only as a social problem, and to some extent which parts of government are active.

Venue Access

Media indicators give one a good idea of what Cobb and Elder call the systemic agenda, but for measures of venue we need a separate indicator for each governmental institution involved in the policy. This proved overwhelmingly difficult to assemble for all of the issues we studied. Hence we adopted a more eclectic approach. We gathered what we could, used what was relevant, and relied on more qualitative assessment when we had to.

We were able to assess congressional attention to each of the issues we studied. Congressional activity can be accurately and easily traced over time by reference to the *Congressional Information Service Abstracts* (CIS annual). These are available both in printed volumes familiar to Congress watchers and in electronic format. The electronic files, with subject headings, prove ideal for tracing congressional attention to given issues over time. Just as we traced both attention and valence using media indices, we can use the abstracts of congressional hearings in a number of ways. Obviously, we are interested in the number of hearings, since this can be used as an indicator of the degree of attention Congress as a whole paid to an issue. Next, we can note the topics of the hearings, according to a relatively complex coding system reported in appendix A. This allows us to distinguish between enthusiastic hearings and critical ones, just as we coded media attention by tone. Finally, we can keep track of the committees and subcommittees holding the hearings in order to note how issues move even within the Congress. Jurisdictional changes among committees and subcommittees turn out to be an important part of the politics of venues within the Washington community, so we pay careful attention to them. Generally, we trace three separate topics in our analysis of congressional hearings over time: levels of attention (the number of hearings), tone of attention (whether it is positive or negative attention), and venue of attention (which committees and subcommittees are holding the hearings).

Indicators of federal executive branch activities proved considerably more difficult to gather than those for congressional activity. First, activity varies by issue: the Department of Agriculture and the Environmental Protection Agency are involved in issues concerning pesticides, but the surgeon general and the National Institutes of Health are active in the area of smoking. Second, many sources were not easily accessible for the longer time periods we wished to study. We sought indicators over time for such things as the number of employees in the relevant oversight or enforcement divisions, the number of regulations published per year, and other signs of activity, but these often proved of limited value. Administrative reorganizations also made it difficult in some cases to establish comparable data over long time series. In some instances (particularly our examination of urban issues), we used expenditure measures to assess government activity.

Things get even more difficult in the area of state and local level activities. We can take advantage of a variety of studies on particular topics showing detailed information about state and local government activities, but in this area even more than in the federal area, it is impossible to gather standardized and systematic information.

In some cases, we can use the stock market as an indicator of financial outcomes. This is important because investor sentiment toward an industry can be affected by governmental action, prompting further government action. In the broadest of terms, the markets become a venue for action. Market indicators proved to be of limited utility, because there are generally no sets of publicly owned companies whose stocks can be traced to see the impact of policy developments. For example, for child abuse, we expect no company to be affected by any changes in levels of government attention to this problem. On the other hand, we have been able to show great changes in the financial fortunes of electrical utilities with large investments in nuclear power plants. So we use these data where they represent something meaningful.

Public opinion data can be gathered from published sources such as the Gallup Poll Index, but again, our use of these data is not systematic, since the polling typically is not comparable over time. Still, as in other cases, we use public opinion data where available.

In sum, then, we have been eclectic in our use of information that can illuminate the long-run dynamics of issue development in American politics. There are two sources that we used for all issues: indicators of media interest and of congressional activity. Otherwise we have used indicators of other venues when the information was available and could be useful in studying an issue over time.

The Nature of the Problem

We use a variety of sources to study the severity of the social condition or the policy problem of concern. For example, we might expect government attention to traffic safety to rise when there are more deaths on the roads. However, this is not the usual case. Often both media and policy attention peak a considerable time after the problem has peaked. Hence a complicated theory of agenda-setting must perform better than a simple null hypothesis that states the government reacts to those problems that grow more severe. For each issue, therefore, we attempt to gather indicators of the nature of the problem at hand, be it the number of deaths attributable to smoking cigarettes, the amount of pesticide residues in human tissue, surveys of drug use, or reports of abuse or neglect of children, airplane crashes, traffic accidents, or whatever.

Policy Outputs

Our principal argument that policymaking in the United States is punctuated by bursts of activity that modify issue understandings and lead to nonincremental policy change requires attention to measures of policy outputs. In some cases, alterations in the structure of policymaking are the most important indicator of policy change. For example, we discuss in chapter 4 the dismantling of the Atomic Energy Commission, which changed the receptivity of the national government to programs favorable to the domestic nuclear power industry. Second, we examine expenditure patterns associated with agenda access. This proved particularly powerful in our studies of urban affairs and the federal system, where the amounts are so large that "symbolic reassurance" cannot be a serious possibility. Finally, we have occasionally examined changes in the activities of government officials, either quantitatively (as in the case of nuclear inspections) or qualitatively (as in the case of health policies toward smoking, where the rhetoric of the surgeon general was more important than any expenditure measures we could have gathered).

Secular Changes in Institutional Structures

Changing institutional and political environments are important determinants of many of the changes in political agendas noted in this book. Because of our long-term historical perspective, we need to pay careful attention to the changing contexts of policymaking. One of the most important ways in which the political environment of policymaking has changed is through the interest-group system. We use a variety of sources to note these changes. First, we trace the growth of the environmental movement, important for many of our issues, through reports in the *Encyclopedia of Associations* (Bureh, Kock, and Novallo, annual), the most thorough directory of groups active in the United States. By noting the number, resources, and variety of groups in ten-year intervals in the *Encyclopedia*, we can observe important changes from approximately 1960 to the present. In addition to this source, we take advantage of a survey of interest groups active at the national level conducted by Jack Walker in 1985. Because the groups indicated their creation dates, we can trace the changing nature of a variety of policy communities by noting the differential growth rates of different types of groups. Finally, we take advantage of the published studies in our various issue areas, studies that generally give considerable attention to the interest-group and political environments surrounding the issues at various times.

Governmental institutions have likewise changed over time. For example, budgetary information is useful in showing the relative importance of different levels of government in spending on various programs. Simple information on the number of congressional committees and subcommittees can be used to assess the changing availability of access to Congress. Apart from interest groups, we focus on two further institutional changes within the structures of government. Congressional procedures and resources underwent important and long-lasting changes in the 1970s. Congressional procedures are our second focus. Similarly the relations between the federal government and the states through the intergovernmental grant structure have shown important variation over time. The different levels of government have traditionally focused on different policy problems, with distinctly different spending patterns. However, the federal government has used its grants to alter the priorities of the states in important ways, so we focus on the changing relations within the federal system as the third major secular change in institutional structures.

Conclusion

This chapter focused on the problems of study design that plague researchers and students of policymaking and agenda-setting in America. We have proposed a strategy that allows us to combine both the longitudinal and the cross-sectional approaches.

Coming chapters make clear the uses to which these data can be put. We start out with a detailed discussion of a single case, that of nuclear power. We describe this case in greater detail than any other, in order to demonstrate the theoretical points we find most important. Then, each succeeding chapter focuses on a single element of our argument and discusses that factor across a range of issues. Each time, we present evidence across a number of issues, similar to that presented for nuclear power in chapter 4. So we start with a case study, liable to all the problems of generalizability that we know. Little by little, however, we hope to convince our readers that nuclear power is not the only case that corresponds to our theories of interaction between image and venue. By the end of the book, we will have presented both intensive information about a small number of issues and extensive information about a larger number of issues, taking the best of two conflicting research traditions. This approach leads us not only to greater confidence in our findings than if we had chosen a more monolithic design, but it points clearly to some revisions to our understandings of the agenda-setting process in American politics.

PART TWO

Tracing Policy Change in America

T his section, composed of five chapters, traces the histories of various public policies in America throughout the twentieth century, showing how they have emerged and receded from the public agenda and how these periods of agenda access have corresponded to long-lasting changes in the institutional structures of policymaking. We begin with an in-depth study of nuclear power in chapter 4. Chapter 5 includes similar, but less extensive, information concerning two more policy issues: pesticides and smoking. It shows how two types of mobilization are common in American politics: the wave of enthusiasm, which often leads to the buildup of policy subsystems, and the tide of fear, which often leads to their demise. Chapter 6 focuses on how several issues have been dealt with in the media, noting some of the biases of media coverage, and how these are related to policy change. Chapter 7 focuses on urban affairs, an important issue for our analysis because it combines important policy changes with strong partisan overtones in American politics. Chapter 8 considers three issues where no partisan cleavage is to be expected, but notes nonetheless that agenda dynamics play important roles in determining the public response even to the valence issues of drug abuse, alcohol abuse, and child abuse.

The five chapters of part 2 are designed to show similar patterns of change across a range of public policy issues that have concerned Americans throughout the twentieth century. Whether they be health-related issues, environmental questions, morality questions, highly partisan issues, or nonpartisan debates, every issue that we discuss shows long periods of stability in public policy understandings and behavior punctuated by short periods when dramatic changes take place.

4

The Construction and Collapse of a Policy Monopoly

Policy monopolies are continually being constructed and destroyed in American politics. These dynamics are driven by the changing allocation of attention by national political leaders, the media, and the public, and by the ability of policymakers to appeal to different institutional venues for decision making by raising new understandings of old issues. In this chapter we detail the creation and destruction of one policy system, that directed at regulating and promoting the production of civilian nuclear power. We present evidence for a single case in greater detail than in chapters to come in order to show most clearly the interaction of image and venue over time and to show with a concrete example followed from beginning to end how we believe this process works. Subsequent chapters deal with similar questions for a range of issues. Rather than following a case from beginning to end, however, those chapters focus on one part of the theory at a time, considering a number of cases rather than only a single one.

In this chapter we show how image and venue changes interacted first to make possible the construction of a powerful monopoly of policymaking surrounding nuclear power during the 1940s and 1950s. Extremely positive public understandings of nuclear power questions were associated with institutional changes meant to allow proponents of the industry to exert complete control over its expansion. After the creation of this policy monopoly, attention died down as expected, but when the issue emerged a second time on the public agenda in the 1960s and 1970s, the tone of this attention had shifted from enthusiastic to critical. With this shift in image came shifts in venue, as a number of congressional committees, state governments, and elected officials began to claim jurisdiction over nuclear questions. The cumulative shifts in image and venue conspired to destroy what the same forces had created only two decades before—the nuclear power policy monopoly.

Nuclear power provides an excellent opportunity to demonstrate these changes over time, since the issue has been variously treated as part of a tightly knit subgovernment and as part of an extremely conflictual policy network. Similarly, public and elite understandings of the issue have changed greatly over the years. By the middle 1950s, a tight subgovernment had been constructed centering on the civilian uses of nuclear power. The subgovernment consisted of the Atomic Energy Commission (AEC), charged with both regulation and promotion of nuclear power production as well as with the production of military nuclear needs; the Joint Congressional Committee on Atomic Energy (JCAE), a unique oversight committee consisting of both Senate and House members; elements of the scientific and technological communities in government, universities, and the private sector; and public utility companies interested in exploiting the new technology (Hamm 1983). By 1974, not only had the subgovernment collapsed, but the civilian nuclear option was, for all practical purposes, dead. No new nuclear power plants have been ordered in the United States since 1977, and more than a hundred previously ordered plants have been abandoned or canceled (Campbell 1988, 4). *Forbes* magazine labeled the failure of the nuclear power program "the largest managerial disaster in business history" (Morone and Woodhouse 1989, 1).

We report data from a variety of sources to trace the changing image and the shifting institutional venues within which nuclear power policy developed from 1945 to 1986. As strategic actors raised the issue in various institutional arenas, regulatory agencies, congressional committees, state public utility commissions, federal and state courts, the attentive mass media, private investors, and the broader public became involved in making nuclear power policy in the United States. The growth in the list of active participants in the debate was associated with dramatic changes in the image of nuclear power portrayed by interested parties and through the media. It led to a complete reversal in public policy outcomes.

Closely examining the validity of a theory in one context constitutes only a limited test of it, of course. Negative evidence would certainly discredit the theory, but positive evidence offers only limited confirmation. The data presented below, however, are nevertheless the most extensive ever assembled on changes in subsystem governance and point the way for more extensive tests of the interaction of image and venue in producing public policies in America. The chapters following assess these questions of generalizability by applying a similar analysis to a greater number of cases.

The Nuclear Image

In his analysis of the history of images of nuclear power in the modern era, historian of science Spencer Weart (1988) carefully shows how the image of nuclear power changed during the twentieth century from solidly positive to overwhelmingly negative. He argues that this shift is not based so much on changing realities as on changing images. Inglehart (1984) documents myths and misinformation on nuclear power among the mass publics of ten Western nations, and suggests that misinformation and sensationalism in the mass media are partially responsible for a lack of factual basis in mass responses to the technology. Public opinion polls have consistently shown both considerable support for nuclear power and widespread fear of the technology. In order to assess the ambiguous nature of the clusters of positive and negative images associated with civilian nuclear power among the general public, we asked a series of questions in the Texas Poll, a quarterly survey of 1,006 respondents in the state of Texas conducted by the Public Policy Resources Laboratory at Texas A&M University. Table 4.1 presents the results of the Texas Poll questions on nuclear energy.

While 70 percent of the respondents thought nuclear power plants are either "very" or "somewhat" safe, 72 percent also felt there is either "great" or "some" danger in living near them. While 72 percent say that the industry is "a high technology industry which creates economic benefits," 81 percent also agree that it creates "dangerous radioactive waste." Clearly, nuclear power plants are associated with both positive and negative images in the public mind. Depending on how the issue is presented in a public debate, either the positive or the negative images may come to dominate, as the history of nuclear power in the United States has shown. Citizens are not overly constrained by the facts in their perceptions of this complex technology, as Weart (1988) found. Fewer than 40 percent of the respondents indicated that they knew very much about nuclear power. Sixty-two percent said they knew "not very much" or "nothing at all" about the industry in a state which recently saw two plants put on line with considerable media attention. The lack of knowledge is apparent when 55 percent agreed with the statement "They produce a risk of explosion similar to an atomic bomb" and only 34 percent disagreed. Similarly, respondents were split virtually even between those who thought "They lead to higher electricity bills" and those who did not. Forty-four percent agreed with this statement, 37 percent disagreed, and 19 percent were unsure. Increased electricity bills may be the single thing that can be taken for granted when new nuclear plants enter into service in the United States. Image is clearly a matter of perception and is only slightly constrained by the facts in this area. Public attitudes toward nuclear power show the contradictory signs that one would expect any complex technology to generate. At any given time, however, one or another of these broadly contradictory clusters of images tends to dominate. Public opinion polls show how people can shift their attention from one group of consequences to another. The key link in this process seems to be media coverage.

Media coverage of political issues has two dimensions—attention and tone. Changes in the tone of issues matter little if attention is low. However, Mazur

Table 4.1 Public reactions to nuclear power plants in Texas (N = 1,006)

A. General questions

	Great Deal	Some	Not Very Much	Nothing at All	DK, NA
1. On a different topic, there are a number of nuclear power plants that produce electricity in Texas. How knowledgeable would you say you are about the issues involved in nuclear energy? Would you say you know	5.7	32.1	41.7	20.1	0.5
	Very Safe	Somewhat Safe	Not Very Safe	Not Safe at All	DK, NA
2. All in all, from what you have heard or read, how safe are nuclear power plants that produce electricity?	18.0	52.3	18.8	5.4	5.6
	Great Danger	Some Danger	Little Danger	No Danger	DK, NA
3. Could you please tell me how much danger you feel there is living near a nuclear energy plant? Do you feel there is	22.3	49.8	20.9	4.3	2.8

B. Positive images

	Strongly Agree	Agree	Disagree	Strongly Disagree	DK, NA
1. Nuclear power plants maintain our independence from imported oil.	4.3	42.9	29.9	2.1	20.8

	Strongly Agree	Agree	Disagree	Strongly Disagree	DK, NA
2. They employ a lot of people and help reduce unemployment.	3.3	58.5	26.5	1.7	9.9
3. They are a high-technology industry which creates economic benefits.	5.3	67.7	14.6	2.0	10.4
4. They do not produce air pollution the way coal does.	5.6	55.7	19.1	2.3	17.4

C. Negative images

	Strongly Agree	Agree	Disagree	Strongly Disagree	DK, NA
1. Nuclear power plants produce dangerous radioactive waste.	14.4	66.7	8.0	0.9	10.0
2. They lead to higher electric bills.	6.3	37.8	34.6	2.2	19.2
3. They produce a risk of explosion similar to an atomic bomb.	6.7	48.1	28.5	5.5	11.2
4. They are not really needed since there is sufficient energy available without them.	2.7	26.1	51.3	7.7	12.2
5. They subject those who work in the industry to health problems due to radiation.	6.4	53.1	25.9	2.7	11.9
6. They cause health problems for those who live near them.	5.4	45.0	33.6	3.8	12.2

Source: Texas Poll, conducted 21 January–3 February 1989.
Notes: DK = don't know; NA = not applicable.

(1981b) presents evidence that, at least for technical issues, any increases in media coverage tend to cause declines in public support for the policy (see also Freudenberg and Rosa 1984). As attention increases (whether positive or negative), public acceptance declines. For the nuclear industry as for other established policy subsystems in technologically complex areas, the adage "No news is good news" could not ring more true. In the early years of the industry, however, this relationship between attention and criticism did not hold. In fact, early attention to nuclear power focused on the tremendous potential of the new source of energy to solve a variety of human problems.

The peaceful use of nuclear power was initiated on a wave of positive propaganda: atoms for peace; electricity too cheap to meter; a clean, high-tech technology; low-cost source of energy for the future. But there were always competing images: the enormous destruction of nuclear weapons; a society of fall-out shelters; giveaways to private business of a public technology; government secrecy; and genetic mutations. At the beginning of the civilian nuclear era, these negative images were far outweighed by the positive. As time went on, the image changed, and this degradation of image was associated with later changes in venue access. As the venues of nuclear power policy expanded, image degradation accelerated. Finally, the industry was in deep trouble.

Weart (1988) coded positive and negative titles listed in the *Readers' Guide to Periodical Literature* for both military and civilian uses of nuclear power and has made his data available to us. Figure 4.1 shows the total number of titles concerning civilian nuclear power listed in the *Readers' Guide,* thus measuring attention. In addition, it assesses tone by presenting the percentage of these titles coded positive (neutral and uncodeable titles are omitted from the calculation of percentages). Appendix A provides details of the coding and use of the *Readers' Guide.* The figure shows an increase in attention to the issue of civilian nuclear power in the late 1940s, coinciding with the passage of the McMahon Act establishing the Atomic Energy Commission in 1946. In the early 1950s, a second major increase in attention occurred, coinciding with major amendments to the McMahon Act in 1954.[1] Both of these increases in attention were associated with positive images. This is the period of "atoms for peace."

During the late 1950s and early to mid–1960s, attention to the issue fell. Then, in 1968, the dynamics of the nuclear image changed. Attention began to increase, and negative titles began to dominate. In 1968 the number of negative titles exceeded the number of positive titles for the first time in the

1. The number of titles in the *Readers' Guide* changes over the years, so there is a risk of misinterpretation by using the raw numbers of titles on nuclear power. However, when we express the data in figure 4.1 as a percentage of all titles in the *Guide,* the shape of the two lines is remarkably similar.

The Construction and Collapse of a Policy Monopoly

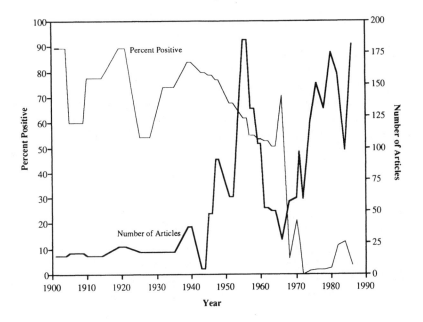

Figure 4.1. Annual number of articles on civilian nuclear power and percentage of articles coded positive, from the *Readers' Guide,* 1900–1986. *Source:* Weart 1988. *Notes:* Data for selected years only; see Weart 1988, 387.

century. Since that year, the trend has been an increasing dominance of negative titles over positive ones, until, in the 1980s, negative titles outnumbered positive ones by more that twenty to one. The opponents of nuclear power had succeeded in convincing writers for the mass media that the future of nuclear power was not the shining city on the hill, but death, destruction, and debt.

During the early years of the AEC, science journalists were enthusiastic about the possibilities of nuclear power, and their articles reflected the official optimism of the AEC. Journalists covering nuclear power questions tended themselves to be from an elite corps of science journalists who shared many of the preconceptions and hopes of the scientists and engineers about whom they wrote (Lanouette 1990). However, negative images of nuclear power and radiation had always been important as well. During the early years of the AEC, these negatives were rarely the object of journalistic focus. In later years, the predispositions of the journalistic community would shift dramatically: Based on their comprehensive analysis of attitudes toward technological change, Rothman and Lichter (1982) report that "the scientific community is highly supportive of nuclear energy development," with support strongest among scientists most knowledgeable about energy matters. However, "journalists in the prestige press are far more skeptical of nuclear energy" (Roth-man and Lichter 1982, 52; see also Rothman and Lichter 1987). These changes can be readily traced in figure 4.1 and in the literature.

Weart describes news coverage surrounding the use of radium as a medicine in the early 1900s: "in the absence of knowledge, fantasy had free play" (1988, 37). Opponents and proponents made incredible claims for both the curative powers and the dangers of this new "potion." Few of these were based on facts, but rather on symbols and exaggerations. Similar patterns of debate through the manipulation of symbols of good and bad have recurred through-out the history of nuclear power. As he points out, "rational argument became less and less prominent in the controversy" (249).

The initial technological advances making commercial nuclear power pos-sible were developed by the national government for military uses, with heavy reliance on contracting to private corporations. In the McMahon Atomic En-ergy Act of 1946, Congress established the Atomic Energy Commission and granted it a governmental monopoly on the development of nuclear power (Polsby 1984, 18–35). After lobbying by private utilities at the AEC, within the executive branch and with members of the Congressional Joint Commis-sion on Atomic Energy, Congress amended the McMahon Act in 1954 to pro-vide for a private nuclear industry, of which the AEC became the facilitator and the patron. The issue had been assigned to the private sector for decision, with a small group of executive and legislative branch officials charged with boosterism, facilitation, and almost incidentally, oversight. (This initial as-signment did not occur without considerable controversy; see Morone and Woodhouse 1989, 47–50.)

The initial institutional assignment of civilian nuclear power questions could not have been more favorable to the development of the industry. Insti-tutions were purposefully designed to ensure control by those most strongly interested in advancing the technology. Government agencies were specifi-cally organized to facilitate private development, and the nation's most pow-erful corporations pushed forward in concert with an encouraging executive branch agency and with a special joint committee of Congress also inclined to give them every assistance. Campbell describes the situation as one of differ-ential access to decision making: "Corporate, political, and technocratic elites advocating nuclear power had privileged access to the most insulated and cen-tralized interiors of the policy process" (1988, 78). Nuclear power was seen as the future guarantor of America's energy needs, while the negative images associated with it were pushed away from the national agenda. The technol-ogy of destruction which had put an end to the war would be put to use through a government–private sector partnership to put an end to scarcity and hunger. "Atoms for peace" would produce electricity "too cheap to meter." Journalists covering science topics played an important role in reinforcing the positive images of the time (see Lanouette 1990).

JoAnne Brown notes the tremendous enthusiasm and the powerful use of symbols of the first chairman of the AEC, David Lilienthal: "I suppose there is nothing of a physical nature that is more friendly to man, or more necessary to his well being than the sun. From the sun you and I get every bit of our energy . . . the energy that gives life and sustains life, the energy that builds skyscrapers and churches, that writes poems and symphonies. The sun is the friend of man. In its rays is the magic stuff of life itself. . . . The life-giving sun is itself a huge atomic energy plant. The sun, I repeat, is an atomic energy plant" (quoted in Brown 1990, 46–47).

According to Brown, this analogy of the sun was well accepted in the early years of the civilian industry. It led to an "almost casual attitude toward atomic radiation" at which people only a decade later would cringe: "Children growing up in the early 1950s had shoes fitted by x-ray. Women went to beauty parlors to have superfluous hair removed from their legs by x-ray. Children had their tonsils literally burned out by x-ray" (Brown 1990, 48).

Figure 4.1 shows the wave of enthusiasm in the popular media that greeted the construction of the subgovernment. Total levels of attention were high, and the tone was extremely positive for the industry. The combination of high levels of attention and enthusiasm for a new technology is precisely what we expect to be required for the establishment of a powerful subgovernment. Under such conditions, incentives for political leaders are first to pay attention to the program, since media attention is so high, and second to facilitate it, since the tone of public attention is so positive. Under these conditions, experts are given great advantage. They argue that the technically complex decisions necessary should be left to them, and that the nation's political leaders can best do their job by establishing relatively independent, if not self-regulating, institutions bestowed with considerable budgetary authority. Political leaders benefit by supporting a popular new program that promises great potential payoffs. Potential critics, especially those within the community of experts, are often ignored during such periods of mass enthusiasm.

These were the conditions that allowed the construction of the nuclear power subsystem in the United States in the 1950s. Mass enthusiasm, based on a massive public relations campaign by government and industry leaders, created the conditions for extremely favorable decisions toward the industry. It was soon to disappoint, however. From overwhelmingly positive, the public and media image of nuclear power began to degrade slowly, following a pattern of expansion of conflict similar to that described by Schattschneider and Cobb and Elder for other issues.

In his excellent case study of nuclear power policy, John Campbell clearly shows that political conflict expanded from the closed subsystem outward as AEC technical staff began to question the agency's safety decisions. He describes this as an internal legitimacy crisis (Campbell 1988, 51). These scientists and safety experts began to feel that government funds were going disproportionately toward the development of bigger and newer reactor designs, with insufficient attention to the safety questions for which they were responsible (see Campbell 1988, 51ff.). Some scientists believed that the variety of designs permitted by the AEC made safety more problematic, since each construction project was unique (Mooz 1979; Morone and Woodhouse 1989).

From the outset of the establishment of the policy subsystem, opponents had voiced objections. First labor unions complained about government subsidies for private businesses (Morone and Woodhouse 1989, 47–50). Later environmentalists and local activists, displeased at the location of plants close to urban areas, objected. Their complaints fell on deaf ears as policymakers deferred to the scientific experts. However, scientists concerned with safety issues could not be viewed as opponents to the industry, since they were nuclear engineers themselves. Hence their complaints had special legitimacy. In their efforts to ensure a larger share of the budgetary pie for safety questions, these bureaucratic entrepreneurs enlisted the support of members of the Joint Committee on Atomic Energy. Members of the Joint Committee objected to the authorization of the Fermi breeder reactor near Detroit, over the reservations of the AEC's Advisory Committee on Reactor Safeguards (Mitchell 1981). With the first appeals from within the community of nuclear power experts, the monopoly of decision-making authority began to be whittled away.

Campbell sets 1965 as the date at which significant concern on reactor safety crystallized in AEC's regulatory arm (Campbell 1988, 53). However, earlier changes in rules of operation concerning licensing allowed external opponents access to the policymaking system. For example, in 1957 the AEC began holding public licensing hearings; in 1962 the AEC established routine and open licensing hearings. This gave safety advocates the opportunity to strike where the public was potentially most concerned: reactor safety at particular locations. Between 1967 and 1971, around a third of all license applications were challenged (Rolph 1979, 102). The conflict had expanded outward as scientists in the agency leaked information to the Union of Concerned Scientists and other antinuclear groups (Campbell 1988, 61). This connection gave external opponents the credibility they needed to attack the system. According to Campbell, an external legitimacy crisis developed by 1972, as the Union of Concerned Scientists and their allies in the emerging environmental movement contested all license hearings. In 1973, Ralph Nader and other environmental groups filed suit in court based on the safety concerns (Campbell 1988, 63). As Campbell puts it, the internal legitimacy crisis had been transformed into an external one.

From the overwhelmingly positive image the industry had enjoyed at the creation of the subsystem in the 1950s, it began to slide toward the negative. While the positive still probably outweighed the negative in the minds of most Americans in the late 1960s or early 1970s, public understanding of nuclear power was moving rapidly toward the negative. As the tone of nuclear power shifted, attention began to increase as well. Figure 4.1 shows two peaks of attention to nuclear power: the first associated with the enthusiasm of setting up a new peacetime industry, but the second, during the 1970s, associated with the beginning of the end of the nuclear policy monopoly. This expansion in public and media interest was built on criticism, not enthusiasm. A combination of high public and media interest in nuclear power and a critical tone of such interest created dramatically different incentives for political leaders in the 1970s than those that existed in the 1950s. A variety of institutional changes followed, each of which reinforced the negative image of the industry and gave greater access to opponents in the policymaking process. Combined, these changes in venue and in image lead to the destruction of this once-powerful subsystem.

Changes in regulatory procedures had their impacts not only in the regulatory environment itself, but also in a number of other venues. State and local governments, courts, and Congress all began to play a more important role, and most were hostile to the industry as the theory of conflict expansion leads us to expect. In 1969, Congress enacted the National Environmental Policy Act, requiring environmental impact assessments for all federal licensing procedures. The courts, initially supportive of the AEC, became increasingly hostile, beginning with the D.C. Court of Appeals ruling in 1971 that NEPA applied retroactively to AEC licensing procedures (Rolph 1979, 106). The AEC responded to the use of its licensing procedures by environmentalists and the Union of Concerned Scientists by trying to close off the venue opportunity. It proposed eliminating the opportunity for public intervention in operating license hearings in 1971, but this received no support from even the Joint Committee (Rolph 1979, 116). In 1974 the AEC was dismantled, its regulatory functions assigned to the Nuclear Regulatory Commission, and its development functions to the Energy Research and Development Agency (ERDA), which later became the Department of Energy. A major reason for these changes was the low esteem in which the AEC and the entire nuclear industry was held by many congressmen. In 1977 the Joint Committee was abolished because of the general perception that the committee members were too close to the industry. A number of congressional committees claimed responsibility for oversight. Venue shopping clearly played an important role in this process, and its importance was understood by those on both sides.

Opponents followed the classic pattern of expanding the conflict by altering the institutional venue. Simultaneously they worked to reformulate the image of nuclear power from one of progress and efficiency to one of danger and waste. Ironically, as Weart points out, much of the reason for the shifting image of the nuclear power industry came from the almost perverse pride that the leaders of the industry took in its early years in proclaiming that they were going to harness "the world's most dangerous technology." The industry prided itself on its preparations for worst-case scenarios, but opponents were able to make effective use of "Maximum Credible Accident" calculations when it suited their strategic needs (see Weart 1988, 288ff.). Unfortunately for those in favor of the industry, public attention focused on the seeming admission by the government and industry that these accidents could indeed occur, rather than on the preparations being made for them, or on how unlikely they might be.

Even though it was not clear at the time, and even though most analysts today do not fully comprehend it, the fate of nuclear power was sealed prior to 1974. When the industry lost control of the issue, when the venue had been expanded by opponents to include licensing, oversight, and rate making, the future was determined. Utilities ordered only fifteen more plants after 1974. Opponents had won primarily by getting their vision of the issue accepted, and by altering the nature of the decision-making process by expanding the range of participants involved. We present data in the sections to follow which assess the changing nature of the nuclear power policy community in the United States. The image changes evident in Weart's data presented above correspond to the emergence of nuclear power questions in a variety of institutional arenas.

The Changing Regulatory Environment

Nuclear power at its inception was regulated by an agency intent on avoiding public discussion of any problems in the nuclear industry and driven by a desire to see the civilian program grow. The Atomic Energy Commission issued few regulations, its inspection staff was small, and its annual reports to Congress showed little reason to be concerned with any problems in the industry. Since the agency was responsible for both safety questions and the promotion of the growth of the industry, however, internal conflicts existed from the start. By the mid–1960s, the AEC was showing the first signs of greater oversight of the industry which it simultaneously sought to stimulate and regulate. While small and seemingly inconsequential at first, these changes multiplied rapidly in following years.

AEC/NRC annual reports and other sources can be consulted to document the transformation of the regulatory environment of the nuclear industry over time. By almost any measure available, the regulatory environment had gone through a major transformation during the early 1970s. Figure 4.2 presents three such indicators. The total number of regulations and amendments issued by the AEC/NRC per year is a rough indicator of how rapidly the regulatory environment is changing. Figure 4.2 shows the number of regulations and amendments enacted in each year since 1957 (unfortunately, the 1973 data were not available in AEC annual reports). After an initial period of only fifteen or fewer new regulations per year, the agency shifted in the late 1960s

The Construction and Collapse of a Policy Monopoly

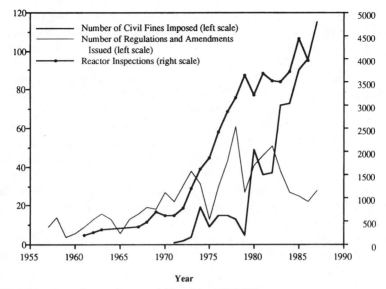

Figure 4.2. Increasing regulatory activities of the AEC/NRC.

toward much greater activity. By the mid–1970s, regulatory activity as measured with this simple indicator was much more erratic, but generally at about four times the previous level.

Corresponding to the change in the total number of regulations and amendments are the results of an independent study which sought to classify each new regulation in terms of the scope of its impact. This study covered only the period 1967–77; fortunately this is the period during which the regulatory environment was transformed in the United States. Bennett and Kettler (1978) created a "weighted regulation index" that counts those regulations with greater impact on the industry more heavily than those with smaller impact. The weighted regulatory index grew almost geometrically from the late 1960s to the mid–1970s, from a value of 3 in 1967 to 12 in 1970, 29 in 1972, 47 in 1975, and 49 in 1977. These figures are not included in figure 4.2, but as that figure indicates, the annual output of regulations and amendments increased in a similar way at about the same time. The two series of data combined show the changes surrounding the activities of the AEC/NRC as the breakup of the nuclear energy subgovernment approached. Of course this activity has a much greater cumulative effect than only annual figures suggest. A major shift in regulatory behavior started in the late 1960s and was complete by the mid–1970s.

Other indicators also point to an increasingly tight regulatory environment over time. The annual number of reactor inspections done by AEC/NRC staff went from about five hundred per year in the early 1970s to over three thousand per year in the 1980s, according to annual reports. As can be seen in figure 4.2, this dramatic shift in activity began in the early 1970s, just as other indicators of regulatory activities were also changing. By 1974 the number of reactor inspections passed one thousand and continued to grow. Not shown in the graph, inspections of fuel facilities and other nuclear sites besides reactors under the jurisdiction of the AEC/NRC follow a similar pattern. Finally, the percentage of NRC staff in the Inspection and Enforcement Division shows a steady increase, from 20.9 percent in 1975 to 32.8 percent in 1986. During the early period, much of the federal government's investment in nuclear energy was in research and other activities, but by the late 1970s the NRC had become a watchdog agency. The mid–1970s was a period of transition.[2]

Figure 4.2 shows a lagging indicator of regulatory activities: the number of civil fines imposed by the AEC/NRC was zero before 1971, then in the area of ten per year during the 1970s, but it increased dramatically after 1980. This presents an excellent example of the positive feedback mechanisms between Congress and the bureaucracy, so we consider it in some detail here. Since the AEC was designed both to promote and regulate the industry, internal battles between those charged with the promotion and growth of the industry and those charged with ensuring the public safety were common. As an example of the initial preoccupation with promotion of the industry, the original mandate of the AEC included no authority for the safety regulators to fine those operators not complying with safety regulations. The leaders of the AEC viewed their role as facilitators, not as watchdogs. Over the years, the relative power of the safety inspectors within the agency grew, but still they had little statutory authority. Congress approved in 1969 the first civil penalties, though these were limited to symbolic levels of $5,000 per violation and to a total of $25,000 over thirty days. Still, this was the beginning of an important change; Congress was the object of an appeal by a bureaucratic loser and reacted by changing the rules to increase the power of that former loser. Figure 4.2 shows the moderate use of this highly symbolic power during the 1970s, beginning as soon as the law became applicable, in 1971. Once the precedent had been set for the use of fines, however, safety regulators were able to return to Congress to argue for greater authority. The idea of using financial incentives to force industry to comply with safety regulations also happened to correspond to general thinking about using market forces in government that were popular at the time. In 1980, again at the request of the Inspection and Enforcement

2. The regulatory data also allow us to eliminate a potential rival hypothesis: that changes in control of the White House caused changes in the regulatory activities. From the mid-1960s to the mid-1970s, regulatory actions increased. A process which had begun in the Johnson administration was continued and accelerated under Nixon until the system was transformed. The data do suggest a lightening of the regulatory load in the Carter and particularly the Reagan administrations (see Wood 1988); however, the nuclear industry subsystem had already been dismantled before then.

Division of the NRC, the law was changed to increase the upper limit on fines to $100,000 per violation, with no limitation on the number of fines within any time period. Almost immediately, the safety inspectors of the NRC began to impose millions of dollars of fines against safety violators. Figure 4.2 shows this increase clearly.

Congress played a key role in the shift in relative powers of the safety versus the promotion activities of the AEC/NRC. The two venues are tightly linked, and changes in one are rapidly seen in the other. As congressional attention to nuclear power has grown, the tone of its inquiry has shifted from positive to negative. Further, this increased attention has resulted in shifting powers within the executive branch as well. Both the internal dynamics of the bureaucracy and congressional influence led the AEC/NRC to shift from a promotional arm of the industry itself to a much more stringent regulator during the 1970s. These changes were cumulative and self-reinforcing. Similar changes took place within the Congress in response to the changes within the NRC.

The Changing Nature of Congressional Oversight

The dramatic changes in the regulatory agencies surrounding nuclear power in the United States were paralleled by changes in congressional activities. In order to pinpoint the period when nuclear power emerged on the congressional agenda, we have coded and analyzed all hearings on civilian nuclear power topics by all congressional committees from 1945 to 1987. There were a total of 1,237 hearings on civilian nuclear power in Congress during this period, which we have identified by reading their abstracts and descriptions in annual publications (Congressional Information Service annual). For each hearing, we have coded its date, the committee(s) and subcommittee(s) which held it, and up to five topics that were discussed. These topics were noted as positive, negative, or neutral in tone. Each hearing then could contain both negative and positive topics, so our dataset contains a greater number of topics than hearings. Positive hearings were those focusing on such things as the use of nuclear power to desalinate seawater, to propel commercial ships and aircraft, or to promote new technologies necessary for the industry, or on growing demand for electricity. Negative topics include such things as reactor accidents, regulatory reform, safety for workers, export policy criticisms, waste disposal, or transportation problems. Neutral topics were those such as annual appropriations hearings or others where no clear tone could be identified.

Early in the postwar period, there was little congressional attention to nuclear power questions, with an average of only 3 hearings per year from 1945 to 1954 (except for the year 1949, when there were 28 hearings). Very few committees were involved in this process, generally fewer than two House and Senate committees holding hearings in any given year. As time progressed, however, the controlled nature of the agenda and the relative inattention to nuclear questions were transformed dramatically. The number of congressional hearings increased to an average of 16 per year during the period of 1955 to 1968, and to 51 per year from 1969 to 1986. The number of different committees and subcommittees claiming jurisdiction over nuclear affairs increased dramatically as well. Table 4.2 presents information concerning the emergence of nuclear power on the congressional agenda.

During the early years of the nuclear power industry in the United States, congressional activity could not have been organized in a way more favorable to the industry. There were few hearings on the topic, and a small number of committees and subcommittees were able to maintain the exclusive right to oversee "their" industry. During the late 1950s and the 1960s, this system began to break up, as evidenced by the increasing number of hearings on nuclear topics, but probably more importantly, by the increasing number of different bodies claiming jurisdiction over some part of the industry. By the 1970s, the previously independent subgovernment intent on supporting the industry had completely disappeared, as two dozen different committees or subcommittees of the Congress held hearings on some aspect of the civilian nuclear program in a typical year. In 1979, no fewer than 36 different congressional bodies held a total of 94 hearings on nuclear power questions.

Not only did the number of hearings and the number of committees and subcommittees claiming jurisdiction over the civilian nuclear industry increase dramatically in the postwar period, but this change in attention coincided with a shift in tone. Negative topics came to dominate congressional attention to nuclear power. Figure 4.3 shows Congress's increasingly negative view as nuclear power emerged onto its agenda in the mid-1970s. It presents the number of positive and negative topics that were discussed in congressional hearings from 1945 to 1986. (A small number of hearings clearly had more than one topic; therefore the number of topics coded in fig. 4.3 is slightly higher than the number of hearings indicated in table 4.2.)

As congressional actors became increasingly interested in questions nuclear, their purpose was not to promote the industry. They were breaking into a subgovernment which had shown its favorable inclinations toward the industry, and those committees and subcommittees which sought to encroach on this jurisdiction did so as the result of appeals from those on the losing side of the previous policy battles. Institutional changes within the Congress during the 1970s increased dramatically the number of committees and subcommittees able to claim jurisdiction over at least some aspects of nuclear power policy in the United States. The Congress as a whole represented a venue to which opponents of the industry appealed when they could not win within the Atomic Energy Commission. By taking advantage of regulatory rules which allowed for public participation and by increasing their presence in Congress, opponents to nuclear power succeeded over a number of years in breaking down a powerful subgovernment. The changes were not dramatic at first.

Table 4.2 Expansion of congressional attention to nuclear power, 1944–86

Dates	Average Number of Hearings on Nuclear Power	Average Number of Committees Holding Hearings per Year	Average Number of Committees and Subcommittees Holding Hearings
1944–54	5.8	1.8	1.9
1955–68	15.9	5.3	8.6
1969–86	51.3	14.3	24.2

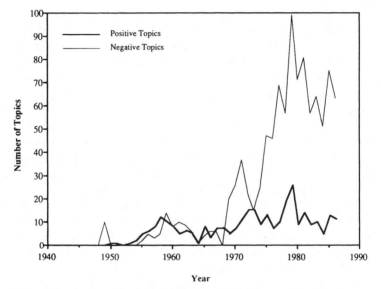

Figure 4.3. Increasingly negative tone of congressional hearings on nuclear power.

However, the cumulative effects of small changes in congressional oversight during the 1960s, then alterations in regulatory activities during the early 1970s, and finally an explosion in the number of congressional masters overseeing the regulatory agencies in the 1970s signaled a complete breakup of the pronuclear iron triangle in the United States. These changes were similar to changes occurring at other levels of government and were soon to have their impact through the financial markets.

The Increasing Activism of State and Local Governments

Beginning with rules requiring public participation and local hearings for individual plants, environmental activists were able to mount increasingly successful campaigns against plants in particular areas. While the national policymaking system was being altered on the one hand, some of the greatest successes of antinuclear activists were due to their skills in using state and local levels of government to slow down or stop construction of many plants. They pressed the rhetoric of public participation to force the opening of numerous previously closed governmental processes, allowing greater and greater intervention by opponents at all stages of the policy process (Nelkin and Fallows 1978). Massive local protests were mounted at specific plants (Nelkin 1971; see also Kitschelt 1986).

In California, strong environmental and consumer movements and the availability of the initiative and referendum allowed citizens to vote on two antinuclear propositions, one in 1972 and a second in 1976 (Kuklinski, Metlay, and Kay 1982). Although these referenda failed, California environmentalists continued to press their case at licensing hearings and rate-setting hearings before the public service commission. Consumer advocates in many states began focusing on state public utility commissions in order to force them to take a tougher stance against the electric utility monopolies which they regulated. They began to intervene regularly in rate-making procedures, especially when nuclear plants were involved, with more success in some states than in others. As capital costs for nuclear facilities escalated during the 1970s, nuclear opponents benefited from public service commission rules that prohibited passing on costs of facilities to ratepayers until the plants were completed. They also picked up some valuable allies in the form of manufacturing corporations interested in keeping their electricity costs low. Antinuclear activists, once a diverse collection of environmentalists, now included General Motors, Dow Chemical, and other large industrial users of electricity who knew that with each nuclear power plant granted an operating license, state regulators would allow significant rate increases so the utilities could recoup their enormous investments.

Expansion of the nuclear power policy community did not only occur in national policymaking institutions. Federal and state courts became more involved, and state and local governments were mobilized. In short, opponents were successful in seeking out not only one more favorable venue for their views, but literally hundreds of them, breaking up the previously tightly controlled subgovernment in the process. These changes were to have dramatic impacts on the economic performance of those utilities operating or constructing nuclear facilities.

The Changing Reactions of the Financial Markets

Ultimately, nuclear power was abandoned in the United States because the industry became uncompetitive with alternative sources of energy. The financial plight of the nuclear power industry occurred during a period of long-term problems in the electric power industry. In 1965, electric utilities as a group represented extremely safe investments, with only 11 percent of major electric utilities rated at the lowest investment grade of (Baa) by Moody. A decade later, half these utilities were rated this poorly and, therefore, were forced to offer higher rates on their bonds (Campbell 1988, 99). Utilities had lost their luster to the financial community. Part of the reason for the declining economic performance of the utilities had to do with their heavy nuclear investments and the changing regulatory environment, as noted above (Montgomery and Rose 1979; Golay 1980; Weingast 1980; Komonoff 1981; Paik and Schriver 1981; see also Goodman and Wrightson 1987). The financial markets reacted to the huge cost overruns associated with nuclear investments in a way which reinforced some of the negative images associated with the industry, even though the business and financial community had no particular aversion to the technology per se. Those utilities most committed to nuclear power fared even worse than others during this time.

Figure 4.4 compares the stock market performance of several standard stock indices with an index of nuclear utility stock prices which we have created, from 1962 to 1988. It shows the Standard and Poor's 500 stock index and the Dow Jones Industrials, the two widest indices of industrial stock performance. The Dow-Jones Utility Index is comprised of fifteen utilities and thus may not be fully representative of the utilities industry. A comparison with the more inclusive Standard and Poor's utility index yielded no significant differences, however. Our nuclear utility index was constructed by averaging the stock market performances of those thirty-six utilities listed on the New York Stock Exchange that rely most heavily on nuclear power for electrical generation. While the Dow-Jones Utility Index includes a number of utilities with large nuclear investments, it also includes those with none of their generating capacity coming from nuclear power. The thirty-six utilities which we have combined into the "nuclear utilities" index include some of the largest utilities in the country, including Commonwealth Edison, Consolidated Edison, Houston Industries, Southern California Edison, and Duke Power. They were chosen by assembling a list of all the utilities with nuclear power plants and taking those with the highest proportion of their total generation capacity coming from this source. Ironically, these utilities may represent some of the most successful nuclear utilities, since by definition they have managed to get their plants constructed and into operation. Many other utilities invested heavily in nuclear power plant construction, only to abandon the projects, in some cases after billions of dollars had been spent. We have also analyzed the performance of those eleven utilities which abandoned nuclear power projects after the longest periods of construction (and therefore presumably the greatest lost investments). We find no significant difference between the stock market performance of these eleven utilities with abandonments and those thirty-six utilities with the greatest commitment to nuclear power included in figure 4.4. Both groups perform poorly.

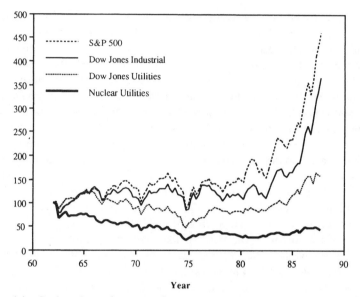

Figure 4.4. Stock market performances of nuclear utilities versus other indices, 1962–1988.

Figure 4.4 reports quarterly values of stocks for the four indices, adjusted to report their values as compared to their starting points in 1962. None of the indices did well before 1974, when utility stock prices hit bottom; still, theoretical investors in Standard and Poor's 500 stocks would have had $1.50 in 1973 for each 1962 dollar they invested, while nuclear utility index investors would have had only about 45 cents. These differences become even more dramatic in the recovery phase, making clear the investment community's new aversion to nuclear power. The two broad industrial indices perform roughly similarly, each increasing in value from 1974 to 1988 by a factor of three or four. Utilities stocks in general did not share this rapid growth, but those utilities with heavy nuclear investments performed even worse than other utilities. The Dow utilities end the series at a point roughly three times their 1974 values, but the nuclear utilities recover hardly at all. So while the broad stock indices increased their values rapidly throughout the 1980s, and while utilities in general also improved during this period, those utilities heavily committed to nuclear power distinguished themselves by seeing their stocks decline to less than one-half their 1962 values. Utilities with heavy nuclear investments became the pariahs of the investment community.

The investment community did not react negatively to nuclear projects before the breakup of the subgovernment which controlled the industry before the early 1970s, but later avoided them with a passion. The breakup of the pronuclear governmental iron triangle seems to have affected the financial performance of the utilities. While utilities in general recovered from the poor performance before the oil crisis of 1973 and 1974, and on average their stocks were worth over three times as much in 1988 as in 1974, those most heavily involved in nuclear power have made no discernible recovery. In 1988 their stocks remained, on average, at less than one-half their 1962 values.

Clearly, the economics of nuclear power did not drive its politics. On the contrary, politics had an important impact on the adverse reactions of the market. As regulatory activity increased and as the federal government jettisoned its boosterism of the industry, it became clear to investors that utilities operating, constructing, or planning nuclear plants could be in serious financial trouble. The market constitutes one more element in the positive reinforcement process. As elite understandings of nuclear power questions were altered in the 1960s, new actors began to intervene, thereby changing the nature of the regulatory and the governmental environment for the industry, making it considerably less favorable. This led to serious changes in the financial outlook for the industry. So changes in the political environment and in the processes and rules of policymaking eventually found their reflection in the financial markets, as an image problem became a serious economic concern. Prudent business managers began to shy away from nuclear investments, where previously the tightly controlled and supportive governmental structure in charge of promoting the industry had made the investments so attractive to this same group. So we see clearly the link between politics and markets, as the markets are a part of the single process of interaction among the multiple venues of decision making in any complex society.

The Changing Public Image of Nuclear Power

We have argued so far that the breakup of the pro-nuclear-policy subsystem in the United States proceeded as follows: opponents exploited divisions within the community of experts; images in the popular media changed; opponents were able to obtain the attention first of regulators and then of Congress, the courts, and state regulators; finally, the market responded.

What about the public? Far from anticipating or causing the changes in venue which we have identified with respect to nuclear power in the United States, public attitudes toward nuclear power responded to elite activity. The expansion of conflict often includes the mass public, but its inclusion in the policy debate is not always necessary. In the case of nuclear power, opinion polls assembled by William Rankin and his colleagues (1984) show clearly that a majority of the public supported the construction of more nuclear power plants until after the incident at Three Mile Island (TMI). However, the proportion opposing started rising after 1974. Moreover, there existed a minority opposition of just under 20 percent as early as 1970. In response to the question, "Do you favor or oppose the construction of more nuclear power plants?" positive responses outnumbered negative ones by approximately 60 to 18 in 1970; 60 to 27 in 1974; 45 to 35 in 1975; 60 to 28 in 1977; and 50 to 30 in 1979 before TMI. After TMI, opponents outnumbered supporters by 60 to 30 (see Rankin, Nealy, and Melber 1984, 48). Throughout the period when changes in the nature of the policy process in Washington were at their most dramatic, the public became increasingly concerned in a pattern that suggests response to elite conflict.

There was significant public concern about the siting of nuclear power plants "in this area," which show increasing opposition to the industry throughout the 1970s. In this series of polls presented by Rankin, in response to the question, "Suppose your local electric company said it wanted to build a nuclear power plant in this area. Would building such a plant be all right with you, or would you be against it?" large majorities were in favor of such a decision in 1971 (58 to 23) and 1973 (56 to 24). Then opposition began to rise steadily throughout the mid- and late 1970s, reaching greater opposition than support in the last poll before TMI, in 1978 (see Rankin, Nealy, and Melber 1984, 52). The critical weakness, ably exploited by opponents, was the location of power plants near heavily populated areas.

The mass public represents but one of a number of potential arenas of political discourse in the American political system, and not always the key one. Strategic policymakers can have tremendous success, and even upend powerful subgovernments made up of cohesive groups of executive branch officials and strong economic interests, through the strategic manipulation of images and venues of local and national governments. They are not limited to appealing directly to the mass public in their efforts to expand conflicts beyond their original bounds. Available data on nuclear power suggest that mass opinion followed elite exploitation of venue opportunities. However, the case can be made that the potential for conflict expansion to the mass public is an important calculus in the entire venue search/conflict expansion process. That is, participants may be keenly aware of the consequences of mass mobilization on an issue.

The Successive Venues of Consideration of Nuclear Power

We have argued that Schattschneider's notions of conflict expansion need to be modified to include the multiple policy venues that can be activated in the United States. We suggested that policy venues tend to become involved sequentially in an issue because of their differing perspectives and responsibilities. Finally, we argued that image change and venue access proceed simultaneously and in an interactive fashion. Changes in policy images facilitate changes in venue assignment. Changes in venue then reinforce changes in image, leading to an interactive process characterized by positive feedbacks.

The information concerning nuclear power presented above can be sum-

The Construction and Collapse of a Policy Monopoly

Table 4.3 Tracing the demise of a policy subsystem: Venue succession for nuclear power

Date	Event	Sources
Pre-1965	Tight control by AEC/JCAE; positive images	Hamm 1983; figs. 4.1–4.3
1965	Internal questioning of safety at AEC	Campbell 1988
1966	Regulatory activity accelerates	Fig. 4.2
	Media coverage increases	Fig. 4.1
1968	Negative press coverage exceeds positive	Fig. 4.1
1969	Negative congressional hearings exceed positive	Fig. 4.3
1971	Court of appeals rules that EIS applies to AEC	Campbell 1988
1972	Union of Concerned Scientists begins to intervene in licensing hearings	Campbell 1988
1972	California antinuclear initiative	Kuklinski, Metlay, and Kay 1982
1973	Nader's court suit	
1974	AEC reorganized into NRC and ERDA	Campbell 1988
	Only 15 nuclear plants ordered after 1974	
1975	Nuclear stock prices fail to recover after nadir	Fig. 4.4
	Congressional hearings exceed 40 per year	Fig. 4.3, table 4.1
1977	Joint Committee on Atomic Energy disbanded	
1978	Public opinion on building local plants turns negative	Rankin, Nealey, and Melber 1984
1979	Three Mile Island	
1979	Public opinion on nuclear power turns negative	Rankin, Nealey, and Melber 1984

marized in table 4.3, which presents a simplified history of the demise of the nuclear power policy monopoly. It shows the dates at which a variety of important changes in image and venue occurred, making it easier to trace the history of the industry. The direct, quantitative evidence we have assembled here is supplemented by particulars from other sources, as noted in the table. These indicators are only rough benchmarks of changes in a very complex policy process, and the table presents a simplified version of the events described in this chapter. Nevertheless, the table illustrates how conflict surrounding nuclear power expanded sequentially, venue by venue, rather than dichotomously, from elite control to the mass public. Further, it shows the relation between image and venue. Finally, it points to the quick interaction of the two, since so many of the important changes occurred within a three-year period in the mid-1970s.

The case of nuclear power policy in the United States demonstrates graphically the power of tracing the changing policy image and its interaction with venue opportunities over an extended period of time. Agendas, policy attention, and the creation and destruction of policy subsystems were tightly linked in this case. In the chapters that follow, we show that what happened to nuclear power policy was not unique. While not all groups are able to achieve the type of policy monopoly that nuclear power proponents were, and while not all such policy monopolies were destroyed in such a dramatic way, each of the issues we discuss in following chapters shows the dynamics of image and venue.

5

Two Models of Issue Expansion

In chapter 4 we followed the development of the nuclear power subsystem in American politics. Our analysis of other issues in a range of areas has convinced us that many aspects of the buildup and breakdown of the nuclear subsystem are not peculiar to that issue, but common to many. Specifically, policymakers take advantage of periods of agenda access in order to build new institutions or to alter those already in existence. These institutions may remain for decades after public interest has died away. As long as the institutional structures and patterns of apathy remain constant, policy is likely to change only slowly. As pressure for more dramatic change builds up, it may be resisted for some time. If the pressures are sufficient, however, they may lead not only to a change in policy, but also to institutional changes designed to reinforce and stabilize the policy around some new point of equilibrium. Structure-induced equilibrium leads to dramatic punctuations in policy outcomes and to long-lasting changes in the very institutions of policymaking, as these are continually redesigned to protect new interests.

Waves of popular enthusiasm surrounding a given issue provide the circumstances for policymakers to create new institutions to support their programs. These institutions then structure participation and policymaking, often ensuring privileged access to the policy process for those who helped set them up. After public interest and enthusiasm fade, the institutions remain, pushing forward with their preferred policies. These institutional legacies of agenda access may structure participation so that a powerful subsystem can remain relatively independent of popular control for decades. During the time when such a policy monopoly is in operation, there may be stability or incrementalism in policy outcomes, which many analysts have mistaken for equilibrium. We know, however, that the issue may reach the public agenda again some years later, and that the consequences of this second period of agenda access could be the dismantling of those very institutions that owe their existence to the first period of enthusiastic popular acceptance. Agenda-setting often has long-lasting institutional consequences, in other words, and can explain the lurching nature of punctuated equilibria in politics.

In this chapter we discuss two types of agenda access in American politics. One is associated with enthusiasm, the other with criticism. When issues reach the public agenda on a wave of popular enthusiasm, conditions are at their best for the construction of a new policy subsystem. Political leaders react to feelings of enthusiasm by doing whatever they can to provide support for specialists who convince them that they have the power to solve a major national problem. Leaders want to be seen as facilitating, not hindering, the work of experts when the public believes that something good may come of it. We saw in chapter 4 how the nuclear power subsystem was created in the 1940s and 1950s, and here we discuss a similar process in the area of pesticides.

When an issue emerges on the national agenda in an atmosphere of criticism, on the other hand, the policy implications are opposite: conditions are ripe for the destruction or dilution of any policy subsystem that may have been created in the past. Criticism of experts encourages political leaders to pay more attention to the details of policymaking within specialized policy communities, whereas enthusiasm leads political leaders to delegate power to experts. Both types of mobilization can have equally important policy consequences, though these may be opposite in terms of substance.

We make two important points in this chapter: First, institutions are often the children of agenda access, and the means through which short periods of attention affect outcomes and government policies for decades. Institutions remain after attention dies away, structuring participation in policymaking, making sure that some have privileged access while others are shut out. Second, agenda-setting comes with a tone; enthusiasm and criticism lead to opposite institutional responses. Waves of enthusiasm lead to the creation of governmental institutions and subsystems, but waves of criticism lead to their breakup.

When we use such terms as *good* and *bad, enthusiasm* and *criticism,* or *positive* and *negative,* we imply no endorsement of a particular point of view; rather the terms are related to our expectation of what the tone of attention will do to the industry or practice concerned. Use of these terms obviously depends on the viewpoint of the user. We follow a simple rule, as described in chapter 2: we look at the issue from the point of view of the industry involved. When studying tobacco, news about crops, export markets, and the glamour value of smoking are all good things. News about studies linking cigarettes to cancer is bad news. Were we looking at the health industry, we might easily use the terms in the opposite way. For example, a "wave of enthusiasm" about curing cancer is positive when considered from the point of view of health professionals. From the point of view of the tobacco industry, however, this would look more like a "tide of criticism." Optimism about limiting deaths on the highways through enacting mandatory seat-belt laws is positive from the public health point of view, but negative from that of the auto industry or from that of civil libertarians. A tax revolt might be considered positive from the point of view of conservatives with a desire to see smaller government, but negative from the point of view of the beneficiaries of government programs or spending. Obviously there is room for confusion with these terms of polarity, so we need a simple rule to keep them straight.

We use these terms because policymakers use them and because they have clear implications for policy outcomes. From the point of view of someone involved in the policy process, it is clear whether new developments help or hurt the cause. The fact that the same development may be good for one group but bad for another is part of the constant dynamic of the creation, the reshuffling, and the destruction of subsystems in American politics. Changes in the mobilization of bias have two simultaneous results: they encourage the creation of government programs to enact the solutions called for by the "wave of enthusiasm," and, at the same time, they promote the destruction of any previously created subsystem in the area being criticized. The antinuclear movement could be seen as critical (from the point of view of the nuclear industry), but also as enthusiastic (from the point of view of the growing environmental bureaucracy). When we use the terms *good* and *bad,* therefore, we should be understood always to be speaking from the point of view of the industry; we could just as easily have adopted the opposite convention. It is important only to remain consistent.

While the previous chapter looked closely at a single issue, we base our analysis in this chapter on two additional cases. Like nuclear power (an issue to which we return from time to time in this chapter), pesticides policy and smoking and tobacco policy have variously been considered as either the solutions to important national problems (and therefore accepted and promoted with enthusiasm) or the sources of tremendous social, economic, and health problems themselves. In later chapters, we note that such changes in public understandings over time are not peculiar to these three issues. Before proceeding with the evidence from the smoking and pesticide policy areas, let us consider the background for our distinction between enthusiasm and criticism, and the reasons why we assert that emergence on the agenda under positive and negative conditions naturally leads policymakers to react differently.

The initial establishment of many policy monopolies came about with remarkable speed in the United States, as we saw in the case of nuclear power in chapter 4. Policy entrepreneurs take advantage of favorable public attention and quickly move to ensure a quick assignment by government officials to an encouraging institutional venue. In the absence of opposition to new policy ideas, policy entrepreneurs can move swiftly to manipulate elite and mass opinion toward a surge of enthusiasm for the new policy. The desired outcome is, of course, a policy monopoly; the political weapons are concerted promotional campaigns. At these times, increases in the investment of political resources can yield increasing marginal returns as the wave of enthusiasm sweeps the policy community, the press, and national decision-makers.

As attention is generated for the initial creation of a new policy system, surrounding, for example, a new industry, increasing attention is associated with great enthusiasm. This positive attention may attract the interest of a broad range of governmental and private officials for a time, but quickly the issue is assigned a restricted venue for control, nurturing, and encouragement. Public and media attention may be high in volume, and extremely positive in tone for a time, but it will not be permanent. As the monopoly is set up and decisions are routinized, the issue will fade from the public agenda.

Just as the successful creation of a monopoly may occur with remarkable quickness, so may its destruction. Once the process of interaction between image and venue is put into motion, it may obtain a logic of its own. Policymakers and institutions which had shown no interest in the matter may descend in droves, as a new way of understanding the issue gives it much greater political appeal. Environmentalism is a clear example of a politically popular idea which, if linked to a particular policy, may quickly lead to its demise.

Where existing policy monopolies are being attacked, we expect that a rise in negative attention is related to an increase in the number of venues claiming jurisdiction. As attention increases due to appeals by those disgruntled with the activities of the previously insulated policy monopoly, the tone of attention and the dominant public image of the policy may shift from positive to negative. Strategically minded policymakers know that only by claiming that there is a serious problem with the policy will they attract the attention of those in other institutional venues. So as attention increases in volume, its tone may shift from positive to negative, and the number of venues in which the issue is discussed may increase. Policy monopolies are created during periods of positive attention, but can be radically changed when attention increases and shifts in tone. All in all, a single process may produce the creation of policy monopolies, their maintenance over long periods of time, and their rapid demise.

The Dual Mobilization Theories of Downs and Schattschneider

In his classic article "Up and Down with Ecology," Anthony Downs (1972) argues that public attention to political issues typically follows a cyclical pattern. In Downs's approach, a preproblem stage is characterized by low attention. Then a state of alarmed discovery and euphoria generates much attention, followed by a realization of the costs of solving the problem and a gradual decline in public interest. This is a decidedly pessimistic view of the agenda-setting process. According to Downs, hitting the agenda is of little policy relevance, for the public and the national political leaders are likely soon to reach the conclusion that action is futile, that the costs of solving the problem are too high, or that some other problem requires their attention even more urgently. Taken to its logical conclusion, this view of agenda-setting implies a never-ending series of "alarmed discoveries" during which the public suddenly focuses on an issue, but after which serious action may never take place. Attention simply fades as the difficulties of action become clear or as some new crisis pushes the old one out of the limelight.

Certainly some issues have followed the pattern described by Downs, but on the other hand, some issues remain on the agenda for quite some time. Now twenty years after his discussion of "ecology," environmental issues remain much higher on the national political agenda than they were at any time before Downs wrote about them, for example. So the cyclical pattern described by Downs is not the only possible outcome of the agenda-setting process. Agenda dynamics have important policy consequences; they are not simple exercises in futility. Some issues remain high on the public agenda for considerable periods of time, and some problems really do get solved, surprising as this might sound.

In one of the few attempts to test Downs's theory empirically, Peters and Hogwood (1985) examined variations in governmental attention to important problems over time. Just as Downs postulated periods of intense activity followed by periods of lower activity, they found that "almost all policy areas have at least one clear peak decade of organizational activity" (251). In virtually each area of government they studied, in other words, there were identifiable periods during which many organizations were created, reorganized, or terminated. Further, these periods generally coincided with Gallup Poll data showing public concern with the same problems. According to this study, governments have periods that resemble "alarmed discovery." While hopes of solving the problem are high, governments create new agencies, reorganize other ones, and try in various ways to address the problem.

Downs's theory suggests that there should be a decline of public interest after the peak, but Peters and Hogwood found that governmental activity did not usually drop off to previous levels. Rather, considerable activity was still apparent in following decades. In other words, public attention to a given issue may fade, but even a short-lived spurt of interest may leave an institutional legacy. Institutions, especially government bureaucracies, do not simply "fade away" like public interest or media attention. So there may be cycles of public attention, but one important element of "alarmed discovery" may be the institutionalization of programs meant to deal with the problem. Perhaps government growth is part of this Downsian cycle. [Where attention suddenly focuses on a new problem, policymakers create new institutions or adopt old ones as potential solutions. As the institutions begin their work, request operating budgets, and get a better understanding of the problem at hand, then the costs become clear, the euphoria fades away, and attention shifts to something else. But the institutions remain. Downs overlooks this key element of the agenda process.

When public attention focuses on some new problem in the way described by Downs, feelings of optimism lead policymakers to fund the research or to implement the programs of specialists who claim to have a solution. Specialists with potential solutions of course waste no time in asking for programs to be implemented, and, as John Kingdon (1984) describes, policies then result from the combinations of the problems that interest political leaders and the solutions proposed by the bureaucratic and other experts. The institution of new programs, policies, and agencies is thus strongly associated with the agenda-setting process.

Downs's theory of cycles may be approximately correct when dealing with public attention to problems that lack a feasible solution. Attention surges, then declines as the futility of action becomes clear. Where solutions are present in the form of existing governmental programs, initiatives, and institutions, however, a surge in public attention to a problem may lead to the enactment of new programs and to the growth of new institutions. As described by Cohen, March, and Olsen (1972), the logical consequence of attention to a problem in the absence of a solution is flight; but where a solution is available, action is much more likely. Even short-lived periods of public interest to a given problem can therefore lead to the bureaucratic institutionalization of solutions and to long-term policy consequences.

In the previous chapter, we discussed the development and breakup of the civilian nuclear power subsystem in the United States. That issue went through at least two distinct periods of emergence on the national political agenda, each associated with opposite results for the industry. As shown graphically in figure 4.1, and as discussed in the text surrounding that figure, a period of enthusiasm for the potentials of nuclear power led government leaders to create an extremely favorable set of institutions in order to support and develop the industry. In the pages to come we call such a mobilization of enthusiasm a Downsian mobilization. In such mobilizations, government is called on to solve problems or take advantage of new technologies.

Public attention to nuclear power then faded, as the plants took years to build, as cost overruns multiplied, and as other issues came to the forefront of the nation's political agenda. But the institutional subsystem remained, and it worked quietly for about two decades implementing the new policy of encouraging greater use of nuclear power, building and ordering more nuclear plants in the United States than in any other country in the world. So the period of optimism and positive mobilization did not last for long, but it left a tremendous institutional legacy.

Nuclear power of course is no longer associated with the positive image it enjoyed in the early postwar years. Neither has it receded permanently from the agenda, as we noted in chapter 4. Its reemergence on the political agenda in the 1970s was certainly not associated with enthusiasm, but with fear, mistrust, complaints, and criticism. We call this a Schattschneider mobilization, since it often stems from the efforts of opponents of the status quo to expand the scope of conflict (Schattschneider 1960). Here the government is already involved in the solution, and some have begun to see the solution as the problem. Hence the issue must be expanded beyond the confines of the existing policymaking system.

Internal critics are often able to combine forces with external critics of an industry (Cobb, Ross, and Ross 1976), in a process that can lead to self-reinforcement. Not only do these critics attack the policies, but they ask for changes in the procedures and rules that have made them possible. Substantive and procedural arguments are combined, as opponents seek both types of reforms. As Riker argued, "One can expect that losers on a series of decisions under a particular set of rules will attempt (often successfully) to change institutions and hence the kind of decisions produced under them" (1980, 444–45). If successful in attracting the attention of government policymakers in search of popular new issues, critics even of a powerful subsystem like the nuclear one can be very successful. With changes in the institutions that helped maintain a policy monopoly, the policy monopoly may be destroyed or rendered much weaker. Institutional changes, coming only periodically, can explain why policies may be relatively stable during long periods while the institutions are stable, but then change dramatically during those periods when the institutional revisions occur.

Just as the Downsian mobilization led to the creation of the favorable institutional structure that the industry enjoyed for decades, the Schattschneider mobilization led to the destruction of these favorable structures. Two waves of mobilization, one positive for the industry, one negative, led to the emergence of the issue on the public agenda twice during the postwar period, each time with important institutional and policy changes. In between these periods of emergence, changes in nuclear power policy were mostly incremental. The system appeared to be near equilibrium during each period of low public attention, but this apparent equilibrium was punctuated by the emergence of the issue on the public agenda, when dramatic policy changes occurred.

Testing the Dual Mobilization Thesis

For the two issues discussed in detail in this chapter, we have coded the total number and the tones of articles mentioned in the *Readers' Guide to Periodical Literature* just as we did for nuclear power in chapter 4. In addition, we have supplemented this source with the *New York Times Index* for the issue of smoking, in order to test for any differences in coverage.⌉As in chapter 4, we use the terms *positive* and *negative* as an industry representative would. Positive articles are those that pesticide or tobacco industry leaders would be happy to see appear; negative articles are those that clearly detract from their position. Intercoder reliability was over 95 percent for each of the cases, and the percentage of articles not codeable as either positive or negative was typically small, on the order of 10 percent or less. The following chapter uses a more detailed coding system for the same issues, and appendix A describes all of our data collection and coding practices in detail.

For the assessment of formal agenda access, we have used the topics covered in congressional hearings. Other researchers have used coverage in the *Congressional Record* (Larson and Grier 1990) and the introduction of bills and resolutions (see Waste 1990). Hearings may not guarantee subsequent policy action, but they do provide a good indicator of congressional interest. Since they typically must be arranged well in advance, and since they usually represent a substantial commitment of effort, hearings provide a good indication of congressional interest, much like what one might find if one studied hours of floor debate, introduction of bills, or some other possible measure. Hearings have several features that make them preferable to these alternatives, however. First of all, there are more hearings on a greater variety of topics than there could possibly be floor debate, since hearings are conducted by smaller groups. Second, because they concern these smaller groups, in committees or subcommittees, we can trace the venues of congressional consideration in a relatively detailed manner. Third, we can code the tone of congressional attention in addition to its volume. Some hearings are held because of problems; others are held because the organizers want to promote attention to the positive aspects of a given program. Finally, we can note the differential participation in the variety of hearings held in different bodies of Congress by noting the list of witnesses. For these reasons, therefore, we make considerable use of congressional hearings in the pages to come. Using other indicators of congressional interest would lead to similar, but less complete, findings. We have used the *Congressional Information Service Abstracts* as our source for information concerning hearings and have made our coding systems correspond with those we used for the media. Some of these data are reported in this chapter; a more detailed and complete discussion of congressional activities is presented in chapter 10.

Smoking and Tobacco Policies in the Twentieth Century

The tobacco industry in the United States benefits from a series of favorable institutional arrangements centering on agricultural subsidies to farmers. At the same time, the government is active in antismoking campaigns. When we look at the history of public attention and government action toward smoking

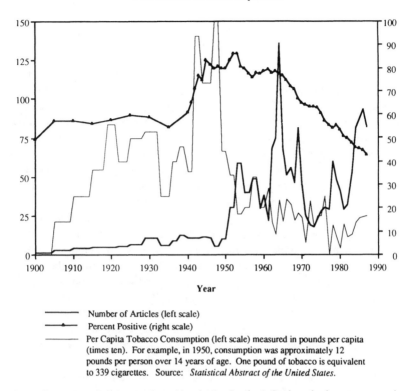

Number of Articles (left scale)
Percent Positive (right scale)
Per Capita Tobacco Consumption (left scale) measured in pounds per capita
(times ten). For example, in 1950, consumption was approximately 12
pounds per person over 14 years of age. One pound of tobacco is equivalent
to 339 cigarettes. Source: *Statistical Abstract of the United States*.

Figure 5.1. Annual coverage of smoking in the *Readers' Guide* and tobacco consumption, 1900–1986.

since the turn of the century, we develop a better understanding of how these diverse governmental reactions came to be. Tobacco once generated almost no coverage in the media, and government actions were almost entirely supportive of the agricultural subsidy program. Tobacco, like wheat or corn, was seen as an important crop that generated export earnings, supported millions of farmers, and on which whole communities and even some state economies were dependent. With tobacco seen as an economic issue, the role of political leaders was clear: they should defer to experts and allow the agricultural subsystem to run its course. This is precisely what happened during the entire first half of the century.

As can be seen in figure 5.1, media attention to smoking and tobacco questions has varied widely during the century. A total of 2,020 articles has appeared in the *Readers' Guide*, but these have been distributed very unevenly across the years. Coverage during the pre-1950 period averaged only about 6 articles per year, but annual articles on smoking averaged 38 in the 1950s, 62 in the 1960s, 31 in the 1970s, and 58 from 1980 to 1987. In 1964 alone, the year of the surgeon general's report on smoking, there were 136 articles listed in the *Readers' Guide*, more than twenty times the prewar average. (Our study of the *New York Times Index* from 1946 to 1987 indicated a similar pattern across time, as we discuss in appendix A.)

Smoking received scant press coverage prior to the 1950s, and what coverage it received was decidedly mixed in tone. Press attention to cigarettes and smoking during World War Two was overwhelmingly positive, focusing on the use of cigarettes as barter by GIs in Europe, on shortages and rationing, on the size of the tobacco crop, and on other items that could not be considered bad for industry. Essentially, figure 5.1 shows that smoking has never been seen with great enthusiasm in the national media, but it was mostly a nonissue for the first fifty years of this century. A few negative articles might have appeared each year, but so did a few positive ones.

Figure 5.1 also shows how media attention to smoking and tobacco questions seems to have been related to the behavior itself. During the postwar years, the industry and the habit were glamorized in popular culture. Per capita consumption of tobacco in the United States increased from about eight pounds per person during the 1930s to eleven or twelve pounds during the 1950s (figures are from the *Statistical Abstract* [Bureau of the Census 1991]). Smoking was not a new industry to be built from scratch after World War Two. Rather, a powerful subsystem was already in place before the war, centering on agricultural subsidies for tobacco farmers (Fritschler 1989; Ripley and Franklin 1991, 88–90). The buildup of the tobacco subsystem appears to have its roots before the turn of the century, so we cannot discuss it as we did for nuclear power. We can see its continued operation and expansion during the first half of the century, however, and we can certainly observe its demise.

The dramatic increases in levels of coverage of smoking issues in the media that occurred in the years following World War Two were driven almost exclusively by negatives. Health warnings had always been a part of the media's coverage of this issue, but these suddenly became the dominant force during the 1960s. As more people began to smoke, health officials mobilized in an extremely effective manner. The number of articles we have coded as negative grew from an average of only 2 per year before 1950 to 20 during the 1950s, to 41 during the 1960s, 19 during the 1970s, and 44 during the 1980s. (There was also a slight increase in the number of positive stories on smoking, from 2 per year before 1950 to an average of 6 in the years from 1950 to 1987, but growth in the negatives far outstripped growth in the positives.) Following this explosion of emphasis on the health risks of smoking, per capita consumption of tobacco began its remarkable decline, which has continued unabated for three decades.

In the case of smoking, a Schattschneider mobilization was clearly evident: opponents of the industry were able to generate lots of bad news. This increase in public awareness led to a dramatic change in public behavior. Industry leaders had benefited from a long period of low public attention to the public health and public policy consequences of smoking policy during the prewar years and had benefited from a true glorification of smoking immediately after the war. This period of positive attention did not last, however, and the industry was not able to control the expansion of conflict once public attention shifted to public health questions.

This short discussion of smoking policy in the media shows that the issue has emerged only in the postwar years as an item on our national systemic agenda. (We have considerably more to say about media coverage of smoking in the following chapter; for this chapter, the simple point of levels and tone of coverage is most important.) The systemic agenda is closely related to the formal agenda, according to Cobb and Elder, so we consider congressional activities next.

While smoking became part of the systemic agenda during the 1960s, and even to some extent during the 1950s, it was not until the mid-1970s that the issue burst onto the congressional agenda. When it did, however, it followed a pattern remarkably similar to the one we observed for nuclear power, in chapter 4. As the total number of hearings increased, the hearings were held before an increasing number of different congressional bodies. During the period when there was little congressional attention to smoking and tobacco questions, a large proportion of congressional hearings were relatively positive toward the industry; however, as participation expanded, this expansion was associated almost exclusively with criticism. Criticism did not come from previous allies changing their minds; rather it stemmed from conflict expansion, as previously uninvolved persons began to assert themselves.

The percentage of topics that our coders coded as proindustry in the congressional hearings declined steadily as the number of hearings increased, as the bottom part of figure 5.2 shows. This is precisely the pattern we expect to be associated with a Schattschneider mobilization. Opponents of the industry are able to appeal to congressional allies to hold hearings and generate adverse publicity. The more they are successful in generating adverse publicity and consideration on the systemic agenda, the more they are likely to be heard on the formal agenda. The more they are heard on the formal agenda, the more adverse publicity is likely to be generated in the media. So the Schattschneider mobilization process is a self-reinforcing mechanism, leading to dramatic, not only incremental, change.

Pesticides

Beginning in the early part of the twentieth century, demand for pesticides began to increase dramatically as the size and variety of farms changed from family producers to large-scale commercial ventures (Bosso 1987). Compared to modern chemicals, of course, the first pesticides were extremely mild and

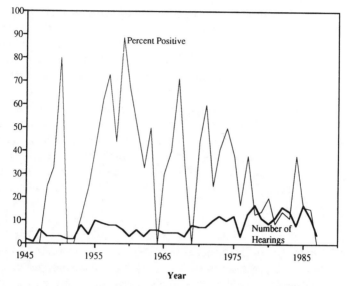

Figure 5.2. Congressional hearings on smoking.

ineffectual, but they did increase crop yields significantly, and their use spread rapidly. As the chemicals became popular, a great number of manufacturers entered the market, and farmers were presented with a confusing variety of products. The first problems associated with the pesticides industry stemmed mostly from farmers not knowing the harmful effects of combining two pesticides, or not knowing the toxicity to skin or from ingestion of the chemicals. By the first decade of this century there was considerable fraud in the industry, with poor labeling of products one of the main sources of problems. Congress first regulated the pesticides industry when it passed the Insecticide Act of 1910, mostly a truth-in-labeling act (Bosso 1987; Dunlap 1981). Enforcement was entrusted to the Bureau of Chemistry in the Department of Agriculture. Agriculture officials saw their mission as one of protecting the farmer from unsafe products even while encouraging the increased use of chemical pesticide. One small voice within the USDA, the Food and Drug Administration, was concerned with the residue levels of toxic agents left on food, but the FDA did not have jurisdiction over pesticide questions, and its studies were generally ignored by USDA officials.

Research during World War Two yielded a new generation of pesticides— synthetic organics such as DDT. These chemicals were stronger and more persistent than their predecessors, and were thought to be nontoxic to humans. Proponents made optimistic claims for the new generation of pesticides, claiming that they would end malaria, increase food production to the point of ending world hunger, and even completely eradicate those persistent pests, the housefly and the mosquito. These arguments should sound familiar to our

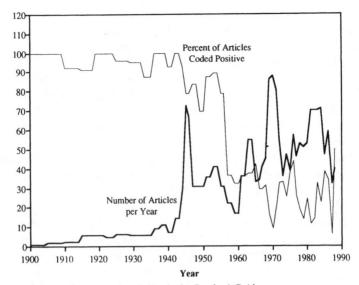

Figure 5.3. Annual coverage of pesticides in the *Readers' Guide*.

readers by now. They had the same effect as those arguments in favor of nuclear power. They were also responsible for a later backlash against the industry. Just as in the case of nuclear power, the postwar years saw a great American enthusiasm for the progress of science, this time as represented in
the pesticides industry. American science and industry would turn its efforts
from the war in Europe and Japan to another war, this one with the
purpose of eradicating world hunger and disease through increased use of
pesticides.

The strength of this wave of enthusiasm for progress through chemistry is
graphically depicted in figure 5.3. Like smoking, pesticides were mostly a
nonissue throughout the beginning of the century, and what little attention
they did receive in the popular press came mostly from farm magazines,
where their virtues were almost uniformly extolled. Popular coverage of the
issue shot up dramatically in the late war years and has remained higher ever
since.

The wave of popular attention to the pesticides industry in the late war years
was overwhelmingly positive in tone. In this environment Congress passed its
second major piece of legislation concerning the industry. The Federal Insecticide, Fungicide, and Rodenticide Act of 1947 (FIFRA) passed with the
strong support of both agricultural and chemical industry interests. Christopher Bosso writes that "the shared assumptions about pesticides as a panacea,
and the imperatives motivating their widespread use, provided the parameters
for policy debate" (1987, 59). A cozy triangle governing pesticides (the Department of Agriculture; farm interests and chemical companies; and the

congressional agriculture and appropriations committees) quickly controlled the regulation and use of these powerful new chemicals. Consumer interests, represented by the FDA, and environmental interests, basically unorganized, were excluded from participation. In other words, a Downsian mobilization took place in the late 1940s for pesticides. Great popular and official enthusiasm about the potentials of the industry to do good led government officials in Congress and the executive branch to facilitate the growth of the industry. They set up an institutional structure, based in the Agriculture Department, that promoted the industry for decades to come.

During the 1950s, the "golden age" of pesticides, widespread campaigns were developed to promote the use of pesticides, and local extension agents fanned out across the country encouraging and teaching farmers to increase their use of the chemicals. The degree of official optimism about the glories of pesticides is dramatically illustrated by two major policy disasters of the late 1950s. In 1957 the USDA launched two huge pest eradication campaigns, one in the Northeast, directed at the gypsy moth, and one in the South, aimed at the fire ant. Both involved massive aerial spraying; both resulted in huge fish kills, enormous crop damage, and the devastation of wildlife. Neither campaign was successful in eradicating the pest (see Bosso 1987). Figure 5.3 shows the decline in the positive tone of pesticide coverage in the press, coinciding exactly with the eradication programs—a decline in public image from which the industry never recovered. Another blow to the pesticides industry occurred in late 1959 when the FDA for the first time banned the sale of a crop because of pesticide residues. The cranberry scare, coming just before the holiday season, devastated annual sales of an entire crop, but more importantly it solidified the public's newly negative view of pesticides.

One simple example gives an idea of how small beginnings of criticism can be compounded through the interaction of image and venue. In reaction to the negative attention associated with the failed eradication campaigns in the late 1950s, of course a number of congressmen began to pay attention to pesticide issues where they had ignored them in the past. One of these was Rep. James Delaney, who became interested in the possible contamination of food through residues. The Delaney hearings in 1958, which led to the Food Additive Amendment, were home to a fierce battle among agricultural interests, health officials, and the food industry. The substantive legislative outcome of the hearings was a single important new rule: "no additive shall be deemed safe if it is found to induce cancer when ingested by man or animal" (Bosso 1987, 97). The institutional outcome of these debates was that the Food and Drug Administration, long the bureaucratic loser in its conflicts with Agriculture officials, was given expanded authority to restrict toxic residues in food. The cranberry scare, coming in 1959, could be seen as an adept piece of bureaucratic expansionism from a group that understood that increasing public attention to a problem in an especially dramatic way is one way to shift the issue from the bureaucratic institutions, where they continually lose, to the front pages of the papers and to congressional hearings, where their side might stand a better chance. From one change in levels of attention, new participants are called into a debate, then their participation leads to changes in the rules, leading to further changes in participation and public understanding of the issue: a pattern of self-reinforcement that we see again and again.

The golden age of pesticides in the United States was relatively short. The wave of popular enthusiasm about the benefits of the new industry lasted only from about 1945 until about 1956. After that, popular attention to the pesticide question was much more likely to focus on the problems than on the promises of the industry. However, our Downsian mobilization hypothesis implies that a powerful set of institutions may be set up during the initial period of popular enthusiasm, and this group of industry boosters may be powerful for years to come. This is exactly what occurred in the case of pesticides. It was several years before the Schattschneider mobilization of public outcry against the industry was able to make a significant difference.

The Schattschneider mobilization followed the abrupt reversal in the public image of pesticides that was associated with the three disasters of the late 1950s: the gypsy moth and fire ant campaigns and the cranberry scare. Attention did not reach its peak until the late 1960s, however. Rachel Carson's 1962 book, *Silent Spring* (parts of which were published in the 16, 23, and 30 June 1962 issues of *The New Yorker*), did not really change ideas about pesticides—the news was already bad for the industry, as can be seen in figure 5.3. Rather, it solidified a movement that had already gathered considerable steam. A rancorous debate between environmentalists and industry scientists ensued, a debate that went to the heart of the issue of scientific objectivity. Peak attention occurred in 1969, coinciding with the announcement of the banning of DDT, while the tone of media attention reached its all-time low of about 90 percent negative. Environmental groups pressed Congress, the courts, executive agencies, and state agencies during this time, with increased success, on air and water pollution, nuclear power, industrial wastes, and pesticides. In consequence, numerous major laws, regulations, and court decisions were issued during the late 1960s and early 1970s. Major revisions of pesticide regulation occurred in the National Environmental Policy Act (1969) and the Federal Environmental Pesticides Control Act (1972). Although the law was a result of compromises between the old agriculture-pesticides subsystem and environmentalists, it provided a new regulatory environment. The pesticides–Agriculture Department link was certainly not destroyed, but the Schattschneider mobilization of the late 1960s led to the breakup of much of the legacy of the Downsian mobilization of twenty years before.

For most of the history of pesticide policy, congressional attention has been low, and most hearings have been aimed at regulating and limiting the industry rather than promoting it. Unlike nuclear power or tobacco, the pesticides industry is not itself the center of a large body of government action. Rather, it is part of a large variety of agriculture policies centering on monoculture and price supports for a variety of crops. One example among many of how pesticide are heavily affected by government agriculture programs is the limitation of acreage in farm price-support programs. These limits encourage farmers to use more pesticides and fertilizers in order to maximize the yields from the land remaining under cultivation.

Because pesticides as such are rarely the exclusive focus of Congress in the normal process of administering programs, most hearings focusing specifically on pesticide issues are directed at problems in the industry. Figure 5.4 shows the levels and tone of congressional attention to pesticides during the twentieth century. Congress paid virtually no attention to pesticides until there were significant public worries about the industry in the 1960s. Despite passage of two major laws concerning the industry, in 1910 and 1947, there were almost no hearings before 1960. Congressional hearings seem to play an important role in the expansion of conflict, but Congress in its role of supporter or booster of an industry is not Congress in committees. Supportive laws seem to be passed with relatively limited discussion, while critical legislation tends to follow extensive hearings and debates.

Between 1960 and 1975, no hearings could be classified as supportive of the pesticides industry. This is the period of *Silent Spring*, the DDT bans, and major environmental legislation. Congress acted as a venue of appeal for those interests not represented within the pesticide subsystem established after the 1947 legislation. Eventually, rules were changed to allow greater openness within that system of policymaking, and the result is considerably more conflict even within the pesticide policy community. Since 1975, Congress has held some hearings supportive of the industry, as actors on both sides now appeal to allies in the different committees and subcommittees. From a one-sided mobilization of interests centering on promoting the use of pesticides, Congress played a key role in expanding the opportunities for criticism. The once-powerful subsystem regulating and promoting the industry now is home to much more internal debate than was once the case.

The case of pesticides shows remarkable similarities to that of nuclear power. Both cases show tremendous growth of positive attention during the postwar period. Attention, as measured by press coverage, increased by factors of 10 to 20, as the industries were established and began to grow. The Downsian mobilization process worked almost identically in both cases. Attention dropped off after this initial surge, as the pesticides and nuclear power subsystems became firmly established. Later, the Schattschneider mobilization occurred. In both cases, we can note a second period of increased attention beginning in the 1960s and 1970s (slightly later for nuclear power than

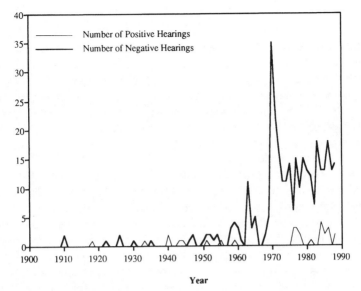

Figure 5.4. Congressional hearings on pesticides.

for pesticides), dominated by negative images. Pesticides and nuclear power emerged on the public agenda twice during the postwar period. The first time was the result of one-sided mobilization by proponents of the industry, as they sought and gained favorable government actions and institutionalized their control over these new industries. In the second phase of agenda access, however, the Schattschneider mobilization process led to major alterations in the proindustry subsystems.

Another regularity in each policy area is that the tone of press coverage turned negative before, not after, the major rise in attention associated with the Schattschneider mobilization. That is, the industry in question began to receive bad press at a low level before the conflict expanded out of its control. A Schattschneider mobilization, with its increase in attention, is most likely to occur in an environment already stressing problems rather than potentials. This finding gives empirical meaning to the observation made by John Kingdon (1984) that windows of opportunity occur within which major policy change is possible. The kinds of opportunities, moreover, are tightly constrained by the prevailing tone in media coverage. When a policy community has already come to be dominated by significant divisions, when experts have begun to criticize their own industry, then appeals to the public are most likely. Where internal divisions are minor, no member has the incentive to break apart the policy monopoly they already enjoy by generating greater public awareness of their issue.

Conclusions

Issues can hit the agenda on a wave of positive publicity, or they can be raised in an environment of bad news. These two different mechanisms of agenda access have different policy consequences. High attention and positive tone can lead to the creation of powerful institutions of government given broad jurisdictions over the policy, while high attention and negative tone often lead to subsystem dissolution. These relations were demonstrated in the case of nuclear power in chapter 4, and we extended the analysis to the cases of tobacco policy and pesticides here.

In the cases of pesticides and nuclear power, we found that both types of mobilization were observable simply by tracing media attention and congressional hearings over time. In the case of tobacco, we were able to observe only the second type, the mobilization of criticism. We can conclude from this either that the Downsian mobilization had occurred before the turn of the century or that it is not a necessary condition for subsystem construction. Pesticides and nuclear power both form a part of a broad set of issues that benefited from a general confidence in the progress of science after World War Two, so we should not build a general theory of issue mobilization around only them. Clearly, there is more than one way to build a powerful subsystem. While the Downsian mobilization process is a good one, it is not the only way to enforce or encourage the mobilization of bias in American politics.

In each of the three policies we have studied so far, on the other hand, the consequences of a Schattschneider mobilization have been similarly devastating for the industry involved. Increasing negative attention, which seems to follow a period during which the tone of public coverage of the issue shifts from positive to negative even while attention is low, leads either to the dissolution of the policy subsystem or to protracted conflict. Protracted conflict has characterized pesticide policy, as agricultural interests and chemical companies have opposed a coalition of environmentalists and local government entities concerned with water pollution, human health, and other problems. We cannot say that the pesticides subsystem has been completely destroyed, though it is certainly not as strong as it once was. Similarly, tobacco policy is much more conflictual than it once was, although tobacco companies retain considerable influence and economic power.

In the case of nuclear power, the opponents appear to have scored the greatest policy victory. The pronuclear coalition that once dominated the issue now is extremely weak, if we look at such indicators as the number of new power plants ordered in the United States (zero since 1978). Of course, one lesson of tracing these policies over time has clearly been that those who appear powerful at one time may see the tables turned, so we should not rule out a dramatic change in public attitudes toward nuclear power in the years to come. It has happened before. In any case, our study of three major issues so far has shown that the Schattschneider mobilization process can cause powerful policy subsystems to be transformed either into conflictual issue networks (as in the cases of smoking and pesticides) or into weak vestiges of their former selves (as in the case of nuclear power).

Our assessment of formal agenda access through the examination of congressional hearings suggested that Congress plays an especially important role only in a Schattschneider-type mobilization, that is, agenda access under negative publicity. We found scant evidence of increased congressional activity during the subsystem construction period for each of these three policies. This is not to say that Congress plays no role in the establishment of powerful subgovernments; certainly its members play a key role there. But, as we saw in the case of nuclear power, its most important function is to restrict participation only to those willing to support and nurture the programs. In the second kind of mobilization, however, Congress plays an especially important role, visible as hearing activities increase and as the tone of these hearings becomes negative. Seeking out congressional allies seems to be a privileged tactic for disgruntled policymakers trying to expand a conflict from within the bureaucracy. This finding fits the common observation that the institutional reforms of American political institutions during the 1970s may have the effect of allowing opponents of policies more venues within which to raise objections, potentially contributing to paralyzed government. But it may also contribute to a dynamism in American pluralism often accused of being unresponsive to excluded interests.

Schattschneider (1960) gave to political science the concept of conflict expansion. Losers, he thought, had motive to try to expand the number of participants in a search for allies. To do this, criticism of the existing arrangements is a necessity. Certainly, we have found numerous examples of exactly the type of issue expansion he proposed. Issue expansion, however, may occur in a second way—with an aura of enthusiasm and with few opponents. Participation is often expanded not to defeat oligarchies, but rather to incorporate supporters and to wrest ever-greater resources from the political system. This is the phenomenon we have called Downsian mobilization, and we have seen that it occurs as well.

Both Schattschneider and Downs are right, but only half right. There are clearly two types of agenda access, and the same issue studied over a relatively long period of time may show both. The remarkable element of each of these mobilizations, besides the tremendous policy implications that can follow from them, is their rapidity once they begin. Policymaking in many areas of American politics may not always be ruled by incrementalism, decreasing marginal returns, and slow changes (although these features remain important); rather, there are critical periods of mobilization of antagonists during which dramatic changes are put into effect. At any one time, there may be little change, but periods of relative stability may be punctuated by fitful bursts of mobilization that change the structure of bias for decades to come. Institutions are the legacies of short periods of attention by the public to a given issue. They remain intact until attention increases at some later date to cause more institutional changes. Periods between agenda access may be characterized by stability, but this is not indicative of any equilibrium of values, tastes, or preferences. Rather, it is induced by the institutions that purposive entrepreneurs push through when they are able to take advantage of favorable conditions. So we can expect long periods of stability punctuated by short bursts of institutional change leading to important changes in outputs before the policy settles into another period of stability. We saw this to be the case for nuclear power in the previous chapter; this chapter showed the dynamics of subsystem creation and collapse for smoking and pesticides. In the following chapter, we look at the structure of these rapid changes more carefully, in order to show how they can develop so quickly.

6

The Dynamics of Media Attention

A major source of instability in American politics is the shifting attention of the media. Media outlets generally base their stories on a limited number of sources and imitate each other, so ideas and issues often spread quickly once they become a topic of interest. Different groups of reporters, with different foci and interests, tend to report on different types of issues. When an issue is moved from one journalistic beat to another (for example, when a science project becomes the focus of a corruption inquiry, or when a business story becomes the focus for articles on gender equality), the tone of the stories written on the topic may shift dramatically because the articles are written by different journalists. Finally, media must sell. Not only must reporters simplify often complex arguments of specialists so that the general reader or viewer may understand them, but they need ultimately to make things interesting enough to maintain sales and viewerships. For these and other reasons, the media reflect most forcefully the intense hopes and fears present in policy arguments surrounding public policies in America.

In this chapter, we show how the media play an integral role in the policy process by directing attention alternately toward different aspects of the same issues over time and by shifting attention from one issue to another. First, we discuss the reasons that make us expect the media to lurch from issue to issue, or from a positive tone of coverage on a given issue to a negative one. These reasons include the need to simplify complex issues, often by focusing only on a single aspect of a multidimensional issue, and the routines of dividing the news into discrete "beats," a system which allows different journalists to focus on alternative aspects of the same issue without any overarching synthesis ever considered. These characteristics are not peculiar to the media; indeed they reflect and reinforce similar tendencies apparent in other institutions of policymaking.

Another feature common to the media as well as to other institutions is a fascination with conflict and competition. We describe how this interest often makes reporters useful allies to policymakers seeking to alter the prevailing conception of an issue and to move it from one venue to another. Whether cause or effect of shifting venues of policymaking, media images of and attention to public policy problems tend to change in nonincremental ways. As they shift, they both reflect and reinforce the lurching behavior we have described in previous chapters for other policymaking institutions.

In sum, the nation's media play an integral role in reinforcing tendencies already apparent in other areas of the policymaking system. In addition to general consideration of the three main points just discussed, we illustrate these processes focusing on three important public policies: pesticides, smoking, and automobile safety. We introduce a more detailed system of coding published stories in order to trace not just the tone of media coverage, but which aspects of a multidimensional debate are the focus of media attention.

Choosing a Single Focus in a Multifaceted Debate

Because of the complicated nature of many policy debates, rational consideration of all the costs and benefits often is not possible. At least, it is not common. Rather, media attention tends to focus for some periods of time on the positives associated with an issue, but later may shift to consider almost exclusively the negatives, as we showed in the last chapter. The period during which both positives and negatives are considered simultaneously may be very short. Of course there are some cases where this period may be extended, particularly where the organization and the mobilization of interests on both sides of the issue are relatively even and stable. In many cases, however, only one side of the issue is considered at a time: either a wave of enthusiasm, or a tide of fear.

Herbert Simon has reminded political scientists of the limitations of human cognition. "People are endowed with very large long-term memories, but with very narrow capacities for simultaneous attention to different information. . . . Of all the things we know, or can see or hear around us, only a tiny fraction influences our behavior over any short interval of time" (1985, 301). What Simon calls the "bottleneck of attention" is a characteristic of how individuals process information, but it also describes political systems and the media. He writes that the important implication of the bottleneck of attention is that "only one or a very few things can be attended to simultaneously. The limits can be broadened a bit, but only modestly, by time-sharing—switching attention periodically. The narrowness of the span of attention accounts for a great deal of human unreason that considers only one facet of a multi-faceted matter before a decision is reached" (302).

What Simon describes as a characteristic of human cognition has been noted by others as a characteristic of the political system, where agenda-setting is the "bottleneck." McCombs has written that "the public agenda seems to be an oligopoly limited to approximately a half-dozen major concerns at any particular moment" (1981, 122). Whatever the causes of this inability to consider many alternatives at a single time, it seems to be an important feature of both how individuals think and how the political system responds to problems. It helps explain lurching from fascination with one set of alternatives to an equally obsessive preoccupation with a contrasting set of images of the same set of issues. Rarely do individuals, political systems, or the media focus for long on many aspects of the same issue. More often, things are considered piecemeal.

Studies of media coverage of complex events stress the role of symbol and metaphor. By portraying issues in particular ways, policy entrepreneurs attempt to take advantage of the routines of journalists in order to move their issues into more receptive venues. Dorothy Nelkin (1987) has noted the particular vulnerability of technically complex issues to this tendency. Moreover, she writes that "a surprising feature of science journalism is its homogeneity. . . . Most articles on a given subject focus on the same issues, use the same sources of information, and interpret the material in similar terms" (1987, 9).

Perhaps the most common and persistent example of the continuing battle of competing metaphors in postwar American politics is that between economic growth and jobs on the one hand versus environmental and social costs on the other. Since so many issues can be portrayed as contributing to economic growth, this image is constantly invoked by those seeking to gain support for a policy. During the postwar period, there have been times where the economic-growth-and-jobs cluster of images has been far more powerful than its indirectly opposing cluster. There have also been times of much greater attention to the environmental cluster. As these broad swings occur in the public mood, policy options are differentially favored or put at a disadvantage.

As issues move from consideration among only elites and specialists to the broader public arena, routines of journalists, the importance of conflict, and the desire to garner ratings and sell more newspapers all lead to an increase in the tendency to exaggerate claims. While underlying facts may change only slowly, media coverage of those facts may shift dramatically from positive to negative, or from little attention to a sudden fascination. Nelkin (1987) notes a shift in emphasis in science journalism over time from an emphasis on scientific revolutions and breakthroughs to a concern over social and environmental risks, and then to a newfound faith in innovation and high-technology solutions. Journalistic emphasis has changed much faster than the pace of scientific discovery. The result is a tendency for the media to amplify, to impose more intense coverage than changing circumstances would objectively warrant.

These features of journalistic homogeneity imply positive feedback: with each success in attracting the attention of new media outlets, still more are likely to become interested. So the media play a key role in creating the positive feedback mechanisms we have noted throughout the earlier chapters.

Some students of the role of the mass media in communicating political images to policymakers claim that the media are neutral actors simply reporting the facts; others contend that all news is socially constructed. Molotch and Lester argue that events are considered newsworthy "because of the practical purposes they serve, rather than their inherent objective importance." They go on to note that news is "the result of practical, purposive, and creative activities on the part of news promoters, news assemblers, and news consumers" (1974, 101). In this view, everything is based on the strategic incentives of policy entrepreneurs striving to take advantage of events in order to push their policy proposals (or news stories, or social issues) to the top of the political agenda.

One need not adopt the strident social construction perspective to appreciate the degree to which the attention and language used by the media are at least partially determined by those who have an interest in promulgating a particular image of a public issue. Schoenfeld, Meier, and Griffin (1979) studied the emergence of environmentalism in the news, and found that the language used to describe environmental news reflected the language used by environmental interest groups. The media followed the lead of the most active environmental groups in conceiving of environmentalism as a public issue. In other words, as environmentalism grew into a major media story (and public preoccupation) during the 1960s and 1970s, media outlets adopted the terms and outlook of those interest groups active in environmental issues. By adopting their language and ideas, they of course gave credence to a point of view that had previously not been articulated or taken seriously in the political system.

Hilgartner and Bosk (1988) present a model of competition of social problems for space on the restricted public agenda. For them, public attention is a scarce resource, and the gatekeeping processes of the media are a key determinant of which issues will receive public attention and which will not. Different venues of consideration of public policy problems have different "carrying capacities," according to them; newspapers are limited by the number of pages they print, by the number of reporters and editors they employ, by the amount of time available to prepare stories, by their travel budgets, and by similar resource constraints. Congressional committees are limited by similar constraints: staff resources, the number of days available for hearings, the budget, and so forth (1988, 60). Different venues have different carrying capacities, of course, and some may focus on one problem while others may ignore it (66), so there is no guarantee that various venues will always be linked. Many are isolated, at least during certain times. On the other hand, different venues often move in concert: as one pays more attention to a given issue, others pay more attention to that same issue. Gaining simultaneous attention of a number of venues at once occurs because of the interactions among the various venues:

> Each institution is populated by a community of operatives who scrutinize the activities of their counterparts in other organizations and arenas. Journalists read each other's work in a constant search for story ideas. Television producers scan the symbolic landscape for fresh subjects for dramas. Legislators seek ideas from neighboring states. Activists "network" to gather information, maintain contacts, and spread ideas.
>
> Nor is this attention only passive and reactive. Indeed, an active attempt to influence events in other arenas is the rule, rather than the exception. Congressional aides, for example, routinely attempt to generate and shape media coverage of their employer's activities. Public opinion polls and news coverage are carefully monitored, and the politician's selection and presentation of issues are heavily influenced by considerations of what will get good press. (Hilgartner and Bosk 1988, 67)

In sum, venues are often tightly linked, and shifts in attention in one are likely quickly followed by shifts in others. The media help link all the other venues together, for they are the privileged means of communication, the way by which disjointed actors keep tabs on each other and on what they consider the "public mood." These features help explain why policy entrepreneurs have such incentives to influence what is presented in the media. While media attention is partly subject to such manipulation, it is not wholly so. The cannons of professional professionalism have their biases; these can sometimes be taken advantage of by strategic policymakers, but sometimes they work against the interests of those who would like to see media attention focus on some new topic. In sum, the set of images of public issues put forward in the media is determined by a mix of factual circumstances and by the interpretations attached to these circumstances by policy entrepreneurs.

Noncontradictory Arguments

Policymakers often challenge the accuracy of their opponents' facts; however, it is generally more effective in a debate simply to shift the focus. One example of direct contradiction with policy consequences comes from the area of policies concerning the elderly. Cook and Skogan (1989) document the importance of the facts in attempting to portray the elderly as criminal victims. Just as policy entrepreneurs were beginning to succeed in focusing government attention on this new "problem," clear survey evidence came out showing that the elderly were less likely, rather than more likely, to be victims of crime. Official attention shifted quickly to other problems.

Certainly, clear refutation of a proposed set of facts with unambiguous evidence is important, and we saw in the case of smoking that as scientific consensus built up on one side, the character of the public debate changed. However, opponents to smoking do not argue that the tobacco industry fails to produce jobs or profits for American companies. Rather than contradicting those facts, opponents seek to direct attention toward other facts, such as health risks, increased medical insurance premiums, and other costs associated with the industry. Environmentalists do not deny that nuclear plants, tobacco companies, or pesticide factories produce jobs, wages, and tax revenues, or that these are worthwhile goals. They prefer to focus public attention on the health and environmental consequences of these activities. Rhetorical battles therefore are often indirect. Policy entrepreneurs often try to ignore, rather than discredit, competing sets of images.

In this process of noncontradictory argumentation, different groups speak to different audiences. The media are an important part of this targeting process, since they reinforce the differences in receptivity of the various venues of policymaking. For example, we noted in chapter 4 that the journalists focusing on science issues at the time of the expansion of nuclear power were particularly enthusiastic about the new technology. Describing the group of science writers who dominated reporting on nuclear power questions during the 1950s, Weart writes: "Such journalists were the last to doubt that atomic energy was going to do wondrous things" (1988, 167). As long as nuclear power was a science question assigned to the science beat in the major newspapers, the industry could expect positive coverage. However, when the issue became one of bureaucratic secrecy, civil disobedience, electoral politics, or investment decisions by utility companies, different reporters began to write on the topic. They did not share the favorable preconceptions about the industry. More importantly, even if they did, these were no longer the important points in writing the article. If nuclear power is unpopular among the electorate, the question of whether or not it is technologically feasible is uninteresting, or at least irrelevant for a political reporter writing about the issues in an election campaign. So the question is one of focus; where the media focus on one aspect of the issue, the positive or negative tone of the coverage is almost dictated. Science articles on nuclear power often have a can-do or gee-whiz undertone. Political articles focusing on electoral implications of the same issue, even if written by the same journalist, are likely to be much more critical. Tone and topic are tandem.

These tendencies for different individuals to focus on different aspects of the same issue help explain why a single issue is rarely treated systematically in the political system. Attention focuses on one side of the issue for a while, and later on another aspect unrelated to the first. For the strategically minded policymaker interested in generating news coverage on a particular issue, there are many different types of reporters. In seeking to appeal to a new audience, one of the most important allies in this process may be a sympathetic reporter who shares the source's interest in generating some new controversy where previously there had been little attention.

During some periods of time, particular images may come to dominate all other ways of viewing a given policy, while conflicting images are ignored. This does not mean that the conflicting images are not there. Rather, in the overwhelming focus on one side of the issue, all other sides are ignored. Those who hold opposing views find few sympathetic ears, and those who are not experts in the area find it presumptuous to question the consensus of the "experts." Over time, however, images may shift, and those who were previously ignored may find many receptive venues in which to air their concerns. These dissidents seem to appear from nowhere once attention shifts to other topics concerning the same issue. Often, they have been making similar statements for years, but were simply ignored in the general focus on some other side of the same issue.

One of the most important implications of the media's tendency to focus attention on only one dimension of a policy is instability. When attention shifts to another dimension of the same policy, the tone of the coverage can be reversed dramatically. Even in the absence of new findings, new scientific evidence, or new arguments, the nature of debate surrounding an issue can shift dramatically if only it shifts in focus. This is because policy debates often are not contradictory, that is, often they do not include simultaneous consideration of both sides. As attention shifts from one dimension to another, different policymakers become interested, different media outlets (and different journalists within them) begin to generate different types of stories, the self-reinforcing processes that link all these venues together can contribute to rapid changes in policy outcomes of the type we described in chapter 1. In sum, the routines of the media help explain how policy images change over time and why they tend to change so quickly once the process of change has begun. They play an important role in creating the positive-reinforcement mechanisms that create the politics of disequilibrium.

A Second Look at Pesticides and Smoking in the Media

We turn now to a second look at two issues we have already discussed, pesticides and smoking. In this chapter, our interest is in how media attention shifted focus. Using a more elaborate coding scheme than that used in chapter 5, we show how there are a number of contrasting topics of possible coverage of each issue. As the media shifted attention from one aspect of smoking and pesticide policy to another, the tone of coverage was reversed. Attention did not shift simply from positive to negative without any shift in topics of interest. Rather, the shift in tone of coverage came about as a result of changes in the topics of coverage. Policymakers in each case were better served by pushing attention away from aspects of the debate that their opponents might choose rather than by attempting to contradict their evidence. In this process of noncontradictory policy debates, facts matter less than the ability to control the topics of media attention. This is not because facts are irrelevant but because, in a complicated policy debate, there are generally many aspects of the debate, and the facts within any single part are often clearly on one side or the other. Since each broad area of attention may have clear positive or negative implications for the industry, the fortunes of those involved in the policy debate rise and fall as attention shifts from one topic to another.

Pesticides

As we described in chapter 5, the growth of the American pesticides industry in the postwar years was associated with a cluster of overwhelmingly positive images about the new products being produced. Pesticides meant agricultural bounty, an end to hunger, and possibly the complete eradication of such pests as the housefly, the fire ant, and a variety of agricultural pests as well as an end to human diseases borne by insects such as the mosquito. Further, it meant greater agricultural productivity, allowing American farms to produce far more, even while the rural population flocked to the cities. Overseas export markets were enormous, and American firms dominated the industry, so pesticides also meant export earnings. American military personnel hoped to knock out diseases such as malaria and typhus by eradicating the insects which carried them. The army engaged in large-scale programs to eradicate these diseases from overseas populations.

During the 1950s, pesticides were associated in the public mind with positive images such as these. Further, these positive images were firmly based in fact. No opponent of the industry could reasonably assert that pesticides did not in fact constitute a way to higher profits and crop yields for farmers, that they were not a major source of export earnings for U.S. companies, or that eradication of the fly and mosquito would not reduce malaria and other diseases in third world countries.

Over time, however, aspects of the policy which were once not known or were ignored began to attract more attention. Pesticides contribute to toxic waste; they pollute farmland and later the groundwater; they do not eradicate pests as promised; they require ever-increasing applications to achieve the same results and therefore generate more in profits for the chemical companies which manufacture them than for the farmers who must pay for them; they are associated with a variety of diseases when used improperly. Of course the positive aspects of pesticides are still with us, just as the negative side was with us in the 1950s, but public understandings often tend to focus on one side or the other.

In sum, there are clusters of good and bad things one can say about pesticides, as with most issues. The positive cluster focuses on scientific progress, growth, and productivity. The negative cluster revolves around environmental hazards and distrust of big business. Rare is the person who ascribes equal importance to these two clusters or who even considers both of them at the same time. People on different sides of the debate tend to focus exclusively on one set of images. While not necessarily denying that the other set exists or is true, they simply ignore it. In any case, this is how public discourse and media coverage of the issue behave.

Our expanded coding scheme for the *Readers' Guide* articles goes beyond that reported in chapter 5. In addition to noting whether a given article was generally favorable or critical toward the industry, we noted three possible foci: (1) financial or economic analysis (for example, reports of the effectiveness of pesticides, profits made by companies, new products being introduced, or other reports of the business side of the industry); (2) government actions (for example, calls for increased regulation by local, state, or the national government, statements by government authorities concerning health problems of pesticides, new laws, court cases, complaints about any of these, or any other discussion of government actions, including farm programs); and (3) health and environmental issues (for example, scientific reports linking pesticide use to pollution of groundwater, reports of damage done by DDT or other specific pesticides, or any other health news not including that focusing on actions by government officials). Table 6.1 reports the close relationship between the topic of coverage and its tone.

When articles are published in newspapers and magazines focusing on economic and financial questions of the pesticides industry, over 80 percent of them are positive in tone. Even those we coded negative in this category include titles that are not particularly critical, simply bad news: decline in profits, sales not as high as hoped, and similar titles would be counted as bad news, even though they are not critical. So our coding scheme is very conservative, but still shows that when attention is on the business side of the industry, the tone is over 80 percent probusiness.

When government actions are discussed, on the other hand, these are almost always bad news for the industry. Fewer than 20 percent of the articles in this category were counted as good news for the industry, and again this is probably an overstatement: an article describing industry success in diluting proposals for stricter government regulation would be counted as positive according to our conservative coding scheme. Finally, when attention shifts to health issues, 80 percent of the articles published are bad news for the industry (with a similar caveat for our coding scheme: industry assertions that health threats from pesticides have not been proved would be coded as a positive article, even though the whole topic might be better avoided from an industry standpoint).

Table 6.1 shows that as public attention shifts from one set of issues to

Table 6.1   Topic and tone of pesticide coverage in the *Readers' Guide to Periodical Literature*, 1900–1988

	Tone		
Topic of Coverage	Positive	Negative	Total
Economic, or financial	81.7%	18.3%	100.0% (1026)
Government actions	17.7	82.3	100.0 (232)
Health, or environmental	20.5	79.5	100.0 (1132)
TOTAL	46.5	53.5	100.0 (2390)

Gamma = 0.82
Tau-b = 0.56
Chi-square (2 d.f.) = 895.58 (prob. < .0001)

Notes: The percentage of articles coded identically by two coders is 95.6. "Positive" means articles supportive of the industry. The subject headings used were "pesticides," "herbicides," "insecticides," "fungicides," "DDT," "DDD," "Dieldrin," "Chlorodane," "organophosphates," "rodenticides." The subject headings for the individual pesticides appear only during periods in which those pesticides were in use.

another concerning pesticides, chances are strong that the tone of coverage will shift as well. However, it lumps together all coverage over the entire century in order to make that comparison as simply as possible. We can show more directly how attention within the media shifted so dramatically from positives to negatives during that period by looking at data over time. Figure 6.1 shows the changing foci of pesticide coverage over time. From an exclusive focus on the business aspects of the new industry and on its benefits for farmers, media coverage of pesticides shifted in the late 1950s to look more closely at the health and environmental aspects of the industry. By the 1970s, attention had shifted even further toward a focus on health aspects, to the virtual exclusion of the business side of the story.

During the boom years of the pesticides industry, media attention rarely focused on the industry (see fig. 5.3 for a summary of total annual levels of coverage), but when it did, it was essentially concerned with reporting the relatively good economic news associated with new products, increased productivity, and the like. Health concerns rarely hit the newspapers. As the years went by, attention shifted from this total preoccupation with the economic aspects of the industry to an equally one-sided concern with the health and environmental aspects of pesticides, the vast majority of which are of course negative for the industry. As attention shifted from the good to the bad, government actions were called for. So pesticides went in the media from being

The Dynamics of Media Attention

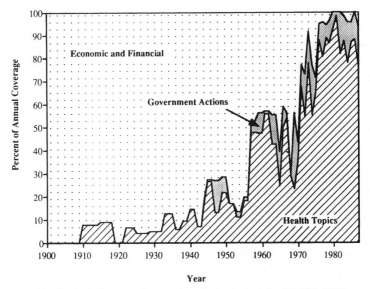

Figure 6.1. Shifting topics of pesticide coverage in the *Readers' Guide*, 1900–1987.

an economic good, which the government should of course support through benign neglect, to a major national problem that the government should solve. A social problem was born where once people had only seen an economic fact.

Pesticides pollute streams and injure people when used improperly. They also increase productivity and allow Americans to enjoy abundant and inexpensive food. If a person were to read a representative sample of articles on pesticides during any single year in the twentieth century, chances are that one would be flooded with information concerning one side of the story. The media, like individual people, tend to focus only on one side of a complicated argument at a time. Rational consideration of all sides is too complex and cannot be expected. Instead, reporters lurch from a fascination with one side of the story to a preoccupation with a contrasting side of the same story. Attention to pesticide questions did not simply switch from positive to negative without any explanation. Rather the shift in tone came about from shift in focus, without any contradiction or refutation of the previously accepted way of looking at the issue. No one in the 1970s or 1980s denied that pesticides produce jobs and profits. Rather, attention simply shifted from these positive aspects of the industry to the negatives of health and environmental damage. This aspect of media coverage is not limited to pesticides, as we shall see in the next few pages. Further, it helps explain why the political system as a whole follows a similar pattern in its attention to public policy problems.

Smoking

Just as in the case of pesticides or nuclear power, there are clusters of good and bad things one can say about smoking. The positive images associated with smoking were long dominant in the United States: freedom, sex, adulthood, sophistication, indulgence, pleasure, and others. Reinforcing these images was the tremendous economic strength of a large industry employing thousands of people in many congressional districts and generating large amounts of tax income for many levels of government. The negative images of smoking have long been around as well: cancer, disease, overindulgence, death. Increased attention to some of the negative aspects of the industry, in particular those associated with its health effects, has led to a rapid erosion of what seemed for a long time to be an iron-clad rhetorical dominance centering on freedom, maturity, and glamour. Even the economic arguments in favor of the industry have been called into question. Instead of representing jobs and tax revenues, smoking is considered by a growing number of Americans to be the cause of increased health insurance premiums, lost worker productivity, and other economic costs never taken seriously in those decades where positive images were more dominant. Challenges to one positive image lend more credibility to other challenges. In this way, positive and negative images are linked with each other. In this interactive process, rapid reversals in policy images are possible, and even common.

We coded titles for tobacco and smoking in a manner similar to our coding for pesticides. Because of the relative importance of litigation in the area of smoking, we separated reports of court cases from other forms of government action. Finally, we coded both the *Readers' Guide* and the *New York Times Index* in terms of tone; we coded only the *Times* in this more complicated way, after noting that overall levels and general tone of coverage were similar. (Appendix A provides details about these comparisons.) Table 6.2 reports the results of this simple coding for coverage reported in the *New York Times Index*.

As in the case of pesticides, the tone of coverage of smoking articles is clearly associated with the topic of coverage. Of 482 articles on the economics and finance of the tobacco industry that we were able to code as positive or negative, 382 (or 79 percent) were positive. Similarly, of 402 codeable articles on health, 350 (87 percent) were negative. In sum, knowing what topics are being considered allows one to know with great certainty whether the news being reported is good or bad for the industry.

Just as with pesticides, we can show the changes in topics of interest over time in smoking coverage in the *Times*. Figure 6.2 shows how these topics have changed during the postwar years.

During the early postwar years, tobacco was a wonder crop, and it promised great economic benefits. Press coverage of it focused on profits, introduction

The Dynamics of Media Attention

Table 6.2 Topic and tone of smoking and tobacco coverage in the
New York Times Index, 1946–1987

Topic of Coverage	Tone			
	Positive	Neutral or Uncodeable	Negative	Total
Economic, or financial	65.0%	18.0%	17.0%	100.0% (588)
Government actions	23.3	23.1	53.6	100.0 (1035)
Court proceedings	34.2	22.8	43.0	100.0 (79)
Health	11.8	8.8	79.4	100.0 (441)
Other	20.1	51.8	28.2	100.0 (369)
TOTAL	30.9	23.6	45.5	100.0 (2512)

Gamma = 0.35
Tau-b = 0.25
Chi-square (8 d.f.) = 734.78 (prob. < .0001)

Notes: Generally, only every third year was coded because of the large number of articles on this topic. Years coded are 1946, 1949, 1952, 1955, 1958, 1961, 1964, 1967, 1970, 1973, 1976, 1979, 1982, 1985, 1986, 1987. The percentage of articles coded identically by two coders is 97.5. Subject headings used are "smoking," "tobacco," "cigarettes," "cigars."

"Positive" tone means protobacco industry. This includes reports of profits, increased sales, record crops, court proceedings in favor of the industry. Where government officials issue health warnings, these are included under government actions, so the category "health" includes only those statements from nongovernment sources.

Coding of the *Readers' Guide* from 1900 to 1987 yielded the following results: 343 (17.0%) positive articles; 1,192 (59.0%) negatives; 485 (24.0%) neutral articles for a total of 2,020. These articles were not coded by topic.

of new products, winning of export markets, government efforts to improve the lot of tobacco farmers, and so on. Health concerns were not in evidence in *Times* coverage until the mid- to late 1950s; they represented consistently less than 5 percent of annual coverage before 1955, but generally in the range of 20 to 30 percent after that year. One reason for this lack of apparent coverage of health issues is that health statements made by government officials are treated as part of government actions here. In fact, government actions have consistently been the largest single category of coverage in the media. Whether the government is supporting new research on tobacco crops, granting subsidies to tobacco farmers, prohibiting smoking in public places, or reporting research results linking smoking to cancer, the government at some level has long been involved in promoting or regulating the tobacco industry.

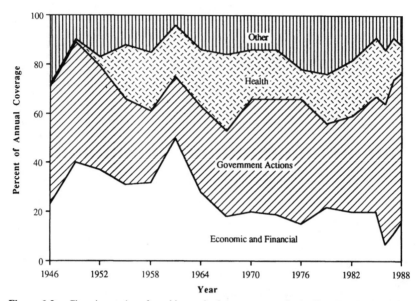

Figure 6.2. Changing topics of smoking and tobacco coverage in the *New York Times Index,* 1946–1988.

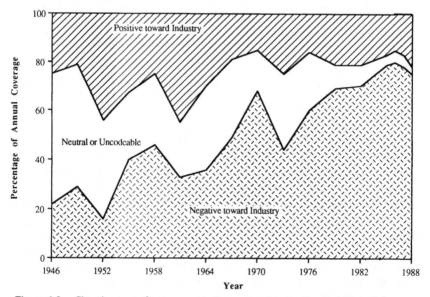

Figure 6.3. Changing tone of government actions reported in the *New York Times Index* coverage of smoking, 1946–1988.

The government has been involved in a great variety of programs and actions both in support of and in opposition to smoking, as was clear from table 6.2. However, the tone of these actions has changed over time. We trace government actions toward the smoking industry separately in figure 6.3.

The vast majority of reports of government activities during the early postwar years were either neutral in tone or favorable to the industry: reports of price subsidies, Department of Agriculture research, and such. As the years went on, and in particular with the 1964 statement by the surgeon general critical of smoking, those units within the government responsible for health began to take a much more active media role. They had always been generating a few articles essentially critical of the industry, but after 1964 the tone of articles reporting government regulation shifted from slightly positive to overwhelmingly negative. Before 1964 there were 88 positive articles associated with government actions as opposed to 82 negatives. After 1964 there were 153 positives and 473 negatives. Agriculture officials, once generating approximately the same level of press coverage as health officials, saw themselves outmaneuvred and overrun by an activist group of government health officials, regulators, and politicians able to generate much more media attention than they. Media attention to government actions shifted from the USDA, Commerce Department, and trade representatives and toward the surgeon general, the Centers for Disease Control, state health department officials, and other governmental officials critical of the industry. The result was a change in the nature of public discourse concerning smoking and tobacco policy.

As in the case of pesticides, media coverage of smoking and tobacco issues has shifted dramatically over time from positive to negative in tone. As in the case of pesticides, this shift has not come from a contradiction in facts or from a refutation of the strengths of the economic arguments in favor of the jobs produced by that industry. Rather, it has come by a shift in attention, with an increased awareness of things that had been true all along but that had been ignored in the past. Health concerns displaced economic growth as the primary topic of coverage for the issues of smoking and tobacco in the media. Tobacco growers and cigarette companies continued to contribute substantially to the gross national product during the 1970s and 1980s, but these aspects of the industry no longer received coverage. They had dominated press coverage of the issue in the earlier years, but no more. With these shifts in topics of interest come changes in the mobilization of bias in American politics. One side benefits as long as the topic of discussion is health, whereas the other side benefits as the topic shifts to jobs. No side has an interest in a full-blown discussion, and the incentives of reporters similarly are served by a piecemeal approach to covering important policy issues. Generally speaking, only one side of an issue is considered in public discourse at a time.

A Media Fascination with Risk or Conflict?

In the three cases we have considered so far in this book, there has been a similar trend over time from a media focus on jobs, economic growth, and "progress" to an increasing concern with health risks, environmental degradation, and other questions of public safety. A reasonable person might conclude that we are simply observing long-run secular changes in how American society evaluates risk, or that increased levels of scientific and medical knowledge now alert us to risks that we previously endured unknowingly. There is of course much to these arguments; there is no question that we know more now that we did at the turn of the century about a wide variety of health risks, and that this increased knowledge has made us all more wary of many activities. However, media attention to public policy controversies is not driven only by greater scientific knowledge.

The media's coverage of questions of risk is highly selective and temporary. They focus on some issues that involve less objective risk than many other issues that generate little or no media interest, and they focus for short periods of time on issues that are constant in their threat to the public health. In part, this is because there are no widely accepted definitions of objective or actual risk. In the absence of statistics and objective indicators, policy entrepreneurs and journalists are free to focus on issues that may be well down the list in terms of actual threats. This tendency is most clearly illustrated where isolated incidents produce dramatic events. One of the reasons the public is more likely to underestimate the risks associated with driving a car and overestimate those from flying in an airplane is that the media are more apt to focus on one rather than the other. Similarly with many health risks: opponents to nuclear power can generate more adverse publicity by focusing on the threats associated with a spectacular and dreadful nuclear accident than opponents to coal mining can by focusing on repeated, but mundane, cases of black lung disease among miners. "People often overestimate the frequency and seriousness of dramatic, sensational, dreaded well-publicized causes of death and underestimate the risks from more familiar, accepted causes that claim lives one by one," explained one EPA official familiar with these problems (quoted in Clymer 1989).

Besides spectacular events that obviously attract media attention, conflict among specialists also does. Journalists like to write stories that people can understand, so many debates are framed as conflicts between opposing sides, where attention, like in presidential campaigns, is more likely to focus on the "horse race" than on the merits of the two positions. This fascination with conflict has important implications, since policymakers who might gain from increased media attention can often attract that attention if only they can make the issue appear controversial.

Studies of public reactions to scientific controversies indicate the public has an inherently conservative bias in evaluating technologies which it cannot be expected to understand. Mazur describes how the appearance of any level of controversy among "scientific experts" gives the public the impression that safety must be imperiled. Opponents to an industry such as nuclear power therefore have an advantage if they can shift the debate toward the public agenda: "Detailed studies of a few technical controversies suggest that there is at least one simple effect of media coverage on attitudes which works in a reliable manner. When media coverage of a controversy increases, public opposition to the technology in question (as measured by opinion polls) increases; when media coverage wanes, public opposition falls off" (Mazur 1981b, 109). However, as we noted in chapter 4, media coverage itself tends to change uniformly. Both nuclear power and pesticides experienced a distinct decline of supportive media coverage during the 1960s and 1970s. Controversy on issues may increase negative press coverage, and it can be this coverage that activates antagonistic public responses. All press coverage does not focus on controversy, and certainly the popular enthusiasm that surrounded the golden days of both these industries was well reflected in the press. So we cannot say that the media in general have an inherent bias against these industries. We can say, however, that the media's fascination with conflict, competition, and criticism leads to a public perception that scientific consensus is weaker than it may be.

Few things frustrate those in favor of nuclear power or other complex technologies more than the ability of opponents to exploit public fears of the technology, and the media's interest in controversy. From their point of view, the media's attitude seems unduly hostile to the industry. Its interest in reporting on conflict and disagreement makes it a natural ally of those opposed to the status quo in technological controversies. David Vogel describes business leaders' frustrations with what they considered the biased and sensational nature of media coverage of business news (1989, 214–15). Similarly, Bernard Cohen (1981) complains that the media often give the impression that there is no "scientific consensus" about complex issues when in fact there might be only a small number of scientists disagree with the dominant view. The media "frequently quote one of the small handful of renegade scientists to promote the scare angle" (Cohen 1981, 71). Further, the relative risks associated with different technologies are rarely put into perspective. Nuclear power is associated in the media with a number of negative images, and Cohen asks why other risks are not treated equally, citing figures on causes of death listed in the *Statistical Abstract of the United States:* "Another problem with journalistic coverage is the use of inflammatory language—'deadly radiation,' 'lethal radioactivity'—for a danger that hasn't killed anyone for many years. We never hear about 'deadly automobiles,' or 'lethal electricity,' even though

1,200 Americans suffer electrocution each year. Or how about 'lethal water,' referring to the 8,000 annual drownings, or 'deadly falls,' which kill 15,000 per year?" (Cohen 1981, 71).

There have been a number of studies comparing media coverage of health risks with actual incidents of death and injury stemming from those risks. Typical of these studies is that by Michael Greenberg and his colleagues in which they studied all the stories on environmental risks that aired on the three major television network news programs from January 1984 to February 1986 (M. Greenberg et al. 1989). They concluded that it takes a crisis or a focusing event to generate news coverage and that significant risk to public health by itself is not enough. They counted 482 stories on airplane safety questions, compared with an average of 220 deaths per year from air crashes. By contrast, there were 15 stories on asbestos, from which approximately 9,000 Americans die annually, and 57 stories on smoking, from which over 300,000 Americans die every year. "If coverage matched risk (measured by total number of deaths), then there should have been 26.5 minutes on smoking and 41 seconds about asbestos for each second devoted to airplane accidents" (1989, 271–72). They conclude that "the disproportionate coverage . . . of chemical incidents, earthquakes, and airplane accidents probably reinforces the public's well-documented tendency to overestimate sudden and violent risks and underestimate chronic ones" (276).

The morbid fascination with large-scale disaster among segments of the public has encouraged considerable sensationalism in the media. (And, we may add, an attempt to profit: the *New York Times* has produced an instructional video for journalists titled "Covering a Radiation Accident." The advertising copy began: "If you're sent out to cover a minor nuclear incident or a major accident like Three Mile Island, you risk exposure to radiation. Are you prepared to do your job . . . ?" Cost of the video: $249, with a discount for multiple copies . . . See *New York Times*, 9 April, 1990.)

Rothman and Lichter (1982) argue that there is in fact much greater agreement among scientists on the issue of nuclear power than is generally portrayed by the press. Two factors interact to give the impression of greater disagreement among experts than is true. Dissidents seek out media attention for their views, while those agreeing with the dominant view prefer to ignore "outsiders," and journalists have incentives to focus on conflict. So a small group of scientists who disagree with the dominant image may be able to create the impression of much greater disagreement among experts than is true. Media reporters, interested in conflict and disagreement become the witting or unwitting allies of those who want to create the impression of greater disagreement and who want to focus public attention on sensational fears. So media attention amplifies elite-level disagreements, according to Rothman and Lichter.

Where large-scale disaster is not a possibility, changing conceptions of risk come more slowly. The risks of smoking to health are far greater than the risks of nuclear power, yet smoking habits have responded only glacially to a concerted public relations campaign by public health officials. And unlike nuclear power, the scientific community is pretty well united behind the idea that smoking is a threat to health. It is likely that the public continues to underestimate the health danger of tobacco while overestimating the danger of nuclear power. So there probably have been long-term changes in the willingness of the American public to accept risks inherent in technological advance. However, all risks are not treated equally: some are constantly in the media while others are commonly overlooked and accepted (see Cohen 1980; Fischhoff et al. 1978; Johnson and Tversky 1984).

Just when public discourse shifts from enthusiasm about "progress" and economic growth toward health risks and dangers is a fundamental problem for policymakers, since so many policy debates can be linked to these simple images. Many of these arguments are affected by changes in scientific knowledge: we become concerned about health risks when we realize their existence or when a potential way to avoid them is invented or brought to our attention. Even in the absence of new technologies or greater scientific knowledge, however, media attention to "progress" versus "risk" varies over time. The alternative images of a single policy debate dominate media coverage at different times. We can show this process clearly by picking an issue that is not so technologically complex, that has posed similar trade-offs throughout most of the twentieth century, and for which there are reasonably objective and well-accepted measures of risk. We turn to the case of automobile safety in order to show the cyclic nature of media attention to the issue. These cycles of attention clearly cannot be explained by objective standards of risk to the public's health, since the risk to public health has changed only slowly and steadily throughout the same period.

Automobile Safety

Fifty-thousand Americans are killed every year on the roads, and the number has only recently stabilized at that level, after decades of increase. Statistically speaking, driving is one of the more dangerous human activities, and most Americans know someone who has been killed or injured in a car accident. In any given year, however, media attention to automobile safety questions is unlikely to be even one-tenth as high as that given to many other topics constituting less of a threat to public health. Further, the rises and falls in media attention to this question cannot be explained by changes in the severity of the problem.

Figure 6.4 shows the number of articles concerning automobile safety listed in the *Readers' Guide* since 1910, along with information concerning the number of deaths on the roads. While the number of deaths has increased, many more Americans have cars. We therefore also present the number of deaths standardized by the number of vehicles in operation (standardizing by the number of miles driven provides a curve almost exactly similar in shape to that of the number of vehicles). While the decline in deaths per vehicles in operation has been steady almost throughout the century, media attention to traffic fatalities has not been.

Media attention to traffic fatalities has swung wildly, moving up and down in approximately fifteen-year cycles, while the severity of the problem has been relatively steady (steadily improving, if measured by deaths per miles driven; steadily worsening if measured by raw numbers of fatalities). Figure 6.4 shows clear surges and declines in media interest in automobile safety, with dramatic changes in levels of coverage that correspond with neither of our two indicators of the severity of the problem. Particularly impressive is the spike of concern during the 1930s, but spikes also occurred in the early 1950s, in the 1960s with the consumer movement and the publication of Ralph Nader's *Unsafe at Any Speed* (1965), and again in the mid–1980s. The problem changes only slowly over time, but attention lurches.

We have attempted to note whether the nature of media coverage of traffic fatalities has changed over time, but can discern no significant trends. Traffic fatalities may be blamed on poor drivers (for example, those with multiple tickets, those who speed recklessly, or those who have been drinking), on poor cars (for example, those without seat belts or padded dashboards, or with other design problems), and on poor roads (for example, poor lighting, poorly designed intersections, sharp curves in dangerous areas, overcrowding). We coded each of the articles on traffic fatalities according to this scheme (with another category for simple reports of accidents or other topics) in order to observe whether media coverage shifted from blaming the driver or the roads in earlier times to blaming the cars in later times, or whether there were any shifts of this type. With the exception of the period before 1930, there were very few articles on infrastructure as a problem.

One important exception to static media perception of the causes of traffic accidents was the discussion of the interstate highway system in the mid-1950s, when a surge of interest in fatalities was indeed associated with a shift in emphasis from accidents and other causes to unsafe roads. Beginning in the early 1950s, construction contractors, truckers, truck manufacturers, and others who wanted lower taxes, fewer toll roads, and more federal highway dollars mobilized into a formidable political force. They were able to focus public discussion of automobile questions so much that our data show a surge in media articles on infrastructure problems in the mid-1950s. This aspect of auto safety had previously not been a particular focus of the media, and it gave way later to other concerns, but a persistent, powerful, and well-organized lobby was able to push these infrastructure questions onto the public agenda in the early to mid-1950s. By no mere coincidence, Congress

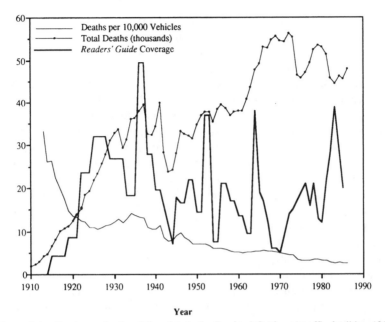

Figure 6.4. Coverage of automobile safety in the *Readers' Guide* and traffic fatalities, 1910–1986.

passed the Interstate Highway Act of 1956 (on the mobilization of truckers in the Project Adequate Roads, see Rose 1979).

Even during the period of the consumer movement and the seat belt controversies in the 1960s, the percentage of traffic articles dealing with unsafe automobiles as a cause of fatalities did not increase significantly. Again, in the 1980s, the Mothers against Drunk Driving campaigns focusing on unsafe drivers as a cause of accidents did not lead to a noticeable shift in topics of coverage in media articles on the topic. Both of these movements did indeed lead to increased coverage and attention to traffic fatalities as a public problem, but unlike in the pesticides and smoking cases we discussed earlier in this chapter, these increases in attention did not come with a shift in focus. Traffic fatalities, an issue that all Americans understand easily from their own experience, has not been significantly transformed over time. Attention to the topic waxes and wanes considerably, but these changes in levels of attention do not seem related to any shifts in topic or tone.

A lack of change in media focus has not stopped federal, state, or local policymakers from choosing different solutions to the problems of traffic safety over time. Walker (1977) showed how increasing attention to traffic safety questions in the mid-1960s led Congress to enact more stringent safety legislation aimed mostly at the automobile manufacturers. However, the choice of a culprit was not so clearly reflected in the mass media. Attention certainly did focus on fatalities during the mid-1960s, but there are many possible causes for fatalities. As Kingdon has written, the links between a social or political problem and its policy solution are often weak (1984). In the case of traffic safety, the problem seems to emerge on the media agenda at irregular intervals in the postwar period. Each time, officials are pushed to enact some kinds of solutions; depending on the circumstances, the solutions may focus on building more highways (the solution of the 1950s), requiring safer cars (the solution of the 1960s), or putting drunk drivers behind bars (that of the 1980s and 1990s). Traffic safety is clearly an issue where many potential solutions can reasonably be linked to the problem. There is little disagreement about whether the problem should be solved; the real question is which group will take advantage of increased public concern in order to promote its favorite solution.

The lack of changes in the relative emphasis on the causes of accidents in the popular press implies that the waves of concern in the popular press were not associated with changes in the understanding of the issue. On the other hand, highways, traffic control systems, automobiles, and probably drivers are all safer every year than they were the year before. Moreover, public policies toward automobile safety have been affected by waves of press attention—the enactment of speed limits by the states and localities in the 1920s and 1930s; the demand for limited access superhighways in the 1950s; the regulation of automotive safety by the national government in the 1960s; the fifty-five mile-an-hour speed limit in the 1970s; the toughening of drunk driving laws in the 1980s. Waves of media concern are roughly associated with waves of governmental activity, but these waves do not seem to be associated with the one-sided understanding of issues that we documented for nuclear power, smoking and tobacco, and pesticides.

Popular press coverage of automobile safety seems more balanced than its coverage of nuclear power, pesticides, or smoking. Nonetheless, neither coverage in the popular press nor governmental activity is incremental, but is subject to destabilizing waves. Even in the absence of focusing events, media attention to a problem that remains relatively constant over the years is characterized by lurching. These rises and falls in media attention are, strangely, related to public policies notable for their incremental impacts. This apparent contradiction is easy to explain: waves of public activity leave behind implementing institutions, which then act quietly to improve the situation. The result, over the long run, has been considerable progress on improving the safety of automobiles in modern society, as each surge in attention has prompted the government to enact some new solutions. Over the years, the cumulative impact of these many solutions may actually have led to safer roads.

Lurching Attention and the Politics of Disequilibria

Subtlety, ambiguity, and reasoned argument are not the most salient character-istics of the way issues are treated as they emerge on the public agenda. Public attention and elite understandings of policy problems can shift focus over time, with no discrediting of previously accepted facts. Or when one new fact is discovered, suddenly a variety of other issues not related to the new discov-ery attain much greater prominence. During some periods, negatives are ig-nored; during others, positives. Of course change is not inevitable. Sometimes only one side of an issue is given serious consideration for decades. When the public perception of an issue changes, however, it often changes in a radical fashion rather than slowly. Further, the change in image stems not from any direct contradiction of facts or through anything one might describe as a ra-tional argument. Sometimes a single new discovery, an accident or natural disaster, or a speech by a major public figure may set into motion a dramatic process of reversal in the tone of public debate. Instead of simultaneous con-sideration of the positive and negative, there seem to be waves of enthusiasm or apprehension—periods during which issues seem entirely positive to the public and to decision makers, and periods when they are just as entirely neg-ative. This has been the case for nuclear power, pesticides, and smoking.

Such severe positive feedback effects are not, however, inevitable. Our study of automobile safety suggests waves of concern in the media, waves roughly associated with periods of heightened public-sector activity. Yet these mobilizations were never as one-sided as those for the other issues we studied. During periods in which the automobile was viewed as unsafe, plenty of ar-ticles were written about problems with drivers. So attention may rise and fall even without important changes in how the issue is framed. In any case, atten-tion often is sporadic, not sustained.

Because of the important role of the media in this process of allocating attention, we have focused on them in this chapter. In each of the three cases discussed here (and in the case of nuclear power, as we saw in chap. 4), media attention was fitful, never sustained. The sudden fascination with a given issue was usually, but not always, associated with changes in how the issue was discussed. Different aspects of the same issue were emphasized during times of low and high attention, except in the case of automobile safety. The fitful nature of media coverage of public policies is linked to the fitful concerns of governmental institutions of decision making. As an issue surges onto the media agenda, so does it lurch onto the agendas of federal and state agencies that had previously not been concerned with it. Media attention sometimes precedes and sometimes follows changes in attention by government agen-cies, so we do not mean to imply any simple causation here. Rather, each can affect the other, reinforcing the pattern of positive feedback and punctuated equilibrium that we have observed over and over.

7

Cities as a National Political Problem

All of the policies described in this book thus far are or have been organized through subsystems. For nuclear power, smoking and tobacco, pesticides, and automobile safety, there are affected industries, specific concerned agencies, and activities by individual congressional committees. Now we turn to a broad policy area not so tied into a limited policy network—urban affairs. Rather than organized within a policy subsystem, national urban policies have been structured by the larger policy institutions—the political parties and the president. Interest groups have taken sides in the national debate over the plight of American cities, but their influence has been dwarfed by the sweep of partisan competition. Rather than driven by interest groups, national urban programs encouraged the formation of new interest arrangements that became known as the intergovernmental lobby. But, as we shall see, these interests proved weak when urban programs, like other intergovernmental aid programs, were attacked by the conservative Republican coalition headed by President Ronald Reagan.

There was but a brief span of modern American history in which urban affairs rose to prominence in the policy priorities of American governmental institutions. From the mid-1960s to the mid-1970s, the plight of the cities held favored status on the national agenda, and then it was driven from the scene in the partisan rancor of the 1980s. This chapter is directed at understanding why the urban initiative happened when it did, and why it so thoroughly collapsed. In doing so, we develop two points. First, the urban initiative was carried on five waves of policy activity, and these waves corresponded to changes in both the definition of the issue and the proposed policy solution. When the urban initiative is examined in this manner, it is difficult to avoid the conclusion that policymaking occurred in jumps, rather than through smooth reaction to changing political and social circumstances.

Second, in broad terms, a window of opportunity opened during the period, and the window was strongly affected by prevailing cleavages of party competition, epitomized by the changing positions of the parties on the issue of race relations. For a brief period, social issues replaced the economy as the first concern of Americans, and race became salient nationally. As the Republican party base shifted toward the South and the West and as the 1964 election replaced scores of moderate Republicans with Democrats in the North, the parties in Congress switched sides on the issue of race (Carmines and Stimson 1989). All of this occurred as American postwar prosperity was reaching its zenith. If America's big cities benefited enormously from federal programs during this period, they also suffered an important image change—cities, after 1967, were associated with racial disharmony. Urban programs were no longer perceived as massive initiatives to improve Americans' lives and rebuild the nation's infrastructure, but rather, in the minds of many Americans, as simple aid programs for blacks.

Unlike the policies we have examined in earlier chapters of this book, urban problems are a vast and amorphous collection of physical and social conditions in modern society. They include housing conditions (overcrowding, decay, abandonment), congestion, crime, racial discrimination, poverty, financial disparities between center city and suburb, mass transportation, and water and sewer quality. The "plight of America's cities" has been a shorthand way of discussing these problems and, most importantly, of emphasizing their interconnections. To the extent that these problems are conceived as a package, the term *urban problems* becomes part of the rhetoric of policymaking. Disaggregating the pathologies of modern life makes it possible to support one set of policy solutions without attending to the more comprehensive situation. Members of Congress may, for example, support crime control without attending to the issue of racial discrimination. Discussing these problems as a syndrome implies a comprehensive approach to treatment, whereas disaggregation implies a smaller effort. Again we see that definition of the issue helps determine the subsequent policy response.

Urban Disorders and the Systemic Political Agenda

"This is not a time for angry reaction. It is a time for action: starting with legislative action to improve the life in our cities. The strength and promise of law are the surest remedies for tragedy in the streets. . . . Let us then act in the Congress, in the city halls, and in every community." Thus responded President Lyndon Johnson to the massive civil disturbances of 1967. This was, in his words, "a week such as no nation should live through: a time of violence and tragedy" (National Advisory Commission on Civil Disorders 1968, 539).

The national government was indeed in the midst of a period of furious activity in domestic policy, much of which was directed at cities. In 1965 the new cabinet post of Housing and Urban Development had been created. Vast sums of money were being directed at urban problems—the war on poverty, model cities, subsidized housing, urban transportation (the Department of Transportation was created in 1966), medical care for the poor, public works programs, manpower training—most working through the intergovernmental grant system. Between 1965 and 1970, intergovernmental grants for social objectives more than doubled in real dollars.

President Johnson viewed the riots as a public problem, and one deserving positive government action. Government was called on not to prepare for the suppression of new outbreaks, but to "improve the life in the cities." Given the choice, the president pursued the broadest definition of the issue possible. Yet, as we shall see, the urban riots did not trigger the large-scale government domestic initiative; that had already begun. They did not cause a turn of attention toward the cities in the media; that was already happening. And while a number of congressional hearings took place on urban matters following the disturbances, the increasing interest of Congress in urban matters had begun years before, in the 1950s. In the language we have developed in this book, the riots took place in the midst of a positive-feedback system during which public and elite attention was turned toward domestic policies generally and the cities in particular. This led to a very different understanding of the 1960s civil disturbances in comparison with the other American urban disturbances of the twentieth century, which did not lead to a reexamination of urban life as a whole.

In the twentieth century, there have been three periods of extensive urban civil disorders: 1917–19, 1943, and 1965–68. Only during the latter period were urban disorders seen as connected to a broad set of urban problems, and only then was a comprehensive urban policy agenda pursued. The first period began in East St. Louis in 1917; 39 blacks and 9 whites died, and over three hundred buildings were destroyed. Violence also occurred in Philadelphia and Chester, Pennsylvania. In 1919 a week of violence took place in Chicago, during which 25 citizens died and hundreds were wounded. Outbreaks also occurred that year in Washington, D.C., Omaha, Nebraska, and Longview, Texas (National Advisory Commission on Civil Disorders 1968).

A second wave of urban violence occurred during the World War Two—in Mobile, Los Angeles, Harlem, and Beaumont. The worst outbreak was in Detroit, in which 29 blacks and 9 whites died, and required federal troops to suppress. The final wave of urban disorders began on a relatively minor scale in 1963 and 1964, then exploded in Watts (Los Angeles) in 1965; 34 citizens were killed, hundreds injured, and $35 million in property damage done. Violence followed the next year in Chicago, and in 1967 the nation experienced the most widespread urban violence ever. Literally hundreds of cities experienced racial violence, with the worst incidents in Newark and Detroit. Forty-three persons were killed in Detroit, making it the worst race violence ever (National Advisory Commission on Civil Disorders 1968).

In translating a social situation into a public issue, "triggering" devices often come into play. These are events that symbolize a situation, forcing it onto the public agenda (Cobb and Elder 1983, 84–85). To what extent were these tragic occurrences "triggering" events, catapulting urban racial problems onto the policy agendas of governments? We use our two standard sources to assess this: media coverage, which measures systemic agenda access, and congressional hearings, one measure of the formal agenda of the national government. These measures, of course, indicate only national agenda events; local responses clearly occurred but are beyond our purview.

Figure 7.1 shows annual coverage in the *Readers' Guide* indexed under the headings "cities," "urban," and "suburban." Use of these keywords in the titles of articles in the popular press suggests the conception of the urban situation as a whole. Other articles have dealt with the problems of housing, discrimination, or crime, but these were not associated so specifically with cities and thus were not included. Of course we also found positive articles on cities: cultural opportunities and urban amenities, for example. Whether dealing with positives or negatives, our rule was the same: we included articles whose focus was on the city as such rather than on the problem or the amenity. As was the case for automobile safety, we found no systematic change in the proportion of articles viewing cities positively across time. Details of our coding scheme appear in appendix A. Figure 7.1 shows, the number of articles in the *Readers' Guide* and the number of congressional hearings on cities and urban affairs.

No increased attention to urban affairs occurred in the popular media during or following the 1917–19 disturbances. The level of interest in urban affairs was low during this period, although interest rose rapidly during the 1920s and sustained a level of about thirty-five to forty articles a year until 1960. No increased attention is discernible during and after the 1943 disturbances. On the other hand, cities became topics of considerable media interest in the 1960s. A sharp rise in the number of articles devoted to urban affairs began in 1961 and continued to a peak in 1966–67. Between 1960 and 1964, however, the number of articles published on cities tripled—before the Watts outbreak. Media interest was certainly intensified by the disorders of 1965–68, but by no means can it be attributed to them. Attention was already at its highest point in this century, although it rose even higher in response to the riots. Cities were on the systemic agenda before the urban disorders of the 1960s. Rather than triggering action, the riots seemed to have symbolized city problems and gave ammunition to those Democratic social activists already in a dominant position nationally.

We have noted the phenomenon of supposed "triggering" events actually occurring after a major change in the extent and tone of media coverage— Three Mile Island in the case of nuclear power, and the publication of Rachel Carson's *Silent Spring* in the case of pesticides. Such events are important

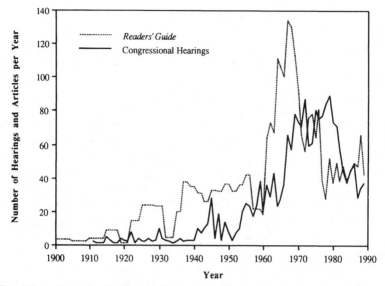

Figure 7.1. Articles in the *Readers' Guide* and congressional hearings on urban affairs.

because they symbolize a particular understanding of a problem. They reinforce a positive-feedback process already occurring, but they are not the trigger for the process. We might term such events "attributed triggers." Triggering events do occur, but they are probably rarer than one might think. More often, they are consolidating events—dramatic symbols of problems that are already rising rapidly to national attention. These events are certainly important, but more because of their timing in relation to other agenda events than because of their intrinsic value. The same event at another time would not have triggered anything.

The Formal Agenda

The formal political agenda includes matters brought before government for serious consideration. When a problem accesses the formal agenda, governmental bodies are scheduling the event for discussion and possible action. In previous chapters, we have used hearing activity in congressional committees as a measure of concern by national governing institutions. Much has been written on the role of the president in setting the national agenda, but, as Hurley and Wilson have noted, "a policy agenda is also defined by Congress" (1989, 247). Moreover, presumably presidential initiatives are generally scheduled for discussion by congressional committees, even if action is not forthcoming. So policy proposals put forth by the executive branch as well as the legislative branch are filtered through the committee process.

Using the CIS Abstracts, we have coded congressional hearings on urban affairs from 1870 to the present, using the following key words: cities, urban, urban problems, urban renewal. Then we independently placed all hearings into the following categories: physical infrastructure (transportation and other infrastructure improvements); race and social (discrimination, disorders, welfare, manpower education, housing); community development and intergovernmental financing (general intergovernmental aid, regional assistance, community development); and environment (water, sewer, and landfill quality). These categories match those used by the Office of Management and Budget in its analysis of federal expenditures, allowing us to examine the connection between hearing categories and expenditures. Hearings were placed in one category only; seldom was there any ambiguity concerning placement. Details of our coding of these hearings appear in appendix A.

Our data allow us to see the reaction of the formal institutions of government as issues surge onto the systemic agenda, as indicated by press coverage. Figure 7.1 shows both media coverage and congressional hearing activity on urban problems for the twentieth century. Throughout the series there is a distinct propensity for media coverage to precede congressional attention. The lag between peaks of press coverage and formal actions suggests that, in general, a sequential process is at work, implying an outside mobilization process (Cobb, Ross, and Ross 1976).

Congressional hearings during the 1940s took place in an environment of considerable media attention, attention that began in the middle 1930s and was sustained at about thirty-five to forty articles a year until the late 1950s. Many of the articles during this period were on urban housing problems; similarly, congressional hearings concerned housing. In 1960, media concern with urban affairs exploded, and preceded the scheduling of congressional hearings by several years. Finally, media interest in urban affairs declined during the 1970s, and congressional hearings followed suit. While the existence of policy waves in urban policymaking complicates the picture, the broad outlines are clear: media discussion precedes congressional attention in the case of urban policymaking.[1]

Now there is of course no specific causality here. Stories do not lead directly to hearings. A far more likely interpretation would stress the effect of the media on context. Returning to figure 7.1, we note that media coverage was sustained at a high level for a number of years prior to the increase in congressional interest. Only after an extended period of discussion in the press did Congress exhibit a rapid increase in addressing urban matters. In the case of a broad policy area such as urban affairs, media coverage is connected to government activity through a very diffuse causal process. Our measure of

1. We have tested two models of the relationship between news coverage and congressional hearings using regression analysis. One model enters media activity simultaneously with congressional hearings; the second uses a lag of five years for the media. The fit is far better for the lagged model. Details appear in appendix B.

media coverage probably reflects changes in social understandings of what came to be termed urban problems. Congressional hearings reflect changes in formal governmental attention, and probably respond more to diffuse social understandings than to specific perceived pressure from the media to initiate action.

Policy Outputs and the Formal Agenda

Hearing activity in Congress may be associated with policy changes, but the connection is not straightforward. Many hearings concern legislation, but many others are general fact-finding operations; others concern the congressional oversight function; still others provide purely symbolic outputs, offering publicity and allowing the airing of complaints rather than passing laws and appropriating money. Even when hearings do concern legislation, they often do not result in specific policy enactments. Hence the connection between placing an issue on the formal agenda and subsequent policy action is an empirical question. On the other hand, agenda theory suggests that concrete action is likely where an issue is extensively discussed by government. Therefore we expect to find a positive relationship between hearing activity and subsequent policy action, although the connection is not likely to happen instantaneously.

We may explore this connection in some detail by comparing congressional hearing activity with federal grants to states and localities. The Office of Management and Budget tabulates expenditures by substantive subcategories within the budgetary category of intergovernmental grants. Comparable assignments are available since 1940. Ideally one would want grants going specifically to cities, but there are two problems with this. First, many federal grants that go to states are in fact targeted at urban problems. Second, comparable tabulations for long periods of time for specific urban grants are unavailable. Our approach is to study federal grants to states and localities in certain OMB categories, which we have combined to correspond to our classification of hearings. The broad categories we have used are social programs, including OMB's categories of income security, health, education, employment training; community development and intergovernmental finance, incorporating general revenue sharing, urban renewal, community development block grants, and certain community-based project grants; infrastructure development, consisting primarily of grants for highways and mass transportation; and environment, where the bulk of funds goes to water and sewerage grants. These are the major policies directed at urban problems, even if not all the funds reached urban areas. We have omitted agriculture programs from our analysis. Coding details appear in appendix A.

Figure 7.2 shows the hearings conducted on urban affairs, previously depicted in figure 7.1 with media coverage, plotted with the inflation-adjusted

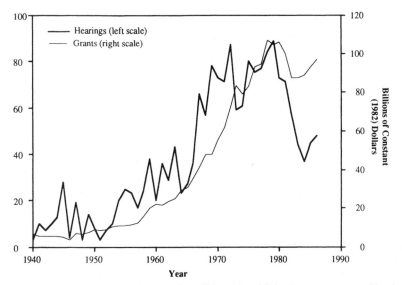

Figure 7.2. Congressional hearings on urban affairs and total federal grants to states and localities.

intergovernmental grants going to states and localities. The figure shows that budgetary action generally followed congressional hearing activity. As hearing activity expanded in the late 1950s, spending for urban-related programs began to grow soon after. Hearing activity expanded during the middle 1960s, and expenditures grew robustly from the late 1960s to the late 1970s. Congressional activity peaked in 1969–72 but was sustained at a very high level until 1979, falling precipitously thereafter. Grant-in-aid programs peaked in the period 1979–81, falling somewhat during the early 1980s, recovering somewhat thereafter.

Congressional attention clearly led budgetary action in urban affairs, and when Congress turned to other matters, program growth ceased. Real dollar declines in grants-in-aid occurred between 1980 and 1982, when Congress was preoccupied with the Reagan budget initiatives. Nevertheless, the dramatic decline in congressional hearing activity on urban affairs was not associated with a correspondingly severe decline in funding for urban programs.

Congressional attention is probably necessary for program creation and large-scale expansion, but may not be necessary for continuance. If this is true, then such comprehensive and large-scale program initiatives follow quite a different agenda logic from policies that are organized through subsystems. In particular, subsystems are often created during a wave of media coverage, but with little congressional attention. They seem to suffer disruption only when the arrangement is put into the limelight by the press and congressional policymakers. For the urban initiative, at least, somewhat the opposite happened. Major funding increases occurred only when major policy attention was directed at cities. Declines in program funding occurred when congressional attention turned away.

Waves of Urban Policymaking

So far we have treated the urban initiative as if it were a single, unified, policy assault on urban ills. That is true only at the most general level. As we shall see, the policymaking process was actually comprised of five waves, each with a different conception of the urban problem and a different set of solutions to the problem. We noted in chapter 6 a similar pattern for automobile safety: each time the issue reached the systemic agenda, a different solution was adopted.

Figure 7.3 presents four separate graphs for the four major areas of activity that we examined. Each presents the number of congressional hearings per year on a topic along with the inflation-adjusted grants-in-aid going to states and localities in the corresponding category.

The Precursors: Subsystems for Housing and Highways

Urban matters first emerged on the national policy agenda in the 1940s. Neither media coverage nor congressional attention followed the 1917–19 period of urban disorder. Following the 1943 riots, however, Congress conducted a large number of hearings. Most of those hearings did not involve the riots directly, but were the prelude to the 1949 Housing Act. This act was concerned with both constructing low-income housing and effecting urban renewal (or, more accurately, slum removal), and thus was connected at least tangentially to the wartime disorders. However, the major outlines of the act were visible as early as 1941, and proposals for slum removal were circulated regularly during the 1930s (Foard and Fefferman 1966). The federal urban agenda concerned primarily housing, but housing was broadly conceived to include the amelioration of blight and slums. (We included all housing hearings in our social program category, presented in fig. 7.3a. Most housing appropriations are included in social programs, but urban renewal funds are included in the community development category, presented in fig. 7.3c.)

As the first major foray by the federal government into urban affairs, the Housing Act of 1949 had critical consequences for urban America. Controversy simmered and occasionally exploded over the issues of "Negro removal" and the use of federal funds for nonhousing construction. The act authorized $500 million in direct grants and $1 billion in loans over five years to local housing authorities, and these amounts were increased over the years.

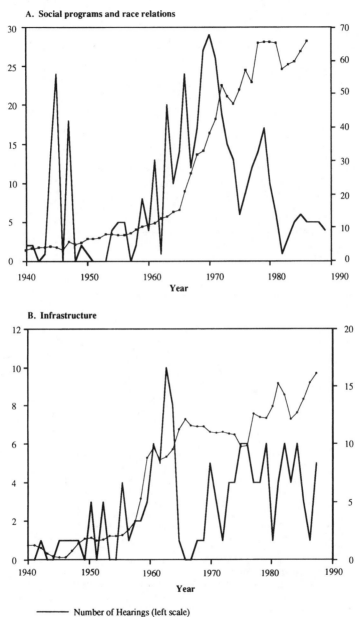

A. Social programs and race relations

B. Infrastructure

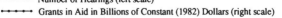

——————— Number of Hearings (left scale)
•—•—•—•—• Grants in Aid in Billions of Constant (1982) Dollars (right scale)

Figure 7.3. Congressional hearings on urban affairs and federal grants to states and localities, by category. (*continued on next page*)

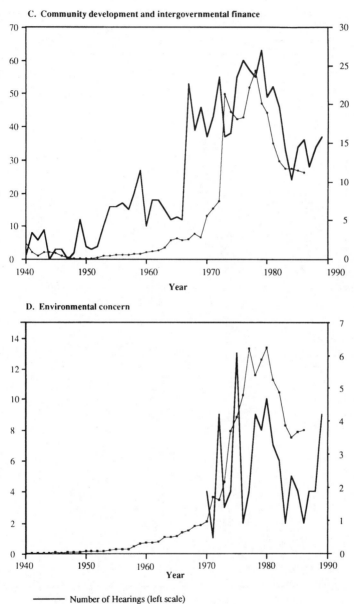

C. Community development and intergovernmental finance

D. Environmental concern

Number of Hearings (left scale)
Grants in Aid in Billions of Constant (1982) Dollars (right scale)

Figure 7.3   continued

In 1953, explicit appropriations for urban renewal appeared for the first time, as a consequence of amendments to the act made in that year.

The urban housing initiatives of the late 1940s took place in the absence of general public concern. Little interest in urban problems is in evidence in the popular media, but Congress held numerous formal hearings on urban matters. While housing problems were widespread, the remedies of the 1949 act were primarily directed at large, older cities in the North and East. The pattern suggests that the mobilization of interests external to government was limited, that broad constituencies were not activated, and that policy participants had a relatively narrow policy objective. The first wave of urban policymaking concern, then, involved a constrained definition of the issue, a small constituency, and relatively small programs from a national perspective—although those cities affected by urban renewal were dramatically changed. This urban renewal policy subsystem incorporated groups with somewhat different understandings of the issue, although all were unified in their focus on rebuilding aging cities.

As figure 7.3a shows, growth in governmental transfers to states and localities was slow from 1940 through the late 1950s. These programs consisted primarily of the modest welfare programs of the New Deal, plus the housing and renewal programs in the 1949 act. Similarly, as figure 7.3b shows, there was little congressional interest in developing the urban physical infrastructure following the war. Highway spending increased substantially after the 1956 Interstate Highway Act. Note that this grant activity actually seems to have spurred congressional hearing activity; indeed, it was the increased highway construction activity that put highways on the national urban agenda. The interstate highway act gave rise to the "neighborhoods versus roads" urban controversy, which reached the congressional agenda in the early 1960s.

Congress was interested in a narrow range of topics affecting cities between 1940 and 1960—almost exclusively housing and highways. These policies were lodged in subsystems—subsystems that incorporated considerable differences of opinion on the implementation of policies, but subsystems nevertheless. Issues were narrowly defined and did not involve macropolitical forces. No broad national strategy for dealing with urban problems emerged during these years. During the 1960s, however, both transportation and housing became part of the solution-set to urban problems. While the number of hearings on urban transportation has always been small, the hearings have occasionally been controversial—especially on the issue of whether funds ought to go for mass transportation or highways.

The Main Waves: Social Programs and Community Development

Beginning in the late 1950s, a major increase in the number of hearings on urban social programs began. As figure 7.3a shows, from 1957 through 1970 hearings on social programs ratcheted upward, with a fallback one year and a recovery and increase above the previous high the next. Then, beginning in 1971, hearing activity fell and has continued to fall with only feeble attempts at recovery until the present. Following hearing activity was a dramatic increase in the dollars going to cities for social programs. From 1940 through 1966 one sees steady incremental growth in appropriations for social programs. Then, in 1967, a dramatic increase occurred, setting a new slope for social expenditures that lasted without interruption until 1974, and until 1980 with only minor fluctuations. As hearings increased, grants increased after a lag of a few years. As hearings declined, grants leveled off—again after a lag of a few years.

One major reason for the dramatic decline in the number of hearings on social programs was that the debate on the urban problem was shifting. Republicans and state and local officials began to cast the debate as one over the level of responsibility, arguing that local governments ought be able to decide their own priorities rather than accept those set by Congress and national bureaucrats. They argued for a block-grant approach to intergovernmental relations, with the federal government providing the revenue from its seemingly inexhaustible supply, and the states and localities spending the money within broad constraints. This shifted the debate from "What do we do about the cities" to "How much leeway should we allow local officials?"

Figure 7.3c documents the shift in the urban debate. There we tabulate the number of hearings and amount of grants going for intergovernmental grants and community development (a broad category indicating substantial local discretion). Note that the issue expanded in Congress in a single year—1967. Moreover, that expansion was followed in 1973 with a dramatic rise in funding—the year Nixon achieved some success in his block-grant program.

With the Nixon block-grant initiatives, the urban initiative was over with one minor exception. During the 1970s, only one urban problem attracted congressional attention—the contribution of city governments to urban pollution. Clearly connected to the environmental movement, this attention resulted primarily in grants for sewerage treatment. While these grants were not of the magnitude of those in the other categories, they did leap up in a nonincremental fashion during the early 1970s, as is indicated by figure 7.3d.

Looking over the curves presented in figure 7.3, it would be hard to conceive of the urban initiative in any other than nonincremental fashion. Even if one were to want to see the increase in funding during the 1960s and 1970s as stepped-up incrementalism driven by increases in real tax revenues, this would not explain the waves of urban concern that are tied to subsequent major jumps in funding. Congressional attention and appropriations lurched as new understandings of urban affairs gained credence and as new solutions were proposed. Moreover, once a solution gained a niche in the national policymaking system through agency creation and funding, it did not disappear.

In three of the four figures, congressional hearing activity after 1960 increased dramatically prior to a nonincremental program expansion. Particularly impressive are the increases in hearing activity on race and social problems in the mid-1960s, and the subsequent growth in grants for social programs during the late 1960s and early 1970s (fig. 7.3a). In a generally similar fashion, congressional attention to intergovernmental finance (including housing and community development), which quadrupled in a single year (1967), was followed with a correspondingly dramatic increase in budgetary commitment to block grants in 1973 (fig. 7.3c).

Considerable differences separate the timing of peak activity in each category of policy activity. Congressional attention to the urban infrastructure peaked in the early 1960s; to race relations and social problems in 1967; to finance in 1967 and again in 1979, with high activity between; and in environmental matters in the 1970s. The urban initiative seems to have been carried on a series of waves, each of which defined the urban problem for the moment and was intertwined with other matters on the congressional agenda at the time. First came concern with infrastructure development, a consequence of the concern with transportation development in the late 1950s. The second wave centered on civil rights and social problems; that wave built steadily from 1958 to a peak in 1970, falling dramatically thereafter. The third wave concerned intergovernmental finance. It literally leaped to the congressional agenda in 1967 and dominated the domestic policy dialogue until the late 1970s. The debate, which divided the parties, concerned not just funding but, more fundamentally, control: should domestic programs be dictated by the federal government, or turned over to the states with appropriate financing and considerable discretionary authority? Finally, the last wave of the urban initiative was environmentalist, perhaps more a spillover from heightened environmental sensitivities than a specific concern with the plight of urban populations.[2]

For urban programs, a dual lag between systemic attention and policy outputs occurred. First, media coverage resulted in congressional interest only after an extended period of time. Second, grant funds increased only after years of congressional interest. Peak media attention to cities occurred in 1967, with almost as much coverage in 1968. Peak grant activity occurred in 1978—a lag of about a decade. Peak-to-peak lags are not very good ways of assessing policy responses for agenda models, however, because one is most

2. As in the case for the relationship between media coverage and congressional attention, we can use regression analysis to examine the connection between hearings and the allocation of grant funds in a more systematic fashion. One expects sustained congressional hearing activity to be necessary to produce increases in budgetary outlays for broad policy initiatives. Hence we compared a regression model in which funds were a simultaneous function of hearings with a model in which funds were a lagged function of hearings. Complete regression results are presented in appendix B for the simultaneous model and a model in which hearings are lagged.

interested in the nonincremental dynamics of getting an issue to the attention of policymakers. The most important measure of policy responsiveness would be the change in slope of the grant curve. For urban programs, this is easy to discern from the graphs in figure 7.3. For social programs, 1966 was the critical year; for community development, 1972.

This pattern of governmental attention and policy responsiveness is consistent with our emphasis on the role of positive-feedback effects in politics. Systemic agenda activity spurted briefly in the early to mid-1960s, but this touched off congressional interest and the activities of national bureaucrats and local officials. Increases in grants were sustained well through the 1970s and dropped only with the Reagan budget initiatives. The rise of urban affairs to the national systemic agenda set in process a positive-feedback system that resulted in a nonincremental wave of policy outputs.

A National Urban Initiative

The urban disorders of the 1960s occurred in a vastly different milieu than did those earlier in the century. Congress, led by two activist Democratic presidents, turned increasingly after 1960 to a broad domestic agenda, of which urban problems were one major aspect. In 1960, Congress held twenty hearings which concerned urban matters either directly or tangentially. In 1970, Congress convened more than four times as many. This is the largest number of hearings on any of the issues we have studied in this book. This intense congressional interest was sustained until 1976, after which a dramatic decline occurred (see fig. 7.1).

The national assault on urban ills was President Lyndon Johnson's success story. Presidents are often thwarted in their attempts to lead in the domestic policy area because of the myriad of forces that act to derail (or transform) their programs. Hence presidents must try to integrate various policy subsystems and direct them toward a comprehensive policy (Jones and Strahan 1985). The housing, transportation, and welfare programs of the early 1960s were dramatically expanded on a wave of enthusiastic attack on domestic problems. Johnson and his congressional allies had succeeded in stimulating a mobilization of enthusiasm whose primary characteristic was its aggregation of numerous social problems into a comprehensive national program.

As a consequence, congressional interest in urban affairs was both broad and deep. In the 1960s, congressional hearings focused on a wide variety of urban problems and programs, as figures 7.2 and 7.3 show. The access of these urban issues to the formal agenda resulted in major legislation and vast new expenditures. All intergovernmental transfers to state and local governments showed major increases in the late 1960s or the 1970s, except for physical infrastructure expenditures. The major vehicle for this expansion was the categorical grant-in-aid. Programs and projects were narrowly defined by federal officials. Implementation was accomplished by state and local bureaucrats, bypassing for the most part elected officials at those levels of government.

In part, this was simply expanding the mechanism used for domestic program implementation since the New Deal. But it also fit into the ideas of many policymakers who had come to Washington in the Kennedy administration. State and local officials, it was thought, were unresponsive to urban needs, partly because of the malapportionment that afflicted state legislatures at the time. Hence it was thought that new programs ought to bypass conservative opposition in state capitals. Categorical programs, by requiring particular forms of administration, did this. Moreover, for the first time federal grants were directed toward city governments, bypassing state governments entirely. And the War on Poverty was designed to deal directly with citizen groups, although control varied considerably from city to city (Greenstone and Peterson 1976).

State and local officials were quite interested in the federal dollars, but had considerable disagreements among themselves and with federal bureaucrats on the administration of programs. Samuel Beer argues that the categorical programs expanded so dramatically during the 1960s gave birth to a new kind of politics. Writing in 1978, he notes that "powerful new centers of influence on what government does have arisen within government itself" (Beer 1978, 17). This "public sector of the polity" (17) took two forms: "the professional and bureaucratic complex, that is, for each program a core of government officials with scientific or professional qualifications, working closely with interested legislators and spokesmen for the beneficiary group; and the intergovernmental lobby, consisting of governors, mayors, county supervisors, city managers, and other officeholders, mainly elective, exercising general responsibilities in state and local governments" (Beer, in Conlon 1988, xviii).

So the national government was subject to influence from two sources: one associated with "the functional specialization in the modern state, . . . the professional-bureaucratic complex. The other results from territorial specialization—the intergovernmental lobby" (Beer 1978, 17). The new programs of the Great Society generated powerful, specialized lobbies from both sources. This peculiarly American version of state expansion had given rise to a particularly powerful set of allies, based both on program and geographic representation (Beer 1977, 1978). This meant, however, that the president's comprehensive approach was disaggregated—in congressional committees, among national bureaucrats, and among state and local officials. Each had interests in specific programs, but none had a stake in comprehensive, coordinated policy.

During the 1960s, then, the federal government undertook a broad urban policy for the only time in the history of the United States. It occurred because an activist president defined a comprehensive domestic program and worked to implement it. Because of the dynamics of the American policy process, the initiative was uncoordinated; it relied on the cooperation of legislatures and bureaucracies at all levels of government. It was focused, but it was focused on specific problems rather than on an overall strategy for dealing with the role of cities in the modern American political system. It was internally contradictory, as highway programs caused new problems in housing and neighborhood preservation. It led to complaints about the administrative overload inherent in the complexity, duplication, and fragmentation inherent in an approach to domestic problems that was both disaggregated and indirect: disaggregated because it was centered in programs directed at specific problems; indirect because it relied on the federal grant structure for implementation. But it was enormous; directly or indirectly, billions of federal dollars were spent to correct city problems from housing to transportation to minority empowerment. The number of federal grant programs tripled between 1960 and 1968, and federal aid more than tripled—from $7 billion to $24 billion—between 1960 and 1970 (Conlon 1988, 6). The national urban initiative of the 1960s, then, was comprehensive but uncoordinated and, as a consequence, generated much criticism both from opponents of large-scale governmental involvement and from state and local officials who felt bypassed in the administrative complexity.

The End of the Urban Initiative

By the early 1970s, media interest, as assessed by the *Readers' Guide,* was declining rapidly, from 120 articles in 1965 to only 60 in 1972 (fig. 7.1). Articles in the popular press leveled off at around 70 during the mid-1970s, then plummeted again in 1978. By that time general interest in cities was only slightly above the level of the 1940s and 1950s. Popular opinion, as gauged by polls, indicated that popular support for domestic policy initiatives was also declining in the 1970s. National surveys concerning the level of spending the public would support in various areas of policy found that 49 percent of those surveyed thought that too little was being spent on the problems of big cities in 1973–74. By the time of the Carter administration, only 40 percent thought so (Bennett and Bennett 1990, 90–91). Urban matters were fading from public consciousness.

Congressional attention also declined—first in infrastructure, then in racial affairs and social programs, then in the intergovernmental fiscal structure. As we noted above, this decline occurred long after declines in media coverage. The sustained congressional interest in the 1970s reflected the agenda of President Nixon, whose major domestic agenda item was the consolidation of the many categorical grant programs of the Great Society into a small number of block grants. Most of the hearings during the 1970s concerned conflict over the structure and funding of these grants. Nixon proposed consolidation in six general policy areas, achieving partial success in only two. Each reform proposal was fought out in a specific policy arena, and the resulting fragmented politics dictated the mixed results achieved by the president (Conlon 1988, 62). The politics of the Nixon administration were dictated in large part by the agenda of the 1960s, even though systemic attention in these matters had declined dramatically.

One might expect that, in the absence of congressional attention, a structured politics similar to single-industry subsystem arrangements might take over. The bureaucratic complex and the intergovernmental lobby would seem to be powerful bases for such arrangements. In urban affairs, as in the federal system generally, stable working arrangements emerged as the system expanded (Anton 1989). These arrangements, occurring as they did over a wide expanse of particularistic programs and costing billions of federal dollars, dominated domestic political calculations between the Johnson and Reagan administrations.

What happened, however, was a partial collapse of the system. After reaching a peak in 1977, real fiscal transfers in block-grant categories (fig. 7.3c) from federal to state and local governments dropped dramatically. Viewed from the vantage point of local governments, the decline was especially stark. In 1978, the ratio of federal aid to own-source revenues for American municipalities was .26, that is, for every $1.00 raised in local taxes, an additional $0.26 came to the city through direct federal aid (even more came indirectly via the state government). By 1984, the ratio had declined to .15—a decline of 58 percent (Wright 1988, 165). The complex, supportive web comprised of both the "professional-bureaucratic complex" and the "intergovernmental lobby" (Beer 1978) was unable to sustain the fiscal transfer system that had been established during the urban initiative. Declines in real funding also occurred in the other categories (figs. 7.3a, b, and d), but were far less severe. In the case of social programs, growth in grants resumed during the mid–1980s, at about the same rate of growth as during the 1970s. This growth is almost exclusively due to the Medicaid program.

What happened, then, was a decrease in the three categories that provide collective goods—infrastructure, environment, and community development—and growth in redistributive or collective consumption programs. We return to this point in chapter 11. These three policy categories have traditionally been associated more closely with the policy priorities of city governments than social programs. Because these policies also give greater discretion to local officials, they are the programs that have been most favored by the intergovernmental lobby. The contraction in the grant structure was primarily limited to urban programs providing collective benefits and local discretion.

Perhaps most surprising, the collapse occurred as congressional attention declined. In other issues featuring powerful subsystems that we have studied, congressional attention was relatively low at the creation of the subsystem, but increased as conflict expanded beyond the confines of the subsystem. Urban politics has worked in opposite fashion: congressional interest was very high at the creation, but decreased as the system came under attack. This is even more remarkable given the expansion of congressional ability to hold hearings after 1974. (Indeed, the fact that urban hearings uniformly decline during a period of increased capacity is important evidence that the patterns observed for subsystem politics are not due to the simple expansion of capacity for attention, but must be due to changing patterns of congressional attention.)

A Window of Opportunity

The findings presented above raise three fundamental questions about the rise and decline of a national urban agenda. First, why did the urban initiatives occur when they did? Clearly urban problems, if anything, were improving— blacks, for example, made their largest income gains during the early 1960s. Disorders had occurred before without getting swept up in a national domestic initiative. Second, why did the initiative collapse? The reputedly all-powerful combination of the bureaucratic-professional complex and the intergovernmental lobby proved utterly unsuccessful in protecting its turf. These public-sector political forces were supposed to be particularly entrenched, but they saw their issue fade away, taking with it a large part of the grant funds that had been dedicated to them. Finally, why did the collapse of the urban initiative occur without provoking more congressional attention? One might expect that increased conflict associated with the dramatic downsizing of the urban grant system would be reflected in congressional hearing activity, but our evidence indicates otherwise.

One cannot understand the rise and decline of the national urban initiative without appreciating the particular confluence of factors that occurred during the 1960s. An unprecedented window of opportunity opened during that time, in which three major social trends came into juxtaposition: America's postwar prosperity; social attitudes that, for a brief moment in history, turned from economics to social issues; and the high watermark of the Democratic Rooseveltian coalition, led by an activist president with an ambitious domestic agenda. One might say that the economic, the social, and the political came into phase to allow cities to be pushed forward as a major national priority.

Some indication of the receptivity of the nation to the urban agenda can be gleaned from figure 7.4, which shows the percentage of citizens indicating that either the economy or social issues were the major problem facing the country, from the 1930s through 1984 (Smith 1985).

Since the mid-1930s, the Gallup polling organization has questioned the

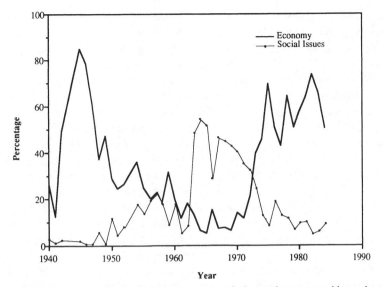

Figure 7.4. Responses to Gallup Poll question on America's most important problems, domestic issues only. *Source:* Smith 1985. *Note:* In years when more than one poll was reported, we have averaged the results in order to smooth out minor fluctuations. Analysis is based on a total of 171 polls reported in Smith 1985.

American public concerning the country's major problems. The Gallup organization has been able to use no more than eleven categories during the fifty years the data have been kept, and most of the responses have been put in five categories (foreign affairs, the economy, social control, civil rights, and government). In figure 7.4, social control and civil rights are combined, as justified by scaling work by Weisberg and Rusk (1970). Economic issues outweigh social questions in the public mind throughout the 1930s, the 1940s, and for most of the 1950s. During the second half of the 1950s, social questions begin to preoccupy a greater number of Americans, but it is only in the early 1960s that these issues shoot up on the public agenda. For a brief period, approximately 1963 to 1972, social issues dominate the public agenda, far outweighing the state of the economy in the mind of the public. Figure 7.4 shows how unusual that period was; after 1972, public concerns reverted to the more traditional economic issues.

Not only was the public particularly concerned with social problems during this brief period of the 1960s, but, as Bennett and Bennett (1990) suggest, public attitudes toward government were considerably more favorable during this period than they were before or after. Although these polling data cannot be viewed as conclusive evidence, they do suggest that during the early 1960s Americans were both trusting of government as an instrument to solve problems and more concerned with social issues than with economic ones. Concern with a problem seems to have coincided with optimism that government might be able to provide a good solution. Neither the concern nor the optimism was to be long-lasting, of course, but while these conditions existed, they provided the perfect climate for a national urban initiative.

When rapid changes in the policy environment occur, the attachment of policy solutions to problems is critical. This is the role of political leaders and, in national politics, the president. Presidents, of course, can play an important role in raising issues to the systemic agenda, but they do not control the process alone. Still, they are in a unique position to attach the solutions they prefer to problems as they emerge high on the national agenda. It is illuminating to return to the quotation from President Lyndon Johnson at the first of this chapter. The president aggressively defined the social issue as one that could be ameliorated by positive government action, not public repression: "legislative action to improve the life in our cities." The Democratic coalition, infused in 1964 with a huge class of northern Democrats replacing, for the most part, moderate northern Republicans, followed enthusiastically.

If the election of 1964 left the Democrats all-powerful for the short run, it defined the end of the Rooseveltian dominance in the long run. With the Democrats defining the issue as one of not enough government, Republicans exploited the opening left them. The Democratic approach to domestic issues centered on a service strategy, which relied on professionals to intervene and correct social problems. Critics viewed this approach as social engineering (Beer 1976). Republicans deftly unified the social issue with traditional conservative economic policies: Nixon rallied the South and West and claimed to speak for the forgotten Silent Majority. Even if these were worthy aims, the social engineering of the liberal Democrats had not worked, wasting billions of tax dollars, Republican critics claimed.

Much of the increased partisan conflict centered on the issue of racial relations. The parties struggled not only with the new role of the federal government in domestic life, but also with the incorporation of blacks into American politics. The civil rights movement peaked as blacks began to assume considerable political power in cities. The fusion of the issues of the larger role of the federal government in domestic policies and the incorporation of blacks together yielded a new understanding of the issue bases of the political parties. The most persuasive evidence for the new definition of issues comes from the work of Carmines and Stimson (1989). These authors show how the congressional political parties shifted positions on the race issue between 1960 and 1970. As the Democrats became more liberal, the Republicans became more conservative.

In the tumult of the period, the urban initiative got swept up in the emerging new partisan dimensions of conflict. Cities benefited as the Democratic majority pushed through its ambitious domestic agenda: city problems, to the Johnson Democrats, were national problems. But there was always a second side to cities: home to immigrants, minorities, crime, and corrupt machine politics. It was this side of cities that came to the fore with the Republican emphasis on social order.

Having become part of the new partisan conflict, cities stayed there. The Johnson activism stimulated a long-run Republican strategy to push back the domestic policy agenda. In some areas, such as Social Security, the Republican strategy was singularly unsuccessful. But in the intergovernmental grant system, it was a rousing success—especially in housing and in general grants for community and regional development. One would have to conclude that the intergovernmental lobby in the late 1970s was enormously powerful, composed of literally thousands of paid professionals from across the nation. Their failure to defend their gains could hardly have been predicted at the time. Their difficulties almost certainly centered on the problems in defending the image of place rather than people, and the generally negative view of cities that intensified later in the period.

Defenders of urban and other intergovernmental programs seemed to have failed to resurrect both systemic and formal attention to urban problems. Exactly why this occurred is not completely clear, but one critical component of the equation was the Republican attempt to redefine urban problems as local problems. President Nixon took the first and most important step. His New Federalism was basically an attempt to separate funding from policy priorities. In his block-grant approach, the federal government would provide the funds, but the states and localities would, within broad guidelines, deliver the services. In later years, Republicans could claim that the national government had no business funding local projects.

Unlike Nixon, President Reagan and his allies had in mind a reduction in the size and scope of government when they pushed for turning back responsibilities to the states and localities. Their arguments over the proper level of government for policy activities were clearly aimed at increasing the powers of those levels of government that they believed were more likely to follow conservative policies (Conlon 1988). We might call this venue shopping on a grand scale. Unfortunately for the Republicans, this did not work exactly as had been hoped, since the states and localities were forced to expand their activities throughout the 1980s in precisely those areas where the national government was reducing its commitments (chap. 11 discusses these links in more detail). Moreover, federal grants for social programs resumed their upward spiral after a hiatus of only a few years, driven by cost increases in the Medicaid program.

Looking at our measures of the rise and fall of the urban agenda, we see that no countermobilization seems to have occurred. That is, as urban matters were aggressively pushed off the national agenda in the Reagan era, proponents mustered no serious counterassault. Press coverage did not rebound from late 1970s lows. Similarly, congressional hearings did not soar as housing programs, community development, and other elements of the intergovernmental grant structure were dismantled or severely constrained. The supposedly powerful intergovernmental lobby seems to have been unable to put urban matters back on the national systemic or formal agendas.

Our data, of course, cannot tell us why something did not occur. But it seems reasonable to speculate that ignoring urban affairs was a consequence of the full Republican broadside on the Democratic welfare state. The Reagan Republicans did not attack specific programs, as had the Nixonians. They attacked the entire philosophy of the positive state, and they did so through budget and tax policies rather than through debate on statutory provisions concerning programs. Nixon, moreover, had been able to define the federalism issue to Reagan's great advantage: one of solving local problems without national bureaucratic interference. Finally, cities had the disadvantage of being fully associated with interracial strife. Given the pressure on all fronts, the Democrats chose to defend only the programs generating the broadest popular appeal, and that was primarily Social Security.

Concluding Comments

The rise and decline of the urban initiative, unlike any other issue we study in this book, was intimately tied up with broad partisan conflict. Neither its birth nor decline can be understood outside of the national debate on the proper scope of governmental action. Neither can be understood without reference to the changing positions of the parties on the issue of racial relations, which became bound up in the debate over the proper role of the federal government in domestic policy. And neither can be understood without reference to the programs of the presidents: Johnson, who initiated the assault on urban ills; Nixon, who tried to channel the federal domestic initiative through the states and localities; Carter, who tried to place his own stamp on urban programs through the formulation of a national urban strategy; and Reagan, who saw fiscal federalism as a variant of big, intrusive, government that was ripe for elimination.

Most importantly, the rise and decline of the urban initiative is one more example of the lurches toward policy that the American political system tends to make. It is different only in its scale. The urban initiative of the 1960s was characterized by extreme positive-feedback effects, as concern mounted until cities were major targets of domestic policy action. Press attention and policy response fed on one another throughout the 1960s.

The initiative can be explained neither by a simple triggering event nor by worsening social conditions. The rise in both systemic and formal attention predated the most obvious candidate for a triggering event, the urban disorders. Conditions in cities were far better than ever before. Fewer citizens occupied substandard housing, and the incomes of both whites and blacks were rising at an unprecedented rate. We have speculated that the initiative was born of a unique configuration of events: postwar prosperity; the rising political consciousness of blacks; public concern with noneconomic issues; a short-lived optimism that government programs might be able to solve major social problems; and the rise of the liberal democratic coalition. This confluence could not have been predicted before it became apparent. The instability we have documented in earlier chapters for policy subsystems also holds for broad domestic policy initiatives.

The demise of the urban initiative was almost as sudden as its emergence. The 1970s were a period of declining press interest and consolidation in Congress. Advocates were unable to mount a satisfactory defense of urban programs in the Reagan attack on the domestic federal role during the 1980s, and congressional attention to urban affairs declined dramatically along with federal funding. Yet urban problems are as severe, if not more so, than they were in the 1960s. Moreover, a vast network of powerful interests organized at both the national and state and local levels had been spawned by the Democratic domestic policy initiative. Could any honest social scientist have predicted the weakness of these public-sector forces in the mid-1970s?

8

Connecting Solutions to Problems: Three Valence Issues

Valence issues have been defined as those in which only one side of the debate is legitimate (Nelson 1984). In such cases, issue redefinition would seem impossible. However, in this chapter we see that a given problem may be associated with many different solutions. Agenda-setting for valence issues often involves important decisions about what solutions are most appropriate to combat a uniformly agreed-upon problem. There is no question about whether drug abuse is bad or good; exactly what should be the nature of the governmental response remains an important question, however. There are various approaches to the drug problem: incarceration of users and dealers; interdiction; treatment; education. How solutions are attached to problems influences later policy dynamics.

In this chapter, we examine briefly three valence issues: drug abuse, alcohol abuse, and child abuse. In all three cases, the definition of the issue means that those who might countermobilize have extreme difficulty in establishing any degree of legitimacy for their position. While there exist opposing positions, they differ in their solutions rather than in their conception of the issue. For example, even though all might decry child abuse, the call for intervention runs counter to social norms stressing the sanctity of the family and the rights of parents to rear their children free from state intervention. Similarly in the cases of drug and alcohol abuse, excessive concern with an enforcement approach can lead to invasion of privacy or political interference in medical treatment, as has often been the case in the area of drug abuse regulation. Certainly the national experiment with prohibition of alcohol was not labeled a success by most of those who lived through it, even though there was probably a reduction in alcohol consumption; graft, corruption, and gang violence were seen as the other side of strict enforcement. While no one is in favor of abuse in any form, the public policy reaction differs greatly if one considers the abuser to be a criminal or to suffer from a disease. For the medical community, alcoholics and drug abusers have sometimes been seen as patients who need treatment, not as criminals who need incarceration.

Valence issues do seem to have some peculiar aspects; however, almost any issue can take on the characteristics of a valence question. In many of the cases we discussed in earlier chapters, one side was so dominant that to defend an opposing viewpoint was seen as almost "un-American." Nuclear power certainly fits this pattern; considering the isse in the 1950s, who was against the technology? So we need to be careful in identifying a given issue as a valence question in the first place.

Even though a valence issue is always viewed in negative terms, it can nevertheless be understood differently at different periods of time. These understandings imply different policy solutions. For example, concern with the well-being of children was once focused on the problem of employment conditions and the outlawing of child labor. Lately, this concern has shifted to the problems of poverty and nutrition, and their effects on educational attainment. In all these cases, well-meaning people have focused on some aspect of the well-being of children, but the particular focus has changed over the years. A strategic definition of the issue, rather than some fundamental characteristic of the nature of the problem, often dictates whether an issue is considered a valence question or not. Certainly if government officials were considering a broad-ranging "family policy," this definition of the question would lead to a greater range of reactions than if their concern appeared limited to fighting the abuse of children.

Many valence issues offer a final paradox. They are tempting issues for politicians to raise, but they are not easy problems to solve. Anthony Downs's (1972) arguments concerning the "issue attention cycle" were developed in reference to the problems of the environment, but they could easily be applied to such lasting problems as these. Politicians and the public may become preoccupied with a serious problem, but after they begin to devote resources to solving it, they often realize that it will not be so easy to solve. After years of frustration, they move their attention to something else. We discussed this theory in some detail in chapter 5, and we noted that Downs overlooked an important element of the attention cycle: waves of popular concern often lead to the creation of long-lasting and powerful institutions that continue to focus on the problem even decades after public concern has died down.

We will see in each of the cases here that powerful communities of specialists dealing with the prevention of abuse, with the treatment of abusers and abused, or with the enforcement of laws prohibiting abuse remain after public concern has withered away. These communities of professionals come to dominate official thinking about the policy responses to abuse. Public and media concern with the problem may lurch from low to high; however, government decisions about the solutions to be adopted will follow a different pattern. Still, the adoption of different policy solutions will be affected powerfully by the emergence of the problem on the systemic agenda. This is one of the most important ways in which the agenda-setting process affects policy outcomes. It also helps explain why the political system often lurches from one period of relative stability to another.

Murray Edelman (1964, 1989) has developed a perspective that might be applied to many of these issues: the government offers symbolic assurances to those who seek to fight certain ills but has little concern about solving the problem. There is no doubt that many candidates for office are careful to state their enthusiastic support for such measures as the death penalty for "drug kingpins" and the eradication of coca fields in Turkey or Peru. However, we should be careful before we dismiss all these efforts as merely symbolic. They may not be effective, but the cumulative impact of all the programs and budgets initiated during a wave of popular concern with an issue like drug abuse is enormous, as we show below. To dismiss it as purely symbolic is overly simplistic.

Drug Abuse

More than any other issue discussed in this book, the issue of drug abuse has periodically surged onto the national agenda, briefly preoccupying the media, the public, lawmakers, and even the president. Over 250 articles per year have sometimes appeared in the *Readers' Guide* on the topic of drug abuse, indicating a virtual obsession with the topic in a broad range of national publications. During these periods of national mobilization, various public policies have been adopted, ranging from complete legalization (the status quo at the beginning of this century), to stern enforcement (for example, during Prohibition, when drug abuse was also stigmatized), to tolerance bordering on glorification (during the 1960s), to enthusiasm about the possibilities of treating addiction as a disease (under President Nixon), and finally to a renewed emphasis on interdiction, enforcement, and punishment.

In his comprehensive history of drug abuse legislation, policy, and attitudes in the twentieth century, David Musto notes that we have never reached any sort of equilibrium of values or policies concerning drugs. Even during the nineteenth century, when the United States was the only major Western country that had not outlawed drugs, the unhindered play of the market was far from sufficient to create an equilibrium. For example, cocaine was considered almost a wonder drug in the 1880s when it was introduced, but this fascination and enthusiasm in medical circles soon were transformed into doubt, and finally into repulsion: "by 1900 it was considered to be the most dangerous of all drugs" (Musto 1987, x). According to Musto, we "oscillate from periods of drug tolerance to drug intolerance. Equilibrium is a state in which drugs, including alcohol, have rarely been found in the United States" (1987, x).

We noted in chapter 2 that many possible issues of public concern may be considered either private misfortunes (and therefore suitable for action by charities, but not demanding governmental intervention) or social problems (see D. Stone 1989). Drugs have oscillated in the public consciousness between these two points. During some periods, addicts have been dismissed as "weak souls" who may have ruined their own lives, but whose actions need not concern the government. During other periods, drug abuse is seen as sapping American productivity, as endangering the social control of minorities, or as contributing to urban violence and criminality. When these social rather than individual issues come to the fore, governmental action has typically been called for to address the problem. Government action, in turn, has oscillated from emphasis on enforcement and incarceration on the one hand to treatment, prevention, and education on the other.

Figure 8.1 shows how drugs have been treated in the *Readers' Guide* and in congressional hearings during the twentieth century. Drugs were not a primary concern of the nation's media during the first part of the century. Small blips of attention occurred in the 1930s, the 1940s, and the 1950s, but it was not until the mid-1960s that drug abuse emerged as a major story in the media. Even this attention was short-lived, however, as the issue declined during the 1970s. It then began its rapid and remarkable increase in the late 1970s, reaching a maximum of over 250 articles per year in 1986, and again in 1989. So drugs have generally not been on the systemic agenda in this century, except for two periods: the late 1960s, and the late 1980s. The second period corresponds to a much greater preoccupation with the problem than the first.

Drugs did not concern congressional decision-makers to any great degree until the late 1960s. Figure 8.1 shows that congressional attention as measured by hearings on drug abuse topics surged dramatically around 1969. Unlike media attention, however, congressional attention remained much higher for the entire period following its initial surge onto the formal agenda. Drug abuse receded from the systemic agenda during the 1970s, but it never declined from the formal agendas of the congressional committees.

During the years before drug abuse emerged as a topic of major public or media concern, federal policies centered on punishment, not on treatment or education. Popular conceptions that people who take drugs are "dope fiends," whereas people who drink come from all types and social classes, made severe enforcement of the antidrug laws possible. Drug law enforcement was much more severe than that ever attempted for alcohol, even during Prohibition. Henry J. Anslinger, the first commissioner of narcotics, was a central figure in federal drug abuse policy from 1930 to 1962. Anslinger had previously been active in Prohibition, where he distinguished himself by proposing six-month jail sentences for first-time convictions for purchasers (not sellers or producers) of alcohol. "While the public did not agree with this attitude for liquor prohibition, it did support the policy in regard to narcotic control. . . . In the Federal Bureau of Narcotics, Ansliger's opinions on how best to put

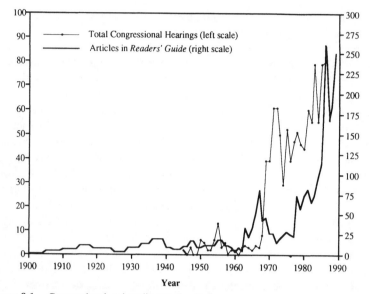

Figure 8.1. Congressional and media attention to drug use.

teeth into the law met with almost no objection" (Musto 1987, 212). Anslinger's personal position epitomized federal policy toward drugs in this period (see Sharp 1991).

Federal agents responsible for enforcement were able to maintain a virtual dominance of antidrug policies for decades by maintaining a relatively low profile and by encouraging outside temperance groups to attack energetically any lawmakers who attempted to propose other ways of dealing with the "drug menace." Many of the same groups that had been active in Prohibition were natural allies of the enforcement community within the federal government. The Anti-Saloon League and the Women's Christian Temperance Union (WTCU) were particularly powerful constituency groups that could be counted on to protect the interests of the enforcement community from any threats to change the focus of federal policy (Musto 1987, 214).

Narcotics enforcement was never a tremendous emphasis of the federal government during the first half of the century, even though enforcement always fared better than treatment programs. While the enforcement community could protect itself from congressional attack, it had few strong supporters in Congress, and as figure 8.1 showed, drug abuse was not a major national concern at the time. When the issue emerged on the agenda in the 1960s, however, the federal response changed dramatically. The seeds for this change in solutions to the same public policy problem were laid in the decades before. As John Kingdon (1984) asserts, new policy proposals often need years of "softening up." The postwar period saw the development of many new approaches toward the treatment of drug abusers. This research was to enter full scale into federal antidrug policy as a result of the dramatic surge of media and public concern with the problem in the 1960s.

Beginning after World War Two, mental health spending in the federal government began to grow tremendously, and a community of mental health experts was available and willing to argue that the drug problem could be solved not by incarceration, but by treatment. Drug abuse officials knew they faced a formidable opponent in Henry Anslinger if they sought to shift the federal emphasis from enforcement to treatment. However, as people realized that he would retire in 1962, a variety of pressures built up: many people apparently saw this as a window of opportunity for shifting emphasis (see Kingdon 1984). Media coverage of drug abuse topics rose from only five titles in the *Readers' Guide* in 1962 to thirty-three articles in 1963 (more than any previous year in the century); figure 8.1 shows that this surge in media attention was maintained for years. In the five years following Anslinger's retirement, a variety of changes were made in the federal antidrug posture. Virtually without exception, these shifted emphasis toward giving increased powers to mental health professionals (see Musto 1987, 238). Federal drug treatment facilities were created during the mid-1960s throughout the country; the Bureau of Drug Abuse Control was created in 1965 and attached not to an enforcement agency, but to the Department of Health, Education, and Welfare.

In sum, national policies toward drug abuse underwent a sea change during the 1960s. For the first time, "advocates of severe punishment for addicts found themselves unheeded" (Musto 1987, 230). As the issue emerged high onto the systemic agenda in the 1960s, new solutions to the long-standing drug problem were proposed, and these differed radically from the previous governmental stance toward drug addicts. Education and treatment emerged as the solution of choice after this surge in media attention. President Nixon played an especially important role in framing the issue as one of education and treatment rather than enforcement (Sharp n.d.).

While the Nixon war on drugs was associated with emphasis on education and treatment, the first major surge of national attention to drugs under President Reagan came with a renewed emphasis on enforcement rather than education. This change in tone was evident in Congress, where members competed with each other over who could propose the most severe and punitive amendments to the drug and crime bills. Claude Pepper, the long-serving Florida Democrat, said, "'Right now, you could put an amendment through to hang, draw, and quarter. . . . That's what happens when you get on an emotional issue like this'" (quoted in Kerr 1986).

Emphasis was so great on enforcement questions that the president announced a new program to spend $100 million in 1986 to increase interdiction efforts along the Gulf Coast before his office had even received proposals from the relevant federal agencies to spend the money:

No one in the enforcement agencies is unhappy to get the hundreds of millions of dollars in additional money, but some officials
note that they are not entirely sure what to do with it. . . . [After
the presidential announcement concerning Gulf Coast interdiction
efforts,] the heads of Federal enforcement agencies, who were
meeting in September, all realized that the money had not been
allotted to any specific agency yet.

"Suddenly it was like a basketball had popped loose, and everyone was all over the floor trying to grab it," a senior drug law-
enforcement official said. Each of the agencies was asked to draft
a plan for spending the money. (Brinkley 1986)

President George Bush continued the Reagan emphasis on law enforcement
over education and treatment, as drug-abuse budgets soared even during the
tight financial times of the 1980s. In his first prime-time speech to the nation,
on 5 September, 1989, President Bush unveiled his war on drugs. If his desire
was to increase attention to drugs, he surely succeeded. After the speech there
was an eightfold increase in the amount of television coverage on drugs (Barrett 1990). Already the problem was on the mind of the public: In June 1989 a
New York Times/CBS News poll found that abuse of drugs was seen as the
most important problem facing the country by 20 percent of those polled. This
exceeded the percentage who believed the economy and questions of deficit
and taxation were the most important. But after President Bush's speech,
those noting drugs as the primary problem of the nation soared to over 60
percent—strong testimony to the ability of the president to capture the national agenda when he so desires (see Sharp n.d. for a similar discussion of
Nixon's success in raising public concern with the drug problem in 1972).
Concern immediately began to decline to around 30 percent in January 1990
and to just 10 percent in August 1990 (Oreskes 1990).

The tremendous range of media attention to the issue of drug abuse could
not have been achieved without the power of the presidency. Presidents
Nixon, Reagan, and Bush have each instituted highly touted "wars on drugs,"
backed with personal television appearances, numerous speeches, and genu-
ine concern. The media react strongly to such presidential commitment, as
does the public. Most importantly, this concern varies from virtual paranoia
to complacency, with no simple relationship to changes in the severity of the
problem, as we see in the following section.

The Severity of the Problem

One of the reasons drug control policy can surge and decline so rapidly
from the national agenda is that statistics and reliable indicators of the extent
of the drug problem are few and far between. Policymakers rely on a series of
different sources of data on drugs. Each source is flawed, since the sources

themselves are subject to change depending on the degree to which the political system focuses on drugs. Drug-related arrests rise and decline partly depending on the number of police assigned to drug-related tasks and on police inclinations to note that crimes were "drug induced." Hospital statistics on drug overdoses and on emergency room treatments for drug problems vary partly as a function of doctors' realization that drugs are a national health problem. Finally, surveys of high school seniors or of the general population were not conducted until the drug problem was considered serious enough to warrant them, and peer pressure may encourage socially acceptable responses (no drug use) in some periods more than others.

The number of federal defendants convicted of drug offenses increased 134 percent between 1980 and 1986, while the number of convictions for all offenses increased only 46 percent. Drug convictions were 17.5 percent of all federal convictions in 1980, but 28 percent in 1986 (Bureau of Justice Statistics 1986, 4). Arrests reported in the Uniform Crime Reports for the entire United States went up 32.2 percent between 1981 and 1989, but drug arrests soared 243.2 percent. According to one important indicator of drug abuse, the problem worsened throughout the early 1980s. Given these statistics, the increase in media concern during the 1980s seems entirely justified.

Surveys of drug use have been funded by the federal government since 1974. The very existence of such surveys is due to the attention policymakers have given illicit drug use since the late 1960s. Nevertheless, surveys are the least sensitive to the phenomenon of measurement instruments affected by attention to the problem. While arrest statistics may reflect the behavior of prosecutors, police departments, and federal granting agencies as much as they reflect the behavior of drug addicts, survey responses are amenable to fewer outside influences. According to survey evidence, the drug problem in America has been declining since 1979. In 1974, just over 45 percent of high school seniors reported using illicit drugs during the previous year. In 1979, 54 percent reported doing so. Then a steep and steady decline set in, so that by 1990 just under 33 percent indicated usage during the last year (National Institute on Drug Abuse 1989; Treaster 1991).

Surveys of the general population show similar declines. In 1979, almost 47 percent of the highest-use age cohort (ages eighteen to twenty-five) indicated that they had used marijuana during the past year. By 1988 that figure had dropped to 27.9 percent. All drugs show the same pattern, including cocaine, whose usage figures are 20 percent in 1979 versus 12 percent in 1988. Similarly, heroin use dropped from 0.8 percent in 1979 to 0.3 percent in 1988 in that cohort (National Institute of Drug Abuse 1989). Between 1985 and 1988, drug usage dropped in every age and ethnic category, accelerating the trend that began in 1979. Young black males (ages eighteen to twenty-five), the highest-use group, saw a decline from 15.2 percent to 8.1 percent among those reporting cocaine use at least once during the year.

A final indicator that often crops up in official reports is emergency room treatments for drug overdoses. According to this indicator, drug use was rising alarmingly between 1984 and 1988. Emergency room admission reports mentioning cocaine more than quadrupled, from 8,831 to 46,020 (National Institute of Drug Abuse 1989). Admittances related to cocaine smoking went up from 549 in 1984 to 15,306 in 1988; but cocaine injections also soared—from 3,717 to 12,461.

Drug abuse statistics are often contradictory. Since the particular forms of abuse change over relatively short periods of time, there is almost always a "crisis" of one sort or another that can form the basis for an alarming report to the public. Broad-scale indicators tend to show that the severity of the drug problem declined throughout the 1980s, even though there were serious pockets of trouble stemming from increased use of crack cocaine. While President Bush made his war on drugs a high priority and convinced a majority of Americans that it was the most serious problem facing the nation, virtually every indicator of drug abuse showed that the severity of the problem was declining.

Congressional Reactions

As drug abuse has emerged and receded on the systemic agenda as measured by the *Readers' Guide* articles displayed in figure 8.1, it has also emerged as an important concern of Congress. Figure 8.1 shows how the number of congressional hearings shot up in response to the wave of media concern with drugs in the mid-1960s. Clearly, increased media concern led to the emergence of drug abuse as a major topic on the congressional agenda. As this occurred, various forces within Congress were activated, as they attempted to define the national response to the drug problem.

In order to distinguish between the two competing broad solutions to drug abuse within the federal government, we have coded all congressional hearings on drug abuse questions, 1,044 hearings in all. Coded categories represent those hearings focusing mostly on education and treatment questions versus those focusing more on incarceration, interdiction, and law enforcement. In this way, we can trace the degree of congressional attention to the topic in general (as in fig. 8.1) as well as note the relative emphasis on these two competing solutions. Figure 8.2 shows congressional attention to drug abuse topics over time. (Appendix A gives details of coding; congressional hearings on drug abuse are also discussed in more detail in chapter 10. For a similar analysis conducted independently, see Sharp 1991.)

As drug abuse rose high on the systemic agenda in the 1960s (as seen in fig. 8.1), it also rose on the formal agenda in the late 1960s. While the issue declined in salience on the systemic agenda after Nixon's war on drugs, it never receded from congressional attention. The top line in figure 8.2 shows total congressional hearings per year (also reported in fig. 8.1). Beginning in

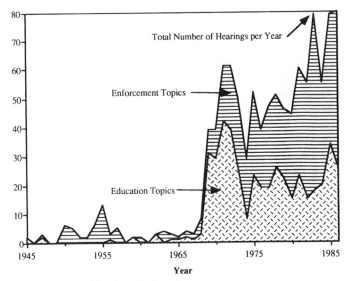

Figure 8.2. Congressional hearings on drug abuse.

1969, Congress began to hold dozens of hearings every year on drug abuse topics. Only once from World War Two until 1968 were there as many as ten hearings on the topic; never after 1969 were there fewer than thirty hearings per year. The two components of figure 8.2 show the numbers of hearings focusing on education versus enforcement solutions to the drug problem. From them, one can see how dramatically the tone of congressional attention shifted as the issue emerged onto the formal agenda in the 1970s and 1980s. The initial surge of attention in Congress in the late 1960s was due almost entirely to the enthusiasm of many members of Congress that education and treatment programs might work to solve the drug abuse problem. Over the years following this increase in official attention, however, enforcement solutions quietly became more prominent. While media attention to drug abuse questions dropped away during the Ford and Carter administrations, a silent revolution in drug abuse policy took place in Congress.

The data in figure 8.2 make clear that the initial surge of interest in congressional activities toward drug abuse policy was related to the possibilities of education and treatment responses. However, after the first few years of such enthusiasm, the traditional emphasis on enforcement, border controls, and incarceration was reestablished. A simple statistical analysis shows that the initial surge in 1969 was associated with an increase of twenty-five additional hearings on education questions, but only six additional hearings on enforcement. In following years, however, education hearings decline by one per year and enforcement hearings increase by an average of two per year. An overall continuation of congressional attention each year after 1969 was made up of two inversely related components, as the enforcement solution set gradually out-placed the education set as the government's preferred policy response to the drug problem. (Appendix B presents the details of the statistical interpretation of fig. 8.2.)

Drug abuse surged onto the systemic and formal agendas of American politics in the late 1960s. Media attention waned after a period of about five years, but official attention remained high. As the government began to spend large amounts of money on drug abuse treatment, eradication, and enforcement, large numbers of specialists in a great variety of policies became active in Congress. Each wanted a slice of what became a huge drug policy budget. Figure 8.2 shows how much more successful the enforcement community has been than the education group. We discuss the dynamics of congressional attention in greater detail in chapter 10; for now the simple point is that the public may become concerned with a given problem, but the solutions adopted in response to that problem are not cast in stone. At different times in history and depending on the degree of media interest in the problem, official attention focuses on the problem. What set of solutions will be adopted seems to follow a different logic, one much less tied to public and media attention, but relying more on inside-the-beltway influence, as Kingdon (1984) also argues. We saw a similar pattern in the case of highway safety policy in chapter 6. The problem may emerge more than once on the national agenda, but the policy solutions chosen at different periods made vary greatly from one period to another.

Budgets and Solution Sets

The changes in relative emphasis on treatment versus enforcement, apparent in figure 8.2, are reflected in federal budgets. In addition, total levels of attention translate almost directly into dollars and budget requests. During the late 1960s and early 1970s, federal expenditures on drug control increased dramatically. The Nixon war on drugs had two major components: enforcement and treatment, with emphasis slightly greater on treatment programs. Between 1970 (the last Johnson budget) and 1974, appropriations for prevention and treatment rose from $59 million to $462 million, while enforcement expenditures rose from $43 million to $292 million (Musto 1987, 257–58). The Nixon administration more than doubled the ratio of education-to-enforcement spending on drug control, pushing this number from 0.78 in 1970 to 1.75 in 1973 (Sharp n.d., 7; Goldberg 1980, 57).

Federal expenditures on drug control have increased dramatically since Nixon, but most importantly, they have shifted emphasis. Under the Reagan and Bush administrations, appropriations for drug-related programs increased eightfold (from $1.5 billion to $11.7 billion). About nine-tenths of this increase went to enforcement agencies rather than to education and treatment efforts (see Sharp n.d.; Falco 1989). Treatment and prevention accounted for 36.4 percent of the total in 1981 (already a significant decline from the Nixon emphasis on education), but only 27.2 percent in the administration's request in 1992. President Bush's 1992 request to Congress included $7.168 billion in enforcement expenditures as compared to only $3.17 billion for education and treatment programs (Marcus 1991).

The public fascination with drug abuse policy and prevention cannot be explained by the severity of the problem itself. However, public and elite attention to the problem did indeed lead to tremendous budgetary and policy outputs. Far from offering only symbolic attention to an important national problem, federal and state officials have spent billions of dollars on treatment and enforcement programs in the 1980s and 1990s. Drug policy was not considered in a small group of experts during the 1980s. It was a featured element of election campaigns and presidential speeches. This high agenda status led to budgetary windfalls for enforcement agencies. Unlike the problems of urban areas discussed in chapter 7, which also were the topic of considerable high-level preoccupation during some periods of time, official attention to drug policy has yet to fade away. Once drug abuse was thrust high on the agenda of Congress in the late 1960s, it stayed there. Attention to the problem remained high in official circles for some time, but the relative strength of two competing sets of solutions changed over time. The loss of interest and commitment in the face of difficult problems hypothesized by Downs (1972) in his issue-attention cycle is simply not in evidence for drug abuse. Rather than fading away, drug abuse policy has become a justification for huge sums spent on law enforcement and border control.

Alcohol Abuse

Alcohol abuse has long been a more serious problem in America than drug abuse, at least in terms of the number of Americans suffering from it. However, we saw in chapter 6 that routine, familiar, risks are more easily accepted than unusual or unfamiliar ones; alcohol abuse seems much more easily accepted by our political system than drug abuse. We might not have written these words in the 1920s, however, when Prohibition made even the sale of beer illegal. Even in the case of alcohol, we have gone through waves of hostility and toleration. Though the amplitude of the swings has not been as great as with drug abuse, alcohol abuse has risen and receded from the media and congressional agenda in a fashion that makes clear that rapid and long-lasting alterations to the previous point of stability are at least as common as incrementalism in policy outputs and preoccupations.

Figure 8.3 shows annual levels of media and congressional attention to alcohol abuse problems in the twentieth century.

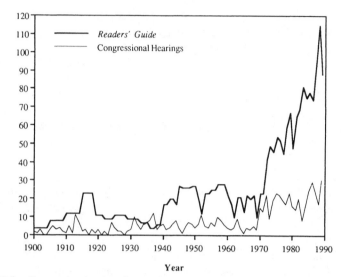

Figure 8.3.   Congressional and media attention to alcohol abuse.

Alcohol use has always been controversial in the United States, and opponents of the industry have long used moral and spiritual arguments in working for strict police controls on drinkers. Joseph Gusfield has argued that the temperance movement was a symbolic crusade in that success would come mostly through a reconceptualization of the issue of alcohol (Gusfield 1963, 1981). Seen from a religious standpoint, alcohol is bad; seen from another view, government interference in people's normal and common behavior is equally bad. As in other cases, the mobilization of interests demanding increased state control or activity must generally push the issue higher on the agenda; those who seek to get government out of the business of regulating might best be served by a lower agenda status. We can see partial confirmation for these ideas in figure 8.3. Media coverage rose before the enactment of the 18th Amendment, then fell (even during the repeal campaign). Ironically, the period of Prohibition did not see high levels of media coverage of alcohol abuse stories. Interest rose in the early 1940s, and stabilized at around twenty articles a year, with some variability, until the mid-1970s. Since then a dramatic rise has taken place, with a real explosion in articles during the 1980s.

The rapid increase in media attention to alcohol abuse questions in the 1970s and 1980s closely parallels the pattern for drug abuse. Figure 8.1 shows that drug abuse articles were much more numerous than alcohol articles, but both series followed very similar patterns. Beginning in the early 1970s, drug articles began to increase, from about twenty-five per year to ten times that level. Similarly, alcohol articles increased from fewer than twenty in 1970 to over a hundred in 1988.

Congressional attention to alcohol questions has been traditionally higher than that for drug abuse, partly because of a routine background of hearings on taxation questions. Since there are federal taxes on alcohol, Congress often discusses of raising or lowering them. Figure 8.3 shows an average of 4 hearings per year on alcohol from the turn of the century until 1969. From 1970 to 1989, there were an average of 19 hearings per year. (Similarly, the number of articles listed in the *Readers' Guide* averaged 15 per year before 1970, but 62 per year after that date.) Drug abuse hearings in the mid-1980s, shown in figure 8.2, were consistently above 50 per year.

Why does drug abuse generate more hearings in Congress than alcohol abuse? For one, congressmen have little to fear when they propose incarcerating "dope fiends;" raising taxes on beer is another matter. In general, however, congressional and media attention to both drug and alcohol abuse shows more similarities than differences. In both cases, underlying problems change only slowly. However, our figures show that media and government attention to those problems lurches with little relation to any changes in the severity of the underlying problem. In particular, once government attention rises to historical highs, it rarely recedes to its erstwhile lows. This is the institutional legacy of agenda access: during periods of high governmental attention, institutions are created, agencies reorganized, and budgets appropriated. All these new organizations work in the future to ensure their own continued survival, which generally means maintaining some degree of official interest in the issue.

Finally, both drugs and alcohol can be understood as an individual or a social problem. Only when they become understood as a social problem is government attention to them likely to be increased. In the case of drugs, criminality has long been the link that has turned an individual problem into a social one. The government must enforce strict antidrug laws to stop drug addicts from committing crimes against innocent victims. In the case of alcohol, there has not always been such a social link. In the 1970s and 1980s the issue seems to have emerged with some significant socializing arguments, however. The most powerful is drunk driving.

The drunk driving issue moved to the national level in 1966 with the passage of the National Highway Safety Act. That act established the National Highway Safety Bureau, which funded research on drunk driving (Jacobs 1989). The NHSB promoted the drunk driving issue before Congress and in other venues (Laurence 1988). The National Institute on Alcohol Abuse and Alcoholism (NIAAA) was established by the Comprehensive Alcohol Abuse and Alcoholism Prevention, Treatment, and Rehabilitation Act of 1970 to direct federal treatment, research, and educational efforts against alcohol abuse (Lender and Martin 1987, 190). Figure 8.3 shows that congressional attention to alcohol never receded after 1970 to the levels where it had been before the passage of this act and the creation of the NIAAA. In other words, alcohol abuse, like drug abuse before it, was institutionalized on the formal agenda of the federal government. The nationalization of the two problems occurred in the same period of time, with considerable activity during the Johnson years and institutionalization during the Nixon presidency. Congressional attention leads to new laws and to the creation of new federal agencies to administer them. Unlike popular or media attention, no one has ever accused a federal agency of being fickle; they do not "fade away."

Child Abuse

In her excellent study of how the issue of child abuse surged onto the public agenda in the 1980s, Barbara Nelson (1984) argues that the media redefined and amplified the issue and that numerous governmental institutions became active in the area at the same time. Congress, executive agencies, states, and localities all became preoccupied with child abuse questions rapidly at about the same time. In the terminology of this book, image changes interacted with venue searching to produce a rapid change in public consciousness and government policy toward a long-standing public problem.

Nelson argues that "the media both created and responded to the urgency over child abuse. . . . The media's role varied, sometimes prodding governmental action, at other times passively reporting governmental interest" (1984, 51). She notes that child abuse has been considered an important national problem before, but it has never preoccupied policymakers as much as in the 1980s. Our study of the *New York Times Index* and the *Readers' Guide* shows that she is right for the entire twentieth century. Nelson (1984) reports that a celebrated case of abuse pushed the issue into the spotlight in the 1870s. A small wave of coverage occurred during the 1920s, and the *Times* carried about twenty articles per year until the 1950s. Then for some reason coverage died away to near zero, but began a steady increase during the mid–1960s until the 1980s. See figure 8.4.

Figure 8.4 presents annual levels of coverage of all child abuse topics for the *New York Times Index* and the *Readers' Guide*. There was no coverage of the topic at all in the *Readers' Guide* before 1959, so our series begins only then (it is possible that some articles appeared in the publications indexed in the *Guide,* but there was no subject heading for them; see Nelson 1984). In any case, levels of coverage in the two media outlets are remarkably similar for the years since 1959. Both show very low levels during the 1960s, then an upward trend beginning in 1972. Both show a tremendous peak of coverage in the same year—1984.

Child abuse, like drugs or alcohol, can be seen as a private misfortune or a public problem. As Deborah Stone (1989) has alerted us, the same issue can be treated in different ways on the basis of this simple, but important, distinction (see also Kingdon 1984). The key element of public understanding that has changed over the years in the case of child abuse is that what was once

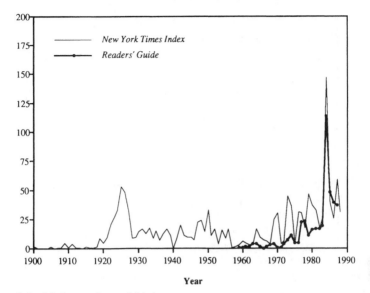

Figure 8.4. Media attention to child abuse.

considered a private tragedy is now often seen as a public outrage. Especially when cases of abuse occur in a public setting, such as in a school or day-care center, calls for public regulation and increased state vigilance are easier to justify than when the abuse occurs in the home. Still, even there public attitudes show that we have grown more willing to treat the problem as a public one demanding a governmental response.

In order to trace the changes we expected to find in the nature of public discourse surrounding the issue of child abuse, we have coded every article in the *New York Times Index* in a more complicated way than for other issues. Rather than noting whether the articles were pro- or anti- the activity in question, as we did for issues discussed in other chapters, we developed the following scheme. First are simple reports of abuse or neglect. Second are reports of child abandonment with no mention of other kinds of abuse. Third are court cases, and fourth are discussions of the activities of government officials, demands for more stringent government regulation, or any other discussion of government actions concerning child abuse. A small number of cases were not codeable. Of 1,447 articles on child abuse topics in the *New York Times,* 268 were simple reports of abuse; 266 were reports of abandonment; 615 discussed court cases; 275 discussed government regulation; and 23 were uncodeable. If we trace these separate categories of coverage over time, we can see how the issue has been redefined over the years. Figure 8.5 shows separately each of the four series.

From figure 8.5 we can see, first, that public discussion of child abuse once

A. Reports of abandonments and abuse

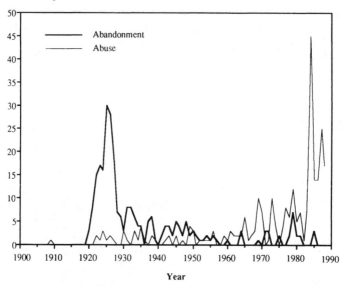

B. Coverage of court cases and government regulations

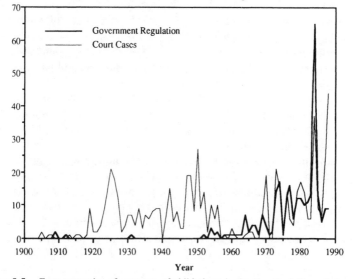

Figure 8.5. Four categories of coverage of child abuse in the *New York Times Index*, 1900–1988.

Connecting Solutions to Problems

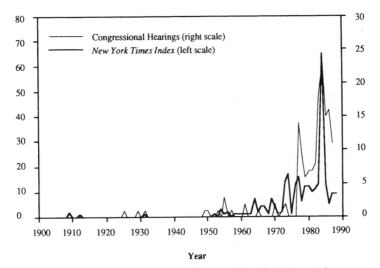

Figure 8.6. Congressional hearings on child abuse and *New York Times Index* coverage of government action.

focused almost exclusively on the problem of abandonment. Discussion of abuse is a recent phenomenon. The largest category of articles on child abuse, that of court cases, seems to provide the bulk of the background noise in figure 8.4. Court cases on child abuse, while not absolutely constant over the years, regularly generate a number of articles on the topic, keeping the issue somewhat in the public eye. Court cases need imply no particular demand for increased government regulation, and we can see that the movement of child abuse from a "social condition" to a "public problem" seems to be an entirely recent phenomenon.

An issue that was consistently treated as an unfortunate social condition became transformed during the 1970s into one where people routinely have called for greater governmental action to curb the incidence of abuse. As the media began to discuss governmental actions, governmental officials became much more active. Figure 8.6 shows the number of congressional hearings on child abuse topics as well as the number of articles on government regulation concerning child abuse.

Nelson dates serious congressional recognition of the issue of child abuse to 1964, when the District of Columbia Committee considered a bill on reporting incidents of abuse for the District (1984, 98). We can see from figure 8.6 that Congress was indeed absent from the issue of child abuse throughout the first two-thirds of the century and that media coverage of abuse questions almost never referred to government actions, except court cases. While there were important individual bills and a few hearings before this date, Congress as a whole never showed any great interest in child abuse questions until 1977. In that year, its committees held fourteen hearings on the topic, almost doubling in one year the total number of hearings that it had held in the century. Just as in the cases of drugs and alcohol discussed earlier in this chapter, this initial spurt of congressional interest was preceded by a rapid rise in media coverage on the topic. Once Congress became active, however, its activity did not fade.

The Child Abuse Prevention and Treatment Act (CAPTA) passed in 1973 required periodic reauthorization (see Nelson 1984, 112–21). In fact, the first reauthorization of CAPTA, in 1977, explains the spurt of congressional activities shown in figure 8.6. In 1978 the revised Child Abuse Prevention and Treatment and Adoption Reform Act (CAPTARA) was passed, and Congress was thereafter in the business of holding hearings on the issue every year, reaching a peak of over twenty hearings in 1984, the same year media discussions of government regulation concerning child abuse and media coverage of abuse cases reached their peaks.

As Congress became active, the very laws that it passed required, or made possible, continued congressional activity. These institutional reforms were reinforced by increased media coverage of child abuse questions, which were themselves partly generated by the congressional actions. A large and growing group of professionals developed. Joel Best describes this growth:

> Foundations and government agencies funded research and pilot projects, universities began offering courses, professionals enrolled in workshops to learn to detect and deal with child abuse, and protective-services agencies expanded. There were now more people—many of them officials with greater resources and more broadly defined prerogatives—involved in child-abuse prevention and detection and in protective services. In turn, this new child abuse establishment became a base from which further claims-making could be staged, so that each successive movement against threats to children benefited from the support of a growing number of professionals and lay people already concerned with child protection. (1990, 179–80)

In other words, a self-reinforcing set of changes made policymakers at all levels of government aware that the issue had been transformed: communities of social workers, welfare administrators, psychologists, and school officials argued successfully that child abuse was not only a private problem, but a public one requiring governmental intervention. Nelson describes how the 1970s saw a rapid increase in concern, both in Congress and in the states and localities, about child abuse. The combined impact of these federal, state, and local activities is much greater than any one of them would have alone, a question to which we return in chapter 11.

Conclusions

Public, media, and governmental concern for the long-standing social problems of drug addiction, alcoholism, and child abuse has varied much more than the underlying social realities have changed. In all three cases, we have observed what seems to be a recurring characteristic of the agenda-setting process—attention lurches. After an initial period of increased media attention to a given issue official attention begins to rise. Policymakers hoping for greater governmental activity in the area take advantage of a momentary burst of public or media concern with the issue and push for new legislation. Generally speaking, this new legislation commits funds and creates new institutions. These new institutions and the people who work for them do not disappear, even if public or media concern with the issue fades away. In fact, they can easily perpetuate themselves, because for the first time they may be able to generate statistics and reports that substantiate what they have suspected all along: that their issue is of alarming proportions, and increased governmental vigilance is called for.

Drug enforcement officials can take credit for a reduction in addiction rates, casual use rates, and all sorts of other evidence that drug abuse has been on the decline since its peak around 1979. However, they are more likely to focus on the huge increases in the numbers of drug arrests and convictions, since these numbers may buttress their claims for greater and greater budgetary support. Education and treatment programs are likely to remain a part of the federal response to drug abuse, since these were part of the initial surge of federal programs in the late 1960s. In both cases, the solutions themselves take on an importance separate from the problem, just as Kingdon (1984) argues.

Critical in the definition of a policy solution is the stance of the president. Drug programs have traditionally received more federal dollars than have alcohol abuse programs; federal programs on child abuse have centered solely on information collection and dissemination. There have been no wars on child abuse; there is no federal alcohol czar in the Office of the President. No president has taken on these causes. When a president does assume responsibility for pressing an issue, he can get media attention. But media attention can also come from other sources such as the death of a celebrity or the introduction of new drugs. More importantly, the president's position can lead to vast budgetary commitments toward the solution set he is proposing. Clearly that could not have been done without Congress. But a comparison of the drug policies of Republican presidents Nixon, Ford, Reagan, and Bush, all of whom led Democratic Congresses, illustrates the impact on public policy of the president's policy stance on a valence issue. (This probably works more through the establishment of a tone than through specific policy proposals; see Edwards 1989.)

In the cases of both drug and child abuse, one of the main elements of federal legislation has been to encourage better statistics on the incidence of the problem. Without clear evidence of the problem's severity, policymakers cannot know whether their programs are effective. However, during the first several years when reporting mechanisms are being put in place, and as social workers, law enforcement officials, teachers, and others begin to look for signs of possible abuse where previously they had not, the statistics will show dramatic increases for a number of years, not because the problem is worsening, but because the statistics are growing more accurate. For example, national estimates of child-abuse-and-neglect reports increased regularly from 669,000 in 1976 to 2,170,000 in 1987; rates per thousand children more than tripled during this time (American Humane Association 1989, 5–6). With more accurate statistics comes increased political clout, since official reports stating that the problem is growing more and more severe constitute strong arguments in favor of greater governmental action.

There is a risk in accurate statistics: they may show less of a problem than advocates expect. As survey after survey since 1979 has shown a decline in drug use among teenagers and among the general public, drug policy officials have had to revise their public strategies. Drug Czar William Bennett claimed in 1989 that there were two drug wars: one against the casual user, which the government was winning, and one against the hard-core addict, which had not yet been won. Bennett buttressed his claim with statistics on arrests and hospital admissions, but most policy professionals were agreeing that the problem was abating. As we noted in chapter 6, unambiguous data can cause a potential agenda item to lose its appeal, as occurred with criminal victimization of the elderly (Cook and Skogan 1989). Accurate and accepted indicators of the severity of a social problem can provide justification for supporters of new causes that official attention should shift, or at the very least they may provide fewer incentives for politicians to jump onto this issue as opposed to some other concern in their search for popular and newsworthy causes to support.

Governmental interest in social problems such as those discussed in this chapter follows a self-reinforcing pattern where each increase in attention leads to incentives for even greater levels of attention in the future. These increases may not be uniform, but with increased budgets come the creation of whole new policy communities made up of professionals charged with ameliorating the problem under question. These professionals, be they social workers, psychologists, law enforcement officials, welfare administrators, or whatever, are likely to demand continued governmental vigilance in their area.

In chapter 5 we discussed the "dual mobilization" ideas of Downs and Schattschneider. Initial public enthusiasm with the potential of a new technology leads policymakers to create institutions and to support research into how best to take advantage of them. Then public attention dies away, leaving those in the new institutions to carry on with significant public support, but with little political oversight. Later, however, public interest in the issue may grow anew, this time calling for institutional changes to dilute the power of those in charge. Through this process, we described how governmental actions lurch because of the dynamics of agenda-setting. This chapter adds a further wrinkle to the story. As previously accepted social conditions are redefined as public problems, the political agenda becomes more crowded. Congress now holds an average of about twenty hearings per year on alcohol abuse, about fifteen hearings on child abuse, and about sixty on drugs. Earlier in the century there was little official attention to any of these problems. Public and media attention may decline rapidly after some short-lived fascination with a given issue, but we have designed a political system that shows a remarkable capacity to handle many issues at once.

As government officials become active in more issues over the years, media coverage, scientific research, and popular opinion are affected both by the social problem itself and by reports of government activities to solve the problem. Americans are often left with the impression that problems are worse, when they may simply have been ignored in the past. In any case, this chapter has shown another element of the self-reinforcing aspects of agenda-setting and public policy. Public and media attention leads to increased government activities, and these in turn lead to greater public and media attention in the future. The initial surge of an issue onto the governmental agenda may be observed as a result of increased media attention, but once this has happened, causal relations become blurred, making prediction difficult.

In the next chapter we turn to another element of self-reinforcing change: the interest-group environment in the United States has been transformed during the twentieth century. These changes are both cause and effect of the rises and declines of many issues from the public agenda. Some issues, such as pesticides, nuclear power, and smoking have been transformed by an increasingly fractious political debate over the years. Each was once considered only by a small, relatively homogeneous group of experts in its area (be they agriculture professionals, nuclear engineers and utility officials, or tobacco farmers), but today each is subject to rancorous policy debates as a greater variety of interests has intervened. Other issues, such as the three discussed in this chapter, have seen increased governmental activities over time. This, in turn, has led to the creation of very large state, local, and national bureaucracies charged with implementing or enforcing the law, or with conducting research into the potential ways of solving the problems of abuse. In all these cases, there have been long-term transformations of the nature of the interest-group environment. As issues surge onto the agenda, new interest groups are formed. As more groups of a greater variety are formed and become active, issues that were previously not controversial become so. The changing nature of the American interest-group environment forms a key element in the self-reinforcing nature of the cycles of rapid change and long-term stability that we have noted again and again in this book.

PART THREE

Structural and Contextual Changes
in Politics

The five chapters of part 2 of this book have shown how common dramatic changes are in public policy responses to important national problems. In this section we focus on long-term changes in the structures and the context of American political institutions themselves. Policymaking in America takes place within an ever-changing social and political environment. During certain periods of our history, the social and political institutions that structure participation in the policymaking process have themselves undergone dramatic changes. These contextual changes then have affected policies across the range of American politics. We focus on three of them here: chapter 9 discusses the growth of the environmental movement and considers changes in the interest-group system more generally; chapter 10 considers changes in the structures of congressional behavior; and chapter 11 considers the relations among the levels of government within the federal system. In each case, we note important changes in the contexts within which policies are made. Given the importance of context and structures in producing stable policy outcomes that we noted in the first two parts of this book, these changes have dramatic and sometimes unintended consequences. Americans have often complained that their system of government was becoming unwieldy; the chapters in part 3 give some idea of why. The structures of bias have been radically altered, giving voice to many groups that previously had been shut out of the political system. The structures of politics determine much of the outcome of the political game, so these three chapters give their attention exclusively to these structual questions, showing how they can change over time.

9

Interest Groups and Agenda-Setting

Throughout this book, we have noted how the policy processes surrounding important public issues have been transformed over time. In this chapter we focus on one important cause of policy change: how interests are organized and mobilized for political action. First, we note that different issue areas are home to different configurations of bias. Some generate the interest of a great variety of competing and conflictual interest groups, but other areas witness the mobilization of only one side of an issue. Second, we note that the mobilization of bias can change over time. A single issue area may be altered over the years from a one-sided mobilization of interests to a much more conflictual and multifaceted configuration.

Policy communities surrounding many important public policies in the United States are constantly undergoing change. While some professions are newly organized, others have been well represented in the Washington community since before the turn of the century. As different groups have organized for political action at different periods during our political history, the mobilization of bias has changed. Few political scientists have studied how the organization of interests has changed because it is difficult to find convincing evidence about the relative mobilization of interests. This is the task we set for ourselves in this chapter.

Some policy communities are organized into extremely prestigious professional societies that have no organized adversaries. Doctors, for example, are sometimes in conflict with insurance companies or others who worry about the costs of health care, but no group is constantly in conflict with virtually everything that doctors as a group might attempt to do. Similarly, lawyers, architects, and members of many professions rarely face the same opponents. They may enter into conflict with various groups on different issues, as their professional interests clash with those of some other group in a different profession or with those who simply want the government to spend less money, but no single set of groups is dedicated to opposing their interests systematically. Such is not the case in all areas; many policy areas are marked by intense conflict from within. Labor unions face predictable opposition from the same business opponents year in and year out. Similarly, pesticide manufacturers may expect environmentalists to object to many of their proposals. Tobacco companies now may expect health authorities to disagree with much of what they find appealing. In sum, some policy communities are more conflictual than others.

We have discussed in earlier chapters how some policy subsystems are unified, powerful, and autonomous, while others are more adversarial and less autonomous (see also Meier 1985; Thurber 1991). Conflict may be organized into or out of policy communities, and this important variable may change over time as new interests are mobilized. So there are both cross-sectional and longitudinal ways of looking at the same question. Each of these views shows that the internal makeup of a policy community has important implications for policy autonomy. Constant internal bickering reduces subsystem independence from the broader political system. Groups of experts that are able to exhibit a united front toward the outside world are better able to get what they want from the political system. So internal dynamics affect subsystem effectiveness.

The degree of diversity of interests apparent within a community of experts plays a fundamental role in determining the public response to an issue. Consensual policy communities are better able to foster a positive public image of their issue and to insulate themselves from broad political concerns. Communities marked by intense internal conflicts, on the other hand, are much more likely to be the subject of broad political debates. As different interests are mobilized or recede from action over the years, the consensual or conflictual nature of a policy community may be changed. Therefore, we must pay attention to changes in the mobilization of interests if we hope to understand changes in public responses to important public problems.

We consider a range of evidence to show that the interest groups and policy communities surrounding many important public policies have changed over the decades. The creation of many of the most powerful subsystems in American politics, some of which are described in earlier chapters, coincides with the most one-sided mobilization of interests in recent history. During the middle part of our century, profit-sector organizations were especially likely to form and grow, while organizations representing consumers, the environment, and other broad interests were in a period of stagnation. The 1960s and 1970s saw a tremendous shift in relative mobilization patterns, however. Policy areas previously dominated by a one-sided representation of interests have been overwhelmed by a vast mobilization of citizens' and consumers' groups in recent decades (see Vogel 1989 for a description of the widely varying levels of influence of the business versus consumers' and environmental lobbies since the 1960s).

As government has grown in America during the twentieth century, the number and diversity of interest groups pressing demands or protecting themselves from others have grown as well. This expansion has not occurred in a uniform manner, however; different types of groups have mobilized for political action during different periods. Jack Walker has argued (1983) that professionals of the nonprofit sector, for example, those working in state welfare agencies, public schools, or hospitals, mobilized in the early part of this century. The postwar years saw a tremendous burgeoning of profit-sector organizations (see also Hansen 1985; Aldrich and Staber 1986), and the period following the 1960s saw the development of the citizens' sector.

Robert Salisbury gives some indication of the increasingly crowded Washington policy process: From approximately 628 groups listed as active in Washington lobbying in 1942, the numbers grew to 1,180 in 1947–48, to over 7,000 organizations in 1981. Of these, 1,600 were trade associations, whose combined employment was 40,000 (see Salisbury 1984, 72–73). In other words, an army of lobbyists had descended on Washington where previously there had only been a few divisions. Baumgartner and Walker (1988, 1990) estimated that the percentage of Americans joining or contributing money to interest groups increased dramatically during this period, from fewer than one membership per adult in the early 1950s to well over two memberships during the mid-1980s. Counting simple financial contributions, an important source of support for many groups outside the profit sector, the number of affiliations per adult American had increased to more than three by the mid-1980s. Translated into interest groups, this expanding mass base clearly means more resources, more staff, more groups, and more activities. Shaiko (1991) reports that over 40 million Americans now contribute 4 billion dollars per year to public interest groups alone. One simple indicator of the growth of the group system is the number of trade associations listed in the *Encyclopedia of Associations* (Bureh, Kock, and Novallo, annual). Figure 9.1 shows the growth in this type of organization since the late 1960s.

Trade associations perform a number of nonpolitical functions; indeed the bulk of their work tends to be on purely professional matters. However, they are also active in following policy developments in Washington and the state capitals. The simple numbers of trade associations in existence do not measure their influence, but the increase apparent in figure 9.1 should make clear that a great number of policy communities are now more crowded than in the past. Where once there may have been only a few major organizations concerned with federal policy in a given area, the multiplication of organized interests apparent in this figure shows how the policy process has grown more crowded.

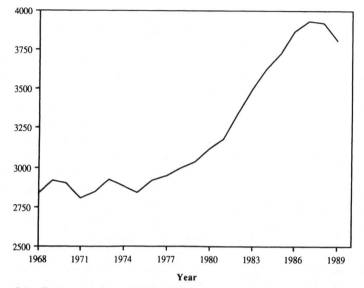

Figure 9.1. Trade associations in the United States.

Increasingly, policy communities once able to exist independently of one another interact because of the greater complexity and interdependence of areas of the economy. Even as government has grown, competition for public resources has become more stiff. Health care policy, for example, is so expensive in the United States that many groups that once paid little attention to health procedures or policies now are much more active. Business and government officials, alarmed at the increasing costs of services, intervene more and more in this area. Previously, the issue was dominated exclusively by hospital administrators, doctors, and insurance company officials, but no more (see Wilsford 1991). Social Security policy, once made by a very small group, now inevitably involves greater numbers of participants, as the size of the program has grown (see Derthick 1979). So policy communities may change in their composition because their large budgets attract the attention of outsiders. The increasing complexity and interdependence of the economy have created conflicts across policy communities and blurred the boundaries of where a policy community stops and its political environment begins. Where in the past experts on a given topic may have shared important views toward their issue and been able to make policies with little interference from other areas of the economy, both of these elements of subsystem strength are less likely to occur in the 1990s.

In the absence of conflict, issues are likely to reach the agenda only through what we have termed a mobilization of enthusiasm. For issues considered within consensual interest-group environments, in other words, we should expect that normally they would be treated far from the glare of public attention, that they would more often be able to maintain a combination of positive tone and low attention—the classic subgovernment. When they do emerge on the public agenda, we expect it to be on the wave of popular enthusiasm led by proponents of some new policy, and that this would lead to the subsequent institutionalization of a policy subsystem designed to support the industry or policy in question. From that time onward, subsystem proponents would attempt to insulate themselves from the political system, and we expect to see little agenda access.

This same thinking leads us to expect that issues treated within interest-group environments marked by intense conflict should less often be able to maintain their independence from broader political forces, and that they should emerge on the public agenda relatively often, as a result of the expansion-of-conflict model first proposed by Schattschneider. Downsian and Schattschneider mobilizations, then, should be associated with distinctive interest-group environments. As the environments change, so should the likelihoods of the two types of mobilization.

Gathering systematic and comparable data on the organization and mobilization of interests surrounding different issues is not easy, which explains why it has so rarely been attempted. The following sections provide some new evidence, however, concerning the development of the present configurations of groups in broad areas of the economy. We first make use of Jack Walker's 1985 survey of interest groups active in Washington. This source allows us to compare a number of broad areas of the economy and to note when groups of different types were formed. Next, we focus on the development of the environmental lobby through an analysis of the groups listed in the *Encyclopedia of Associations* in 1961, 1970, 1980, and 1990. This is the period identified by the first survey as that of the greatest mobilization of these interests, and we document these changes further. These changes in the American interest-group system give an empirical basis to our discussion of how American politics has been transformed over the years.

The Transformation of the American Interest-Group System

Using a variety of indicators, we can note the tremendous changes in the composition of policy communities in the United States during the twentieth century. Virtually without exception, growth in the number of groups has led to increasing diversity of views within previously homogeneous policy subsystems. By noting the creation dates of interest groups now active in Washington policymaking, we can see not only the increasing representation of diverse interests in the years since 1960, but also how one-sided was the mobilization of bias during many periods earlier in the century. We can see that the current constellation of interest groups active in national policymaking is radically different from that which existed in earlier periods. Further, those periods for which we have already noted the most enthusiastic buildup of policy subsystems and the largest grantings of government advantage correspond with those times when the mobilization of interests in the United States was the most one-sided of the twentieth century. As the mobilization of groups changed beginning in the 1960s, so did the strength of these powerful subsystems.

Walker (1983) has already shown how different sectors of the American group system have had different growth rates during different periods of history. Essentially, citizens' groups are latecomers to the Washington community. Based on his 1979 survey, Walker showed the much faster rates of creation in the citizens' sector since 1960, and he discussed how this could have transformed many areas of policymaking. In this section we take advantage of his 1985 dataset to show the effects of these developments (see also Walker 1991). Walker has documented the rapid growth in the numbers of groups representing the profit and nonprofit sectors of the economy during the early years of the twentieth century and their continued growth throughout the postwar years. Citizens' groups, on the other hand, were created at a relatively slow pace during these years; however, since 1960 they have multiplied at a more rapid pace than have their competitors.

We can get a clear picture of the relative mobilization of bias in the interest-group system by one simple comparison: the ratio of profit-sector to citizens'-sector groups during different periods of history. (Walker's typology also included a nonprofit sector, in which the periods of growth were roughly similar to those of the profit sector. Comparison of the citizens' groups to the non-profit groups would therefore show a pattern virtually identical to that pictured here.) Figure 9.2 presents these figures for the twentieth century.

The beginning of the twentieth century saw a mobilization of bias in the Washington community of approximately two profit-sector groups active for each group claiming to speak for a broad group of citizens, regardless of their occupational status. By the 1930s, this ratio had increased to about three to one, and the relative mobilization of bias remained at such a skewed level for approximately forty years. Only after the beginnings of the current environmental and consumer movements after 1960 did this ratio begin to change. And change it did, with the rapid growth of the citizens' sector of the group system far outstripping the continued growth of the occupational sectors. By 1980, the ratio of profit-sector groups to citizens' groups had declined to only about 1.6 to 1, the lowest level of the century, and almost half its level of only twenty years before.

We can get a slightly different view of the changing patterns of mobilization of interest groups in America by tracing the numbers of groups listed in the broad categories of the compilers of the *Encyclopedia of Associations* (Bureh, Kock, and Novallo, annual). The number of agriculture and trade associations listed in the 1974 edition of the *Encyclopedia* was 3,531; by 1992, it was

Figure 9.2. Ratio of profit to citizens' groups over time. *Source:* Walker 1985 dataset.

4,996. Therefore, there was a 41 percent increase in the numbers of these groups. Other professional associations grew by 82 percent, however: from 5,134 to 9,328. Fastest growth occurred among the "public affairs" associations: they grew by 176 percent, from 792 in 1974 to 2,182 in 1992. Other types of groups listed increased similarly from 3,171 to 5,872 (85 percent growth). In all, the numbers of groups listed increased from 12,628 to 22,348, or by 77 percent. The 41 percent increase in the numbers of trade and agricultural associations, which seems impressive at first, in fact pales in comparison to the dynamic growth occurring in other areas of the interest-group system.

These data give some indication why political scientists and others studying policymaking and interest groups in Washington during the 1940s and 1950s discussed iron triangles, subgovernments, and the like, while those discussing the same topics during the 1970s and 1980s were more likely to describe diffuse policy networks and advocacy coalitions (see chap. 3). Certainly not all conflicts, probably not even most conflicts within the group system, can be ascribed to the dynamics laid out in figure 9.2. Many battles pit one profit-sector organization against another (as oil versus gas interests in energy policy), or a profit-sector group against a nonprofit (as tobacco interests versus health professionals in smoking policy). Still, the changes in the mobilization of bias in the Washington community, which can best be observed only by taking a long-term historical perspective as in these figures, have contributed greatly to the creation and destruction of many systems of limited participation in American politics.

Reconstructing the past on the basis of a 1985 survey leaves open the possibility of some alternative explanations for the pattern shown in figure 9.2. After all, groups might simply have different death rates, and it could be that a greater number of citizens' groups have come and gone, or that profit-sector groups are more likely to be long-lived. Therefore our estimates might overestimate the degree of bias, since by definition they are based only on those groups still in existence when the survey was conducted in 1985. However, the great advantage in creation rates and representation in the Washington community of the profit sector of the economy during the middle part of this century surely could not be explained only by the differential death rates of the various sorts of groups. Certainly some citizens' groups have come and gone in the ensuing years, but so are many profit-sector groups no longer in existence. Further, the profit sector of the economy is represented in Washington by more than only the voluntary associations and trade groups present in this survey; the citizens' sector is represented almost exclusively by these groups. We can provide some evidence about the death rates of groups by looking at lists of groups in existence compiled at different times. Our analysis of the *Encyclopedia of Associations,* described below, reassures us that only a small proportion of the groups existing in 1960 had ceased operations by 1990. Differential death rates do not explain the pattern of figure 9.2. Rather, they correspond in general to important changes in the mobilization of different types of interests in American politics.

The ratio of the number of profit-sector groups to the number of citizens' groups in a given area gives at least a glimpse of the relative mobilization of bias. That is, in some areas there may be well-organized profit-sector groups and few organizations in opposition to them; in other areas there may be more conflict. Figure 9.2 presents data for the entire Walker survey, but we can break these down to some extent by issue area, since the group leaders responding to that survey were asked to note the relative interest of their group in ten areas of the economy. Table 9.1 shows the number of groups of each type which reported they were very interested in each of these topics.

As seen in table 9.1, different areas of the economy are home to widely varying interest-group configurations. The Walker typology of groups by itself does not capture all sorts of conflict that may exist among interest groups, of course, but it summarizes some of the most important points of cleavage that have historically divided policymakers in the United States. We can have no surprise after seeing these results that transportation policy, for example, is often cited as home to one-sided mobilization of truckers, producers, and highway contractors to the detriment of the public, while education policy is home to a wide range of divergent views.

Just as we reported in figure 9.2 how the group system as a whole developed over time, we can repeat this analysis for individual sectors of the economy. For example, table 9.1 shows that there were 62 citizens' groups and 98

Table 9.1 Percentages of profit, nonprofit, and citizens' sector groups very interested in different subject areas

Very Interested In	Membership Base				Ratio of Profit to Citizens' Sector Groups
	Profit	Nonprofit	Citizens'	Total	
Management of the economy	63%	28%	9%	100% (225)	7.05
Transportation	65	19	16	100 (142)	4.00
Agriculture	50	22	28	100 (116)	1.81
Energy	48	22	30	100 (205)	1.58
Organization of the government	36	33	31	100 (144)	1.18
Housing	31	32	37	100 (106)	0.85
Health	26	43	31	100 (275)	0.82
Foreign affairs	26	32	42	100 (159)	0.64
Education	12	61	27	100 (233)	0.46
Civil rights	17	41	42	100 (177)	0.40
TOTAL	40	35	25	100 (808)	1.59

Source: Walker 1985 dataset (Walker 1991).

profit-sector groups in the Walker survey expressing very great interest in energy questions. The area of energy policy includes a broad range of groups, then, almost exactly the same ratio of profit to citizens' groups as in the entire dataset (1.59 to 1 for the dataset as a whole; 1.58 to 1 in energy). Tracing the creation dates of these groups, we find that the area was once dominated almost exclusively by the profit-sector groups. Among those in existence before 1900, there were 2.5 private-sector groups for each citizens' group. This ratio changes over time, but remains relatively constant in the range of 2.5 to 3.6 from 1900 to 1960. Beginning in 1960, the citizens' sector shows much faster growth than the profit sector, and by 1970 the ratio has declined to 2.2, and to 1.6 by 1984. In other words, the energy field shows a pattern virtually identical to that shown for all groups in the study in figure 9.2.

When we repeat this analysis in the area of agriculture, we note again the same pattern of growth across types of groups. Table 9.1 shows 32 citizens' groups and 58 profit-sector groups in this area. For the entire sample, therefore, there was a ratio of 1.8 profit-sector groups per citizens' group. Before 1940, this ratio was over 3.5; it declined to 3.5 in 1950, to 3.1 in 1960, and to 2.2 in 1970. In other words, a steadily more conflictual mobilization of interests came about in the area of agriculture as more and more citizens' and consumers' groups became involved in an area that once interested only farmers and others with an economic interest in production. Whether we consider the entire sample of interest groups in the Walker survey or limit ourselves to some area of the economy, we note a similar pattern. Beginning around 1960, a tremendous advantage in the mobilization of interests in favor of various profit-sector interests began to be chipped away by the increasing mobilization of citizens' and consumers' groups. These groups have become active in many areas of the economy, changing what had previously been relatively insulated subsystems into much more conflictual policy networks, marked for the first time by significant disagreements over policy goals.

Policymaking for different issues varies not only because the structures of government are different and the issues are of greater or lesser complexity. The relative mobilization of diverse interests also matters, and in this section we have shown that this mobilization varies both across time and across issue areas at a single time. Longitudinal variation in the mobilization of interests is especially important in explaining many of the changes we have observed in this book. Issues once understood in a consensual, proindustry manner later became more controversial. One of the reasons nuclear power policy became much more conflictual starting in the 1960s was that the interest-group environment changed. As citizens' groups grew and mobilized increasing numbers of opponents, they pushed their issues onto the public agenda. Similarly in the cases of pesticide policy and smoking and tobacco, discussed in chapter 5, changes in the mobilization of interests in the area of agriculture correspond to the changes in how those policies were treated. So the mobilization of interests appears to play an important role in determining policy images, venues, and outcomes.

The Growth of Environmental Groups

Policymaking in many areas of American politics has been transformed during the postwar years by an ever-increasing mobilization of Americans in voluntary associations. Nowhere has this been more apparent than in the area of environmental quality, although this increased mobilization has not been limited to that area. Many citizens groups are organized around general ideological purposes (such as the Moral Majority or the American Civil Liberties Union) or around consumers' or taxpayers' interests (such as Common Cause). The largest, most visible, and fastest growing part of the citizen's sector is the environmental movement, however. In this section we focus on environmental groups in order to illustrate the growth of the citizens' sector more generally, and because these groups have been instrumental in changing the established patterns of policymaking in so many areas of American politics since World War Two.

In order to get some systematic evidence on the growth of the environmental movement in the United States, we used the *Encyclopedia of Associations* (Bureh, Kock, and Novallo, annual). Beginning in 1961, these annual volumes list every association active at the national level in the United States. While there may be gaps in the coverage of any single such publication, this is by far the broadest and most complete of its type. Its 1990 edition, for example, listed over 25,000 organizations. Our coders read through the 1990, 1980, 1970, and 1961 editions of the *Encyclopedia* in order to trace the development of the movement over time. They scanned for all groups active in the area of the environment. (Appendix A gives details of the selection of groups.) In all, 461 groups were found. These groups ranged from the obscure, such as the American Phytopathological Society, to the well known, such as the Sierra Club. Virtually all the major groups that appear regularly in the news or in other compendia of interest groups are included in the *Encyclopedia,* so we have confidence that few if any major groups are overlooked in our analysis (on this point, see also Walker 1991 and Knoke 1990).

We were particularly careful to exclude from our dataset those organizations sponsored by the profit sector to conduct environmental research. For example, groups clearly sponsored by timber companies, coal manufacturing interests, chemical companies, and the like were excluded. In short, we have constructed a dataset that allows us to trace the development of the environmental movement in the United States from 1961 to 1990, and we can be sure that our environmental groups listed here are not actually producer-sponsored public relations or research arms, but are true advocacy groups for the environment, wildlife, or land conservation.

The largest set of associations was that concerned with wildlife or animal protection and conservation (158 groups). Second were those groups concerned with general environmental quality or protection (131 groups), followed by plant and land conservation groups (110 groups). There were 27 groups particularly concerned with questions of water quality; other groups covered a range of interests, some very broad and others very narrowly focused on a particular toxin, solar energy research, or some other particular aspect of the environmental movement. Clearly, the environmental movement in the United States has strong roots in the conservation movement, since we coded 268 groups, or 58 percent of the total, as essentially concerned with plant, animal, or land conservation. Of the 75 groups created before 1950, 68 were focused on conservation rather than on general environmental quality, as were 8 of 10 groups created before the turn of the century. Conservation groups clearly formed the base on which the modern environmental movement has grown. (This may be a general phenomenon; see Lowe and Goyder 1983 for Great Britain.)

We have constructed a panel dataset from the four editions of the *Encyclo-*

pedia that we have coded, allowing us to trace the staff sizes, memberships, and activities of individual groups over three decades. In addition, we can trace the growth of the system as a whole, as more groups were listed in each succeeding edition (and we can check for the possible errors of oversight by the compilers of the *Encyclopedia* by comparing groups' creation dates with the year of their first inclusion in the *Encyclopedia*). In the early years of the *Encyclopedia*'s coverage, groups were added with creation dates that made it clear they had been overlooked in previous editions; however, the 1990 edition contained no additional groups created before 1980. In other words, the first few editions of the *Encyclopedia* may not have been complete, but we feel reasonably secure that by the 1970s the editors were accurate in their claim to have compiled a census of all groups active nationally. This analysis allows us to test for the problem of death rates as well, since we can observe when groups listed in one edition of the *Encyclopedia* disappear from the next.

The first and most striking observation about the development of environmental groups in the United States is that there are more than three times as many of them now than there were in 1961: 119 groups listed in 1961; 221 in 1970; 380 in 1980; and 396 listed in 1990. The rapid growth of the group system during the 1960s and 1970s is not simply an artifact of the increasing accuracy of the *Encyclopedia,* since the same pattern of growth is apparent when we base our analysis on the groups' dates of creation. Table 9.2 shows creation dates for all groups that reported this information (448 of 461 groups listed in at least one edition of the *Encyclopedia* reported their creation date) and for those groups still in existence in 1990 (388 of the 396 groups in operation in 1990 reported their creation date).[1]

A small core of venerable conservation organizations has been around since before the turn of the century. By World War Two, approximately 80 organizations focusing on the environment had initiated operations. This number increased by half in the next decade, to 119. In the 1960s it almost doubled, to 219, then it almost doubled again during the 1970s to 390. Fewer groups were formed during the Reagan era, but there was overall growth in the number of environmental organizations even during this difficult time. Figure 9.1 shows an increase in the number of trade associations active in the United States; they grew from about 2,800 to almost 4,000 from the 1960s to the 1980s. Walker (1991) shows further evidence of the rapid growth in the num-

---

1. Of the groups that ceased operations at some point during this period, 5 were subsumed into larger groups, 31 became defunct, and 23 were simply not listed in the 1990 edition of the *Encyclopedia,* though they were included in 1980. It is possible that some of this last set of groups might still be in existence but had changed names or purposes, or simply had failed to respond to the queries of the compilers of the *Encyclopedia*. Others were probably defunct. We therefore must assume that the number of environmental groups having ceased operations lies somewhere between 36, of which we are certain of the defunct status, and 59, which includes those groups which may be defunct. So the number of groups having ceased operations lies between 8 percent and 13 percent of the total of 461 in existence at some point from 1961 to 1990.

Table 9.2 Creation dates of environmental groups

	Pre-1990	1900–1949	1950–1959	1960–1969	1970–1979	1980–1989
All groups listed in 1961, 1970, 1980, or 1990	10	70	39	100	171	58
Cumulative totals	10	80	119	219	390	448
Only those groups still in operation in 1990	10	65	30	81	144	58
Cumulative totals	10	75	105	186	330	388

Source: Compiled from Bureh, Kock, and Novallo, various years.

Table 9.3 Environmental group staff sizes, 1961–1990

Year	Numbers of Groups Reporting				Total Staff of All Groups Combined
	1 or More FTE	11 or More	25 or More	100 or More	
1961	23	8	2	0	316
1970	36	16	6	1	668
1980	116	38	10	2	1,732
1990	151	50	20	6	2,917

Source: Bureh, Kock, and Novallo, various years.

bers of interest groups of all types. Table 9.2 shows that the most rapid growth may well have been in the area of the environment; the environmental movement increased its size by almost 400 percent from 1960 to 1990.

The growth in numbers of environmental groups is impressive; however, it is dwarfed by the growth in resources at these groups' command. Both in terms of memberships and staff sizes, the environmental movement of the 1980s and 1990s bears little resemblance to that of the 1950s and 1960s. One of the most important yet least noted changes in the area of the environment has been the increasing professionalism of the environmental movement as it is organized and represented in Washington. Shaiko (1991) reports comparisons of studies done in 1972 and 1985, indicating rapid growth in staffing levels of the public interest sector. Nineteen of 82 public interest groups in Berry's 1972 study had over ten staff members, whereas 151 of 219 groups in a 1985 study had more than ten full-time staff, according to Shaiko. Table 9.3 reports data on staffing levels for all environmental groups listed in the *Encyclopedia of Associations* in the years indicated.

Environmental interests are represented not only by more groups with broader memberships, but they employed over nine times as many full-time staff members in 1990 than they did three decades before. The number of groups at various levels of staff size has increased steadily over the years, as has the total number of staff working in the movement. As this has occurred, groups have become more professional and more specialized, avoiding costly duplication of effort (see Bosso 1991). In any case, they now represent a force not only at the mass level, but can be expected to use their professional staff to conduct research, testify at hearings, and play the inside Washington game just as well as their grass-roots counterparts can play the outside game.

Growth in the environmental movement has come through both the creation and expansion of new groups and the reinforcement of the oldest groups. The movement has its roots in the conservation movement of the 1930s, but the growth of new types of groups, such as Greenpeace, has not come at the expense of the older groups. For example, the Wilderness Society, founded in 1935, reported 7 staff members in the 1961 edition of the *Encyclopedia,* but this number grew steadily to 30 in 1970, to 42 in 1980, and to 112 in 1990. Table 9.4 shows the growth of staff size of selected, long-established, conservation and environmental groups and gives totals of staff size for all groups created before and after 1960.

Growth in the environmental movement has not come about through a complete refocusing of efforts. Old groups have been invigorated just as new groups have been created. Certainly there is a wider range of environmental concerns being expressed through the group system than there was in the 1940s or before, but these changes have come through an expansion in the overall size of the movement, not at the expense of the most established groups. Many venerable groups, such as the Audobon Society, face increasing competition for contributions from a variety of groups with much more modern images and are wracked by internal debates about the need to diversify from only a conservation group to a more broadly concerned environmental organization (see Raver 1991). Still, the decades-old conservation groups remain at the core of the environmental movement. Historically, it was by building on the membership base these groups had established that the diverse groups now constituting the American environmental movement were able to grow. About half the increase in staffing levels of environmental organizations over the years from 1960 to the present represents the addition of new groups; about half comes from expansion in the size of previously existing organizations.

We can get some information about the budgets of environmental organizations, although the *Encyclopedia* does not report budgetary information in the 1980 edition or before. Further, many groups did not report their budgets (although since many have nonprofit, 501(c)(3) tax-exempt status, their budgets are public information and a surprisingly high number did report). In any case, we have budget information for 206 groups out of 396 listed in the 1990 *Encyclopedia* (52 percent); the remainder either had no budgets or did not report them. Of those groups that reported budgetary information, the median

Table 9.4 Growth in staff size for selected groups and for all groups created
before and after 1960

Group Name	Creation Date	Staff Size			
		1961	1970	1980	1990
A. Groups reporting over 100 staff members in 1990					
National Wildlife Federation	1936	80	20	400	500
Sierra Club	1892	15	60	130	250
Ducks Unlimited	1937	10	12	55	210
Trust for Public Land	1973	—	—	46	130
Natural Resources Defense					
Council	1970	—	—	80	125
Wilderness Society	1935	7	30	42	112
Cousteau Society	1973	—	—	20	100
B. Totals for all groups					
Groups created before 1960		316	617	1,069	1,563
Groups created 1960 or later		—	51	662	1,353

Source: Bureh, Kock, and Novallo, various years.

budget was approximately $100,000 (though the arithmetic mean was $1.8 million). Fully 16 percent of those groups reported budgets in excess of $1 million. Eighty-one groups reported both staff and budget, and the correlation between the two is .93 (when we exclude three extremely high outliers, which might be expected to skew the results of this correlation, the number actually increases to .96). We cannot assess growth in group budgets over time, but the extremely high correlation between budgets and staffing levels makes us think that the figures reported in table 9.3 are good indicators of the growth in overall resources of the environmental movement from the 1950s to the 1990s. Whether we study group numbers, staff sizes, or budgets, our conclusions are identical. A massive shift in the mobilization of bias has occurred.

Agenda-Setting and the Mobilization of Bias

Interest-group environments structure the incentives and possibilities of policymakers seeking to expand or contract participation. Generating support for the nuclear industry was much easier in 1948 than it could have been in 1988. Opponents to the use of nuclear power have a much more powerful institutional infrastructure on which to rely in their efforts to affect policy. Similarly, pesticide manufacturers and agricultural interests face a much more critical environment in the 1980s than they did in the 1950s. There is no coincidence that Schattschneider mobilizations described in chapter 5 came at a time when the interest-group environment had already been transformed. Mobilizations of enthusiasm are most likely under conditions of one-sided organization of interests. As the mobilization of bias changes over time, so too does the like-

lihood of political conflict and agenda-setting under conditions of criticism—
a Schattschneider mobilization.

In this chapter we chose the environmental movement for discussion because of its size, its importance, and its readily identifiable membership, but
we could have traced the development of another interest-group environment,
for example, around cities and urban development, around health issues related to smoking and tobacco, or around any other of the cases discussed in
this book. At any rate, we would have found at least one thing in common.
The mobilization of interests changes over time, and with these changes come
differences in the likelihood of certain issues to hit the public agenda. Interest
groups play an important role in formulating questions, affecting public opinion, and defining the terms of debate. Where interests are well mobilized on
one side of an issue and poorly organized on the other, conflict and political
debate are unlikely. Rather, subsystem politics is likely to be the rule, as was
the case with pesticide and nuclear power before the 1970s. As the mobilization of bias changes, so often does our understanding of the underlying issues.
So the interest-group environment plays an important role in structuring the
choices available to policymakers and the public's understanding of what is at
stake in a public policy debate.

Of course the nuclear power and pesticide cases do not demonstrate simply
that mobilization of criticism is easier when there is a powerful set of interest
groups in operation. Indeed, these battles were among those that caused the
environmental movement to grow so strong in the first place. As the antinuclear movement grew during the 1960s and 1970s, so too did the environmental movement in general. Similarly, the reaction against the aerial spraying campaigns in the late 1950s and the publication of Rachel Carson's *Silent
Spring* in 1962 helped generate further support for a variety of environmental
groups. So the growth of the group system represents yet another example of
the interdependence among a variety of features in the agenda-setting process.
As opponents seek to generate mobilization, they at first face a difficult task.
With each success comes a greater likelihood of further success, however, as
the positive feedback mechanisms begin to enter operation. Clearly the environmental movement has been an example of a strong positive feedback
mechanism. Groups formed around a given battle remain in operation after
that battle is over, ready to be redirected toward the next. So it becomes easier
to raise environmental concerns over time as more groups are prepared to
mobilize. Similarly, these groups have had great impact on public opinion, as
a result of their initial successes and organizational powers. So environmental
themes are more powerful than they were in the 1940s. This combination has
made policymaking in the 1980s and 1990s much different from what it was
in the 1940s and 1950s, even in the absence of any changes in the underlying
facts or questions. Rather, changes in the mobilization of bias have made one
side more able than it once was to generate opposition to proposals that were
once successfully portrayed as questions of economic growth.

What are the results of the tremendous change in the mobilization of bias apparent in the growth of the environmental movement? Many previously closed systems of limited participation have been opened up, scores of issues that were previously the subject of little or no public discussion or controversy have hit the public agenda, and many other important public policy results have stemmed from these changes. Bosso (1991) has noted that the environment has become institutionalized on the public agenda. Environmental questions are much more likely to be in the public eye today than they were in earlier decades. James Lester and Douglas Costain have traced coverage of environmental issues in the *New York Times* from 1890 to 1990. They show a steady and dramatic increase in the amount of coverage, from 40 column inches per year in the 1940s, 110 in the 1950s, 285 in the 1960s, to over 900 in the 1970s (Lester and Costain 1991, table 4; see also fig. 2). This chapter has explained why. The movement has given itself the resources to mobilize massive numbers of people, it has the staff to conduct credible research, it has appealed to more favorable venues of policymaking within the Congress, within the executive branch (in particular with the creation of the Environmental Protection Agency), and in a variety of state and local institutions. Most importantly, it has altered perceptions of what is acceptable and what is not. In sum, the positive interaction of a number of related factors has combined over a period of twenty years or so to create a sea change in a broad area of policymaking.

Downs (1972) was wrong when he argued that public interest in ecology would quickly wane, since he overlooked what Peters and Hogwood (1985) rightly noted: agenda-setting can have long-lasting organizational implications. These organizational changes need not be only additional governmental agencies, new congressional subcommittees, or reorganized state-level institutions; they may also be in the voluntary sector. The Sierra Club and its allies can be just as effective in raising public awareness of an issue as a governmental institution. Because groups and institutions work in concert, however, we need not construct separate explanations of each. The surge and decline of new issues from the public agenda leave behind a variety of institutional legacies that later affect the chances of new issues from reaching the agenda. Interest groups, like governmental institutions, are among these semi-permanent legacies (see Costain 1991).

In chapter 3 we noted the evolution of terms used by political scientists to describe groups of policymakers: from iron triangle or policy subsystem, we have gradually moved to advocacy coalitions and policy networks. (Charles O. Jones has written of energy policymaking that "the cozy little triangles . . . had become sloppy large hexagons" [1979, 105].) From one-sided mobilizations of interest, in other words, many sectors of American society have moved toward a much more crowded, more complicated, and more representative system of interest representation. In chapter 5 we noted the important distinction between a Downsian and a Schattschneider mobilization. Mobilizations of enthusiasm are most likely under conditions of one-sided organization of interests, while criticisms and conflicts are more likely when many sides are well organized. By focusing on a single issue area in this chapter, we have been able to note how the relative mobilization of bias may change over time. This organizational question, in turn, has had important implications for agenda-setting, as many issues generating controversy in the 1970s and 1980s were easily accepted, even enthusiastically endorsed, in the 1940s and 1950s. So we have a methodological lesson: By focusing on cross-sectoral variation as they often have in the past, political scientists have been likely to conclude that factors related to the contents of the policies themselves are key elements in affecting patterns of conflict. In fact, patterns of mobilization may change over time, so studies that focus on longitudinal analysis may uncover different findings. The changing interest-group environments we have noted in this chapter are not the only historical reforms that have had important consequences for agenda-setting, however. In the next chapter, we consider the important and long-lasting changes in Congress as it has become much more active and decentralized.

10

Congress as a Jurisdictional Battlefield

In the last chapter we noted important and long-lasting changes to the American interest-group system. During the late 1960s and throughout the 1970s, critical changes occurred in the relative mobilization of bias, as we noted for example in figure 9.2. The same social forces that created those changes in the interest-group environment were felt within the halls of Congress. The 1970s saw dramatic shifts in the internal organization of Congress that reinforced and institutionalized the access that new interests demanded throughout the 1960s and 1970s. We focus here on documenting the degree to which long-term changes within Congress correspond to changes in the interest-group system, and how they affected policymaking. In the next chapter, we note how the relations between the federal government and the states also underwent large-scale alterations at about the same time.

The structure of a nation's political institutions affects powerfully the degree to which certain interests are heard where it matters. As new social forces became organized during the 1960s and 1970s, they demanded changes in those structures within Congress. This chapter focuses on those changes and relates them to policy changes in several of our cases. Congress provides one of the most important elements in creating the system of positive feedback, potential instability, and reversals in policy outcomes that we have noted in previous chapters. Congressional jurisdictions are more easily changed than those of executive agencies; members of Congress are active in seeking out new issues with which to associate themselves; and many groups that lose battles within executive agencies are able to find some supportive niches within Congress. Congress has been called the "keystone of the Washington establishment" (Fiorina 1989), and certainly its members play important roles in maintaining powerful policy subsystems. Congress in this sense is a source of stability, a protector of the status quo. However, congressional rivalries are great, jurisdictional battles are common, and policy changes often emerge from conflicts internal to the institution. When these changes do occur, policy systems may lurch from one point of relative stability to another. Congress therefore has the potential to play an important role both in the maintenance of subsystems (and therefore in the creation of incrementalism or stability) and in their destruction or replacement.

Congress is an important part of numerous subsystems, but its competitive and contradictory internal structure also makes it a prime avenue for appeal for those seeking to break apart existing subsystems. We noted in chapter 8 how increased congressional attention to the issues of drugs, alcohol, and child abuse was preceded by a rapid emergence of those issues on the systemic agenda. Once a number of congressional committees became involved in the issues, however, their interest did not fade away even after the degree of media interest in the issues declined. Rather, short periods of agenda access caused the entire policymaking structures surrounding those issues to be transformed. When congressional attention is raised, changes in the structures of policymaking often follow (Jones and Strahan 1985). During critical periods in the history of an issue, previously uninvolved groups within and outside of the legislature are encouraged to participate; other groups, which had been dominant, are structured out of the issue, or they see their own influence vastly diluted. So Congress is important in creating the lurching behaviors we have noted in each issue we have studied so far in this book.

When we study one issue at a time, we can note many such critical points, and we will do so in this chapter. However, there are also periods when general institutional reforms occur that affect a great variety of subsystems in similar ways. One of these periods of institutional reform was the mid–1970s. These reforms made permanent or lawful what had already become standard practice in many cases. We do not belittle their important by any means; however, like Rachel Carson's *Silent Spring,* they may have been more a symptom of change and a reinforcing element of that change than a cause of it. Many policy subsystems were being torn asunder during the 1970s; part of the effort that went into these changes in the relative mobilization of bias was put into decentralizing and democratizing the internal structures of the legislature. These institutional reforms then remained for decades: the institutional legacy of agenda-setting was felt in the structures of Congress, staffing procedures, budgets, and internal rules. We focus on each of these in a section below.

In their study of bureaucrats and politicians in Western democracies, Joel Aberbach and colleagues found that the relations between elected legislators, career civil servants, and appointed executive branch officials were far different in the United States than in any other country. Civil servants in the United States kept much closer contact with both clientele groups and elected officials in Congress than did similarly placed bureaucrats in other Western countries.

These relations were often closer than the contacts the civil servants kept with their own superiors, leading the authors to describe an "end-run model" in the American context (Aberbach, Putnam, and Rockman 1981, 234). According to Aberbach and his colleagues, "institutional incentives generate entrepreneurial instincts in American bureaucrats" (1981, 231). One of the most important instincts any bureaucrat or policymaker in the United States must develop is to pay attention to Congress. Its members may be willing and skillful participants in systems of limited participation, or Congress may be the venue in which opponents to current policy first are able to drive in a wedge.

Congressional relations with executive agency programs are often organized in an exclusive manner in order to limit the number of participants and to enhance the power of those with a vested interest. We saw this, for example, in the case of nuclear power in chapter 4, with the creation of the exclusive Joint Committee on Atomic Energy, granted exceptional powers of jurisdiction on this topic during a time when policymakers considered it especially important to nurture that young industry. On the other hand, Congress also played an important part in the destruction of the nuclear power subsystem. When subgovernments begin to crumble, and we have seen in previous chapters that they often do, the beginnings of the end can often be traced to changes in congressional behavior.

There are two complementary and mutually reinforcing mechanisms that structure changes in congressional behavior. First, jurisdictional boundaries separating the activities of various congressional bodies are not fixed in stone; in fact they are constantly undergoing changes as a result of two factors, one pulling, the other pushing. Disgruntled policymakers, interest groups, and executive agencies pull congressional committees to become active in new areas, asking them to claim jurisdiction in an area where another, more hostile, committee has held sway in the past. Second, entrepreneurial members of Congress and their staff push their committees and subcommittees to become active in new areas when they think there is a potential political payoff from the new activity. The incentive, indeed the necessity, for those inside Congress and those outside to collaborate in altering committee jurisdictions is clear. Without an inside collaborator, no outside group can force changes in areas of committee activity. Without a set of outside groups that stand to gain from the change, few internal entrepreneurs would be able to push through a jurisdictional alteration. Congress therefore plays an integral role in many policy communities.

The interests of policymakers outside of Congress hoping to move their issue into a more favorable venue (or simply to dilute the power of a hostile or antagonistic committee chair) can become linked with those of entrepreneurial members of Congress searching for a potent political issue with which to make their mark (see Walker 1977; Baumgartner 1987 presents similar findings in another context). In previous chapters, we have already noted the important role of Congress in the cases of drug abuse, nuclear power, pesticides, and smoking. In each case, an increase in congressional attention or in the number of different committees and subcommittees claiming jurisdiction over the issue led to important policy changes. Sometimes, this was the destruction of a previously powerful subgovernment (as in nuclear power, pesticides, and smoking); in other cases it involved the creation of new agencies and new groups of professionals to implement important new legislation (as in urban affairs, child abuse, and drugs). In every case, congressional attention contributed to the lurching behavior, as image and venue interacted to produce changes in policy processes.

In this chapter we first look at longitudinal trends in congressional activities in general. Since the middle of the century, Congress has grown in complexity, in staff, in the number of issues with which it deals, and Congress has changed its internal organization and balance of power. This has had important implications for virtually all areas of policymaking, so we consider these secular trends first. Second, we return to our practice of following particular issues over time, and we note important changes in congressional activities that correspond to changes in the relative autonomy of a variety of subsystems in American politics.

Secular Trends in Congressional Activities

We saw in chapter 9 that the interest-group system was dramatically transformed during the 1960s and 1970s in the United States. These changes are reflected in similar changes in congressional resources, behavior, and incentives. Mark Peterson has shown that as the interest-group system has grown more complex, presidential proposals in Congress have more likely been met with opposition or inaction. When the interest-group system was less complex, the president was more likely to be able to generate a consensus in Congress (1990, 117), so congressional reaction to policy proposals is affected by the interest-group environment. As this has grown more complex, congressional reactions have been more diverse. It is not only forces outside Congress that have caused changes in legislative practices in recent decades, however; Congress has reorganized itself internally, reinforcing many of these external changes and contributing greatly to the increasing diversity and complexity of the Washington policy community.

Probably the most dramatic changes relevant to this study are the increasing resources and new internal organization that Congress has given itself in the modern era. Increased budgets, more staff, and greater investigative powers translate into higher chances of bringing issues to the public agenda. As the U.S. Congress has given itself more resources in the postwar years, it has increased its already considerable powers of intervention in agency-centered policy subsystems. Two important types of changes are discussed here: the decentralizing administrative reforms that occurred in the 1970s, and the increased staff and resources with which the newly decentralized Congress has endowed itself.

When House Democrats revolted against the seniority system and particular committee chairmen in 1974, one complaint was the size and control of staff. Powerful committee chairmen typically used their control over staff (and therefore information) as a means of maintaining tight reins over their memberships (for an example, see Krehbiel 1991, 145). In the prereform Congress, powerful committee chairs used their control over staff and investigative budgets as a means of avoiding controversial intrusions into the tight relations they maintained with outside interests. One of the most powerful means by which the power of subcommittees was increased during the decentralizing reforms of the mid-1970s was the expansion of their staff and informational capacities. With greater control over staff came greater ability to break into previously tight subsystems.

Table 10.1 shows the growth in selected categories of congressional staff. Following the 1974 reforms, the staffs of the committees grew at an especially dramatic pace, and they continued to grow until the early 1980s, at which point they were at a level more than five times higher than they had been in 1950. Similar trends took place not only in committee staffing levels, but in the support agencies, where, for example, the staff of the Congressional Research Service grew from 161 in 1950 to 860 in 1985 (Ornstein, Mann, and Malbin 1990, 139).

In 1990, 27 House committees and 158 subcommittees controlled an investigative staff budget of almost $57 million. With this money, they hired 2,109 staff members. With the addition of 30 staff members that each committee was allotted through normal appropriations (or 810 staff), about 2,900 staffers worked for House committees and subcommittees in the 101st Congress (Summary of Comparative Data 1991, 16–17). Member staffs not associated with particular committees grew at a pace even greater than those of committees or the specialized congressional agencies during the twentieth century, but this expansion occurred earlier, mostly during the 1960s. After the 1974 reforms, member staffs of the House and Senate became relatively stable at around 11,000, as compared with 2,020 in 1950 (Ornstein, Mann, and Malbin 1990, 132–33). Budgetary appropriations for U.S. House committees hovered in the area of $8 million per year during the early 1970s, but they shot up to almost $25 million in 1976 and have continued to grow since (see Subcommittee on Legislative Branch Appropriations, annual). The mid–1970s saw some dramatic changes in congressional resources. These increased staffing and budgetary resources made Congress a much more complicated institution.

In sum, we can see from table 10.1 and from other sources of information that Congress had endowed itself with the resources to play a much more active role in a variety of policy areas in the 1980s than was possible in the

Table 10.1   Growth of congressional staff, 1950–1985

Year	Committee and Subcommittee Staff	Personal Member Staff	Selected Support Agencies		
			CRS	OTA	CBO
1950	546	2,030[a]	161	—	—
1960	910	3,556[b]	183	—	—
1970	1,337	7,706[c]	332	—	—
1975	2,737	10,186[d]	741	54	193
1980	3,108	11,117	868	122	218
1985	3,089	11,625	860	143	222

Source: Ornstein, Mann, and Malbin 1990, 132, 136, 139.

Notes: CRS = Congressional Research Service; OTA = Office of Technology Assessment; and CBO = Congressional Budget Office.

a. 1947 data.
b. 1957 data.
c. 1972 data.
d. 1976 data.

1950s or before. These material changes reinforced and were part of the internal organizational renovations aimed at diluting the powers of the most powerful members. Some of these changes were well underway before the 1974 reforms, but were reinforced by them. Others occurred shortly after these rule changes. The bulk of these changes remain in effect to this day, making the present-day Congress considerably more entrepreneurial and difficult to control than it was thirty or forty years ago. One of the most important ways Congress has changed is in its more detailed policy role and in the smaller size and greater number of its various functional jurisdictions.

Congress in subcommittee plays a more detailed and precise role in the policy process than did Congress in committee. For example, even while staffing levels have increased, the number of bills introduced in Congress decreased from the 90th Congress (1967–68) to the 100th (1987–88). The total number of bills enacted decreased slightly from the 80th to the 100th Congress, but the length of each bill increased dramatically. The typical bill was only two to three pages in length during the 1940s, but increased to over eight pages per bill in the 1980s. During this time, the number of committee and subcommittee meetings increased dramatically (Ornstein, Mann, and Malbin 1990, 155). Detailed legislation is now the rule; committee and subcommittee staff resources allow members of Congress to play a much closer role in writing detailed legislation. They can affect particular programs in precise ways, so they play an important part in the policy process and are constantly appealed to by policymakers outside of Congress for protection.

Jurisdictional boundaries between 158 House subcommittees and a large number of Senate bodies are difficult to maintain. Members and staff are jealous of their turfs, but each may try to encroach on that of another. For the strategic policymaker who believes that one committee or subcommittee may be more favorable than another, there are clear incentives to attempt to steer legislation in a particular direction. Since 1975, when the House changed its rules to make this allowance, bills have sometimes been referred simultaneously to more than one committee at a time. Multiple referrals, once nonexistent, grew from a small and insignificant proportion of all legislation to representing approximately one-quarter of all bills (see Schneider 1980; Davidson 1989; and Davidson, Oleszek, and Kephart 1988). From the point of view of a policymaker secure in a position of cooperation with a given congressional committee, these developments portend only trouble. It has become more difficult to maintain isolated and insulated systems of limited participation because of the changes in congressional rules, procedures, budgets, and staff.

Because of the great number of committees and subcommittees, leaders of each of these bodies strive to avoid interference from others. According to Barry Weingast, "One of the major changes of the reform period was the transfer of many of the critical rights over bill writing from 18–22 committees to 125–50 subcommittees. By the time of the Subcommittee Bill of Rights, this change had dramatically altered the ability . . . to enforce bargains" (1989, 809). Decentralization, according to Weingast, has led to dramatic increases in the numbers of floor amendments. In reaction, the smaller bodies have insisted on institutional protections. Increasingly, they ask for limitations on the rights of House members to offer substantive amendments on parts of legislation, and over time the House Rules Committee has been more willing to grant these requests. The number of restrictive rules allowing no amendments, only certain types of amendments, or a limited number of amendments on the House floor has increased dramatically and steadily during this time. In the 95th Congress (1977–78), 85 percent of House bills were debated on the floor under open rules, but this percentage declined steadily over the next decade. Restrictive rules constituted a majority of all rules in the 101st Congress (1989–90) (Summary of Comparative Data 1991, H17; see also Bach and Smith 1988). Power has been greatly diffused, in other words, and the newly powerful subcommittees have worked hard to protect their influence by requesting, and receiving, restrictive rules. Congress affects policy in a much more detailed manner in the 1980s than it ever did before. Increased specialization and decentralization have more often brought subcommittees into jurisdictional battles with each other and with their parent bodies. Amendments and restrictive rules are part of this process.

Though congressional scholars have often focused on how committees and subcommittees with established jurisdictions protect themselves from encroachments from others, some new scholarship shows that jurisdictional change may be common. While the parliamentarian must refer a bill to the committee that has established jurisdiction in that area according to precedent, "authors of bills have learned to draft them cleverly so that they can be referred to the 'right' committee" (Davidson and Oleszek 1977, 51). David King has shown how the jurisdictional battles that others have observed are often resolved not by reinforcement of the status quo, but by the formation of new jurisdictions. In his words, "Committee jurisdictions are continually realigning" (1991, 3). These realignments sometimes stem from the rise of new technologies or new public policy problems that do not fit neatly into preexisting committee jurisdictions, but they often result from strategic efforts to expand common-law jurisdictions.

Committee and subcommittee leaders are active in seeking out new areas for jurisdictional expansion, and they take advantage of new understandings of public issues in order to expand their own powers. The hearing process is one way in which they can demonstrate their willingness to invest resources in a new area and to claim new ground. Any committee may hold hearings on any topic it pleases, even those clearly within the jurisdiction of another committee. However, when a bill is introduced it may or may not be referred for consideration to that committee. Bill referrals are what count; hearings are often held as a means of claiming future jurisdiction so that new bills will be referred to a given committee. King shows that over time, committees have successfully encroached on the jurisdictions of others, or argued so strongly for the relevance of some new issue to their existing jurisdiction that they have expanded their powers over the years. He documents growth in the number of issues within the purview of the House Commerce Committee from 1947 to 1989. Shortly after the 1946 Legislative Reorganization Act that set committee jurisdictions for the postwar period, over 90 percent of the House Commerce Committee's activities were devoted to that set of issues described in the rules (railroads, inland waterways, securities and exchanges, telephones). By the 1980s, however, the committee had expanded its jurisdiction to such an extent that the original set of policy areas constituted less than one-third its efforts (King 1991, 10; for a recent and lively example of jurisdictional conflicts between the Commerce and Banking committees, see Wayne 1991).

Jurisdictional changes within Congress have not stopped members of Congress from cooperating with outside interests as a general rule. Indeed, Joel Aberbach has demonstrated that much congressional oversight activity is focused on offering help, rather than criticism, to agency administrators: "many oversight hearings, no matter what surface appearances might imply, are done in a fundamentally nonhostile, indeed a supportive, context" (1990, 161). One top committee staffer told him: "I think any subcommittee that has its subject, whatever its subject is, they're advocates. I mean, the Aging Subcommittee is advocating for aging programs, the Arts for arts, you know, Education for education, Health for health. They wouldn't be doing their work if they weren't interested" (quoted in Aberbach 1990, 163).

Having a supportive committee in Congress is nice; however, it is of little value if the committee loses its jurisdiction, as sometimes occurs. As Congress has grown more decentralized, as its resources have increased, as it has played a more detailed policy role, and as its members have sought more actively to make names for themselves based on some policy innovations, venue changes have become more likely. These secular trends explain why so many issues discussed in this book saw dramatic changes in agenda access in the 1970s rather than in earlier periods. Congress is not the only avenue for appeal for those seeking to dismantle a powerful subgovernment, such as those focusing on pesticides, smoking, or nuclear power, but it is an important one. Changes in the rules and practices of congressional committees and subcommittees during the 1970s increased the number of venues available for appeal.

Jurisdictional Encroachments and Policy Change

We have seen in previous chapters that important policy changes often come about because of changes in policy image and institutional venue. As one begins to change, changes in the other become more common, and this interaction can cause rapid reversals in policy outcomes. We saw in chapter 4 how nuclear power policy was altered by the increasingly negative public view of the technology, then by the erosion of power of the Joint Committee on Atomic Energy, the reorganization of administrative agencies overseeing the industry, and the increasing activism of opponents of nuclear power throughout the committees of Congress and in state and local governments (see, for example, table 4.2). Similarly, we saw in chapter 5 how policymaking for pesticides was initially dominated by officials in the Department of Agriculture and by leaders of the congressional agriculture committees, but how these officials eventually lost their jurisdictional monopoly. The Delaney hearings in 1958 led to a self-reinforcing process of increased congressional opposition to the pesticides subsystem.

In his study of congressional testimony on nuclear power reactor safety, Steven Del Sesto (1980) found that the pro- and antinuclear witnesses consistently raised different questions. Rather than contradicting each other's testimony, they simply raised different subjects. Where one side focused on the need to limit dependence on foreign sources of energy, the other discussed the hazards of radioactive leaks. The noncontradictory nature of the testimony was so remarkable that Del Sesto concluded that the two sides held differing ideologies rather than different facts. Each stressed points that the other would not dispute, just dismiss as irrelevant. Congress is a haven for many such noncontradictory or self-laudatory "debates." Different committees or subcommittees often promote different ways of looking at the same problem. Policy changes in Congress often come about as a result of jurisdictional battles rather than changes of heart by individual legislators. Jurisdictional and procedural rules structure policy outputs.

In this section, we look more closely at congressional activities surrounding pesticides, drug abuse, smoking, and air transportation in order to demonstrate how shifting jurisdictional boundaries can both create and respond to changes in issue definition. We will see consistently that different committees or subcommittees, each with a distinctive policy bias, sometimes enter into jurisdictional competitions. These battles often lead to rapid changes in policy as a committee that once enjoyed a jurisdictional monopoly is forced to share jurisdiction or, more rarely, loses its jurisdiction altogether. We discussed in chapter 2 how the same issue may have many different implications, but how at different times one aspect of the policy may dominate the policy debate. These various aspects of a single issue are reflected in congressional committees. As previously unimportant aspects of a given issue gain in prominence, new groups within Congress assert their control over the issue. For example, smoking and tobacco policy was once in the exclusive domain of the agriculture committees, since the question was seen as how best to maintain the livelihoods of tobacco farmers. As the issue has been redefined over the years from crop supports to health consequences, so congressional action has shifted toward those committees able to claim jurisdiction over the health questions.

Changing policy definitions are closely linked with congressional jurisdictions. Policy change within the Congress is often driven less by changes in the attitudes, beliefs, or values of members than by jurisdictional or procedural changes that allow advocates of change simply to bypass their opponents. Rather than win over one's enemies to a new way of thinking, the more realistic strategy is simply to appeal around them or over their heads, or avoid their jurisdiction through some other means. The jurisdictional complications of the Congress are the grounds on which policymakers fight many of their most important battles. As Congress has become more decentralized, with a greater variety of powerful subcommittees involved in particular jurisdictions, as described in the previous section, these strategies of appeal have become even more important, and their success more common. Many times, dramatic policy changes occur as a result of the combined activities of a great number of new jurisdictions. As new issues hit the agenda, many congressional bodies may claim some piece of the action. In a study of the governmental response to the energy crisis of the 1970s, Charles O. Jones and Randall Strahan described this jurisdictional inflation: "Meanwhile congressional response took on the character of the Oklahoma land rush. . . . The proliferation of committees and subcommittees claiming jurisdiction over energy policy dramatically expanded the number of members, congressional staff, and lobbyists participating in the issue area" (1985, 155).

In this atmosphere, jurisdictional claims multiplied and new participants with different policy ideas joined the fray. Such jurisdictional turbulence in Congress is characteristic of a Schattschneider mobilization that destroys prevailing subsystem arrangements. It is a positive feedback process within the confines of Congress.

Some significant debates have recently occurred in the literature concerning the degree of policy bias in various congressional committees (see Krehbiel 1990, 1991; Hall and Grofman 1990). Our study, based on committee hearings and witnesses' testimony rather than on the members' roll call votes, leads us to conclude that bias is probably alive and well in most congressional committees, but also that the debate is often miscast (see also Hall and Grofman 1990). The bias of any one congressional committee only matters if it is combined with a jurisdictional monopoly. This last question is probably more important than the views of the individual members, since if there is no monopoly there is little reason to expect that final legislation will reflect the views of the members of that committee very strongly. Finally, jurisdictional changes over time probably swamp individual member bias as an explanation of policy outcomes.

Pesticides: Preaching to the Converted

Almost seven thousand Americans have testified in congressional hearings concerning pesticides since the turn of the century. The vast majority of these witnesses have preached to the converted. Congressional committees with an interest in promoting the use of pesticides have tended to hear from farmers, agricultural interest groups, pesticides manufacturers, and members of Congress with strong agricultural interests. Those committees and subcommittees critical of pesticides have heard overwhelmingly from a different group: environmental activists, health officials, and other critics of the industry. Of course neither group hears exclusively from one side or the other; hearings almost always include a variety of views. However, hearings are not only informational; they are also meant to convey a message, and this message can be clearly discerned by inspecting the list of witnesses at pesticide hearings in Congress.

For every hearing on the topic of pesticides from 1900 to 1988, we have coded each witness as representing a certain kind of interest: (1) agricultural, (2) environmental or health, or (3) other or uncodeable. Agricultural interests included officials from the USDA, from farmers' organizations, and from pesticide manufacturers, as well as those individual members of Congress we could identify as having strong proagriculture views. Environmental or health witnesses included those from environmental organizations, health officials, and others whose affiliations made clear that they were health or environmental experts rather than farming experts. Of a total of 6,973 witnesses, we were able to classify 86 percent of them into one of these two substantive categories. Intercoder reliability for this coding of witnesses was 98.2 percent. (As for all coding questions in this book, details are presented in appendix A; for another example of coding witnesses at congressional hearings, see Jenkins-Smith, St. Clair, and Woods 1991.)

We coded the committees and subcommittees holding the hearings in the same way we coded the witnesses. Some committees were clearly proagriculture, others were clearly preoccupied with health and environmental questions, and still others could not be coded. In all, there were 385 hearings on pesticide topics from 1900 to 1988, held by 39 different committees and 89 different subcommittees. We have coded each of these committees or subcommittees as being part of the proagriculture venue, the health and environmental venue, or part of another or uncodeable venue. This venue coding was done by reference to the title of the committee or subcommittee in question, independent of the topics of the particular hearings. Therefore we are confident that this venue coding is distinct from the question of tone of the topics considered or the witnesses appearing before them. When this venue coding for pesticide hearings was done by a second coder, 95.2 percent of the cases were coded identically.

Finally, we have coded each hearing on pesticides by the tone of its title and description in the *Congressional Information Service Abstracts*. Some hearings clearly concerned with promoting some new technique for applying pesticides; others were mostly about investigating disease, among farm workers, caused by pesticides. We coded each hearing into the same two categories as those for witnesses and venue, based on its tone, asking simply whether a pesticide manufacturer would be pleased or worried that Congress was holding a hearing on this topic. Intercoder reliability for the coding of tone of coverage was 96 percent.

Table 10.2 presents the relationship between the type of witness and the type of venue. It shows that agricultural committees tend to invite propesticide witnesses to testify, while health and environmental committees are more likely to invite those critical of the industry. Committees like to hear from their allies, not their opponents.

When an agriculture committee has hearings on pesticide topics, its members are three times more likely to listen to testimony from representatives from the pesticide industry or from others likely to have a favorable view on pesticides than they are to invite health or environmental representatives. When a health committee holds hearings on a similar topic, the same selection bias in witnesses occurs: almost three-quarters of the witnesses appearing before these committees are health or environmental experts rather than agricultural officials. We can also note from table 10.2 how much more active the health and environmental committees have been in holding hearings on pesticide matters as compared to the agriculture committees. Over 3,700 people have been invited to testify before these committees on pesticide concerns, as compared to fewer than 2,300 before the agriculture committees. Of 385 hearings on pesticide topics coded, 220 have been in the health or environmental venue, as compared to only 102 in the agriculture venue.

Hearings are more often a vehicle for exposing problems and complaining about the status quo than they are for defending the current state of affairs.

Table 10.2 Distribution of witnesses on pesticide hearings in Congress, 1900–1988

Venue of Hearings	Type of Witness			
	Agriculture or Pesticides Representative	Health or Environmental Representative	Other or Uncodeable	Total
Agriculture	1,593 (75.7%)	510 (24.3%)	161 (—)	2,264 (100.0%)
Health or Environmental	861 (27.5%)	2,267 (72.5%)	657 (—)	3,785 (100.0%)
Other or uncodeable	357 (47.9%)	389 (52.1%)	178 (—)	924 (100.0%)
TOTAL	2,811 (47.0%)	3,166 (53.0%)	996 (—)	6,973 (100.0%)

Gamma = .78
Tau-b = .47
Chi-square (1 d.f.) = 1174.2 (prob. < .001)

Note: Percentages within the table and measures of association are calculated on the basis of codeable cases only.

Since the agriculture committees have generally been interested in promoting the use of pesticides, they have not held many hearings on the matter, and when they have they have invited witnesses who could be expected to defend the industry. Congress specializes. When pesticides are to be attacked, one group of committees holds those hearings and one group of members hears their testimony. When pesticides are to be defended, another committee holds those hearings and invites a different group of experts to give testimony. Committees use hearings to garner support for the views they already hold.

The high degree of bias in congressional testimony concerning pesticides would indicate a severe problem in representation if either the agricultural or the environmental venue had a monopoly on jurisdiction over pesticide matters. In fact, jurisdictions are constantly in flux, and we can see the importance of these changes in jurisdictional lines by following these issues over time. We saw in chapter 5 that congressional attention to pesticide matters changed dramatically over time (see, in particular, fig. 5.4), and we noted how the expansion of congressional attention to the industry corresponded with the decline and breakup of the powerful pesticide subgovernment. We can see the important role that jurisdictional changes played in this process by tracing separately the attention to pesticide issues in the two venues described above.

Figure 10.1 shows how the pesticide issue emerged in congressional hearings because of the activities of the environment and health committees, not those within the supportive agriculture venue.

Congress increased its attention to pesticide matters in the 1970s not because of any change in heart by agriculture committee members. Rather, it came about through a change in jurisdiction. Health and environment com-

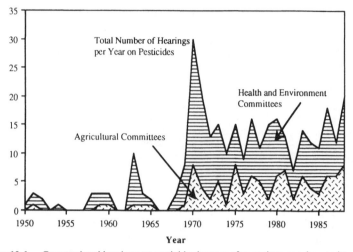

Figure 10.1. Congressional hearings on pesticides by type of committee or subcommittee holding them, 1950–1988.

mittees simply pushed their way into a new issue area. Figure 10.1 clearly shows that once the environmental and health committees were able to claim jurisdiction in the wave of environmental concern beginning in the early 1970s, they never abandoned the field. In chapter 8 we saw how the surge in congressional concern with drug abuse questions of the late 1960s was associated with dramatic shifts in tone. Rather than focusing only on enforcement questions, the rise in attention was associated with a new emphasis on education and treatment of addicts. We see below that this shift in tone was related to a shift in jurisdiction; as the issue was redefined as one of treatment, health and labor committees moved into the area. Exactly the same pattern fits for pesticides; we can see clearly the relationship between tone and venue. Table 10.3 shows how different types of committees focused on different aspects of the pesticide issue.

We saw in table 10.2 that when health and environmental committees or subcommittees hold hearings on pesticide matters, they invite almost three times as many health and environmental witnesses as they do agriculture witnesses; no wonder that 98 percent of the hearings held by these committees that we were able to code as either supportive or critical of the pesticides industry were critical. Congress in its role of supporter of powerful subsystems often does its best by avoiding publicity. When issues hit the congressional hearings circuit, it is more often on a wave of criticism than a tide of good feelings. The vast majority of hearings about pesticides were critical, even when they were held within the most supportive institutional sanctuaries, as table 10.3 shows. We know from table 10.2, however, that when the agricultural committees hold hearings on problems associated with pesticides,

Table 10.3 Venue and tone of congressional hearings on pesticides, 1900–1988

Venue of Hearings	Tone			Total
	Positive	Critical	Neutral	
Agriculture	18 (18.4%)	80 (81.6%)	4 (—)	102 (100.0%)
Health or Environmental	4 (1.9%)	205 (98.1%)	11 (—)	220 (100.0%)
Neutral	7 (11.9%)	52 (88.1%)	4 (—)	63 (100.0%)
TOTAL	29 (7.2%)	337 (92.8%)	19 (—)	385 (100.0%)

Gamma = .84
Tau-b = .30
Chi-square (1 d.f.) = 27.1 (prob. < .001)

Note: Percentages within the table and measures of association are calculated on the basis of codeable cases only.

they are likely to invite witnesses who can defend the industry. Few hearings are organized to sing the praises of pesticides; Congress as a supporter of a powerful industry is at its best in quietly drafting legislation to promote use of pesticides or in creating price-support legislation that promotes monoculture. When the pesticides subsystem was at its strongest, Congress simply did not hold hearings on the topic. As the issue grew more controversial, jurisdictional changes within Congress were set in motion. Hearings within hostile venues are a prime avenue for the expansion of political debates and often spell the beginning of the end for jurisdictional monopolies that are necessary for the maintenance of powerful subsystems.

Drugs: Enforcement versus Education

Congressional hearings on the topic of drugs are all critical, of course. They differ in the extent to which they emphasize law enforcement, interdiction, and smuggling questions as opposed to treatment, heath, and education questions, however. Just as in the case of pesticides, we find that different venues within Congress tend overwhelmingly to focus on different aspects of the same issue, and that jurisdictional monopolies may change or disappear over time. As in the case of pesticides, we have coded all the committees and subcommittees that have held hearings on drugs into one of two venues: the enforcement venue includes committees such as Foreign Affairs, Judiciary, Government Operations, Merchant Marine, and others that deal mostly with enforcement questions; the education and treatment venue includes Labor and Education as well as others. Table 10.4 shows how venue and focus of interest are closely correlated.

Most congressional attention to drug questions comes from committees concerned primarily with questions of enforcement, not education. However,

Table 10.4 Venue and tone of congressional hearings on drug abuse, 1945–1986

	Tone		
Venue of Hearings	Enforcement	Education, Health	Total
Enforcement	419 (74.7%)	142 (25.3%)	561 (100.0%)
Education or Health	44 (15.5%)	239 (84.5%)	283 (100.0%)
Neutral or uncodeable	129 (64.5%)	71 (35.5%)	200 (100.0%)
TOTAL	573 (54.9%)	471 (45.1%)	1,044 (100.0%)

Gamma = .88
Tau-b = .56
Chi-square (1 d.f.) = 265.68 (prob. < .001)

Note: Statistics are based on four coded cells only.

Table 10.5 Congressional hearings on drug abuse in two venues before and after 1968

	Venue			
Time Period	Enforcement Committees	Education or Health Committees	Other or Uncodeable	Total
Before 1968	62 (97%)	2 (3%)	6 (—)	70 (100.0%)
1968 or after	495 (63%)	285 (37%)	194 (—)	974 (100.0%)
TOTAL	557 (66%)	287 (34%)	200 (—)	1,044 (100.0%)

Gamma = 0.89
Tau-b = 0.19
Chi-square (1 d.f.) = 29.4 (prob. < .001)

Note: Statistics are based on four coded cells only.

there are important and powerful venues that deal almost exclusively with education questions: of the 93 hearings held on drugs in the Senate Labor and Human Resources Committee during the postwar period, 84 percent focused on education rather than enforcement questions. Of 42 hearings in the House Foreign Affairs Committee, on the other hand, 98 percent focused on enforcement questions (mostly interdiction, linking foreign aid to eradication programs, and similar questions). Clearly, neither side exerts complete control over the issue of the federal response to drugs. We saw in chapter 8 how competing groups of committees battled during the postwar period for control of drug policy. As the issue burst onto the congressional agenda in late 1960s, this was at least partly a product of the desire of the education and treatment group of committees and subcommittees to intervene in an area that had previously not concerned them. Table 10.5 shows how attention to drug abuse questions in Congress before 1968 was dominated completely by the enforcement venue, but how this monopoly of jurisdiction was whittled away after the issue became a high agenda item.

From 1945 to 1967, there were only 70 hearings on drug topics in Congress. Of the 64 hearings codeable by venue, 97 percent were within the enforcement venue. Beginning in 1968, the issue began to attract the attention of a greater number of committees and subcommittees in both the House and Senate, as we saw in chapter 8. As this occurred, the jurisdictional monopoly for those focusing on enforcement was diluted, as education and treatment questions became more prominent. From 1968 to 1986, there were 974 hearings on drug questions. Of those that were codeable by venue, over one-third were in the education, not the enforcement, venue. From a virtual monopoly of jurisdiction, the enforcement committees became only one of a number of congressional bodies busily holding hearings and enacting legislation within the area of drugs. In an independent analysis of a sample of drug policy hearings, Sharp (1991) classified those giving testimony. Her analysis corresponds closely with ours in that she shows an almost total domination of the enforcement and interdiction interests in the early period. This tightly linked subgovernment was later transformed into a more diverse and conflictual issue network, just as the number of committees and subcommittees claiming jurisdiction over drug issues expanded.

Much of the agenda process is driven by competition among congressional bodies. As one group moves to become more active in a given area, other committees and subcommittees react to protect their turfs or to avoid being outshone by a competitor. Through this process of competition over jurisdictions, congressional attention in hundreds of separate and independent committees and subcommittees is linked. Positive reinforcement mechanisms cause congressional attention to lurch, in a smaller-scale version of similar behavior within the broader policy process. Our analysis, combined with that of Sharp, shows how Congress and the interest-group system are tightly linked.

Smoking: Health or Agriculture?

We noted in chapter 5 that congressional attention to smoking and tobacco issues followed closely on the heels of media attention. These questions were once in the exclusive domain of the agriculture and price-support groups in Congress, but as the issue began to become more controversial, a broader range of committees became involved. These newcomers had much more hostile views toward the tobacco industry. Before 1973, when annual hearings on tobacco issues passed the level of 10 per year, almost 90 percent of all hearings were either in agriculture, foreign trade, or taxation venues, with only 17 hearings (11.4 percent of the total) in health-related committees. The percentage of hearings held in health committees or subcommittees increased to 35 percent of the total in the period 1973 to 1986, however. During this time, the percentage of total hearings held in the agriculture committees declined from 55 to 26—from a majority to only one-quarter of all hearings on the topic. Smoking came onto the congressional agendas in the 1970s as hostile committees attacked a well-entrenched subsystem.

Just as in the other cases we have studied, the new committees seeking to intrude in an area where they had not previously been active could not challenge the established jurisdictions directly. No health committee could claim the right to legislate on price-support legislation. Rather, the intruding committees must discuss new aspects of the same issue. In the case of smoking and tobacco, of course, agriculture and trade committees continued to discuss crops, subsidies, and foreign markets in a generally positive tone for the industry, even after the issue had reached the broader public agenda in the 1970s. The difference was that a new group of committees also raised the negatives associated with the industry. Table 10.6 shows how committees and subcommittees in the two competing venues consistently discussed different aspects of the smoking question.

Among the topics we have been able to code as pro- or antitobacco industry in 313 hearings on the subject since 1945, 84 percent of those discussed in the agriculture or trade committees were positive; 96 percent of those brought up in the health or tax committees were bad news for the industry. Each side of the battle has its allies in Congress. The question of subsystem politics is to know whether one of these groups holds a jurisdictional monopoly. In smoking, there was one in place in the postwar years, but, as in the cases of pesticides, nuclear power, and drug abuse, jurisdictional battles caused the once-powerful group to lose its monopoly. Agenda dynamics always lead to change in the relative mobilization of bias. As issues emerge on the agenda of Congress, new groups within Congress become mobilized. These changes almost always have strong and long-lasting implications for the policy system surrounding that issue.

Air Transportation: Toward a Jurisdictional Free-for-All

In this section, we show how the politics of jurisdictional competition within Congress can create rapid and irreversible change in policy outcomes, even without the intrusion of a new dimension of conflict. As congressional leaders fought each other over control of air transportation issues, this very competition led to more dramatic policy change than might have happened in a more controlled system. John Kingdon has written that "battles over turf, far from leading to stalemate, often actually promote the rise of an item on the governmental agenda. Congressional committee chairs, for instance, compete with one another to claim credit for some initiative that they sense will be popular. In the rush to beat each other to the punch, a subject may become

Table 10.6 Venue and tone of congressional hearings on smoking and tobacco, 1945–1986

Venue	Tone			
	Favorable toward Industry	Antagonistic toward Industry	Neutral	Total
Agriculture	116 (84.1%)	22 (15.9%)	65 (—)	203 (100.0%)
Health, or taxes	3 (3.8%)	76 (96.2%)	25 (—)	104 (100.0%)
Other	—	2 (—)	4 (—)	6 (—)
Total	119 (54.8%)	98 (45.2%)	94 (—)	313 (100.0%)

Gamma = .99
Tau-b = .78
Chi-square (1 d.f.) = 131 (prob. < .001)

Note: Percentages within the table and measures of association are calculated on the basis of codeable cases only.

prominent much more quickly than it would in the absence of this competition" (1984, 164–65). Jones and Strahan have argued similarly that energy policy in the 1970s was affected greatly by competition among congressional subcommittee chairs (1985). In the case of air transportation, such competition was clearly the cause of dramatic changes in federal regulations in the late 1970s. As the ideas of deregulation swept through the federal government in the 1970s, leader after leader searched for industries they might deregulate. Air transportation had long been discussed in Congress in terms of its economic and regulatory implications, but this wave of new participation swept through the system even with no new dimension of conflict emerging.

Air transportation was once part of a well-organized subgovernment centered on the commerce committees in Congress and the Civil Aeronautics Board (CAB) in the executive branch (Redford 1960). As a consequence, Congress held only a total of forty-seven hearings from the turn of the century until 1968. Twenty-one of these hearings (or 45 percent of the total) were in the Commerce committees of the House and Senate; another seven hearings were in the Appropriations Committee of the House, and no other committee held more than five hearings throughout this period. As deregulation became a governmental buzzword in the 1970s, this quiet system was quickly torn asunder. The government deregulated trucking, long-distance phone service, savings and loans, and other industries all during the mid- to late 1970s. Figure 10.2 shows the increase in congressional attention to air transportation in the late 1960s and early 1970s, as revealed in the number of hearings on the subject from 1944 to 1989. In this figure, hearings with a primary focus on safety questions (27 of 229 hearings, or 12 percent of the total) are distinguished from those focusing on economics and regulation (202 hearings, or 88 percent of the total).

At no time was safety the most important topic of interest. Unlike nuclear

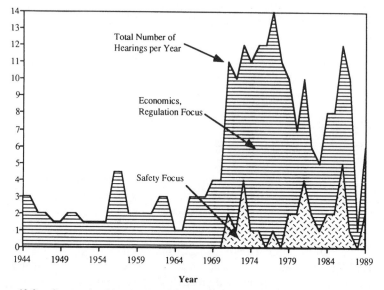

Figure 10.2. Congressional hearings on air transportation, 1944–1989.

power, pesticides, and tobacco, agenda access was not propelled by the introduction of a new dimension of conflict. Rather, there appears in this case to have been a diffusion of deregulation activities from other areas. In any case, jurisdictional rivalries were intense, and the secure subsystem that once controlled air transportation policy was quickly destroyed once deregulation became a major political issue. As the issue burst onto the congressional agenda in the early 1970s, a great number of different bodies claimed a piece of the action.

While the commerce committees and the CAB had shared jurisdiction over air transportation issues with relatively little interference from other congressional bodies throughout the 1940s, 1950s, and 1960s, this jurisdictional oligopoly was soon whittled away. Commerce did not recede entirely from the area; it held 52 hearings from 1969 to 1989. However, the House and Senate committees on public works also held 40 hearings during the later period; 35 hearings were held in various financial committees; 10 in government affairs or operations committees; others were held in committees on science, small business, the judiciary, armed services, and still other bodies. An average of more than six distinct congressional committees held hearings on some aspect of air transportation in each year from 1969 until 1978, when the industry was deregulated. From 1950 to 1968, there had been hearings in fewer than two committees per year. Some of these changes were institutionally designed, as the 1974 reforms gave the newly organized committee on Public Works and Transportation official jurisdiction over many air transport issues (see Davidson and Oleszek 1977). Others stemmed from informal jurisdictional aggrandizement, as many committee and subcommittee chairs exerted authority over some part of the issue. A jurisdictional oligopoly had given way to a jurisdictional free-for-all.

This congressional frenzy was of course matched by considerable action within the executive branch. As we have come to expect, actions in one branch quickly had reverberations in the other. Presidents Nixon and Ford were supportive of deregulation, and President Ford made specific proposals that were considered by Congress in committee in 1975. President Jimmy Carter's appointment of Alfred Kahn to head the CAB was a mandate to eliminate rate regulation for air transportation, but it is clear that the issue had been on the formal agenda for years before Carter's election. Carter's appointment of Kahn further reinforced changes that had already begun to gather a momentum of their own. Congress continued to hold regular hearings on deregulation and other economic aspects of air transportation until deregulation of routes and prices and the elimination of the CAB in 1978. Rapid changes in the levels and venues of congressional interest in an issue once again can be seen to have led to dramatic impacts on the organization of not only future congressional but also executive branch activity. With the dismantling of the CAB and the deregulation of airlines, the industry and the American public entered a new period that could not have been predicted by an incremental view of prevailing federal policies toward the airlines even in the late 1960s, just before the issue surged onto the national agenda.

The air transportation example illustrates well why political systems rarely return to policy equilibrium once the systems are disturbed. The very nature of the policy process is altered forever, making it literally impossible to return to the status quo ante. The CAB, formerly the centerpiece of the regulation subsystem, was disbanded. New institutions were created, generating a new configuration of political forces. At first, competition increased, new airlines were established, and fares fell. Then a wave of mergers beset the industry, and the remaining carriers developed hub-and-spoke systems routing all transportation through terminals where they controlled gate access. As competition declined, prices rose. The Reagan administration steadfastly refused to use antitrust legislation to interfere, allowing the industry to develop into an oligopoly, with barriers to entry maintained by the hub-and-spoke systems and "frequent flier" programs to encourage loyalty to a limited number of carriers.

Airline deregulation lurched onto the formal agenda in a manner similar to other issues we have studied. During the period when the issue moved high onto the agenda, institutions governing the policy process were radically altered. As a wave of interest in deregulation rushed through the federal government in the 1970s, new groups pushed their way into what had been a relatively tight and controlled subsystem centered around a single federal agency and congressional Commerce committees. In only a few years, this quiet system had been torn asunder through the competition for political advantage through jurisdictional change.

Congress and Subgovernment Stability

Policymaking has the potential for instability because different venues within the American political system harbor different biases. These distinctive characteristics are seen in microcosm within the Congress. The great variety of congressional bodies creates the possibility for instability in congressional activities, just as the fifty states, the three branches of government, and the thousands of local governments allow for instability in the larger political system outside of Washington, D.C. Particular issues are often treated within the Congress by specialized committees or subcommittees with little interference by those not part of the small network. Later, when an issue hits the congressional agenda through the strategic appeals of those unhappy with the status quo, a great variety of congressional bodies may begin to interfere, a process we have seen again and again in this book. Of course there are important and limiting rules of jurisdictional precedence that give great advantages to those bodies with long-standing jurisdictions in the area; specialized committees can protect their turf. However, we have seen in this chapter that change in congressional activities can be dramatic because jurisdictions are not, and cannot be, cast in stone. As issues are redefined over time, different groups within the Congress are able to claim jurisdiction over them. Policy change within Congress stems often from these changes in jurisdictional authority.

In the previous chapter, we noted the increasing complexity and competition within the interest-group environment. Congressional reforms have not created by themselves a more complicated policy process. Rather, Congress reacted to the same forces that caused changes in other areas. As citizens mobilized in the environmental movement described in chapter 9, they generated publicity for a great variety of problems that previously had been ignored, avoided, or, within policy subsystems, dominated by other interests. The general social conditions that led to the growth of the environmental movement are the same that led to the changes in congressional practices in the 1970s. In other words, all parts of the policy process are linked. Changes in one part of the system tend rapidly to be reflected in other parts. When the interest-group system began to change, as we described in chapter 9, similar forces led to great changes in congressional practices, as described in this chapter. In the following chapter, we focus on the politics of federalism, noting how the relative importance of the national versus the state governments in a variety of policy arenas has changed over time.

Changes in the structure of the policy process affect individual policy subsystems by moving consideration of issues from one venue to another, by diluting the influence of the most powerful members, or by destroying them altogether. The cumulative impact of institutional and social changes such as those described in this and in the previous chapter can be much greater than the sum of their parts. Many systems of limited participation were destroyed or weakened in the United States in the 1970s. More important than any single one of these occurrences is the fact that the American political system may be more difficult to control in the 1980s and 1990s than it was in the 1940s or 1950s. While the general public agenda could never deal with all important matters of public policy, and while policy specialization (with its attendant problems of bias) will therefore always be present in any political system, monopolies of jurisdiction may be more or less secure. In a system with many venues, each in competition and each seeking to please a different constituency, policies are more difficult to maintain away from public view than in a system where jurisdictional boundaries are clear-cut and where appeals by minorities have little chance of success. There are important and powerful subsystems in American politics; however, these may be more difficult to maintain, on average, in the 1990s than they were in the 1950s because of the changes in mobilization of bias described in chapter 9 and the changes in congressional procedures described in this chapter.

11

Federalism as a System of
Policy Venues

Federalism in America creates a great number of distinct and partially autonomous venues for policy action. Subnational jurisdictions often are the areas where new ideas are tried out, later to be adopted and mimicked by others if they are successful, or abandoned if they are found unworkable. While the various parts of the federal system differ from each other in a number of ways, they are also part of a whole. As parts of a single system, they can all simultaneously be affected by changes in the structure of the federal system itself. In this chapter we see that great changes have indeed occurred in the intergovernmental grant system, causing dramatic changes in the behaviors of state and local governments over time.

This chapter, like the previous two, strikes two complementary chords. First we focus on the cross-sectional variation from issue to issue. Just as some interest-group environments or congressional jurisdictions are more nuturing to stable policy subsystems, so are some aspects of the federal system. Second we focus on longitudinal trends in the entire federal system. Just as the interest-group system and the Congress as a whole went through important changes during the 1960s and 1970s, similar changes occurred within the structures of federalism.

Differences in receptivity to particular policy proposals among governments in the federal structure have two components. First, the states and localities are more receptive to policies directed at the development of the human and physical infrastructure than is the federal government, while the federal government has been more involved with issues of collective consumption policies—policies directed at improving the lives of individuals but which cost more in taxes than they replenish. Second, subnational governments vary in their receptivity to particular policy proposals. Some states or localities within states are more receptive to, for example, welfare programs than are others, because of variability in political culture or class composition.

Differences in receptivity to policy proposals imply that federalism provides an important limit to positive-feedback processes. On the other hand, it also means that the federal structure can provide niches for policy ideas that can later expand to other governmental entities. In the case of nuclear power, the division of power in the federal system actually intensified the process of subsystem destruction as utility regulators in some states came under increasing pressure from the consumer and environmental movements. Most research on the federal system has emphasized its role in limiting comprehensive policy change. Ironically, however, the federal system can promote change because no group can control all parts of the system, closing out consideration of policies that it does not favor. Federalism does not so much limit change as it makes such changes less controllable by anyone. The numerous venues provided by federalism make change far more unpredictable than in a unitary system.

Our approach to understanding policy dynamics has stressed the occurrence of both positive- and negative-feedback effects in a single system of action. In some cases, policy innovations damp out; in others, they spread rapidly through a political system. One critical factor in the positive-feedback process is the degree to which policy venues are linked. When venues are separate and distinct, responding primarily to local pressures, they are less subject to positive-feedback effects than when they are more interdependent. In American federalism, the national and state governments are linked through a complex maze of intergovernmental grants and associated requirements. These bonds are tighter at some times than others, and the strength of these ties affects the flow of policies across venues.

Secular trends in the development of federalism strongly affect the extent to which the multiple venues in the federal system are interdependent. The more interdependent the venues, the more predictable the overall direction of policy change. As we shall show, flow of policies across jurisdictional boundaries is stronger in periods of nationalization and weaker in periods of decentralization.

The Federal Character

There are more than 80,000 governments in the United States: one federal government, fifty states, 40,000 municipalities, 26,000 special districts, and 15,000 school districts. Nearly 50,000 elected officials and more than 13 million appointed officials staff these governments (Anton 1989, 4). On the one hand, these units of government give representation to the diverse elements in the nation, integrating this diversity into a national political system. On the other hand, as Livingston (1952, 93) has argued, governmental diversity creates divergent patterns of loyalties and policy expectations, diversity that is even greater than the social and economic diversity of a complex nation. Governmental institutions offer opportunities for policy entrepreneurs. The mere existence of multiple venues colors policy outcomes independently of variability in social and economic characteristics. On the other hand, the smaller scale of local governments means that they can be more easily influenced by single constituencies. Hence dual forces are at work. By giving the opportunity for policy entrepreneurs to influence more places within the federal structure and by imposing only some common standards, the federal system encourages a great diversity in policy outcomes.

Many writers on federalism have expressed dissatisfaction with the way in which federalism thwarts the implementation of comprehensive national domestic policies. By requiring an extraordinary degree of cooperation among officials at all levels of government, the federal system virtually ensures that national programs will not be implemented uniformly. It also makes certain that bargaining and conflict will be as much a part of the process as consensus and compromise. As the intergovernmental grant system expanded during the late 1960s, James Sundquist wrote, "Is it possible to institutionalize recourse, and flexibility, and responsiveness within a system that is still a single system and an organizational strategy that is still a single strategy?" (Sundquist 1969, 28).

Several authors have argued that central policy control in the United States is achieved by the superior fiscal and political incentives offered by the grant-in-aid system. Carrying this view to its extreme, John Chubb (1985) has modeled the federal system in a principal-agent format with two tiers. The first tier is composed of elected officials who control the behavior of their agents, the national bureaucrats. In the second tier the national elected and appointed officials control the behavior of the myriad of state and local officials. During a period of nationalization, this model may have some validity. However, Dan Wood (1991) has subjected Chubb's approach to careful quantitative scrutiny in the implementation of clean air policy. Wood concludes that the system is a mixed one, with the upper tier distinctly hierarchical and the lower tier driven by a multiplicity of forces.

Trying to impose coordination on a system that allows for the expression of diverse interests and gives those diverse interests the resources to affect policy is indeed frustrating. Indeed, the implementation perspective on intergovernmental relations is not the best vantage-point from which to evaluate the performance of the federal system. An alternate aproach would take us far from Washington, directing our attention to the entrepreneurial activity of state and local officials and other political activists as they seek to achieve benefits from governments (for example, see Anton 1989; Rich 1989).

Secular Change in the Federal System

In the two previous chapters, we have shown that secular changes in the interest-group system and in the internal structure of Congress are related to changes in policy subsystems. Similarly, long-run changes in the organization of federalism have occurred, and these changes have also affected the composition of policy subsystems. These secular changes affect the role of federalism in the making and implementation of public policy, with a move toward and then away from centralized policymaking since the 1930s. Deil Wright (1988) has detailed seven phases of intergovernmental relations in the United States, six of which have occurred since the 1930s. Prior to that time, intergovernmental relations were limited to trying to specify boundaries and spheres of influence. After that period relations became more complex.

We may crudely collapse the development of federalism in the United States since the 1930s into two periods. The first, lasting until 1978, was a period of nationalization or centralization. The federal government took responsibility for more and more governmental functions, many of which the states and localities were happy to relinquish in return for financial relief. Then, about 1978, a period of cutbacks in the intergovernmental system began, with the federal government less willing to assume the burden for problems. We saw in chapter 7 that the late 1970s experienced peaks in congressional hearings on urban affairs policies relating to community development and the intergovernmental grant system. Grants in real dollars peaked at about the same time (see fig. 7.4).

Another way to address the issue of nationalization of the federal system is to examine the extent of congressional interest in federalism. Figure 11.1 displays the number of congressional hearings relating to intergovernmental relations since 1945 (appendix A provides details). From that year until 1969, a steady upward trend occurred. Then the intergovernmental issue leaped onto the congressional agenda during the early Nixon years when the president's proposal to consolidate many of the categorical programs enacted since the New Deal into block grants was the major domestic agenda item. Debates centered on both the specifics of practical programs and the nature of federalism itself (Conlon 1988). A temporary fall took place during the mid–1970s, with a strong resurgence in interest in the issue of federalism culminating in 1979. Since then congressional hearings relating to intergovernmental relations steadily declined under the twin weights of budgetary stringency and the New Federalism program of President Reagan. As we noted in chapter 7, during this period the intergovernmental lobby found few allies in Congress and was unable to mobilize to protect intergovernmental grants from the Reagan era cutbacks.

This ebb and flow of national interest in the intergovernmental system has changed the distribution of advantage in the United States by offering policy

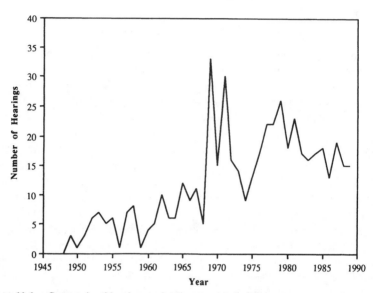

Figure 11.1. Congressional hearings on intergovernmental relations.

entrepreneurs new opportunities for action. In particular, the period of nation-alization linked venues, whereas the period of devolution partially decoupled them. Decoupling has not been complete, because federal agencies and na-tional organizations have not disappeared since 1979, and interaction among policy professionals is facilitated by such organizations.

Policy Specialization

Even during the most centralized period of intergovernmental relations, states and localities had ample authority and resources to pursue independent policy priorities. In fact, institutional features of the federal system push the states and localities toward specialization in certain kinds of policies. The distinct policy specializations of the different levels of government are one of the most fundamental features of American federalism. They often cause national and subnational priorities to diverge, thereby frustrating national policy imple-mentation but also increasing policy diversity and providing greater adaptabil-ity and more opportunities to policy entrepreneurs.

Earlier in this book we noted that one recurrent theme of political conflict during the middle part of the twentieth century has been between proponents of public policies directed at promoting economic growth and those who stress the social and environmental consequences of that growth. Most gov-ernment policies designed to promote growth are indirect. That is, they do not focus on the direct creation of jobs or new businesses; rather they are designed to provide the public infrastructure upon which private commerce may be built. Hence one may categorize public policies by the extent to which they promote economic growth versus the degree to which they provide benefits to groups or individuals but actually detract from the growth process. In chapter 3 we noted problems with all policy categorizations, because the very meaning of issues may change over time. What promoted growth in the past may have become a wasteful expenditure today. As we stressed then, this does not mean that categorization of policies is useless, but rather that one ought to be cautious in extrapolating a categorization that fits at one point in time to either the past or the future.

One consequence of divided powers is that state and local governments are pushed toward the pursuit of policies that promote economic growth, whereas the federal government is more likely to pursue policies that redistribute policy benefits toward disadvantaged citizens. Paul Peterson (1981) has classified public policies according to their anticipated effects on economic growth into (1) developmental policies, which promote growth, and (2) redistributive policies, which benefit the disadvantaged.[1] Peterson then argues that the federal government is more successful in pursuing redistributive policies, while the states and localities are more efficacious in pursuing developmental policies; hence the levels of government tend to specialize in the functions they perform best (Peterson and Wong 1986).

In order to examine the policy performance of different institutional venues within the federal system, we have modified Peterson's classification by dividing governmental expenditures into investment and consumption policies. Conceptually, we define investment policies as those that provide more tax revenue from economic growth than they cost in taxes, while consumption policies are net consumers of tax resources. The distinction between investment and consumption policies parallels Peterson's distinction between developmental and redistributive policies, with one important difference. The term *redistribution* implies that policies that take from the well-off in taxes and give to the less well-off are implicated in economic decline. But all sorts of well-off groups may make claims on government that are not investments in future growth; farm subsidies are an excellent example.

Within the broad class of consumption policies fall government actions that can benefit the poor, the middle class, or the upper class; farmers or laborers; businessmen or landowners. What is important is that with regard to economic effects, these groups are all in the same situation. Their claims, if granted, would result in slower economic growth in the short term (Olson 1982). Similarly, groups may advocate policies that promote economic growth, perhaps because of the distributional benefits they receive. That these

---

1. Peterson includes a third category, allocational policies, which includes public services that maintain economic functions without favoring one group over others. In later work, Peterson and Wong (1986) drop allocational policies from their analysis.

groups pursue growth policies for selfish ends is irrelevant to the economic impacts of the policy.

Federalism and Selection Pressures

We may conceive of institutional arrangements as selection devices, winnowing some kinds of policies and nurturing others. Indeed, the whole notion of venue receptivity can be recast as providing selection pressures on the activities of policy entrepreneurs. Policy entrepreneurs, through a process of trial and error, find that some policy proposals are received favorably within a particular venue, while others are not. In general, the smaller the unit of government in a federal system, the stronger the selection pressures favoring investment policies.

For convenience, let us think of the relative pursuit of the two general types of policies as a ratio: expenditures devoted to investment divided by expenditures devoted to consumption. Different levels of government, if they specialize in different kinds of policies, show distinctly different values on this ratio, which we call the *investment-consumption ratio*. Focusing on the ratio of investment to consumption allows us to observe the policy specialization of different levels of the federal system independently of the overall size of the public sector. The debate over the size of government has obscured the choices between investment and consumption that better capture the overall priorities of governments.

The levels of government differ in several important respects, and these differences are likely to lead to different policy mixes such that the investment-consumption ratio increases as we move down in the federal structure. There are several reasons for expecting this. First, the smaller size of state and local governments leaves them less insulated from economic forces and more prone to engage in competition for economic growth (Peterson 1981). Second, state constitutional limitations on debt mean that economic growth or increased taxes are the only ways to raise additional revenues for ongoing operations. Hence the connection between growth and policies is clearer for state and local politicians than for national leaders.

Third, historical reliance on the states and localities for service production and infrastructure development has meant more attention to investment policies at the subnational level (Scheiber 1987; Kantor 1988; Eisinger 1988). Fourth, local business elites are better able to affect political outcomes in small governments, because their resources are critical to the success of local politicians. According to Stone (1980), local politicians are particularly interested in projects that have high visibility, and they need to mobilize the business community to gain access to the resources necessary for those projects. Local business elites, of course, can be interested in either investment or consumption policies. Logan and Molotch (1987) argue, however, that there exists a shared interest among local business elites in growth promotion. Such interest should lead them to prefer investment over consumption policies.

Fifth, the national government is better able to pursue redistributive policies because of its broader tax base and its relative autonomy from economic forces (Peterson and Wong 1986). Moreover, national governments are able to provide protectionist policies for industries, something the states and localities cannot do. This means the national government is often beset by consumption claims from both business and labor. Finally, some evidence exists that voters have different expectations of politicians at state and national levels with respect to the management of the economy (Stein 1990). These differences in expectation are connected to the assignment of functions in the federal system. To the extent that voters expect politicians to pursue growth-oriented policies at the state and local levels, and consumption policies at the national level, the natural tendencies of institutions to promote such a sorting of policy functions will be reinforced.

To examine the thesis of policy specialization further, we have assembled data on federal expenditures, by object of expenditure, since 1940, and aggregate state and local expenditures, by object of expenditure, since 1934 (Bureau of the Census 1970, 1990). For the states and localities, this is the earliest date for which categories of expenditure were assembled by the U.S. Bureau of the Census. The federal data are based on analysis by the Office of Management and Budget, and are available in equivalent form since 1940 (Office of Management and Budget 1991).

For each level of government, we have put expenditures in either the consumption or investment category (for the federal government we have excluded defense and foreign aid expenditures). (The rationale for this division and the specifics of the policy categories are presented in appendix A.) For both national and subnational levels, we have calculated the investment-consumption ratio discussed above for each year of the period studied. These are presented in figure 11.2, for the period after the disruptions stemming from World War Two. (The figure also presents a curve entitled "grant impact," which we discuss below.)

Figure 11.2 shows, first, that the investment-consumption ratio for state and local governments is consistently much larger than that for the federal government. Throughout the period, the states and localities devote from two to three times as much money for investment than for consumption; for the federal government, the ratio is almost the reverse. Second, the two sets of ratios each change dramatically over time. While not shown on the graph, the state and local ratio is fairly constant during the 1930s and 1940s. It begins to rise during the mid–1940s. By 1955, the ratio reaches a level approximately 50 percent higher than it was in 1945, and it stays at this level until the late 1960s. It declines rapidly during most of the 1970s, then less rapidly during

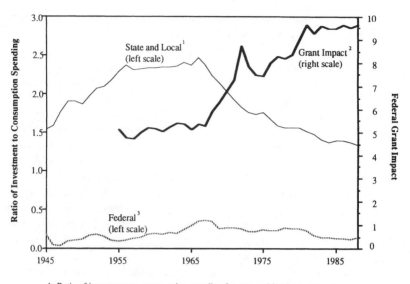

1. Ratio of investment to consumption spending for state and local government.

2. Percent of state and local budgets derived from federal grants to individuals.

3. Ratio of investment to consumption spending for federal government.

Figure 11.2. Impact of federal grants on state and local spending priorities. *Sources:* Bureau of the Census 1970, 1990; Office of Management and Budget 1991.

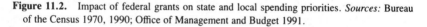

the late 1970s and early 1980s, before leveling off after 1985. The ratio for the federal government falls quickly during the 1940s, recovers marginally from the mid-1950s until the late 1960s, is constant until the 1980s, then falls radically.

Our analysis shows that different levels of government in the United States pursue different strategies of investment. Each level specializes. In the next section, we discuss efforts by the national government to alter the behaviors of the state and local governments, imposing policy priorities from the top of the federal structure.

Federal Influence on State and Local Policy Priorities

The policy priorities of the different levels of government may be different only so long as the higher level does not have the ability and political will to alter the priorities of the lower level. Yet the grant-in-aid system was developed to do exactly that. There is no question that the federal government influences the specific program priorities of the states and localities through grants-in-aid. It is not clear, however, whether the federal government's grant structure affects the basic inclination of the states and localities to pursue investment policies. Nor is it clear whether this influence is variable across time.

Because we have rough summary measures of the generalized priorities of the levels of government in the investment-consumption ratios, we may examine more closely the imposition of priorities from the center and the consequent linkage of venues. Causal interactions are complex, and to some extent state spending was driven by endogenous forces. In Michigan, for example, the liberal-labor coalition achieved its greatest successes during the 1960s and 1970s, when the nationalization of the federal system was greatest (Jones 1986). In part, however, federal priorities, which moved toward consumption spending, were imposed on the states through the intergovernmental grant system.

In order to examine these questions, it is necessary to develop a measure of federal impact on state priorities. One possibility is simply to use the extent to which states and localities rely on federal grants. This may be measured by the proportion of state and local revenue derived from the federal government. State reliance on federal grants has varied since 1955 (when the American Council on Intergovernmental Relations began calculating it) from 10.2 percent in that year to 26.5 percent in 1988.

Unfortunately, this number combines grants for investment with those for consumption. To correct for this, we adjust this figure by the percentage of federal grants going for consumption purposes. Then we get the percentage of state budgets that comes from federal consumption-based grants. The higher this percentage, the greater the imposition of federal consumption priorities on state and local priorities. This is the "grant impact" variable displayed in figure 11.2. All of the grants going to individuals would fall into the consumption domain. Some grants not going to individuals would also fall into the consumption-spending category—such as hospital expenditures —but grants to individuals comprise the great bulk of consumption grant spending.

The percentage of federal grants-in-aid going to individuals declined from 50 percent in 1955 to a low of 31 percent in 1978, then rose again to over 54 percent in 1989 and the years following (by OMB estimates). This pattern resulted from a complex interplay of forces, but roughly declined as the federal government moved money into highways and urban renewal during the 1950s, and into community development during the 1960s and 1970s. Expansion of welfare programs and the enactment of Medicaid caused the percentage to rise beginning in the late 1960s. Then the Reagan cutbacks in intergovernmental aid avoided cuts in grants to individuals, concentrating disproportionately on community development programs.

It is clear from figure 11.2 that the state investment-consumption ratio is strongly affected by the percentage of federal grants designated for consumption purposes. The negative relationship implies that increases in state budgetary reliance on federal grants to individuals cause the states to deviate from their preferred investment policies toward the federal government's consumption-based priorities. The simple coefficient of determination between these two series is .958. Almost 96 percent of the variation in state priorities can be explained by federal government activities through the grant-in-aid structure. When states began to move toward consumption policies in 1967, they did so only because the federal government pushed them in this direction through its grant structure. (It ought to be noted, however, that the range of variability in the investment-consumption ratio, while considerable, never changes so much as to cause the states to mirror the policy priorities of the federal government. Even after the federal government succeeded in changing the priorities of the states to be more like its own, the two levels of government remained miles apart. States spent $1.55 on investment for every $1.00 spent on consumption in 1989, while the corresponding figure for the federal government was $0.18.)

Returning again to figure 11.2, we note that when the grant impact measure is flat, as in the 1955–65 period, and after around 1980, the state investment-consumption ratio is fairly constant. But the grant measure moves rapidly upward in the late 1960s and early 1970s, showing that the states shifted their policy priorities quickly away from investment spending toward consumption spending. Changing priorities of the states and localities are related, at least in part, to the conception of federalism as a system for imposing national policies. Increases in the use of the grant system combined with emphasis on consumption policies led to increases in consumption spending in the states. Declines in the use of the grant structure after the late 1970s were associated with a leveling-off of state-based consumption policies and a drift toward investment-centered policies.[2]

Experts in intergovernmental finance have pointed to a substitutability effect in grants in which the receiving unit substitutes donor (federal) funds for locally generated funds (Anton 1989). The analysis above suggests that states will substitute their own funds for federal investment grants, but will not do so for consumption grants. The period of greatest decline in the state investment-consumption ratio, the late 1960s and the 1970s, saw little change in the percentage of federal grants going to individuals. In 1967 this was 31.3 percent; in 1978 it remained at 31.0 percent. On the other hand, the reliance of states and localities on federal grants grew greatly during this period—from 16.9 percent to 26.5 percent. Hence increases in both categories caused a

2. Our analysis suggests that the degree of reliance on intergovernmental aid exerts a more powerful influence on state and local priorities than does the imposition of grants to individuals. The simple coefficient of determination between grant reliance and the state investment-consumption ratio is .602, but this figure is only .095 for grants to individuals. In a multiple regression with the state investment-consumption ratio as the dependent variable, the coefficients are -0.0979 for reliance on federal grants, but only -0.0484 for grants to individuals, indicating that the first variable has about twice the influence as the second. Both are statistically significant.

deviation of priorities toward consumption spending, because no new money was flowing into investment options. In the 1980s, cutbacks in federal aid for investment policies did not influence the state investment-consumption ratio very much, and for the same reason: the states' traditional investment priorities encouraged re-substitution of state and local funds for declining federal revenues.

The Role of Federalism in Systems of Positive and Negative Feedback

We argued early in this chapter that federalism ought to act as a brake on positive-feedback processes in policy dynamics. Now we have provided strong evidence that buttresses that view: the policy priorities of the levels of government are substantially at variance. Moreover, the phenomenon of policy specialization implies that subnational governments will be more like one another than the federal government, at least with respect to broad expenditure categories. It also implies that policies which pursue investment aims will diffuse among states more quickly than will consumption policies. Given this policy specialization, how can we explain the positive-feedback effects that often occur in American politics?

Certainly the major policies discussed most intensely by state and local officials during the 1980s centered primarily on investment policies. In particular, industrial policies designed to attract commerce and the reform of education were high on the agendas of state and local officials. Diffusion of ideas to attract and retain industry came through interaction among relevant state officials and their professional organizations, with little encouragement by federal officials (Boeckelman 1989). The most important mechanism, however, has been competition. States and localities have perceived themselves as competing for a scarce good—economic growth (Jones and Bachelor 1986). As is the case for the private sector, competition among political systems motivates rapid diffusion of policy ideas. This competition has moved from specific incentive packages to infrastructure more generally, including human services development (Taylor 1991). One does not observe such competition in the consumption policy arena, except to the extent that states and localities make the case for limiting such policies because they interfere with economic growth (Peterson and Rom 1990).

Many of the policies we study in this book are consumption-based policies in that government action has been directed at the amelioration of the ecological and health consequences of capitalist development. In some cases, policies initially directed at promoting economic progress were altered as subsystems collapsed. In the cases of nuclear power and pesticides, government policy clearly changed from solidly oriented toward investment to one based on consumption. A major question, then, is why the positive-feedback processes characteristic of subsystem collapse included the states and localities, given their motives to pursue investment policies. Put another way, it is easy to account for rapid diffusion and nonincremental policy changes among state and local governments where investment policies are concerned, because competition for the fruits of economic growth is a stimulating agent. But it is not so easy to account for diffusion where consumption policies are concerned. What forces the states and localities to deviate from their normally predominant focus on investment policies?

In the first place, the issue of whether a policy falls within the investment or consumption domain is an empirical question. But it is a very difficult empirical question, and this allows ample room for political rhetoric in the policy adoption process. In particular, claimant groups have become adept at justifying their policy proposals in the language of economic growth. Moreover, most policies are mixes of the two fundamental elements (O'Connor 1973). Given this mixture, the justification for a policy can shift over time, assuming different connotations in different periods. The example of education is instructive. Education in the United States has often been justified in relation to the particular American ideal of upward mobility—that is, in terms of equality of opportunity. Occasionally, however, education is justified in terms of its contribution to economic growth. The shift in language carries different implications for policies—one promoting uniformity of experience, the other promoting tracking and more demanding curricula for at least some students. Most importantly, it allows proponents to promote their policy in different terms, depending on the predominant view of those in power.

In the second place, states themselves differ in size and in political culture and institutional development, so some states (large liberal ones) should be more receptive than others (small conservative ones) to such ameliorating policies. Once policies are established in one state, they may diffuse to others. Finally, we have shown above that periods of nationalization have occurred in the federal system. During such periods, consumption policies should have an easier time in the diffusion process, because federal and state venues have been linked through the intergovernmental grant process and the creation of federal agencies responsible for such policies. As we shall see below, many policies that are well established today came to national prominence during the period of nationalization in the federal system, approximately between 1965 and 1975.

Venue Linkages in Policy Subsystems

The nationalization of the federal system joins the growth of the interest-group system and the increasing capacity of Congress as powerful secular forces affecting the composition of policy subsystems. Below we reexamine some of the policies studied earlier in this book, focusing on the question of the diffusion of policy ideas and images in state and local venues.

Nuclear Power and the Nationalization of Interests

As we noted in chapter 4, the decline of civilian nuclear power is the story of venue shopping by activists in a federal system characterized by many separate but overlapping policy centers. The federal government was the scene of monumental debates on nuclear power policy through a variety of committees in Congress and in many executive agencies. The multiple venues of the federal government, which in many ways made possible the success of the antinuclear movement, are dwarfed in number by those of the states and localities. These, too, played a key role. Various state agencies, including the courts and legislatures, but perhaps more importantly state utility commissions and local planning agencies, were important elements in the antinuclear venue shopping of the 1970s.

Public utility regulation has always been primarily a state function. In most states, public utility commissions were highly responsive to the rate requests of electric power utilities. Beginning in the 1960s, however, consumer advocates began focusing on state public utility commissions in order to force them to take a tougher stance against the electric utility monopolies which they regulated. They began to intervene regularly in rate-making procedures. William Berry (1979) has presented an analysis which indicates that states with more professionalized public utility commissions developed rate structures which favored smaller consumers. Berry (1984) has also shown that both the presence of a consumer representative and the openness of the proceedings tend to lower the price of electricity. Finally, a professional commission was able to price electricity more closely according to cost, thereby not inflating profits for firms. All of this suggests professional commissions are more responsive to consumer interests than less professional commissions. As we discussed in chapter 4 and as Gormley (1983) and Campbell (1988) have described more completely, state utility commissions proved to be one of the most effective venues for appeal by those opposed to the nuclear industry, since their decisions hit the utilities straight in the balance sheet.

The venue-exploitation activities of policy entrepreneurs did not stop with state public service commissions. Local governments in the United States are the primary repositories of the power to regulate land use. Planning and zoning laws often require that various approvals to construct nuclear facilities must be granted by local planning boards, and antinuclear activists brought their objections to these boards wherever plants were sited. The common "Not in My Back Yard" (NIMBY) concerns of citizens caused delay and thereby drove up the costs of plants dramatically. Such volatile situations are ripe for exploitation by electoral politicians, and the governors and attorneys general of New York and Massachusetts were particularly vocal about the Shoreham and Seabrook plants being built on Long Island and in New Hampshire.

As we discussed in chapter 9, environmentalism galvanized into a national movement in the 1960s and early 1970s. The greatest growth in environmental groups was in the 1960s and 1970s, with the growth probably most concentrated in the period 1968 through 1975. The fact that domestic nuclear power policy got caught up in a powerful positive-feedback system of venue exploitation and image deterioration was related to the communication and reinforcing actions of environmental groups spread across the nation. Changes in the intergovernmental system, in the organization of Congress, and in the interest-group system all reinforced one another, spelling trouble for nuclear power and many other political subsystems. Separate institutional venues were linked by the national organizing power of the environmental movement. On the other hand, the existence of venues meant that receptive venues could be found, thwarting the power of the subsystem at the national level.

Diffusion through National Coordination: Child Abuse and Traffic Safety

Left to their own devices, state and local governments tend toward the pursuit of investment policies. The intergovernmental grant system, however, has forced or strongly encouraged the states to adopt a variety of health and welfare policies. Beginning with the New Deal, the federal government has used intergovernmental grants to encourage the development of state and local agencies whose mission is the implementation of health and welfare policies. The grant system at one time created both budgetary resources and constituencies for the promotion of such policies. There were in many states, particularly in the East, histories of governmental concern with health and welfare issues, so the grant structure reinforced existing institutions.

The diffusion of child-abuse-reporting statutes is a case in point. In 1962, the Children's Bureau of the Department of Health, Education, and Welfare sponsored a conference on child abuse. A major result was the drafting of a model reporting law for the states. Between 1963 and 1967, every state and the District of Columbia adopted reporting statutes (Myers 1986; Nelson 1984). Apparently the model statute had struck a responsive chord. Important in this extraordinarily rapid diffusion were local advocates in every state and the existence of a national organization with an interest in the issue (the American Humane Association).

The reporting statutes heightened interest in the issue in the states, causing far more controversy than most legislators involved probably expected. "Reporting legislation, which seemed utterly noncontroversial when originally passed, eventually became the field on which many bitter battles between the 'public' and the 'private' were fought" (Nelson 1984, 77). Moreover, child abuse was first considered by Congress in the District of Columbia committees (House and Senate) because of the reporting-statute frenzy (Nelson 1984, 98–99). So a movement went from a federal bureau through a national professional and advocacy association to fifty states, then came to Congress in its role in administering the District of Columbia. We saw in chapter 10 how Congress became heavily involved in the issue shortly after this period.

In the case of child-abuse-reporting statutes, state-based advocates were linked with each other through national organizations and a federal agency, the Children's Health Bureau, which promoted the issue. State-based groups approached their respective state legislatures with considerable success. Separate state policymaking venues were linked through the activities of advocates and the Children's Health Bureau. These policy networks were the vehicles for the diffusion of the reporting laws. Reporting statutes, leading to more reliable official statistics on the severity of the problem of child abuse, later helped keep the issue in the public eye for years to come.

The nationalization of highway safety as a political issue followed broadly similar, if more successful, policy lines. As we showed in chapter 6, highway safety has reached the systemic agenda in waves. Each of the waves had a solution attached to it by transportation officials. The most recent set of safety solutions has emphasized driver responsibility, as opposed to earlier concerns with traffic control, highway engineering, and automobile safety. National concern can be traced to 1966, when the National Highway Safety Act established the National Highway Safety Bureau, which pushed the driver responsibility issue onto the congressional agenda (Jacobs 1989). The NHSB funded university research on drunk driving and other safety issues, and supported the development of state statutes. It thus helped create and coordinate a national policy network devoted to the promotion of highway safety. The greatest national accomplishments of this network were establishing a national drinking age of twenty-one and a fifty-five mile-an-hour speed limit, both of which were enforced through the threatened denial of federal highway funds to states that did not comply. National lawmakers and a national community of policy specialists worked to enact similar changes in driving laws in rapid diffusion across all fifty states.

Pesticides, the Environment, and Three Forms of Diffusion

The complex interplay between state-to-state diffusion, state-to-federal diffusion, and federal-to-state diffusion is perhaps nowhere better illustrated than in the case of environmental regulation. Our earlier discussions of pesticides stressed changes in national policies, but changes were also occurring at the subnational level. By the 1960s, most states adopted laws regulating pesticides; generally these laws were based on a model statute developed by the Council of State Governments (Conn, Leng, and Solga 1983, 7–8). The Council of State Governments had based its model statute on the Federal Insecticide, Fungicide, and Rodenticide Act of 1947 (FIFRA). However, many states had regulated pesticides prior to the 1947 federal act, and the model statute served more to encourage uniformity among those states already regulating pesticides.

After the passage of the National Environmental Protection Act in 1970, policy was strongly guided from the center. Since then, the Environmental Protection Agency has had the responsibility for administration of federal pesticide regulation. By law, states cannot register a product as safe that has not previously been registered by the EPA. States, however, can refuse to register products registered by the EPA. Moreover, states have primacy in enforcing pesticide regulation, and considerable variability in the stringency of enforcement has developed among the states. California's highly developed regulatory system includes a permit requirement for pesticide application and detailed disclosure requirements. Florida has also developed a vigorous pesticide regulatory system (Conn, Leng, and Solga 1983).

The environmental policy deadlock of the 1970s and 1980s meant that initiative in the environmental policy area fell to the states. States such as California and Florida put in place stronger systems of regulation, while in Texas pesticide regulation was left to the lenient Department of Agriculture, and the regulation of chemical manufacturing was almost nonexistent. Pesticide regulation in California was a product of that state's strong environmental movement, which also moved aggressively to limit automobile emissions in the face of changing federal standards concerning urban pollution. The immensity of the air pollution problem in southern California made drastic action feasible. East Coast officials have actively discussed the California plan, and Congress has considered the desirability of a national approach. On the other hand, Houston, which has considerably less pollution than Los Angeles but nevertheless is second among American cities in severity of pollutants from automobiles, has developed very few policies for dealing with the problem. The spirited "road versus rail" debates of the early 1990s have never incorporated the issue of pollution control, centering instead on central city versus suburban cleavages.

In environmental regulation, as in other policy activities, considerable variation exists in the extent of government intervention from state to state. It is clear, however, that these separate venues are linked. Two mechanisms have acted to cause more uniformity in environmental regulation than one might expect from an examination of local political conditions. These are diffusion via professional associations and the activities of the federal government itself. Rather than frustrating attempts at national policy change, the multiple venues of the states and the federal government sometimes coalesce into a single system of positive-feedback, each encouraging the other to enact stronger reforms than might otherwise occur.

Conclusion

In this chapter we have explored the issue of venue receptivity in the American federal system. State and local governments experience competitive pressures regarding maintenance and growth of their tax bases, whereas the federal government does not. Hence the two levels of government pursue fundamentally different mixes of public policies, with the federal government specializing in consumption policies and the states and localities emphasizing investment policies.

But the competitive pressures have played out very differently in different states and cities. Presumably California and Texas have both been subject to these pressures, but their policy mixes are vastly different. Moreover, increased recognition of the power of these competitive pressures has resulted in a different kind of competition than that envisioned by analysts ten years ago. Rather than creating minimal-tax states in the face of competition for capital, states and localities raised taxes and improved their human and capital infrastructures. This helped balance internal pressures for quality-of-life improvements and demands for policies designed to attract capital investment.

Differences in venue receptivity do not end the matter, because venues are linked. What happens at the federal level is not insulated from what is going on in state and local governments. While smaller units of government tend to be oriented toward the provision of investment policies, they are also involved in the provision of welfare services and the regulation of many industries and products. Professionals in state and local government are in contact with one another through professional associations and through their federal counterparts. These connections ensure the flow of policy ideas across venue boundaries.

The result is that the complex mix of governments in the federal system creates as many opportunities as constraints. Analysts who ask if "the government can govern" often focus on the limitations of numerous venues of policy action that must be controlled in order to achieve coherent policies. But numerous linked venues provide many opportunities for active policy entrepreneurs. Some seek election, some seek specific policy action, and in the federal system they are more likely to find a venue receptive to their demands. Sometimes this search is careful and calculated, sometimes it is frenetic and emotional. It always involves trial and error. Failure in one venue can lead to resignation, but it can just as likely lead to a search for a new venue. If the state is unresponsive, what about the courts? Will a federal agency intervene on our behalf? Can we approach the school board as a potential ally? These sorts of calculations go on every day in America. They make the process of federalism (and it is a process as well as a structure) dynamic, not constrained and stultifying.

Our view of federalism is not that it carries no bias. Indeed, every venue is biased. It is this bias that offers opportunities for change. Even the whole complex of institutions that comprise federalism may well be biased in the sense that more (or more important) venues are more easily captured by, say, business interests. But the very existence of multiple venues means that cracks are likely to appear somewhere, and these can be exploited by political activists.

The particular distribution of advantage is affected by the nationalism of federalism. Beginning in the late 1960s, and running through the early 1980s, many politicians and policy advocates urged that federalism be viewed as a mechanism for the implementation of national policy priorities. Democrats promoted this conception practically through the development of domestic programs that relied on the grant-in-aid. Republicans argued for local authority and pushed block-grant programs and severe cutbacks in the intergovernmental system. Because federal expenditure priorities have shifted over time to policies which regulate and ameliorate capitalist development, periods of nationalization tend to move state and local priorities away from their traditional pursuit of investment policies.

It is noteworthy that the federal system was heavily nationalized during the same period that the interest-group system was growing most rapidly and Congress was developing a more articulated institutional structure. The period of the late 1960s through the early 1970s was one of remarkable policy activity in the United States, one that affected governing arrangements from policy subsystems to the very structure of federalism. The positive-feedback systems that can occur for the individual policy communities we have been describing in this book can also occur for the grand secular trends discussed in the last three chapters. We discuss the relationship of this phenomenon to "national moods" in the concluding chapter.

12

Governing through
Institutional Disruption

Much recent literature, both scholarly and popular, has offered discouraging assessments of the ability of democratic institutions to deal with change. This line of argument, summarized in the question "Can the government govern?" contends that democratic government in the United States (and elsewhere) is so plagued with lackluster politicians beholden to powerful interest groups that heroic policy actions have become impossible, at least in domestic affairs. No longer, so the argument goes, do politicians rely on popular sentiment to motivate and justify their actions. Rather, each politician has found a network of interest groups that are willing to offer support, while election campaigns are run less and less on parties and issues and more and more on personalities and finely orchestrated photo opportunities just as potent in emotional symbols as they are lacking in substantive information. Other arguments blame the inability of the government to govern on the increasing complexities of modern society, but many adopt the same conclusion. Modern democratic governments cannot respond to the great challenges of the late twentieth century (see, for example Chubb and Peterson 1989; Is Government Dead? 1989).

We disagree profoundly with this straightjacket view of government. When one takes a longer view, as we have in this book, one is struck by the vast policy changes that have occurred in the United States. These changes occur both incrementally and in bursts, and when the bursts occur, old ways of doing things are swept aside, to be replaced by new organizational forms. In the long sweep of American politics, one is less tempted to claim that cozy arrangements between politicians, interest groups, and the media prevent change and more likely to ask when and how new policy arrangements will emerge, sweeping away those currently in place.

The approach we have developed in this book gives a more sensible base from which to evaluate modern developments in American politics. Our primary thesis is that the American political system, built as it is on a conservative constitutional base designed to limit radical action, is nevertheless continually swept by policy change, change that alternates between incremental drift and rapid alterations of existing arrangements. During quiet periods of policymaking, negative feedback dominates; policy innovations seldom capture the imagination of many individuals, so change is slow or rare. During periods of rapid change, positive feedback dominates; each action generates disproportionately large responses, so change accelerates. Critical points occur before the initiation of a positive-feedback process; such periods are referred to as windows of opportunity. Punctuated equilibrium, rather than stability and immobilism, characterizes the American political system.

Given the myriad problems that face all complex societies, issues must normally be assigned to policy subsystems dominated by issue experts. Such specialization is the only way the system can deal with issues in parallel fashion, rather than serially. Parallel processing is necessary for any system to handle many issues simultaneously; this is just as true for a political system as for a large computer. From time to time, however, issues are normally confined to policy subsystems move higher onto the political agenda, where issues are processed only one or a few at a time. This period of agenda access, when new participants become interested in the debate, is when major changes tend to occur, often disrupting one or more policy subsystems. So the political system, combining as it does systems of parallel and serial consideration of many issues, involves the continual creation and destruction of policy subsystems.

Discussing change in American politics in this manner makes it clear that nonincremental change does not imply comprehensive, rational, decision making, nor does it imply that any particular set of decision makers are in control of the process. Issues considered high on the political agenda tend to be dealt with during periods of tremendous optimism or after waves of pessimism have swept through the political system. They are often the results of the efforts of mobilization by those who were not favored by the policy actions while the issue was limited to expert analysis inside the policy subsystem. Rapid change in policy outcomes implies nothing, therefore, about rationality, comprehensiveness, or quality. Vast policy changes may be initiated with neither comprehensiveness nor coordination. So we disagree with those who argue that the American government is in a straightjacket, but we do not dispute the adage that coordinated plans of action are not feasible.

Indeed, our approach, focusing as it does complex interactions among variables at critical periods, suggests that dynamics during periods of nonincremental change are particularly difficult to control. Of course political actors can discern whether the flow of events is generally favoring their proposals or not, and the most skillful political actors may be able to recognize these trends, or national moods, early enough to take advantage of them. As Shakespeare's Brutus tells Cassius,

> There is a tide in the affairs of men
> Which, taken at the flood, leads on to fortune;
> Omitted, all the voyage of their life
> Is bound in shallows and in miseries.
> On such a full sea are we now afloat,
> And we must take the current when it serves
> Or lose our ventures.
>
> (*Julius Caesar*, IV, iii)

Similarly in politics, there are powerful forces of change that sweep through the entire system. These are not controlled or created by any single group or individual, but are the result of multiple interactions among groups seeking to propose new understandings of issues, political leaders seeking new issues on which to make their name, agencies seeking to expand their jurisdictions, and voters reacting to the whole spectacle. Sometimes skillful leaders can foresee an onrushing tide and use their energies to channel it in a particular direction. Others fail to see the tide or attempt to oppose it, virtually always unsuccessfully. Successful political leaders, then, are often those who recognize the power of political ideas sweeping through the system and who take advantage of them to favor particular policy proposals. Leaders can influence the ways in which the broad tides of politics are channeled, but they cannot reverse the tides themselves.

In sum, the American political system is characterized by punctuated equilibrium. The forces that create stability during some periods are the same that combine during critical periods to force dramatic and long-lasting changes during other periods. Rather than being controlled by any single group, institution, or individual, these forces are the result of a complex interconnection of many institutions in society. When they combine to reinforce the pressures for change, their force appears unstoppable. During these periods of change, they can be channeled in particular directions, and the most skillful political leaders may be those who recognize and channel those forces that present themselves during their tenure in power. So the system as a whole is not conservative in the sense of inhibiting all change, but neither is it amenable to simple direction.

Summary of Approach and Findings

We have described the nature of much policy change in America, but the above discussion does not explain it. Our explanation relies on three sources:

the agenda-setting approach; the analysis of policy subsystems; and the social choice school. The study of policy agendas focuses on the manner in which new policy ideas are selected for adoption; hence it implies change. The analysis of policy subsystems centers on organizational arrangements that act to insulate; it focuses on stability. The social choice perspective has clarified the role of equilibrium processes in politics; it has also raised the possibility that they are rare in politics. Bringing together these three important streams of analysis in modern political thought allows the development of a synthesis that simultaneously leads one to look for punctuated equilibria in politics and offers a satisfying explanation of them. Relying on a variety of data sources about the policies and the institutions responsible for them, we have studied the dynamics of punctuated equilibria for extended periods of time.

Our most important findings can be summarized simply.

The American political system spawns numerous policy subsystems which are characterized by inclusion of the interested and exclusion of the apathetic. All of the subsystems we studied were established in the face of weak objections from excluded groups. In the case of nuclear power, some labor unions claimed that the Atomic Energy Commission was a "giveaway" to big business, but really did not follow through strongly. Agricultural subsystems, such as those for tobacco and pesticides, were developed with little or no controversy. Air passengers had little say in the regulations issued for air transportation by the Civil Aeronautics Board. Even in the case of drug and alcohol abuse, where professionals differed on treatment modalities, no one spoke in favor of drunkenness or the marketing of drugs. Apathy is a key variable in politics. Differential intensities of preference lead specialists to be involved constantly, but those with no vested interests become interested in a given policy area only from time to time.

Policy subsystems are often institutionalized as "structure-induced equilibria" in which a prevailing policy understanding dominates. One of the clearest findings from our research is the extent to which a prevailing conception of a policy issue dominates both press coverage and official behavior during periods when policy subsystems are especially strong. A reexamination of figure 6.1 is worthwhile. During the heyday of pesticides, the discourse concerning them almost completely concerned financial and economic issues. The issue was confined to one dimension: the benefits of the application of pesticides compared to the costs of development and application. We have noted similar patterns in the other policies we studied. During periods when differential intensities of preference are strong, and when a favorable public image causes a subsystem to be viewed with benevolence rather than hostility, specialists hurry to create institutional structures designed to protect them from later encroachments. Institutions are the legacies of agenda access. They remain in place for decades, structuring further participation, creating apparent equilibria that can be changed only by changing the institutions themselves.

Those excluded from the policy subsystem constitute "slack resources" that can be mobilized by policy entrepreneurs. Much, but of course not all, policy change comes about because new participants are attracted to an issue. These previously disinterested and apathetic citizens almost always enter on one side of the issue. Hence it is generally in the interest of one side to expand the conflict (they are losing in the existing venue anyway); it is in the interest of the other side to contain the conflict. Mobilization of the apathetic determines whether a particular issue will remain assigned to its protective policy subsystem or whether it may emerge in other political venues.

Mobilization typically occurs through a redefinition of the prevailing policy image. New participants are attracted to the fray as the issue becomes redefined. Seldom do fresh participants enter a political conflict while an issue is confined to a single dimension. Again, figure 6.1 is instructive. The pesticides subsystem became conflictual as the issue was redefined to include not only economics but also health and environmental damage stemming from the application of pesticides. The new participants seldom argued that pesticides were not economically efficient. Rather, they argued that the environmental and health consequences were so severe that they outweighed the economic gains from pesticide use. We observed similar redefinitions in virtually every case we studied. As policy advocates seek to mobilize new groups in favor of their view of a given policy, they systematically seek to alter the ways in which the issue is discussed. Changes in image affect the mobilizations of the apathetic, and the jurisdictional venues to which the issue may be assigned.

There are two contrasting types of mobilization. We have described the difference between a mobilization of enthusiasm, which often creates new institutions in a previous vacuum, and a mobilization of criticism, which often destroys existing arrangements. We have highlighted incidents where subsystems were created during periods of high media interest, but subsystem creation may also follow an inside strategy (Cobb, Ross, and Ross 1976), as in the case of airline regulation. When policy proponents follow an outside strategy, with great interest outside government, we refer to a Downsian mobilization, or a mobilization of enthusiasm. Subsystem destruction (or major alteration), however, almost always occurs through an expansion of conflict, which we have termed a Schattschneider mobilization. In both cases, movement from subsystem politics to high agenda status leads to the alteration of the institutional structures that structure participation. Downsian mobilizations lead to the construction of favorable institutions designed to enhance the powers and autonomy of experts, and Schattschneider mobilizations tend to lead to the breakup of these institutional structures. Each leads to dramatic and long-lasting changes in policy outcomes, because each leaves a distinctive institutional legacy.

Multiple venues in the American political system constitute many opportunities for policy entrepreneurs to appeal. The federal system has often been assailed for inhibiting change because it requires so many actors in various positions of authority to agree on a policy action. From our analysis, it is easy to see that this confuses nonincremental change with rational and comprehensive change. Federalism may very well inhibit top-down coordination of policies; however, its multiple venues do not prohibit change by any means. Many observers of American politics have noted that the states serve as laboratories of democracy as they move ahead to solve problems that have not been raised to the national agenda. Federalism, together with separated powers, adds great dynamism to American policymaking. Just as commentators have complained about the difficulties of control in a federal system, the conflicting claims to jurisdiction among congressional committees have been seen as deleterious to rational policymaking. Yet jurisdictional disputes among committees is one major way that new definitions of policy issues enter into the policy process. The multiple venues of politics are often seen as inhibitors of change, but this may not be true. Federalism, separation of powers, and jurisdictional overlaps are opportunities for change as much as they are inhibitors of change.

The many venues of politics work against conservatism. The existence of multiple policy venues is especially critical in the process of disrupting policy monopolies. Where opponents have many potential venues for appeal, chances are greater that they may succeed. Where a single institution maintains monopolistic control over a particular issue with no chance of appeal to other venues, those with power stand little chance of losing it. The many venues of the American political system therefore make the system amenable to considerable policy change. The federal structure, separation of powers, and the overlapping jurisdictions of many agencies and legislative committees make institutional control unstable in many areas of politics. Thus we must be careful not to confuse the possibilities of rapid change with the ability to control the political system.

New ideas or policy images may spread rapidly across linked venues, thus setting in motion a positive-feedback process. While it is difficult to control a system in which there are many avenues for appeal, many issues move rapidly from one venue to another, as they all react simultaneously or in quick succession to new policy images. In positive-feedback processes characteristic of many agenda-setting processes, the flow of ideas and images across venues can be very rapid. Therefore the complex structures of federalism, divided powers, and jurisdictional overlap do not always work in the direction of favoring immobilism. Rather, they often influence each other, creating a self-reinforcing system leading to much more rapid change than would otherwise be possible.

Venues may be more or less tightly linked, and these linkages may change over time. One important indicator of critical periods in policy development is the extent of linkage among policy venues. In chapter 11 we saw the policy consequences of a federalism that was based on a theory of the national government as policymaker and the states and localities as implementers. The federal grant structure built on the conception of a national domestic policy led to the imposition of more consumption-based policies than the subnational units would have normally preferred. This had the effect of diffusing consumption policies faster than would normally have been the case, so institutions can affect each other formally. Policy venues do not have to be linked formally, however. Many times new venues are activated as aggressive policy activists search for new arenas in which to gain favorable decisions concerning their projects. Professionals operating in different states still read the same journals, go to the same conferences, and learn of new techniques or new information at the same time. Within tightly knit professional communities, a variety of institutional venues may be covered. We observed this most clearly in the case of the policy areas affected by the environmental movement, but the diffusion of child abuse policies is also instructive. The existence of multiple venues often works for, rather than against, rapid policy diffusion.

The intervention of the macropolitical institutions generally reinforces the possibilities of rapid change. As new understandings of issues diffuse through the system, building up momentum through positive-feedback, major national political actors become aware of them and attempt to use them for their own purposes. This further encourages rapid change, providing another link in the positive-feedback process. In our empirical studies, this is most clearly illustrated in the national government's approach to urban problems. Urban problems are conglomerates of more specific problems such as crime, poverty, housing, and transportation. These problems may be seen individually or as the manifestations of an underlying syndrome. During the 1960s, this broader definition of the problem gained greater acceptance, and the issue moved from the states and localities to the national level for action. From disjointed policies aimed at each of the individual problems, a unified approach, involving much more money, was adopted. In chapter 7 we show how the definition of the urban issue pushed it high on the national agenda in the 1960s, and how its disaggregation through the Nixon block-grant program allowed it to be pushed off the national agenda during the late 1970s and early 1980s.

Presidential involvement can be decisive. The personal involvement of the president can play a key role in further strengthening the positive-feedback processes. No other single actor can focus attention as clearly, or change the motivations of such a great number of other actors, as the president. We saw in several cases, most particularly in drugs and urban affairs, how the involvement of the president pushed those issues high onto the agenda. We also have noted a number of cases where similar processes worked without any significant personal involvement by the president. So we conclude that the president is not a necessary actor in all cases, but when he decides to become involved, his influence can be decisive indeed.

Problems and solutions are linked but are considered separately. The nationalization, and subsequent denationalization, of urban problems also illustrates another important point. Just because major political actors call a policy comprehensive does not mean the system is capable of dealing with it in a comprehensive fashion. The urban problem was dealt with in the 1960s and 1970s through a sequence of waves, each carried by a slightly different issue definition and each handled by a different policy community. In the end, governmental response was disjointed rather than global and generated considerable criticism that the federal government had no single urban program. Even though there developed a global perception of the problems of urban areas, this did not imply that the governmental solutions would be similarly large in scope. Rather, each policy solution focused on a single part of the problem.

During periods of positive feedback, the rapid diffusion of new ideas often appears due to the actions of one or a few actors or events, when in fact its causes are more diffuse. John Kingdon (1984) writes of infinite regress when one tries to trace the ultimate source of a policy idea. There is always a precursor. Similarly, one may point to critical interventions in the development of policies, but no single cause of the activity can be found. Indeed, by engaging in the timeless sport of searching for specific causation in social affairs, one runs the risk of attributing causation to one of many contributing factors. We might term this the "*Silent Spring* phenomenon" because Rachel Carson's book served to focus and symbolize the environmental attack on pesticides, but it did not cause the attack, as is sometimes thought. Other examples abound: The accident at Three Mile Island is often said to have killed the nuclear industry, when we know that its future was bleak even before 1979. Similarly, the urban riots of 1967 are sometimes said to have caused the urban initiatives of the 1970s, but in fact those had their seeds even before 1967. As Samuel Popkin has noted, "in remembering we often revise chronology to let a single symbolic event carry the meaning of a complex process" (1991, 112).

In a recent book challenging much of the literature on the impact of the Supreme Court, Gerald Rosenberg (1991) has argued that many of the most important decisions of the Court concerning civil rights, womens' rights, and other issues were in fact not responsible for later policy changes. From our perspective, Rosenberg could not possibly be wrong, but his conclusion that the Court is unimportant is not substantiated either. In a positive-feedback process, single actors are important when their actions combine with those of others. Rosenberg is certainly correct in stating that the Court's decisions alone would not have led to the great changes that came about in the areas he studied. Rather, they reinforced similar decisions in other areas. In a positive-feedback process, no single decision should ever be expected to be decisive. Rather, all depend on the context. Dramatic events, such as Three Mile Island, the urban riots, or important Supreme Court decisions, often come to symbolize the entire process of change to which they merely contribute. The causes of change are much more complex than the behaviors of any single actor.

Long-run societal changes affect policies across the entire political spectrum. Much of our analysis in chapters 9, 10, and 11 concerns changes in the institutions of American politics that affect issue definitions and the establishment of policy subsystems. We have shown how changes in the composition and operation of the interest-group system, Congress, and the federal system have favored certain definitions of issues over others. But we also note that the process of construction and destruction of policy subsystems feeds into broader trends, amplifying them and allowing them to affect still more areas of the economy. The birth of new policy systems provides an institutional legacy for further development of issues associated with the subsystem. As individual policy subsystems are built up or destroyed in a given period of time, these events affect other areas of the political system as well. The cumulative impact of many small changes can often be dramatic changes in the entire political system. So the political system as a whole, not only particular issue areas, may go through periods of stability and rapid change.

Our findings concerning the importance of surges of activity in issue definition and policy subsystem composition are mirrored in an important study by David Mayhew (1991). In examining the ebb and flow of the enactments of major new policies, Mayhew surmises that there have occurred periods of "continuous high energy activity during quite clearly bounded eras" during the twentieth century (1991, 157). Mayhew writes of "interlocking political movements" that are "capable of permeating and animating the two parties—usually one more than the other, but to a substantial degree both" (163). These findings are similar to those that we have reported throughout this book; our emphasis on periods of positive feedback and lurches in policy action finds reinforcement in Mayhew's work.

These points are not the only lessons we can identify from the preceding chapters, but they include some of the most important ones. There are other, larger-scale, implications of our approach. We consider a few of them in the following pages. First, the question of cycles versus instability in politics; then the idea of national moods. We end with discussions of class bias in politics and the limited attention span of government.

Cycles and Instability in Politics

We have interpreted subsystem government as a policymaking system that excludes, either by rules of participation or by self-selection, broader political forces. Subsystems are generally characterized by low interest of political parties, the president, and the mass media. These forces are present, however, at the creation, major alteration, and destruction of subsystems. If organization is the mobilization of bias, so mobilization can cause the bias of organizations. Each mobilizational surge and decline leaves a new organizational structure certain to be different in its bias than the previous one. There exists a great variety of subsystem arrangements within the American national government, in various phases of change. At the creation of many subsystems, a structure-induced equilibrium may be established, forcing a homogeneity of preferences within the system and excluding divergent voices. Often the exclusion of divergent voices is simple, because many subsystems are created on a wave of enthusiasm. Powerful buttressing ideas that are linked to symbols of national importance, such as economic progress, are attached to the system of governance. This was the case for nuclear power, pesticides, and many other issues, as we documented earlier in this book.

We have argued that subsystem governance features a continuous process of discontinuity, that is, subsystems are continually being created, modified, and destroyed. There exist, however, broader swells of politics that support the creation of many similar subsystems in some political eras and encourage their modification or destruction in others. In chapter 9 we showed graphically the changes in the interest-group system in the 1960s and 1970s that modified or destroyed many industrial subsystems. In chapter 10 we analyzed the committee structure of Congress, which has allowed new issue definitions that are antagonistic to old subsystem arrangements to find an institutional expression. In chapter 11 we showed how the flow of policy ideas across venues was affected by the centralization of the federal system during the 1960s and 1970s.

Several observers have suggested that such broad political changes in the United States follow cyclical patterns. Cyclical models imply reactions to excesses and are thus dynamic equilibrium models. Historian Arthur Schlesinger (1986) depicts periods of rapid progressive governmental action interspersed with pragmatic retrenchment, rest, and renewal. Andrew McFarland (1991) has argued that there are regular cycles in American politics based on the creation of powerful subsystems centered on the support of business interests, then the inevitable reaction against them based on consumer protection, democratic egalitarianism, and other ideals. Urban political economists have described cycles of aggressive city program development demanding large budget increases, and reactions of businesses and taxpayers against the corresponding tax burdens (Shefter 1985; Pecorella, 1987). Samuel Huntington (1981) has also discussed a cyclical theory of American politics.

The evidence presented in our book suggests some support for a cyclical view of politics. In particular, we observe a pattern of punctuated change. But we cannot subscribe to cycle theories of politics because we do not see links to political motivations and structures that would imply cycling. Business cycles have their roots in speculative excesses and reactions to them. The causes of political cycles cannot be linked to similar motivations because of what we have called the institutional legacy of agenda-setting. As subsystems are created, new institutions are created that structure future policymaking and the influence of outside groups. These institutional changes need bear no resemblance to those that existed a generation or two previously because each involves a fresh definition of political issues. McFarland also discusses the possibility of cycles superimposed on secular trends (called "spirals" of history), but even this concept implies that the new institutions are reactions to the old, re-creating those that existed one cycle before. While we certainly agree that the mobilization of interests in American politics is a reaction to existing political arrangements, it need not be related to the mobilizations of a generation before. So there are certainly periods of rapid change, as we have shown again and again. However, we would make a mistake to conclude from this that politics is cyclical. A punctuated equilibrium model of the political system differs dramatically from the type of dynamic equilibrium model implicit in any discussion of cycles.

There is another more important problem in discussing cycles of conservative and liberal "moods" in American politics. The manifestations of these moods must occur in an ever-changing economic and social setting. We have focused in this book on a number of issues, showing the creation and breakup of subgovernments. Many of these issues (nuclear power and pesticides in particular) have been part of the general industrial, manufacturing, base of the American economy during the years of postwar economic growth. Industries such as these seem to have been favored in many ways during the period when optimism about the possibilities of creating wealth through scientific progress and manufacturing was high. Later this optimism soured, as we have shown. We should not conclude from an emphasis on the manufacturing economy that such cycles are inevitable, or that trends affect all areas of the economy and political system simultaneously. We need only consider the financial services industry for a counterexample.

As the American economy has shifted from the massive industrial enterprises that dominated during certain periods to the greater power and importance of financial services in the 1980s, powerful new subgovernments have been created in certain areas even while they were being discredited in others. Writing in 1992, we feel it unnecessary to do more than mention the problems in the savings and loan industry stemming from exactly the type of subgovernmental arrangement that many industries would like to foster. "Thrifts" certainly benefited from a supporting public image centering on encouraging family values through mortgages, and we need not detail the institutional arrangements that ultimately led to the excesses of the 1980s. Similarly in bond trading, in the marketing of government securities (see Wessel 1991), and in a variety of service and financial sectors, we suspect that public involvement was low enough to allow a great variety of subgovernments to be created even while others were being destroyed.

This does not mean that political actors do not react to excesses. They clearly do. But we believe that new issue definitions are more important sources of change than the action-reaction model of cycles. As such, an evolutionary model is more relevant to politics than is the regularity implied by a theory of cycles.

National Moods and Public Policies

The public choice approach to democratic institutions studies the correspondence between preference orderings of voters on policy issues to policy outcomes. Its pessimistic outlook on the possibility of democratic equilibrium concerns the impossibility of this matching. There is, however, a second approach followed by some empirical students of representation. What if broad trends in government match broad swings in the national mood? Can this not be treated as an encompassing democratic equilibrium? From this perspective, the creation or destruction of subgovernments is not as important as broad swings in the role of government in the lives of the citizens. A focus on the national mood demands that one first define the national mood. Is it mass opinions or specialized elite concerns? Is it articulated preferences or preferences held even if not articulated? What if some citizens feel more intensely than others? Are their preferences to be weighted differentially?

In this book, we have consistently used the level of media interest in a given topic as an indicator of agenda status. This is not a perfect indicator because it does not necessarily correspond to the concerns of the mass public, weighted or otherwise. We have generally avoided a discussion of how public concerns are related to media attention, since we have only used media attention as an indicator of systemic agenda status and for that purpose it appears justified. When we want to understand why politicians and policymakers react to issues that reach the systemic agenda, however, we need to know: is media interest an indicator of public concern, or does public concern tend to lag official and media interest? Our conceptions of how public opinion is related to public policy hinge on our understanding of causality and time order here. For example, we noted in chapter 4 that public opinion toward nuclear power became strongly negative only after the incident at Three Mile Island, long after the elite-level game had been played out.

In an exhaustive study of public opinion polls since 1956, James Stimson has presented the case that a generalized policy mood undergirds specific opinions on policy issues, and that these underlying changes are "considerably more 'real' than the measured preferences" (1991, 39). Stimson's measure of policy liberalism, which is based on averages from a large number of polls on specific issues, increases from 1956 until the early 1960s, when it begins a long-term secular decline until 1980, after which there is a steady movement toward greater liberalism (118).

None of our series measuring media attention, congressional interest, or policy outputs corresponds to the changes in public mood that Stimson describes throughout his book. His mood variable reaches its most conservative values exactly at the time that many industrial subsystems are collapsing and as vast amounts of money are being directed at domestic problems. It grows steadily more liberal just as tax limitation movements and Reaganomics begin to take hold during the early 1980s. From the evidence presented, it seems probable that policy mood, according to Stimson's definition, responds to policy changes rather than the other way around. When we compare our measures of federal grants going to states and localities, reported in chapter 7, with Stimson's data on liberalism (based on questions asking whether the government is "doing too much" or "not enough" to solve a variety of problems), we find a correlation of -0.51 between the two. The more the government spends, the more conservative the public becomes, apparently. When we lag the grants to predict public opinion a year later, the fit increases slightly, to $-.58$.[1] From these results we may conclude one of two things, depending on which direction we believe the causality flows. If public mood as measured by Stimson causes government responses, then we must conclude that the government systematically moves in the opposite direction as that called for by the public. If, as we argue, government actions generally precede and cause later changes in public mood, then we can see that the public may call for less when the government begins to do too much, then call for more when it perceives the government is beginning to do too little. Public opinion reacts to public policy more than it causes it.

If public opinion seems to lag official actions, the same cannot be said of media attention. There the relationship is more complicated. In several cases we have seen a significant increase in press coverage before any notable increase in congressional interest or other formal agenda activity during an initial period. This happened at least in the cases of nuclear power, pesticides, smoking and tobacco, drugs, child abuse, and urban politics. Once the issue had become an important part of the formal agenda of Congress, however, the relationship between media attention and governmental attention became complicated. In the case of drug policy, stories in the mass media lag congressional hearings for the period after 1970, when the issue first surged onto the national agenda: the media have reacted to official activities as much as they have preceded them in the last two decades. In the case of urban affairs, on the other hand, intense media interest was followed by governmental action during the 1960s and 1970s. But in the later period, official actions remained high while media attention declined dramatically. The relations between media attention and governmental actions can clearly go in either direction. Sometimes media coverage leads to increased demands on the government to act; at other times government actions stimulate more media attention. To

1. A measure of liberalism on urban problems calculated by Stimson is highly related to the general liberalism measure, with a correlation of .78 for the period both were tabulated, since 1965. Using that measure produces similar results to those reported here.

state this complication is not to complain of it: the rapid interactions of the different parts of the policymaking system are part of any positive-feedback mechanism.

More important than whether public opinion is dependent on policy activities, however, is the question of the meaning of national mood. We believe that national mood is a consequence of the confluence of many factors and should not be associated by scholars with pubic opinion alone. Kingdon notes that

> People in and around government sense a national mood. They are comfortable discussing its content, and believe they know when the mood shifts. The idea goes by different names. . . . But common to all . . . is the notion that a rather large number of people out in the country are thinking along certain common lines, that this national mood changes from one time to another in discernible ways, and that these changes in mood or climate have important impacts on policy agendas and policy outcomes. (Kingdon 1984, 153)

The elites that Kingdon interviewed base their feelings of mood on a great variety of sources. Certainly public opinion polls are one of these. But so are the actions of state legislatures, the courts, activist groups in their constituencies, professional associations, and a variety of other actors. Policymakers are especially attuned to what they perceive as trends, so positive-feedback processes are particularly important in the perception of a changing mood. Public opinion is, as we have argued, one of many venues in a pluralistic society. As a component of the national mood perceived by policymakers, it certainly plays an important role. However, if the policymakers themselves are unwilling to rely on only one source of information, neither should we as analysts. Political leaders may appeal to mass publics, and mass publics certainly have the capacity to respond. Our evidence suggests that mass mobilizations and public opinion reactions often occur late in the issue development process, after many of the most important issues have already been decided during elite-level debates and jurisdictional battles of which we have observed many examples in these pages. E. E. Schattschneider has been credited with asking a question that we can only paraphrase: Why study the audience when the actors are up on the stage? Like many of his comments, this one remains as relevant today as when he first uttered it.

Punctuated Equilibrium and the Question of Bias

The American system, it is said, provides privileged elites special protection through what we have called policy monopolies: exclusive policy subsystems buttressed by powerful images. While Schattschneider was clearly correct in his observation that "organization is the mobilization of bias," his aphorism underestimates the fragility of organization in politics. Indeed, over the long run, the American system seems to provide little respect for those who are able to construct policy monopolies. Like the subsystems of nuclear power, pesticides, and air regulation—and like the intergovernmental lobby and the treatment professionals in drug policy—organization can mobilize bias, but there is no guarantee of its permanence.

Schattschneider pointed to two kinds of political bias, however. The first is the notion that new policy ideas are shut out of the policy process. This, as we have shown, is not always the case. The second is symbolized by his complaint that the "flaw in the pluralist heaven is that the heavenly chorus sings with a strong upper-class accent" (1960, 35). Here Schattschneider considers not the exclusion of ideas but the exclusion of classes. Many issues processed by modern democratic political systems have little to do with class bias. For example, many of the issues we have studied in this book involve the complex interplay of middle-class interests. Further, we have noted how the opinions of the mass public often react to, rather than precede, elite-level political bargaining. We think the policy changes we have observed and documented throughout this book have had important consequences for all Americans. Nevertheless, we cannot help but note that the American political system seems more devoted to the processing of issues of interest to various factions of the middle class than those of benefit to the lower classes.

How one understands an issue goes far in explaining how one thinks that it relates to class interests. Certainly in American politics, issues that are phrased in terms of class interests, or as protecting the lower classes against business interests, have little chance of success. However, we suspect that many issues with important redistributive consequences do indeed get serious treatment in the American political system and that many times the disadvantaged win. These policies may not be phrased in terms of class conflict (and perhaps if they were they would not be adopted), but they may still have such consequences. We noted the growth of the environmental movement in chapter 9. This movement, as others have shown, was largely a middle-class endeavor. Certainly there has not been a similar mobilization of unemployed workers, undereducated service workers, or other groups that are disadvantaged. However, there have been important civil rights movements with at least as much impact on race relations as the environmental movement has had on industrial policies. Current concern in the United States with the health insurance industry may be driven by business and middle-class interests; however, it may very well provide low-cost health insurance to millions of poor people who are currently locked out of the system. The process of mobilization and of punctuated equilibrium that we have described in these pages often involves conflicting elites or middle-class interests. However, its dynamics affect all areas of the political system, and the multiple venues and rapid changes that it makes possible ensure that if lower-class groups certainly do not have equal say, neither do small groups of elites control the process.

Limited Attention Spans and Government

The existence of multiple policy venues in American politics implies that the system can process many different issues at once. It has impressive parallel processing capabilities, in other words, and these seem even to increase over time (see Beecher, Lineberry, and Rich 1981). On the other hand, political leaders must deal with things in serial fashion. The result of these parallel and serial processing systems operating simultaneously is inevitably that political systems appear to have limited short-term attention spans. That is, there are periods during which some problems gain disproportionate attention from many policy venues, in particular from the national leaders. It is easy to complain of a system where high-level attention seems to lurch quickly from issue to issue, with little regard to the seriousness of the emerging issues or to the effectiveness of the policies recently decided on.

Herbert Simon (1985) has described a "bottleneck of attention" in human cognition, in which complex reality is simplified and processed for decision making. Such a bottleneck, the point where parallel processing, made possible by the operation of many autonomous policy subsystems working simultaneously, meets the serial processing of the nation's political leadership, also fits our observations of the political system. To say there is a parallel between how individuals deal with choices and how the entire political system makes similar decisions is not to imply that the same processes determine them. Our point here is simpler: whatever models one may use of political decision-makers or of entire decision-making systems must be consistent with our observations of lurches and lulls. No matter what the ability of experts to work independently, from time to time there must be higher-level political involvement. Since this involvement cannot be constant in more than a handful of cases, the entire system must be subject to lurches and lulls. Just as individuals may act purposefully but not rationally, in that they may not be able to process all the information they have at their disposal, so the political system cannot. Its leaders certainly act to achieve certain goals. However, they cannot deal with all issues equally, so their involvement in any one area is sporadic and destabilizing. The agenda-setting process creates lurches and lulls in politics.

Mass mobilization, like attention, cannot be maintained forever. Issues once in the public eye eventually recede. The continual emergence and recession of a variety of issues from the public agenda allow the broader system to deal with a great variety of issues over time. Further, this mechanism of sporadic interest hinders the stultifying and self-serving incrementalism that could result if issues were permanently of interest only to the same groups. A lurching system is more adaptive than a slothful one, even if neither conforms to any rational ideal.

We come back to a basic feature with which we began this book: the absence of equilibria in politics. We have suggested that our government can best be understood as a series of institutionally enforced stabilities, periodically punctuated by dramatic change. There may be some broad equilibrium, in the sense that, as McFarland writes, cycles of power for one group eventually lead them to commit "excesses" that lead to the countermobilization of others opposed to them. However, in the emphasis on the equilibrium value of these possible waves, analysts have overlooked some important features of the American political system. Its most fundamental features and public policy actions can be affected for decades at a time by critical periods during which new institutions are created and new understandings of old problems are promulgated. These periods of change, when they occur, are likely to leave institutional legacies that will structure, influence, and bias public policy outcomes for decades. Political scientists would do better to explain these disruptive periods and their implications than to try to fit them into models of stability and incrementalism.

PART FOUR

Agendas and Instability
Fifteen Years Later

We based our original inferences on intensive, cross-time studies of several policy subsystems. Can the arguments we made based on those case studies be sustained in light of the passage of time, the conduct of numerous relevant studies, and the availability of better data? What can we conclude about the general dynamics of the public policy process from the evidence that has accumulated since 1993?

In this section, we return to the issues that were at the core of the analysis presented in the previous chapters, and we update and extend our analyses of the policy subsystems we studied in the first edition. In particular, we examine nuclear power, tobacco policy, and urban affairs. Our updates indicate that our original analyses continue to offer insights to the dynamics of policy subsystems, which of course is a major reason for this second edition.

On the other hand, recent developments suggest that the dynamical processes we postulated may be considerably broader than the subsystem-based analysis common in the study of policy processes. After all, all policy areas do not exhibit the kind of powerful policy monopolies or entrenched subsystems as we studied in the cases of tobacco, pesticides, and nuclear power. And the breakup of a subsystem, such as those we have described, does not necessarily create another. In sum, the punctuated equilibrium view is not and should not be limited to analyses of policy monopolies, though the cases we chose for study in this book were dominated by such cases.

How do electoral processes and broader social trends affect the course of public policymaking? In our concluding comments, we suggest a broader perspective, one that we term *disruptive dynamics* to indicate that punctuated policy equilibrium is but one very important component of a more general process. This broader perspective requires the integration of changes driven by

elections and political parties into the standard policymaking focus on interest groups, government officials, and legislative committees. We turn first to a
review of more recent developments in some of the policy areas we originally
studied, and in our last chapter we consider the broader questions of punctuations and dynamics associated with micro- and macrolevel changes to the
political system.

13

Policy Subsystems, Punctuated Equilibrium, and Theories of Policy Change

In the decade and a half since we published the first edition of this book, an outpouring of studies of the dynamics of public policy has appeared. Most of these confirmed our findings here that policy subsystems are subject to long periods of drift and incrementalism, only to be disrupted occasionally by bursts of frenetic policy activity. We will not review these findings here, as we have recently done so elsewhere (True, Jones, and Baumgartner 2007).

One thing that is clear from this literature is that policy punctuations are not confined to the complex and pluralistic American system, but occur in many European parliamentary systems. So our explanations must move beyond the particulars of the American system to some more general aspects of the manner in which policymaking systems operate. Of course, the multiplicity of venues and the lack of party discipline in US politics contrasts with many European systems, so our focus on the interactions of shifting venues and changing policy images can seem peculiarly American. When we or others have looked at other political systems, however, we have found more in common than in contrast. The European Union has created a new level of government available for appeal by strategic entrepreneurs in European policy disputes. Governments everywhere deal with a crush of many complex public policies, ensuring that, just as in America, the small set of issues currently on the agenda will be only a subset of the possible ones and that the dimensions of debate gaining the most attention will be only a small part of the total, and therefore may shift over time. A special issue of the *Journal of European Public Policy* was devoted to comparative studies of policy agendas in 2006 (Baumgartner, Jones, and Green-Pedersen 2006), and we have looked at budgeting processes in over a dozen different political systems, finding strong evidence for punctuated equilibrium in each case (Jones et al. 2007). These systems were not only national systems but also existed at the level of US states and even at the school district financing level (see also Robinson 2004). Clearly, something interesting is going on. In *The Politics of Attention* we focused on explaining the broad applicability of the punctuated equilibrium approach, and our explanation dealt mostly with cognitive characteristics of human decision making in showing why certain features of our model should be visible in so many different contexts, not only the ones that we explored in this book.

Another aspect of our earlier work, sometimes given less attention in subsequent years, is our focus on stability, the forces that maintain most policy issues in equilibrium most of the time. Negative feedback mechanisms abound in American politics; institutions that control given policies do not usually lose control in the kind of disruptive cascades of attention that we have nonetheless documented from time to time. Such events *do* of course occur. But for most issues most of the time, stability rules the day. We have written extensively about the causes of this stability in the years since 1993 when this book first appeared. The most important is scarcity of attention. Most issues, most of the time, are understood the way they were understood in previous periods, and they are controlled by the institutional actors and vested interests who were active in that policy area in the previous period as well. The causes of change, we noted, typically work to reinforce, not to destabilize, established policy subsystems. So while some have suggested that ours is a theory of instability or punctuation, a punctuated equilibrium approach must be understood as placing equal focus on both the punctuations *and* the periods of equilibrium behavior. The key question is whether the interactions among the many actors involved in a given policy issue will be driven by negative feedback producing stability or whether positive feedback processes may break out, creating explosive change (Wood 2006b).

What about the particular subsystems we studied in this book? Can the arguments we made based on those case studies be sustained in light of the passage of time and the availability of better data? In this chapter we return to the issues that are the core of the analysis presented in the previous chapters, and we update and extend our analyses of the policy subsystems we studied in the first edition. In particular, we examine nuclear power, tobacco policy, and urban affairs. Then we suggest a more general understanding of punctuated equilibrium, one that may incorporate changes driven by elections and parties as well as interest groups, government officials, and legislative committees. We have little doubt that our original analyses offer insights not only into the subsequent developments relating to the particular issues and industries we studied in the earlier edition, but more generally as well.

Nuclear Power

In our examination of nuclear power, we detailed the collapse of a policy subsystem as its policy image was transformed in the political debate from benign to malevolent. We showed how environmentalists and consumer activists attacked the network of government subsidies and favorable regulations through a multiplicity of venues, and how in the end it was economic realities that spelled the end of the commitment of utility companies to nuclear power. Utility companies whose production assets included nuclear facilities found that their stock values declined relative to other utilities, a process driven in part by the increased costs associated with increased regulation of the nuclear power industry and the uncertainty caused by activist mobilizations.

Here we add some important details to the nuclear power story, and examine what may be a new life for the industry, due the concerns about climate change (since nuclear facilities don't burn carbon) and increases in the costs of other fuel sources.

Fleshing out the Nuclear Story

We can examine in more detail the nuclear power story using the expanded general capacity of the Policy Agendas Project. In particular, evidence of the "dual mobilization thesis" that we examined in chapter 5 is clearly evident in the new data. We will examine two sources: congressional hearings and statements by presidents in their State of the Union speeches.

Figure 13.1 provides a simple count of the number of hearings on nuclear power. Clearly in evidence on the graph are two periods of intensified congressional interest in nuclear power: the first from 1946 through the late 1950s; the second from the late 1970s through the late 1980s.

Our argument in chapter 5 centered on the notion that these two waves could be characterized by two different policymaking dynamics: one centering on enthusiasm, as government adopted new approaches to policy problems, and one based on criticism, as major problems came to be recognized as policymaking unfolded. A *mobilization of enthusiasm* tended to suppress criticism, and hence was one-sided, whereas a *mobilization of criticism* involved the oftentimes harsh give-and-take between policy proponents and opponents.

An examination of the content of these hearings confirms that the two periods of policymaking attention were characterized by different dynamics. Let us take 1957, the year in which Congress conducted the most hearings after the subsystem start-up period (after World War II) as emblematic of the early period. We find mostly supportive hearings, including such topics as "development, growth, and state of the atomic energy industry"; "participation act for the international atomic energy agency"; and "proposals under power demonstration program." There was congressional discussion of nuclear safety and accidents, but it was in the context of enacting the Price-Anderson Nuclear Industries Indemnity Act that year. A major reason for the act was to ensure potential investors that they would face only limited liability for a nuclear accident. Even when safety was discussed, it was in the frame of promoting the industry.

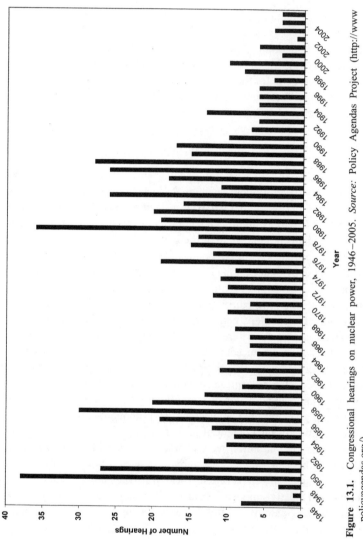

Figure 13.1. Congressional hearings on nuclear power, 1946–2005. *Source:* Policy Agendas Project (http://www .policyagendas.org/).

The tenor of hearings conducted during the second wave of congressional interest was strikingly less supportive. On March 28, 1979, the Three Mile Island (TMI) nuclear power facility near Harrisburg, Pennsylvania experienced what the Nuclear Regulatory Commission later called "the most serious [incident] in U.S. commercial nuclear power plant operating history" (US Nuclear Regulatory Commission 2004). The sequence of events led to a partial meltdown of the reactor core in Unit 2, a small release of radiation, but no deaths or injuries. It led to sweeping regulatory reform.

Readers of chapter 4 know that nuclear power in the United States was in trouble long before the accident (see also Robert Duffy's excellent 1997 book explaining in detail the evolution of the issue). Figure 13.1 shows that congressional attention in nuclear power peaked in 1979, but that it had been building since the early 1970s, and the matters covered in the hearings were nothing short of a nightmare for nuclear utilities and government regulators. According to data provided by the Policy Agendas Project, twenty-eight of the thirty-six hearings during 1979 centered on reactor safety, emergency planning, civil defense, or directly on the TMI accident.

The accident came at a time of heightened scrutiny of the industry. In 1975, Congress investigated a fire at the TVA's Brown's Ferry, Alabama, facility and general safety issues. In 1976, ten of the twelve hearings centered on problems of reactor safety, waste disposal, and the safeguarding of materials. In 1977, hearings centered on the escalating costs of producing nuclear power as well as reactor safety. In 1978, Congress questioned the accuracy of testimony received from the NRC, problems with plant shutdowns, and held five hearings on plant-siting issues. TMI occurred in an increasingly skeptical regulatory and legislative environment.

It is fascinating that this negative legislative environment occurred in the midst of a severe energy crisis. In 1973, the Organization of Petroleum Exporting Countries (OPEC), a producer cartel, pushed the price of oil dramatically higher (the price tripled), and did so again in 1979, doubling the price. Yet we find no hearings on nuclear power as a source of domestic energy until 1980, and even in 1981 most hearings continued to dwell on TMI (this time the cost of the cleanup).

Even though nuclear power was bound up in environmentalism, energy, and technology, the issue generally avoided the politicization associated with partisan conflict. During the wave of enthusiasm associated with the establishment of the nuclear power subsystem, presidents, both Democratic and Republican, served as chief cheerleaders. Table 13.1 provides a count and a general flavor of statements on nuclear power made during the presidents' annual State of the Union speeches. Presidents Truman, Eisenhower, and Kennedy all made supportive statements, and Johnson ignored the issue.

As the subsystem began to collapse in the mid-1970s, President Ford tried to put the industry on sounder footing without ignoring the problems. In 1975,

Table 13.1 Presidents' comments on nuclear power in their State of the Union
addresses, 1946–2005

Date	President	Number of Comments	Representative Comment Summaries
1946	Truman	1	Proposing AEC
1947	Truman	3	"our hope that this new force may ultimately be turned into a blessing for all nations"
1948	Truman	1	Industrial progress
1950	Truman	2	New wonders of peaceful development
1951	Truman	2	Atomic power urgent for government
1955	Eisenhower	1	"There is promise of progress in our country's plan for the peaceful use of atomic energy"
1958	Eisenhower	1	Inspiration of Atoms for Peace
1959	Eisenhower	1	Budget proposal
1961	Kennedy	1	"Atomic energy has improved the ability of the healing professions to combat disease"
1975	Ford	6	Energize a troubled industry
1976	Ford	2	Expedite safe and clear nuclear power
1981	Carter*	10	Comprehensive energy program with nuclear power as a major component, but with safeguards
1989	GW Bush	2	Modernize industry and increase plant safety
1993	Clinton	1	"We are eliminating programs that are no longer needed, such as nuclear power research and development"

*Carter gave a "farewell" State of the Union speech in 1981, even though he had been
defeated the previous November.

he pointed to increasing problems in the industry, and promoted the development of two hundred new nuclear plants in response to the energy crisis; in 1976, he tied nuclear power to the general energy issue, and promoted a program to produce "clean and safe nuclear power." Carter actively promoted the use of nuclear fuel in attempts to formulate a national comprehensive energy plan based both on conservation and production.[1] But Reagan never mentioned nuclear power in his annual speeches. George H. W. Bush again tried to raise the issue of nuclear plant modernization in 1989, but subsequently dropped the issue. Clinton's only mention of nuclear energy was a cryptic mention of eliminating funding for nuclear power research and development as part of an initiative to "eliminate programs that are no longer needed."

A New Era for the Nuclear Power Subsystem?

As late as 1999, almost all congressional hearings on nuclear power centered on safety. But climate change was fast developing as the most important

1. Carter gave an unusual 1981 State of the Union Speech, even though he had been defeated the previous November, in which he detailed his plan.

environmental issue, and nuclear power produces virtually no greenhouse gasses. Moreover, after declining in real dollars from 1980 through 2000, the price of oil began to rise, and has risen steadily since. The course of events had begun to favor the nuclear industry.

Public attitudes were becoming more sympathetic. In a *New York Times–CBS* poll taken in April of 2007, respondents were asked whether they would approve of "building more nuclear plants to generate electricity." Responses indicated that 45 percent approved, while 47 percent disapproved. By June, 51 percent approved while 42 percent disapproved. However, if the question was modified to add "in your community," approval in April dropped to 36 percent, and disapproval jumped to 59 percent (40 percent and 55 percent respectively in June). While this looks rather bleak for the future of nuclear power, the industry fares well in comparison to coal: only 41 percent approved of new coal plants in April, with 51 percent disapproving. In a Bloomberg Poll about a year earlier, respondents were asked if they would "support or oppose the increased use of nuclear power as a source of energy in order to prevent global warming." Adding the phrase "global warming" generates much higher levels of support: 61 percent support and only 30 percent oppose. On the other hand, only 6 percent supported more nuclear plants to relieve energy shortages.[2]

After the terrorist attacks in September of 2001, Congress held a few hearings on reactor security, but by 2005 had begun to focus on nuclear energy as part of a comprehensive national energy policy. Early in the Bush administration, Vice President Cheney had convened an energy task force (which became controversial because of its secrecy). The administration produced an energy program high on increasing productive capacity of carbon-based energy sources and nuclear power within the country (including repeated attempts to allow drilling in the environmentally sensitive Arctic National Wildlife Refuge), but low on promoting alternate energy sources and conservation. In 2006, for the first time, President Bush discussed nuclear power as a component of his "Advanced Energy Initiative." While he did highlight alternate energy sources such as biodiesel, solar, and wind, he discussed neither conservation nor the climate change issue. The energy issue was much more connected to the increased partisan divisions in the nation than when Presidents Nixon and Carter offered more balanced energy initiatives.

By 2005, utilities had begun to explore the possibility of building new nuclear facilities. In December of 2007, Congress passed an appropriations bill containing almost a billion dollars for research, development, and promotion of nuclear industry. Signs were that the nuclear power subsystem was getting back in business.

Without the climate issue it is unlikely that environmentalists would have quietly tolerated (and in some instances, actively promoted) these measures, or that many politicians would have promoted them either, given the long-

2. Reported at Pollingreport.com (http://www.pollingreport.com).

standing public concern about the industry. These new measures were a direct result of new information coming into the political system, and not a result of some sort of restoration of the old order under a conservative Republican administration with roots in the energy industry. As in the 1970s, energy supply alone does not seem to work as an argument in favor of the industry, even when energy costs are rapidly escalating. Rather than a simple partisan explanation (after all, Presidents Reagan and George H. W. Bush had certainly not presided over a resurgence of the nuclear industry, and seven years into his term George W. Bush could not claim to have done so either), the possible return of nuclear power has to do with shifting foci of attention.

We cannot say for sure what the future of civilian nuclear power in the United States will be. However, it is clear that the topic of attention will determine the tone, as has happened in the past. To the extent that public attention focuses on issues of climate change, nuclear power (as a non carbon-producing source of energy) will generate increased positive attention. If attention focuses on questions of international proliferation of nuclear material, terrorist attacks, and waste disposal, on the other hand, criticism and opposition will be more apparent. Signs suggest that issues of climate change have indeed caused some significant attention to nuclear power as a potential solution to global climate problems. However, the disposal of nuclear waste remains a tremendous political problem, evidenced by the lack of final congressional approval and remaining controversy surrounding the proposed Yucca Mountain nuclear waste depository in Nevada. Depending on where attention focuses, the industry might remain stalled or it may come back.[3]

Because tracing the tone of media coverage is so important in assessing the success or failure of a policy image, we have updated our analysis of media coverage in figure 13.2. Figure 4.1 presented the number of articles on civilian nuclear power and the percentage of those articles that were coded positive from the perspective of the industry. In presenting those data, we relied on analyses previously conducted by Spencer Weart (1988), who graciously provided his data. In order to update the figure, we first had to replicate the earlier data to understand exactly the coding rules and procedures used by Weart, so figure 13.2 presents both the original data from figure 4.1, our replication (for the last several data points), and then the update.[4] Figure 13.2a shows the amount of attention to the industry. The original figure showed two surges in attention around 1960 and again around 1980. Our replication of the number of stories is nearly perfect, and the continuation of the trend line shows that

3. We are referring here to the construction of new nuclear power plants in the United States. Internationally, signs are that many countries will begin or expand construction projects. In that sense, the US nuclear industry may well be revived, but it may focus on building plants overseas, especially in China, rather than at home.

4. These data were updated by Penn State student Mary Gardner, who worked under the supervision of Baumgartner; thanks to Mary for allowing us to use them here.

Policy Subsystems, Punctuated Equilibrium, and Policy Change

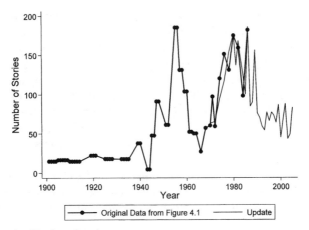

A. Number of stories per year.

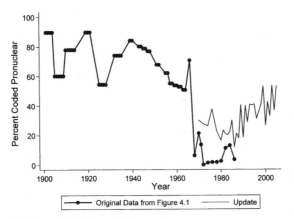

B. Percent of stories coded pronuclear.

Figure 13.2. *Readers' Guide* stories on civilian nuclear power. *Source:* Updated from figure 4.1 using the *Readers' Guide*.

attention has declined to relatively low levels, similar to the situation in the early 1960s before the wave or criticism took place in the 1970s and beyond.

Part B of the figure replicates the tone of the coverage. Here we showed earlier a tremendous drop from relatively pronuclear coverage in the early years until a sudden shift to a much more critical tone beginning in 1968. Our replication of these data was less accurate than with the simple counts of stories. Compared to Weart's original data, we show a somewhat more positive tone of coverage, though the trends are roughly parallel and the numbers are, in either version, quite heavily critical of the industry. Looking at the period since our previous analysis ended, we see a moderate increase in the tone of coverage.

Essentially, media coverage remains split between hopeful coverage of nuclear power as a potential solution to the problems of global warming and critical stories focusing especially on issues of waste disposal.[5] We see the tentative beginnings of resurgence, but no dramatic surge in attention, and great ambivalence so far with about a 60/40 split in the tone of coverage, with more critical rather than supportive stories. This is, of course, a dramatic improvement from the late 1970s when good news was much less common than that.

Nuclear power remains a complex issue. Public, official, and media discussions of it, on the other hand, remain highly stylized. There are two diametrically opposed images associated with the industry, now as in the past. While there are some signs of a nuclear resurgence, the issue has not risen to anywhere near its previous levels of attention, either that associated with its original expansion, some fifty years ago, or its collapse three decades ago.

Tobacco

Our update of tobacco policy confirms most key aspects of our earlier investigation, but it also suggests some modifications. The dynamics of change described in the 1993 edition are pretty much confirmed, but the particular manifestations of them are somewhat different. Updating the story we told in chapter 5, which ended in the early 1990s, changes the story considerably, but reconfirms the pattern of disruptive dynamics we delineated earlier. However, the longer period in which disruptive dynamics have operated in tobacco regulation without a clear restoration of equilibrium indicates that a system can be characterized by disruption and punctuations without settling down into an equilibrium pattern for a very long time.

We may think of a policymaking system as consisting of inputs, based on information about social conditions and perceived problems, and outputs, which are the public policy reactions to that information. Information processing is not smooth and effortless in humans or in political systems; rather, it is disjoint and episodic. There are many reasons for this, but we may classify them into two broad categories (Jones and Baumgartner 2005). First, there are aspects of governing institutions that retard the translation of information into policy responses. In the United States, policy action requires overcoming considerable friction because of supermajority requirements, as is well recognized.

But there is a second source of friction, one that stems from how people process information and think about problems. We term this *cognitive friction.*

5. Note that we do not include, in either analyses, discussion of military or international events relating to the industry. Positive events internationally would be discussions of plans by other countries to build new plants, for example. Negative stories would be focused on safety hazards, nuclear proliferation, or other such aspects. Negatives are likely to far outweigh positives in this realm though we have not done a formal analysis.

Kingdon (1984) notes the barriers to translating factual situations into problems that are viewed as amenable to action by government. We noted above that information relevant to government action is processed through policy images, and these images spur people to action. Not infrequently, people deal with competing images of a policy, and this can lead to considerable ambivalence in processing information about policy targets. These images often compete for ascendancy in media coverage of the topic, as well as for space on the governmental agenda. Or stated more precisely, policy entrepreneurs use images to compete for space on the media and governmental agendas. These policy images carry with them a tone or valence; the prevalence of positive or negative images in the media and in the halls of government are critical components in policy success.

For many polices, the dynamics at play during periods of intense general attention are distinctly different from the politics during periods of inattention. That is clearly the case for tobacco policy, where variation in collective attention to the problem and variations in the tone of the image both motivated policy entrepreneurs and had strong effects on policy outcomes. In effect, seemingly disfavored groups (judged by the standard metric of money and access) were able to offset their disadvantages by transforming the information that was accumulating from the medical community about the health effects of tobacco into images that resonated in the policy process, but this was anything but simple.

Arguments that had previously been tried with scant success gained traction with the accumulation of evidence. In addition, smoking opponents mounted entirely new arguments, or adopted significantly different angles to old arguments. In particular, opponents countered industry arguments that statistical correlations can't prove cancer in individual cases (which had successfully shielded the industry from thousands of individual lawsuits) by suing on behalf of state Medicare funds. These taxpayer-supported systems enrolled millions of members, so that statistical correlations between smoking and health consequences were bound to hold. Similarly, in response to an industry focus that smoking is an individual choice, opponents sought to focus on workers' rights issues: employers could not force workers to work in smoky environments. As these environments include bars and restaurants, in addition to office workplaces, smoking bans have proliferated. These events have enraged many smoking supporters, as their previously successful arguments were turned against them. In any event, the industry has been transformed and the events we described in chapter 5 have only gotten stronger in the ensuing decades.

Tobacco and Health

Literally for centuries people have strongly suspected that tobacco was harmful to human health. In 1604 King James I of England published "A Counter-

Blaste to Tobacco" in which he described smoking as "a custome lothsome to the eye, hateful to the Nose, harmefull to the braine, dangerous to the Lungs, and the blacke stinking fume thereof, nearest resembling the horrible Stigian smoke of the pit that is bottomelesse" (James I 1604/1869). In 1665 the first medical report on the harms of tobacco was published (Glantz et al. 1998). Beginning in the 1940s an outpouring of studies linking cigarette smoking to cancer, heart disease, and a host of other ills came literally pouring out of the medical research community.

The U.S. Center for Disease Control and Prevention (2006) reports that in 2001 160,372 deaths were due to tobacco smoking. Since there were 553,888 cancer deaths in 2004, this computes to over 29 percent of cancer deaths attributable to smoking (National Center for Health Statistics 2004). Add to that the 131,503 cardiovascular-related deaths attributable to tobacco (of 652,486) and some 102,632 deaths related to respiratory diseases, and the grim toll of tobacco becomes vividly clear.

Nevertheless, there has always been a positive side to the tobacco image. As King James railed against tobacco, his colonists were naming a settlement in the New World after him in Virginia, and brought in the first tobacco crop in 1611. Virginia was destined to become one of the great tobacco producing regions of the world, and a great source of income and trade for England; in 1999, it was still the state's fifth-leading agricultural crop (Tobacco in Virginia 2000). Throughout the years, tobacco has been an important agricultural crop, and the manufacture of cigarettes and other tobacco products remains a highly lucrative business. Moreover, tobacco has generally also had a positive social image in the past—smoking was associated in popular lore and in advertising with independence and free choice.

We analyzed these competing images in the media in chapters 5 and 6 from 1900 through 1987, showing that tobacco interests were less successful in maintaining a positive image when attention increased. Expansion of conflict operates against entrenched interests. Figure 13.3 shows that this pattern continued to hold through 2002. This is important because a second wave of policymaking activity occurred in the mid-to-late 1990s, and this wave is important to the story of the declining fortunes of the tobacco industry in governmental affairs. Media coverage during this wave differed from the wave that occurred during the 1960s with the initial Surgeon General's report linking smoking to cancer because it emerged when the image of tobacco in the media was already very low. There was no collapse in the media image because there was no way it could go down.

However the new wave of activity offers an opportunity to reexamine the connection between media coverage and tone. Figure 13.4 plots the number of articles in the *Readers' Guide* against the percentage of those articles deemed to be positive. The figure shows very clear threshold effects, in this case at around eighteen entries in the *Readers' Guide* per year. Once that level was reached, virtually all coverage about tobacco in the media is unfavorable.

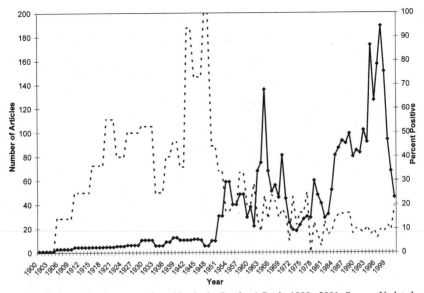

Figure 13.3. Annual coverage of smoking in the *Readers' Guide,* 1900–2001. *Source:* Updated from data provided by Neilson 2002.

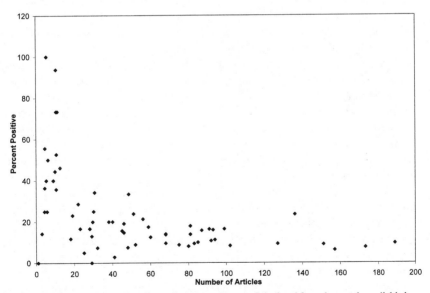

Figure 13.4. Threshold effects in media images. *Source:* Calculated from data made available by Lars B. Nielson.

Table 13.2 Topic and tone of tobacco coverage in the *New York Times Index,* 1946–2001*

Topic of coverage	Positive	Negative	Neutral or Uncodeable	Total
Economical or Financial	51.62%	17.96%	30.42%	100%
	(431)	(150)	(254)	(835)
Governmental actions or Court proceedings	18.12%	62.79%	19.09%	100%
	(469)	(1625)	(494)	(2588)
Health	9.56%	80.72%	9.72%	100%
	(61)	(515)	(62)	(638)
Other	16.11%	44.73%	39.16%	100%
	(130)	(361)	(316)	(807)
Total	22.41%	54.46%	23.13%	100%
	(1091)	(2651)	(1126)	(4868)

*Data from the first edition updated by Neilson (2002).

Neilson's (2002) update of our 1993 data on *New York Times* coverage on smoking and health (table 13.2 and figure 13.5) shows that the pattern we reported in table 6.2 continues to hold, with financial matters continuing to shrink and coverage of government actions and court proceedings occupying an increasingly large proportion of stories. He finds, moreover, that negative coverage increased in every category, indicating that not only were the topics of coverage shifting, but any positive tone within those categories was evaporating. The industry faced a very hostile media environment.

The issue, however, "went dormant" even in an atmosphere of media negativity. It was not enough for health professionals to win the media image war. They had done that by the late 1960s. Yet the tobacco support program remained, and the health warnings on tobacco products were proving a defense in court for companies sued by individuals. When plaintiffs contended that the companies had sold a harmful product and admitted it on the packaging, the companies defended themselves by pointing out that the plaintiff had chosen to smoke even after reading the warning. In effect, the companies had mounted a very successful defense that essentially maintained that "in America, you may chose to damage your own health, and all government is obliged to do is to warn you." While the policy monopoly was broken, and big tobacco could expect little help from government, the drifting of the issue from the agenda after 1971, when they accepted a ban on advertising on television, actually allowed the industry to regroup.

President Lyndon Johnson's Surgeon General, Luther L. Terry, stimulated the first wave of media interest and policymaking activity with the 1964 report of his Advisory Committee, *Smoking and Health* (U.S. Department of Health, Education and Welfare 1964). This began a series of public health reports warning of the dangers of smoking; twenty-nine have been issued from 1964 through

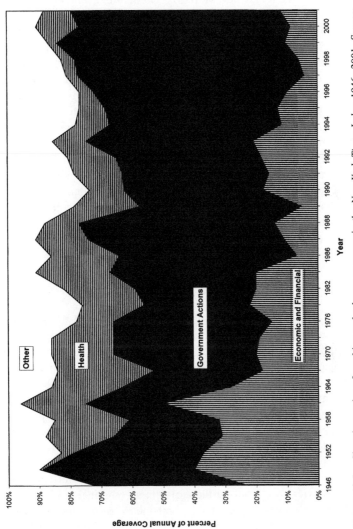

Figure 13.5. Changing topics of smoking and tobacco coverage in the *New York Times Index*, 1946–2001. *Source:* Neilson 2002, updated from figure 6.2, Baumgartner and Jones 1993.

2006.[6] Most of these had little effect beyond the public health community, but the 1980s reports of C. Everett Koop, President Reagan's Surgeon General, on secondhand smoke and nicotine addiction ignited a firestorm (Studlar 2002). The smoker may choose to smoke, but the restaurant patron or bartender in the smoking establishment may not. Moreover, children in the home suffer health effects due to secondhand smoke, and are clearly blameless.

In the smoking wars, it was important for public health officials to connect smoking to cancer and heart disease. That caused a collapse in the positive tone of tobacco, and this led to important public policy outcomes. But that alone was not enough. As Schneider and Ingram (1993) have shown us, the target of the policy matters. When the activity involves one's own health, the general opinion seems to be that warnings are enough. When the activity harms other innocent parties, government regulation is both more justified in economic theory (where these are termed "externalities") and apparently in the general opinion of the public. In the new cigarette wars, workplace safety became the new battleground. Here we see important ways in which scientific evidence, mediated through official government reports with their attendant legitimacy, gave the ammunition to advocates subsequently to seek where these new facts could have their greatest impact. As the tobacco image was reframed, a mixture of facts as well as creative searching for the best arguments and the best venues by policy entrepreneurs was apparent.

Promoting Tobacco

As the negative image increased with the supply of health-related information, the positive images came under attack. The Agricultural Adjustment Act of 1938 established marketing quotas for tobacco and other commodities in order to keep prices for farmers high. The Supreme Court found the quota system for tobacco constitutional in 1939 (*Mulford v. Smith*, 307 U.S. 38).

The system guaranteed tobacco farmers an above-market price and in return agreed to market quotas. Farmers received quotas based on past production; in effect, quotas went with the land. This made land with quotas considerably more valuable than neighboring land without quotas.

In an analysis of the content of congressional hearings on tobacco, Worsham (2006) shows an exclusive focus on economic issues during the 1940s and 1950s, mostly conducted by the agriculture committees. With the 1964 Surgeon General's report, committees in both the House and the Senate turned to health matters, but the House returned to economics during the 1970s. The Senate held hearings on both health and economics. In the 1990s, hearings in both chambers centered on health, and concentrated on regulatory solutions.

This health focus occurred even though the Republicans, far more suspicious

---

6. A list of these reports may be found at http://www.surgeongeneral.gov/library/secondhand smoke/factsheets/29Reports.pdf.

of regulation and elected with a more rural base, had captured both houses of Congress. This leads to an important point: the dynamics of interest groups, issue definition, and subsystem politics do not necessarily map onto partisan divides. A shift in partisan control can certainly boost the fortunes of one interest coalition or another, but multiple venues and shifting issue definitions can operate with considerable independence from the partisan wars.

One reason that this can occur is that the parties can be divided internally on issues. Republicans were split on the issue of tobacco subsidies in particular. The entire system of federal crop supports came under attack by free market conservatives in the House of Representatives, culminating in the Federal Agriculture Improvement and Reform Act of 1996, called The Freedom to Farm Act. The act failed to produce the extent of market-based reforms envisioned by the Republicans in Congress and their ally in the White House on this issue, President Bill Clinton. Republican legislators sensed a clear farm state disadvantage in their support for market-based farming, and began to retreat from the principle. Since then, subsidized farming has made a comeback, with the 2002 Farm Act and in the 2008 reauthorization.

The tobacco quota system came under attack by free-market conservatives as part of the farm subsidy reform movement, but in this case they had as allies health professionals. What sense did it make to subsidize a crop that caused such misery? Seeing the handwriting on the wall, tobacco state legislators supported a buy-out of the existing quotas. All of the cosponsors of the bill proposing the new program were from tobacco-growing regions; The Fair Trade and Equitable Tobacco Reform Act of 2004 (enacted as Title IV of the American Jobs Creation Act of 2004, P.L. 108–357) ended the tobacco quota program and set up a program for buying out the existing quotas. After the buy-out program terminated in 2012, the US government would be out of the business of subsidizing tobacco growing (Womach 2005).

The Tension between Positive and Negative Feedback

Based on his studies of tobacco policy as well as other policy arenas, Jeff Worsham (1998, 2006) has developed a theory of coalition-formation based on the tensions between positive and negative feedback as they are translated into the committee system of Congress. Congressional committees are the arenas where these tensions are played out in the policymaking process. Worsham sees the tension between positive and negative feedback as essentially a struggle between order and disorder, and views the struggle as generating three typical kinds of coalitions among interests.

The *dominant coalition* structure "resembles the classic iron triangle . . . policy interests are made by and in the interest of producers, with little public attention to the process" (Worsham 2006, 440). Because the image of tobacco is positive and centers on the productivity of the industry, this is a classic policy monopoly, and a single congressional committee controls policymaking.

The *competitive coalition* scenario "is distinguished by turf wars featuring pro-tracted and regular competition . . . and often involves a struggle between an industry in direct competition with those who seek to regulate it. . . . Finally, *transitory coalitions* represent a policy system in free fall" (Worsham 2006, 440). Positive feedback has won the struggle, and the subsystem is in collapse.

Worsham's theory is an important extension of punctuated equilibrium theory, and it offers the potential of synthesis with advocacy coalition theory (Sabatier and Jenkins-Smith 1993). Advocacy coalition theory incorporates a model of dueling megacoalitions that seems very similar to Worsham's com-petitive coalition situation with its emphasis on a balance between the forces of order and those of disorder. This bears much further study by those interested in the dynamics of policy change. One open question is the relative mix of dominant, competitive, and transitory coalitions that surround various public policies. In any case, Worsham's analysis brings attention not only to the di-versity of these policy coalitions, but also to how they can change over time, as we have emphasized.

The Second Wave

In the 1993 version of this book, we left tobacco regulation just as the political system was digesting the double strike on tobacco initiated by Surgeon Gen-eral Koop. Koop issued reports in 1984, 1985, and 1986 highlighting the role of secondhand smoke, and struck again in 1988 with a report on the addictive nature of nicotine (US Department of Health and Human Services 1986, 1988). President Reagan did not always approve of Koop's actions, but he deferred to Koop's pursuit of the scientific facts.

Figure 13.6 shows a number of governmental actions taken on behalf of tobacco control. These data are taken from the Policy Agendas Project (http://www.policyagendas.org). As Studlar (2002) maintained, Koop's secondhand smoke reports propelled the issue back into the public limelight. The figure suggests how many different kinds of national level policy venues were be-ing directed at tobacco; several executive branch agencies were attacking the problems of tobacco and health in addition to the Surgeon General: the Cen-ters for Disease Control, the Substance Abuse and Mental Health Services Administration, the Environmental Protection Agency, and the Food and Drug Administration.

As the issue developed, the agencies drawn to it changed. With the emer-gence of concerns about secondhand smoke, the Environmental Protection Agency began focusing on the health consequences of a within-building en-vironment that forced occupants to consume secondhand smoke. In 1992, the EPA issued an important report, "Respiratory Health Effects of Passive Smok-ing: Lung Cancer and Other Disorders." Tobacco companies responded by su-ing, but lost in a barrage of unfavorable coverage.

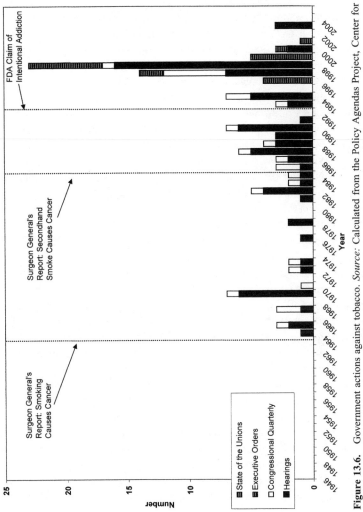

Figure 13.6. Government actions against tobacco. *Source:* Calculated from the Policy Agendas Project, Center for American Politics and Public Policy, University of Washington, Seattle.

This jurisdictional scramble among federal agencies for a piece of the to-bacco control action matches the jurisdictional free-for-all that had erupted in Congress. It indicates that the collapse of a policy subsystem is characterized not just by complex turf wars in Congress, as we argued in chapter 5, but a similar, parallel executive branch competition.

In 1998 Congress was considering the approval of a megadeal with the to-bacco companies stemming from the action of forty-two state attorneys general (see below) in which the companies had agreed to pay $368 billion to the national and state governments. Instead of simply approving the deal, a bidding war erupted to see who could be the toughest on Big Tobacco. The Republican-controlled Senate was considering six separate pieces of legisla-tion, including one to raise the US excise tax on cigarettes from $0.39 to $1.50 from the Budget Committee. Wood (2006a) shows that a "surprising amount" of media coverage during the 1990s was about the settlement, and much of this was negative and from public health advocates. They thought the proposed settlement went too easy on the companies.

The leadership on the initiatives went to Commerce Committee Chair John McCain, who produced a compromise bill that raised the excise tax, imposed potential fines on the industry for violating the agreement with the states, pro-vided no liability protection from lawsuits for companies, and gave the FDA unrestricted control over nicotine (Catanzaro 1998; *Frontline* 1998). A week after the Senate Commerce Committee voted to refer the bill to the floor the tobacco companies pulled support for the deal. The legislation collapsed, and the states signed a separate deal with the companies.

Finally, figure 13.7 depicts the various governmental actions taken against tobacco companies along with media coverage (assessed by articles in the *Readers' Guide*). It is very hard to decide from that graph whether the media is simply indexing its coverage to activities taking place in government (Bennett 1990), or whether media coverage is actually involved in highlighting scien-tific investigations and reports, with government action. We would suggest that intensive media scrutiny does result in heightened sensitivity on the part of policymakers to the information being transmitted in government reports; this certainly seems to be the case for the 1964 Surgeon General's Report. The second period of activity strongly suggests the outbreak of a positive feedback process, and the case material presented above supports that interpretation. As in the case of nuclear power, we are witnessing the complex response of the policymaking system to incoming information (Jones and Wolfe 2007).

The Role of the Food and Drug Administration

Particularly illustrative of disruptive dynamics is the role of the FDA and its director, Dr. David Kessler. Kessler (2001) has left us a first-rate firsthand ac-count of the process. While much of the action at both the state and federal levels centered on the secondhand smoke controversy, it was the 1988 Surgeon

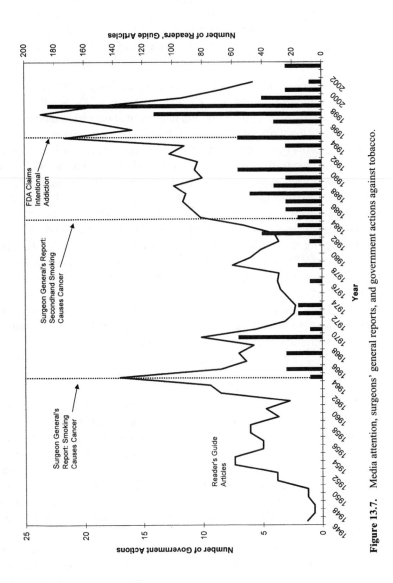

Figure 13.7. Media attention, surgeons' general reports, and government actions against tobacco.

General's report on the addictive nature of nicotine that energized Kessler. He explicitly wanted to interject a new dimension into the tobacco argument:

> For decades the industry had trumpeted the cause of free choice for smokers, and the concept had struck a chord with the public by tapping into a libertarian instinct in American society. I had to reframe the debate. My job was to make the case that nicotine is addictive and that addiction robs people of choice. (Kessler 2001, 155)

Not only did he reframe the debate around nicotine addiction, but he charged that tobacco executives knew the addictive nature of nicotine and that the manufacturing process artificially increased and manipulated the nicotine content of cigarettes. He and his staff embarked on a strategy that sought to regulate cigarettes as "drug delivery devices," since they were designed to deliver a "jolt" of addictive nicotine to the user. In the end, he failed, as the Supreme Court, on a 5–4 vote in *FDA v. Brown and Williamson, et.al* (529 U.S. 120 [2000]), refused to grant the agency the authority to regulate tobacco, indicating that separate legislation was necessary. That legislation was not forthcoming.

In this case the complex nature of divided powers in American government had worked to the tactical advantage of the tobacco companies. Yet Kessler (2001, 383) wrote, "Still I was struck by the extent to which perceptions of tobacco had shifted. . . . The FDA's investigation had changed popular thinking forever." As the FDA's role waned, the importance of other policy venues waxed anew. If the issue had been contained to the national government, indeed the companies would have at least temporarily prevailed, but federalism opened up new avenues of challenge to the industry.

Federalism and Tobacco

In the 1993 edition of this book, we made some radical claims about the federal system. We flatly denied the "veto group" perspective on federalism that claims federalism, by adding organizational complexity, acts to block concerted policy action. While we had sympathy with the "laboratories of democracy" notion of the roles of the states and localities, we thought that such a conception was too linear and orderly. Rather we saw the states and localities as policy venues where policy entrepreneurs could hawk their ideas, occasionally setting off a positive feedback process in which policy mimicking would drive a fast-acting competition.

The tobacco case is an excellent example of how this system works. But we were somewhat off the mark in some respects. Pralle (2006) argues, correctly we think, that interest groups engage in far more trial and error behavior than our perhaps overly rational venue-shopping model implied. Advocates do not always know which venues will be sympathetic ahead of time. And organizations have their own prejudices or inertial factors in their organizational cultures that keep them from trying new venues with which they may not be familiar, even if those venues might well be receptive to their views. So Pralle rightly points to some complications in the venue-shopping model; activists are not completely rational and the venue-shopping process can therefore be highly inefficient.

Moreover, policy venues are far from passive, but are themselves composed of ambitious policy entrepreneurs capable of reaching out and grabbing issues rather than just waiting to be venue shopped. While the courts must be passive, taking only the cases that come to it, political venues such as executive agencies and legislatures can and do seek out new issues in order to expand their jurisdictions and to achieve what they conceive to be good public policy.[7] We can see these processes in the case of tobacco.

Just as the fight over regulating tobacco as a drug (and cigarettes as "drug delivery systems") opened in Washington, Michael Moore, the attorney general of Mississippi, initiated a second assault against big tobacco. Following a suggestion from Michael Lewis, a Mississippi plaintiff's attorney, Moore filed a lawsuit that attempted to recoup losses incurred by taxpayers in treating sick smokers through the Medicare program. Moore then visited attorneys general in other states to convince them to join in the suit. Eventually forty-two states joined the suit.

Tobacco companies had been able to deflect lawsuits by sick smokers based on the harms caused by the product by raising an "informed choice" defense: smokers chose to smoke even though clearly the federally mandated warning label indicated that they could well get sick if they did so. At the national level, Koop's report that indicted cigarettes for being physically as well as psychologically addictive had undermined that defense, but the companies fought back through testimonials from those who had in fact quit the habit. FDA Director Kessler, pursuing the angle that companies had manipulated the addictive part of cigarettes, nicotine, was a distant threat, but Moore's new legal theory was a clear and present danger.

The new theory was innovative and successful because Moore was not seeking compensation for an individual smoker, but for the state Medicare programs which enrolled millions of members. This was a fundamental shift, as there is and can be no statistical proof that any individual cancer has been caused by smoking. In case after case, tobacco lawyers argued that even if there was a statistical correlation this was insufficient to demonstrate that the individual health result for the person in question could be linked to their smoking behavior. After all, some people do not get cancer after smoking for years whereas others get it without smoking at all; the statistical evidence is a tendency, a correlation, not an individual-level demonstration of causality. The epidemiological evidence focused on aggregates, not individuals, after all, and the courts have often been loath to accept aggregate-level evidence for demands for individual redress.

---

7. A point that Valerie Hunt pointed out to us on several occasions.

The tobacco companies' argument was successful for decades in the courts (and, we might add, it is true; statistical correlation is *not* the same as individual-level causation). With Moore's new argument, individual outcomes were not the point, however: with millions of state Medicare participants, there was, indisputably, a linkage between smoking and the aggregate costs for health care for the state Medicare program. And that cost rose into the hundreds of billions of dollars.

In 1994, Moore signed up two other states; the next year, two more. In 1996, thirteen more added their states to the list, and in 1997 twenty-two of the remaining states enlisted. The final two, South Dakota and Nebraska, were added in 1998 (Wood 2006a). In the meantime, Moore took the lead in negotiating with the tobacco companies. In 1998, the states signed the Master Settlement Agreement, in which states won $206 billion spread out over twenty-five years. The tobacco companies also agreed to fund a $1.5 billion antismoking campaign and release previously secret company documents (Attorney General of the State of California n.d.).

Wood (2006a, 433) sees the Master Settlement Agreement as a tipping point that is quite distinct from the typical view of focusing events. He writes that "many events open the door to major policy change but introduce no new issues. Rather, they signal a change in the balance among coalitions competing for agenda space in a domain." The context of the policy change involved a great deal of new information, particularly from the Surgeon General's reports claiming the addictive capacity of nicotine and the health consequences of secondhand smoke. However, the Master Settlement Agreement was the fruit of a new strategy based on old information. It was based solely on the health consequences of smoking, documented in the thirty-year old 1964 Surgeon General's report.

The actions of the state attorneys general illustrate two critical components of disruptive policy dynamics. First, it involved the emergence of a new venue, one that did not passively wait for tobacco-control advocates to discover it. Rather, the "venue," in the form of an ambitious young attorney general, reached out as a policy entrepreneur, redefined the issue, and disrupted the policy space. Schneider, Teske, and Mintrom (1995) developed a full theory of policy entrepreneurship based on disruption and the ability to direct attention to an unappreciated attribute of the policy problem, and certainly Moore's behavior can be taken as a case study in the dynamic they developed.

Second, it shows that, while new information provides fodder for policy entrepreneurs, it is not necessary. Highlighting new perspectives on available information can also serve the entrepreneur's purpose.

Beyond the Master Settlement

Since the collapse of the McCain legislation in 1998 and the refusal of the Supreme Court to allow the FDA to regulate cigarettes, federal activity has been much quieter on the matter of tobacco legislation. However the Bush Justice Department continued a Clinton Administration suit against tobacco companies based on an interpretation of federal racketeering statutes that tobacco companies had conspired to lie to the American public about the health consequences of tobacco; since the lying had occurred through advertising, racketeering laws against wire and mail fraud had been violated (Sebok 2004). The Justice Department demanded "disgorgement" of the profits earned because of these lies. In *US v. Philip Morris USA Inc, et al.* (396 F.3d 1190 [D.C. Cir. 2004]), the US Circuit Court for the District of Columbia held the case to be proven, but denied the remedy, essentially letting the companies off the hook.

At the state level, however, antitobacco legislation has continued unabated. The issue of secondhand smoke had great impact on states. For example, in 2005 the voters of the State of Washington overwhelmingly approved the most stringent smoking ban in private establishments in the United States; a major consideration was the possibility of lawsuits by employees of bars and restaurants due to health harm from secondhand smoke. The American Lung Association reports that as of October 2007, fifty states have laws regulating smoking in public buildings, forty-seven have laws regulating smoking in public workplaces, and forty regulate smoking in private workplaces (American Lung Association). Throughout the European Union, similar smoking bans have taken place. Smoky French cafes, British pubs, and Italian bars are things of the past.

Health professionals take the level of excise taxes on tobacco as an indicator of state-level smoking control activities, because smoking and taxes are highly negatively related (see, for example, Monitoring and Evaluation Program, 2002). Tobacco companies were unable to deter states from raising them after 1998. Excise taxes on tobacco were raised aggressively in the economic downturn of 2001–2, and the increases continued throughout the decade. Only six states failed to raise their tobacco excise taxes between 2001 and 2007, and the average tax per pack doubled. In 2007, state taxes averaged over $1.07 per pack (with a median of 80¢), and in some states were passed explicitly to deter smoking rather than raise revenue. Low taxes exist only in some southern, mostly tobacco-producing states (Alabama, Georgia, Louisiana, Kentucky, North Carolina, South Carolina, Virginia, Florida, and Mississippi all charge less than 42¢ per pack). Even producer Tennessee charges 62¢, and nonproducing Texas charges $1.41, well above the national average.

Was Tobacco a Case of Subsystem Destruction?

In the same issue of the *Policy Studies Journal*, Wood (2006a) contends that the Master Settlement Agreement constituted a "tipping point," basically pushing the tobacco subsystem toward destruction, while Givel (2006a, 2006b) argues that the changes were fundamentally symbolic, and that a business-dominated subsystem remains in place, arguing that health advocates "have not been very successful."

Some of the dispute about whether a given policy has been punctuated or remains operating according to the rules of a previous equilibrium amounts to arguing about whether a single event is sufficient in its impact to constitute a punctuation. Scholars can argue about half-full or half-empty glasses. Surely all can agree that the tobacco industry has been hit with waves of problems, all of them government caused. Compared to, say, the attacks from government on the consumption of alcohol, surely tobacco has come under withering fire. That the defenders of the tobacco industry were able to stave off complete destruction is less relevant than the fact that they suffered grave challenges and experienced huge costs during the "second wave" of tobacco activity. And at two junctures, in 1998 with McCain's tobacco settlement bill and again in 2004 with the Bush Administration's racketeering argument on disgorgement, the domestic industry was under threat of destruction.

Moreover, we think there is little doubt that the subsystem was destroyed. The only active government agencies today in the area of tobacco are all directed at deterring smoking, regulating smokers, and taxing tobacco. Agricultural subsidies are gone, removed by tobacco state representatives with a buy-out plan. Otherwise they could have gotten nothing. Of course, millions of people remain addicted to tobacco, and new recruits respond to advertising every day, so the industry remains in existence. However, to argue that US policy has not been fundamentally altered over the course of the last few decades toward an industry that it once supported so completely is to ignore these important shifts, though it is true that the government has not put the tobacco industry out of business.

More important, perhaps, than the particular conclusion which the evidence supports in the case of tobacco is that the case also demonstrates the complicated self-reinforcing process by which positive feedback operates. Over the past two decades, change has not been caused by a single intervention so much as by many different actors inside and outside of government, making use of a variety of different arguments and bits of evidence in different institutional venues, with varying levels of success. Isolating *the* punctuation that upended the tobacco industry turns out to be harder than pointing to the self-reinforcing processes that caused an explosive process to get underway. There may be many events adding up to more than any single one of them alone. In sum, there is little doubt that change has occurred and that one movement in the direction of promoting health has been followed not by stabilizing counteractions focusing on protobacco arguments but by further health arguments, increasing the momentum in place in an explosive manner. So a positive feedback process has unfolded over many years, not only in a single punctuation.

Perhaps the best characterization of post-1964 tobacco policymaking in the United States is one of bursts of disruption, none of which resulted either in some sort of systematic tobacco control policy at the state or national level nor in the destruction of the domestic tobacco production and manufacturing industries. At the present time, Worsham's (2006) depiction of tobacco politics as one of competing coalitions may be right, but one coalition has clearly been fighting a defensive action for years. The pattern is one of classic disjointed dynamic American pluralism—infuriating to public health advocates, incomplete in its realization, harmful by a thousand large and small cuts for the tobacco industry, and uncoordinated by any level of government. Per capita cigarette consumption peaked in 1965 in the United States; by 2002 it was less than half the 1965 average. The level of smoking among adults fell from 42.4 percent in 1965 to 20.9 percent in 2002 (Information Please Database). The system is messy, imperfect, and frustrating to all those involved. But it can be explosive. And powerful economic interests occasionally are upended, as has been the case here.

Tobacco policy dynamics might be characterized as disjoint, episodic, and disruptive. There was no single punctuation nor was there a lasting equilibrium after any punctuation. This rolling disruptive dynamics is due to the complex interactions of positive and negative feedback processes, as we described in the original edition of this book. But one might want to reconsider the generality of the punctuated equilibrium description. Perhaps the proper conception is to think of punctuated equilibrium as one manifestation of complex evolutionary policy dynamics, one that yields occasional punctuations in at least some policy areas, but which may not settle down to an equilibrium for a very long time.

A Note on Urban Policy

In chapter 7, we examined urban policy as an example of a policy that became intimately bound up with the great partisan issues of the day. Unlike energy or tobacco, policies directed at cities became associated with issues of race, class, and expensive government programs. President Johnson's urban policies were ambitious, expensive, and directed in part at improving the lives of poor and minority citizens. The urban policy subsystem, if there really was one, was inchoate and incoherent, with its different parts—housing, transportation, urban revitalization, crime control, city governance, and education—not well integrated.

Recent research has shown that policy subsystems may be ordered along a "coherence" dimension and that these subsystems have radically different properties and dynamics (May, Sapotichne, and Workman 2006). In particular, policy coherence is dependent on a stable set of legislative actors and the presence of a lead federal agency, both of which were absent in the national urban initiative. It would have been difficult to forge a coherent urban policy out of these disparate parts even under the best of circumstances

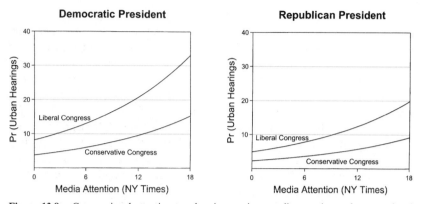

Figure 13.8. Congressional attention to urban issues given media attention and congressional ideology for Democratic and Republican presidents. *Source:* Sapotichne 2006, using data from the Policy Agendas Project. Liberal and conservative congresses are distinguished based on their ADA key vote scores.

(a supportive president and legislative leaders), but it proved impossible under the onslaught of the Republican "Reagan revolution" and the associated increases in legislative partisanship. The component subsystems did not disappear, nor were they substantially curtailed (with the important exception of housing). Transportation and education, in particular, thrived as relatively autonomous subsystems that occasionally accessed the broader macropolitical agenda without the intense partisan rancor that the urban initiative activated.

In a related analysis, Sapotichne (2006) updated and extended the analysis of urban affairs we presented in chapter 7 using data from the Policy Agendas Project. He used the more reliable *New York Times* series available there, and he developed a way of examining the influence of macropolitical forces on national urban policies. He reports that media coverage about cities and congressional hearings on urban affairs are closely related, as we reported. He also finds that the connection between media and congressional interest are more closely related when 1) Congress has a high proportion of liberal members (based on their Americans for Democratic Action [ADA]) scores, and 2) when a Democratic president is in office.

Figure 13.8, from Sapotichne's work, shows how critically ideology and party (in the presidency) influence congressional attention to urban media coverage. The figure shows the expected number of congressional hearings for different levels of media coverage, for liberal and conservative congresses separately. Liberal congresses are distinguished from conservative ones based on their voting records. Liberal congresses are far more sensitive to increases in media coverage than are conservative ones. As media coverage increases, hearings on urban affairs increase, but at a higher rate for liberal congresses.

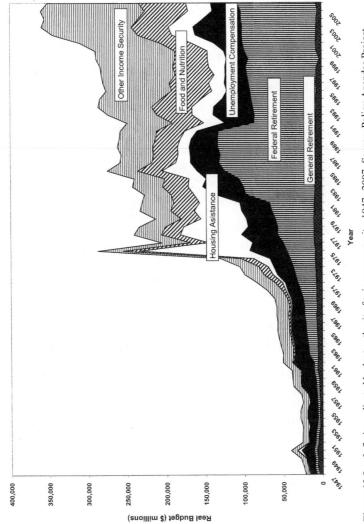

Figure 13.9. Inflation-adjusted budget authority for income security, 1947–2007. *Source:* Policy Agendas Project.

Presidential policies also influence congressional hearings on urban matters. In figure 13.8, the left frame is for Democratic presidents (Truman, Kennedy, Johnson, Carter, and Clinton); the right frame for Republican presidents (Eisenhower, Nixon, Ford, Reagan, George H. W. Bush). Congresses conduct more hearings as media interest increases during Democratic presidencies than Republican ones, regardless of the ideology of the sitting congress.

As in the case of tobacco policy, we see a complex interaction between politics, public policy, and the media. But unlike tobacco policy, urban policies were swept up into the partisan and ideological debates of the day. Unlike tobacco policies, which to a substantial degree crosscut partisan and ideological cleavages, urban affairs reinforced them.

The Politics of Income Security

Figure 13.9 presents further evidence of policy punctuations that are bound up with partisan macropolitics. In the mid-1970s, there was a huge leap in government funding for what the Office of Management and Budget (OMB) terms "Income Security." The largest increase occurred in housing programs, but food assistance (food stamps) and the "other" category, including traditional "welfare" programs, received boosts, as did federal retirement programs. The OMB classifies expenditures by function, but housing programs are urban programs. The data highlight how urban affairs were intimately bound up with the income transfer, class-based programs that were so controversial and partisan during the period.

In the 1980s, Reagan cut housing programs severely, as we noted in chapter 7. Although Republicans failed to reverse spending for income security generally (with the exception of housing), they did dramatically slow the increases in these programs.

Urban programs, along with income security, were all part of the macropolitical dynamics that the political parties organized during the 1960s though the 1980s. Some of this change involved the "appeal" of subsystem participants in systems of limited participation, but most of the change came about in a top-down process, with the parties initiating large-scale policy changes at the behest of their electoral coalitions. Subsystem disequilibrium can cause macropolitical change, in a bottom-up process, but change can also be forged in a top-down, party-driven process.

14

Punctuated Equilibrium
and Disruptive Dynamics

$\mathbb{A}$re the punctuated dynamics that we have described here more general than the particular policymaking pattern that we describe in this book? Our analysis was confined to studies of the construction and destruction of important, but generally limited, arenas of policymaking; after all, this book describes only a fixed number of policy subsystems, not the political system as a whole. There is, however, considerable evidence that punctuated patterns may describe broader political and social processes. Large-scale policy changes sometimes require large-scale political changes, and these changes inevitably involve political parties and the president (though these actors may or may not control the processes in which they participate).

So is there a more general pattern of political change that describes both policymaking in subsystems and change in party and electoral systems? We suggest here that indeed there is, and we point to some directions toward thinking about a more encompassing approach to political change. We refer to these broader patterns as *disruptive dynamics* to distinguish them both from punctuated equilibria in policy subsystems and the glacial, incremental changes that some have argued characterize social processes. Disruptions to established ways of making public policy may come at all levels of scale: some affect only small policy subsystems, some affect larger ones, and some may occasionally affect virtually the entire political system. Surprisingly enough, the dynamics which lead to these changes may be very similar even though they have effects at widely different scales. Natural scientists have observed such processes in many areas, and we believe the political system is affected by similar processes which are "invariant with respect to scale"—that is, the same process may sometimes occur within a limited range of actors, but occasionally have much broader effects. In this book we have focused on single subsystems or policy monopolies, but in the years since it was published we have investigated similar processes with a different approach and we believe the processes do indeed occur at all levels. Here we focus on how they may sometimes affect political leaders and the political party system.

Disruptive Dynamics in Party Systems

In the study of political parties, debates occasionally erupt over the concept of party realignment. Realignments occur when large segments of the public shift their "standing commitments" to support one party over the other. This can happen when many people who identify with one party (or consider themselves independents) shift to the other party. This can cause the macropolitical balance—that is, the aggregate support in the electorate for the parties—to shift from one party to the other, or it can result in even bigger majorities for a prevailing party.

Such electoral realignments are associated with fundamental shifts in the manner in which the electorate, and policymaking elites as well, understand the policy process. In the most important party realignment since the Civil War, that associated with the economic dislocations of the Great Depression, the federal government became far more aggressive in its use of government to manage the economy and provide for the welfare of citizens. That aggressiveness radiated throughout the New Deal, in law and in regulations issued by the newly created regulatory commissions created during the era.

For the most part, however, students of electoral history have not tied the notion of realignment to a broader theory of policy change. The most interesting attempt, albeit one that is controversial, is that of Burnham (1970). He writes that

> the periodic rhythm of American electoral politics, the cycle of oscillation between the normal and the disruptive, corresponds precisely to the existence of largely unfettered developmental change in the socioeconomic system and its absence in the country's political institutions. . . . The socioeconomic system develops but the institutions of electoral politics and policy formation remain essentially unchanged. . . . Then the triggering event occurs, critical realignments follow, and the universe of policy and of electoral coalitions is broadly redefined. (Burnham 1970, 181)

Party realignments imply punctuated policy change. This is an obvious point, but party scholars have, with few exceptions, focused on the potential remaking of electoral coalitions rather than policy change. Perhaps this is one reason that the study of electoral punctuations has been more controversial than the study of punctuations in policy subsystems.

As a consequence, the study of parties and the study of public policy have pretty much proceeded along separate paths. Yet there is something intriguing about beginning to think about integrating these two fields of study. Burnham himself, in an essay in the *Yale Law Journal* in 1999, suggests the integration of these fields, explicitly employing our analysis of punctuated policy patterns, and criticizes constitutional scholar Bruce Ackerman for arguing that constitutional crises lead invariably to the expansion of rights (Burnham 1999). He saw crises as emerging from an evolutionary process, one that, like biological evolution, was indifferent to progress. One immediately sees the connection between Burnham's historical analysis of party changes and our analysis of punctuated equilibria in policy subsystems.

Information Processing in Political Systems

Using the comprehensive datasets of the Policy Agendas Project, we recently developed a theory of information processing in politics that in some key respects resembles Burnham's arguments (Jones and Baumgartner 2005). We show that punctuated policy change is a general pattern in American politics, characterized by many small incremental adjustments and occasionally large, disjoint bursts of action. We further show that these patterns are linked to the nature of American political institutions, characterized by a great deal of resistance to the forces of change. In addition, we show that these punctuations are not invariably related to shifts in party control. Finally, in specific cases, we examined how changing information led to changed policies.

There are several intertwined mechanisms that can lead to patterns of incrementalism interspersed by occasional disruptive change. Sometimes these major changes occur within limited spheres, as was the case for tobacco policy. In other cases, they involved broader social and political actors, as in the case of the demise of nuclear power. But at least in that case, the party system was only partially engaged, and the actions of presidents were not predictable from knowledge of their party affiliations. Finally, some issues fully engage the party system, and can become intertwined in the reorientation of electoral coalitions. We found this to be the case for the rise and decline of a national urban policy. These issues probably engage class, race, and ethnicity to a greater degree than the more contained dynamics characterized by tobacco and energy policies.

Large-scale realignments of the scale discussed by Burnham and in the literature on political parties are rare because they are so large in scale. Even "mandate elections," in which major policy shifts occur whether or not there have been electoral realignments, occur only sporadically—three times since the Second World War (Grossback, Peterson, and Stimson 2006). When major punctuations occur, they may involve party electoral coalitions and policy changes based on those new coalitions (Stimson 2004). But party changes are not the only source of policy disruptions. These may occur within and among policy subsystems, and may only partially activate the electoral coalitions of the parties, something we observed in the cases analyzed in this book.

All of these general patterns involve policy punctuations, but the magnitude of the punctuations differ. In fact, we would expect disruptions in politics to be apparent at every level of scale, from micropolitics through subsystem politics to macropolitics. Similar processes operating throughout the political system should produce many punctuations at the lowest levels of aggregation (e.g., in the realm of small niche-based policy subsystems), fewer as we move up the ladder to sector-level initiatives, and fewer still at the level of the entire political system. But the mixture of equilibrium and punctuated change should be apparent at each level of aggregation throughout the political system.

The processes of positive and negative feedback that operate within the policy system certainly operate in other areas of political life as well, however. Most issues most of the time are dominated by expectations that the system will remain stable. Disruptions or shocks are absorbed and counteracted by opposing forces, and all understand that the system will remain in place: negative feedback dominates and stability ensues. Such is the nature of a negative feedback, or thermostatic, system.

One remarkable aspect about the outbreak of bursts of creative destruction in politics is how seemingly small events and trends, that seem routine at the time, can cascade into larger disruptions. So the same events, interpreted differently by actors who are basing their behaviors on their expectations of how others around them will respond to the changing circumstance, may occasionally lead to cascades of change even if typically they do not.

The first edition of *Agendas and Instability* was one of the first to focus on these processes of positive feedback within politics, and we limited our focus to the study of policy change, but the approach has more general possibilities for the study of politics. One interesting area for future research is in the size of various punctuations. Research in natural science suggests that we should expect similar processes to those we have observed here to operate at every level of scale, and that would be our expectation as well. We have found this pattern in the analyses reported in this book, but also in budgetary changes in the US government comprehensively by topic area since 1947, and in overall levels of spending change annually for the entire government from 1803 to the present. No matter how we look at the political system, whether at a single spending area, at domestic versus defense spending, or at the entire budget as a single annual observation, we see evidence of great stability most of the time, but dramatic shifts occur more commonly than can be explained except within a punctuated equilibrium framework.

Disruptive Dynamics and Information Processing

Because policy punctuations are not confined to partisan realignments, or to mandate elections, or to social movements, they must be put into a broader framework if they are to be explained generally. We propose this general proposition: *Disruptive dynamics are a function of how political systems process information.* Information processing involves a signal concerning some change in a system's environment, which is then attended to by government. The processing of information is disproportionate, which means that political systems can ignore important information for a very long time, but at some point can move rapidly to react to that information. The processes by which social processes come to the attention of government involve many of the most important areas of study in political science: political parties, social movements, professional communities, scientific actors, bureaucratic administrations at all levels of the federal system, and others participate in collecting, analyzing, and using information about developing trends "out there" in order to demand or justify responses by government. But the process is far from smooth, far from neutral, and far from efficient.

Different political structures and different policy preferences lead to different modes of processing information. The American system of separated and divided powers is designed to retard change, even if the multiplicity of venues for policy action sometimes actually encourages it. The human mind tends to resist it, and this reinforces institutional drag. Parties may maintain policies out of inertia, or vested interest, or ideology. But, as John Adams said in his defense of British soldiers accused of the Boston Massacre, "Facts are stubborn things, and whatever may be our wishes, our inclinations, or the dictates of our passion, they cannot alter the state of facts and evidence" (The Quotations Page).

All policymaking systems process information and all are subject to institutional and cognitive friction to some extent. Some systems are designed to produce more friction, as in the case of the United States, and some less. Just how those characteristics act to retard or promote change is at present unclear, but research projects in Denmark, France, the Netherlands, the United Kingdom, Canada, Belgium, Spain, Switzerland, and the State of Pennsylvania using the same general methods developed in *Agendas and Instability* and *The Politics of Attention* are allowing these differences to be explored in a systematic fashion.

The field of policy studies has advanced rapidly since 1993, both theoretically and empirically, and we expect accelerated progress in the years to come. From a base focused on case studies of a small number of US public policies studied over time, we have followed our intellectual curiosity and tried to lay the foundation for a broader theory of government response to changing social conditions. Any good idea should survive only by being incorporated into a broader understanding of a topic. If punctuated equilibrium is replaced by a fuller understanding of the complex evolutionary dynamics that characterize policymaking, we will be pleased indeed.

Appendix A

Data Sources

$\mathbb{A}$ variety of sources were used in creating the various indicators and time series used in this book. This appendix describes those sources, the methods by which the data were collected, the coding systems that were used, and a variety of other details and explanations of our data-gathering procedures so that they might be replicated. First, we discuss coding of media coverage.

Media Coverage

As described in chapter 4, Spencer Weart's (1988) discussion of the positive and negative images associated with nuclear power in the United States convinced us that we could do similar coding for a variety of public policy issues over time. After seeing a small graph in his book (1988, 387), we wrote to request the data. Weart generously complied, and we have used a recoded version of his data for civilian nuclear power in this book. In all, his analysis was based on over three thousand articles in the *Readers' Guide,* generally covering every other volume of the *Guide* from 1900 to 1986. For all other issues, we have trained graduate student assistants to use the following methodology.

Details of Coding Procedures

The first question for any issue is to identify the proper keywords to ensure that all articles on the topic are found. We include in the following section a list of all the keywords we used for each issue studied. In general, we attempted to be as complete as possible. In addition to referring readers to the articles listed under the keywords, the *Readers' Guide* and the *New York Times Index,* our sources for media coverage of issues, often refer readers to other topics, noting

"See also." We included all of these articles, making sure they did not duplicate any we had already included. For example, in the case of child abuse, the "see also" reference might lead the reader to a series of court cases listed separately under the name of the plaintiff or defendant. In some cases, the number of "see also" references was very high.

Once the list of keywords was established (and sometimes these keywords changed over the years—the list below includes all those keywords used at any time during the century), our coders typed the title of each article in abbreviated form into a spreadsheet, along with a numeric code indicating its content. Coders covered one issue at a time, coding each volume of the *Guide* or the *Times* separately. (*New York Times Index* coverage includes not the title of the article, but a short abstract; our coders used the entire abstract to construct their codes, but summarized it in a few words for our files.) Before 1965, the *Readers' Guide* included more than one year per volume. We therefore adjusted all data from the *Guide* by dividing the number of articles in a volume by the number of years covered and reported the result for each year.

In addition to the simple number of articles per year, we were also interested in the tone of coverage. We therefore coded each title for most of our issues according to whether the title indicated support or opposition to the activity in question. For example, an article reporting the introduction of a new, highly effective, pesticide would be coded as a positive article; one describing the damage of a toxic spill would be negative. Details appear below.

In some cases we used an additional, more complicated, coding scheme. For articles on pesticides, for example, we asked our coders to note whether the title indicated concern with economic or financial implications, government actions, health or pollution concerns, or other elements. Thus each general tone (positive or negative) could be subdivided into a more complex scheme, indicating concern with the problem, its economic implications, or the government's appropriate role. In the cases of smoking and child abuse, we further divided the government activities to report court cases separately, since these represented a large proportion of the total government activities reported in the media. This coding scheme allowed us to note whether an issue was being discussed as part of the governmental agenda or only as a social problem, and to some extent which parts of government were active.

Table A.1 presents a summary of our coding of the *Readers' Guide* and the *New York Times Index*. As described in more detail below, there were slight variations in how each issue was coded. For example, in some cases there was no purpose in coding the tones of positive and negative, since few articles appear condoning child abuse, for example. Similarly, media coverage of auto accidents and traffic safety is rarely encouraging (though from time to time a small number of articles note, for example, that accident rates are declining; such an article would have been coded as positive).

Table A.1 makes clear the large scope of our coding of media coverage. Over

Table A.1 Summary of coding media coverage

Issue	Number of Articles Coded				Percent of Articles Coded Identically by Two Coders
	Positive	Negative	Neutral or Uncodeable	Total	
Pesticides	1,111	1,279	0	2,390	95.6%
Economic news	838	188	0	1,026	
Government actions	41	191	0	232	
Health issues	232	900	0	1,132	
Smoking					
Readers' Guide	343	1,192	485	2,020	
New York Times	776	1,145	595	2,516	97.5
Economic news	382	100	106	588	
Government actions	241	557	241	1,039	
Court proceedings	27	34	18	79	
Health issues	52	350	39	441	
Other	74	104	191	369	
Alcohol	458	950	576	1,984	
Drugs	469	1,096	607	2,172	
Urban affairs	2,130	725	1,973	4,828	
Nuclear power	660	1,267	1,336	3,263	
Auto safety				1,264	
Child abuse, *Readers' Guide*				452	
Child abuse, *New York Times*				1,447	96.0
Abandonments	266				
Abuse	268				
Government actions	275				
Court proceedings	615				
Other	22				
Total number of articles coded				22,336	

Note: Articles are from the *Readers' Guide* unless otherwise noted.

twenty-two thousand titles were coded in a variety of ways. In several cases, we had a second coder follow the same rules and recode the same articles, as noted in the right-most column of the table. For the cases of pesticides, smoking, and child abuse, we found over 95 percent agreement between two coders. This reliability score counts as errors those cases where one coder marked an article "positive: economic and financial," while another marked the same article "positive: government regulation." In terms of the simple positive-negative tone coding, reliabilities were even closer to 100 percent. After this encouraging news, we discontinued the practice of performing reliability checks, but had the same coders continue with other issues. In our discussion of congressional attention below, we used a similar method of checking reliability. Results were equally encouraging.

As an example of how this coding was done, consider the case of pesticides.

From table A.1, we can see that there were 2,390 articles on pesticide topics listed in the *Readers' Guide,* and that 1,279 of these were negative in tone, focusing more on unfavorable side-effects of pesticides than on potential benefits. Further, we can see that of the 1,111 positive articles that have appeared during the twentieth century, the bulk has focused on the economic benefits likely to accrue to farmers and consumers. A significant minority of the positive articles about pesticides have concerned their effects on health and the environment (generally reporting that threats are not as high as some have suggested, noting introduction of new pesticides thought to be less toxic to humans, or focusing on some other such health news that the industry would be pleased to see). Finally, most discussion of governmental activities is associated with criticism of the pesticides industry, calls for more regulation, and other demands not likely to appeal to pesticides manufacturers.

Below we report the keywords used to locate articles for each of our issues as well as information on how they were coded.

Pesticides. Keywords: pesticides, herbicides, insecticides, fungicides, rodenticides, organophosphates, DDT, DDE, Chlordane, and Dieldrin. Positive articles were those supportive of the pesticide industry; negatives were those critical of the industry or its products. Economic and financial news includes reports of new products, profitability in the industry, or other business news; government actions include any reports or discussion of regulation, legislation, or court cases; health issues include all questions of toxicity and pollution.

Smoking and Tobacco. Keywords: smoking, tobacco, cigarettes, and cigars. Positive articles include such news as reports of profits, increased sales, record corps, and court proceedings in favor of the tobacco industry. Negative articles include bad crop news, lost productivity, government health warnings, and court cases against the industry. Economic news includes reports of crop size, profits, and sales; government actions include all discussion of actions by government officials, including reports of the surgeon general; court proceedings are reported separately; health issues include any statements by nongovernmental sources on questions of health effects of smoking.

Alcohol. Keywords: alcohol, alcoholics, alcoholic beverages, alcoholics anonymous, alcoholism, alcohol and the following: air pilots, airplane accidents, automobile drivers, crime, employment, religion, sex, sports, aged, women, youth. Positive articles include those relative to favorable effects of alcohol, positive economic information for alcohol manufacturers, and positive aspects of alcoholic products, for example, cooking.

Drugs. Keywords: drugs, drug abuse, drug rehabilitation, drugs and the following: motion pictures, education, physiological effects, air pilots, celebrities, airplane accidents, automobile drivers, children, crime, dancers, mass media, musicians, physicians, politicians, public officers, servicemen, sports, sex, aged, youth, the press, women. Positive articles include articles relating to the use of drugs to improve health and human performance and the introduction of new medical drugs. The negative category contains articles about the dangers associated with the use of cocaine, marijuana, steroids, or other drugs.

Urban Affairs. Keywords: cities, cities and town life, city planning, city traffic, metropolitan areas, suburban homes, suburban life, suburbs, and urban. Positive articles include aspects of city life such as good city planning, urban expansion, and economic growth. Negatives include crime, fiscal problems, and ghettos.

Nuclear Power. Keywords: nuclear power, atomic power, nuclear energy, atomic energy, and others (see Weart 1988). Weart coded articles into several groups: risk versus benefits, reactor accidents, emissions, fuel cycle and waste, environmental, and other. We regrouped these codes into simple positive, negative, and neutral or uncodeable, as in our other cases. Weart included separately coverage of military versus civilian nuclear power; we have used only the civilian nuclear power data.

Automobile Transportation Safety. Keywords: automobile safety, automobile accidents, traffic safety, and traffic accidents. Only totals are reported.

Child Abuse. Keywords: child abuse, child abandonment, cruelty and neglect of children. For the *Readers' Guide,* only totals were counted. In the *New York Times,* we counted separately several types of articles: first, simple abandonments were counted separately from reports of actual abuse. Second, we differentiated between reports of government activity (legislative actions or executive agency activities) and court cases. Since virtually all articles on this topic were of course anti–child abuse, we have not reported coding by tone.

Comparing the Readers' Guide *with other Indices*

The *Readers' Guide to Periodical Literature* is the broadest index of popular periodicals, including in its coverage a wide range of popular and specialized publications. Still, it is not exhaustive. Further, it does not include newspapers and obviously overlooks the electronic media on which most people rely. When we compare the levels and tone of coverage in the *Readers' Guide* with those of other major news outlets, we find that it makes little difference which index one uses, however. Media attention trends follow similar patterns no matter which particular indicator is used. Patterson and Caldeira (1990) used *New York Times* coverage as an index of media attention toward Congress and write that there is "considerable similarity in coverage of Congress across various national news media (see Robinson 1981, 72–75; Tidmarch and Pitney 1985, 471–75; Veblen 1981, 153–55)" (1990, 34).

There are some important differences between the *Times* and the *Guide,* but in general every media indicator we have studied shows similar trends over time. As a newspaper of record, the *Times* covers government actions much more carefully and fully than the periodicals indexed in the *Guide.* Further, its business news is much more complete. However, we have found that changes in relative levels of coverage in the two outlets follow virtually identical patterns over time. We have collected similar data from the *New York Times Index* and from the *Readers' Guide* for two issues (child abuse and smoking) in order to determine whether coverage is similar in each. The results indicate that both reflect similar trends in overall media coverage. Figure 8.4 presents data from both the *Times* and the *Guide* for child abuse questions, showing that the two outlets peaked exactly at the same time and generally followed similar patterns of coverage. The correlation between amount of coverage in the two indices for the period when the *Guide* had a separate category is .88, indicating an extremely high degree of correspondence. The absolute annual figures are not exactly the same, and the *Times* tends consistently to be higher, but the timings of the peaks and valleys are identical. We can feel confident that 1984 was indeed a year of tremendous media attention in child abuse, since two separate indicators come to that striking conclusion independently.

In the case of smoking and tobacco, where we have also collected comparable data from the same two sources, we find similar results. For the *New York Times,* coverage of smoking was so high that after coding each article from 1988 back to 1985 (and finding an average of 169 articles per year), we took only every third year, from 1982 to 1946. For the *Readers' Guide,* on the other hand, we collected complete yearly data from 1900 to 1987. Figure A.1 compares the total levels of coverage of smoking and tobacco from the two sources.

As in the case of child abuse, the degree of attention to the issue of smoking and tobacco reflected in the two sources is similar, with a Pearson's correlation of .73 for the sixteen years for which we have collected data from both sources. Both trends show tremendous peaks of coverage around 1964, corresponding with the surgeon general's report on smoking, then declining coverage during the 1970s, and another increase in the 1980s. There are important differences (for example, overall levels of coverage are consistently higher in the *Times* than the *Guide*), but all in all we can be reassured that either of these media indicators would show peaks and valleys, representing the emergence and decline of an issue to and from the public agenda at the same time. Small shifts in coverage are not the same, but general trends are almost identical.

Rogers, Dearing, and Chang studied coverage of AIDS in six media outlets and found very close correspondence among levels of coverage: "The numbers of new stories about AIDS across time in each of the six media of study are highly correlated with each other. When one medium carried a relatively large number of news stories about AIDS, so did the other media. The highest correlation was .96 between the AIDS coverage of *The New York Times* and the *Washington Post,* and the lowest correlations were .73 between the number of AIDS news stories on ABC and in *The New York Times* and in the *Los Angeles Times.* . . . Correlation between the combined three newspapers and the combined three television networks is .84" (1991, 9). We are confident that a variety of media indices would show similar, if not identical, trends in levels

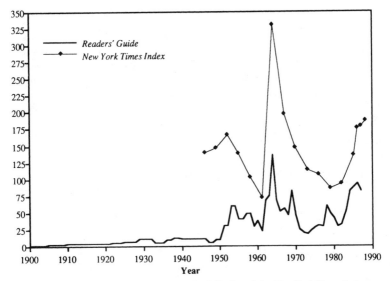

Figure A.1. Coverage of smoking in the *Readers' Guide* and the *New York Times Index*.

of coverage for the range of issues we discuss throughout this book. Available studies and our own research buttress this conclusion. Further, we are careful not to overemphasize small or temporary changes in levels of coverage. For the broad sweep of changes over the decades that are the focus on our argument, we are confident that the *Readers' Guide* and the *New York Times Index* provide reliable information.

Congressional Hearings Data

Data for congressional hearings were taken from the Congressional Information Service reports of congressional activity. The CIS publishes data on every Congress from 1789 to present. The data are available both in published volumes and on computer database in CD-ROM format. Contents of the two versions are identical, but the CD format (used for all issues except nuclear power and drugs) made it possible to conduct the searches much faster. Each hearing is cross-referenced with all the appropriate keywords in the CD format, but in the paper volumes it was necessary to look under several topics, then carefully delete references to hearings that had already been included because they were listed under more than one topic. The detailed method used for each case is as follows.

We constructed a dataset that included the year of the hearing, the name of the committee(s) and subcommittee(s) that held it, and a summary of the topics discussed. In the case of pesticides we conducted a more detailed analysis, including coding each witness into a variety of categories, as described

Table A.2 Summary of coding congressional hearings

Issue	Positive	Negative	Neutral or Uncodeable	Total	Percent of Articles Coded Identically by Two Coders
Pesticides	29	337	19	385	96.0%
Smoking	119	98	94	313	
Drugs				1,044	86.8
Enforcement	573				
Education	471				
Nuclear power	168	694	375	1,237	87.3
Air transportation				229	97.1
Safety	27				
Economics and regulation	202				
Child abuse				155	
Alcohol				679	
Intergovernmental relations				520	
Urban affairs				2,002	
Infrastructure	156				
Social issues	448				
Community development	1,288				
Environmental	110				
Total number of hearings coded				6,565	

Note: Reliability scores count as an error even those cases where one coder coded an article positive or negative and the other coded it neutral. Disagreements in direction of coding were extremely rare.

in chapter 10. In the case of nuclear power, the first issue we analyzed, we allowed our coders to note up to five topics per hearing. We found that the vast majority of the hearings were homogeneous in that all the topics discussed were coded in a similar direction: either supportive of the industry, or critical of it. Therefore in subsequent cases we simply coded the abstract of each hearing in a single direction: positive, negative, or neutral/uncodeable toward the industry in question. In the case of drugs this was altered slightly since, of course, few hearings extol the virtues of drugs. In this case we distinguished between those hearings focusing on enforcement questions and those focusing more on education and treatment aspects of the federal response. In some cases we performed no detailed coding of the hearings, but simply collected annual totals. Table A.2 summarizes our coding of congressional hearings.

In our coding of congressional hearings, we made every effort to follow our coding of media coverage. In most cases we assigned the same coder(s) to work on the same issue in both outlets. Choice of keywords in the CIS was simpler than in the case of the media indices because the CD technology allowed us to use fewer keywords and to avoid the complication of the "see also" references altogether. Comparisons of searches done manually with the paper volumes and those done electronically assured us that such cross-references were all included in our electronic searches. Following is a list of keywords and details for each issue discussed.

Pesticides. Keywords: pesticides, herbicides, insecticides, fungicides, and rodenticides. A single code for the tone of the hearing was made by reading the abstract of each hearing. A positive hearing would discuss some benefits derived from pesticide use while a negative tone would discuss dangers or harm associated with pesticide use. Each subcommittee was assigned to one of two venues based on the title of the committee and subcommittee. The agricultural venue is composed of those committees and subcommittees with a general focus on agriculture questions. There were 102 hearings in the agricultural venue. The health and environmental venue is composed of committees such as Wildlife and Fisheries, Environment, and Interior (these accounted for 220 hearings on pesticides). Some committees or subcommittees fit into neither of these categories (63 hearings were held in an uncodeable venue). Participants were coded by using the affiliation listed by the CIS and by reading the testimony of each witness testifying at the hearing. The participants were grouped into either the agricultural, health and environmental, or other group.

Smoking. Keywords: smoking, tobacco, cigarettes, and cigars. Venue coding involved distinguishing between agricultural or commodities committees generally likely to promote the growth and sale of tobacco and tobacco products and those in the health or tax areas that focus more on regulation. The agriculture/trade venue accounted for 203 hearings; the health/taxes venue for 104 hearings; 6 hearings were held in committees that could not be categorized.

Drugs. Keywords: drugs and drug abuse. The coding of both topics and venues involved distinguishing between enforcement and education hearings. Enforcement-type hearings are concerned with interdiction of drugs at the borders, eradication campaigns, and law enforcement activities. Education-type hearings are concerned with the treatment of drug offenders using hospitals and rehabilitation centers. A single code for each hearing was created by summarizing the hearing abstracts; venue codes were taken from the titles of the committees and subcommittees holding the hearings. Enforcement/interdiction committees held 561 hearings; health/education committees held 263 hearings; 200 hearings were held in committees that could not be classified according to this scheme.

Nuclear Power. Keywords: nuclear power, atomic power, nuclear energy, and atomic energy. Each hearing was coded as either positive or negative, and each subcommittee or committee was similarly coded as either supportive or critical of the industry. A positive hearing, for example, would be in support of nuclear power and its uses, where a negative hearing would question the safety and health of nuclear power. The tones were coded using the hearing abstracts while the venues were coded using the titles of the committees holding hearings. The pronuclear committees, including the Joint Committee on Atomic

Energy, held 611 hearings on nuclear power questions; critical or antinuclear committees held 274 hearings; 352 hearings took place in committees that could not be classified.

Urban Affairs. Keywords: cities, urban, ghetto, slums, urban problems, urban renewal. As in the case of drugs, there was no point in coding by tone in the sense that no hearings are "anti"-cities. Rather, we coded them into four subject areas that correspond to available budgetary data on grants: (1) physical infrastructure, (2) social issues, (3) community development, and (4) urban environment.

The grant-in-aid data are from the Office of Management and Budget's appendices to the U.S. Government Budget (Office of Management and Budget 1991). We combined the OMB categories (excluding agriculture) into four groups as follows: (1) infrastructure (transportation, highways, mass transit); (2) social issues (education, training, employment and social services, health, income security, housing); (3) community development (community and regional development, general purpose financial assistance, energy, general government); and (4) environment (natural resources and environment). OMB analysts attempt to place programs in functional categories so that budget allocations to agencies can be divided among the functional categories. For example, an appropriation for housing policies going to the Department of Housing and Urban Development would generally be divided according to the object of the program. Hence a weatherization program would go to the energy category and would therefore be included in our broader community development category. Grants for low- and moderate-income housing are placed in OMB's income security category and would therefore be included in our broader social programs category. Using the exact OMB grant categories for our coding of urban hearings ensured a close correspondence between congressional hearings activities and policy outputs in the form of grants-in-aid.

Air Transportation. Keyword: air transportation. Topics were coded as focusing on safety issues (27 hearings) or economics and regulation (202 hearings). The latter category included appropriations and organizational hearings, except where safety was explicitly discussed. Hearings were coded by topic, year, and committee/subcommittee.

Alcohol. Keywords: alcohol, alcohol abuse, and alcoholism. Only totals per year were collected.

Child Abuse. Keywords: child abuse and child abandonment. Only totals per year were collected.

Intergovernmental Relations. Keyword: intergovernmental relations. Only totals per year were collected.

The Issue Density Question

In our analysis of congressional hearings and media coverage we report annual totals in order to track the emergence and recession of issues from the government's agenda. Over the years, however, Congress has increased its capabilities to hold hearings, and the number of media outlets available in the United States has risen as well. Therefore one might question our use of totals as opposed to proportions; we discuss here the relative merits of standardizing our measures of agenda status by some measure of the total aggregate levels of media coverage or congressional attention. In general, total levels of coverage have increased over the decades, but these overall increases cannot be used as rival explanations for the patterns we found and reported in the various figures throughout the book. Certainly there are more magazines and journals indexed in the *Readers' Guide* today than in 1920, and there is no question but that Congress holds more hearings today than it did on average in the 1930s (see Ornstein, Mann, and Malbin 1990). Still, the rapid movements we observed in case after case in the chapters of this book cannot be explained by these secular trends.

Table A.3 reports overall statistics for two of our main data sources—the *Readers' Guide,* the *New York Times Index.*

We noted in an earlier section that the *Readers' Guide* has published annual volumes only since 1965. The first volumes of the century included five years; the number of years included in annual volumes gradually decreased as noted in the table. We standardized our coding by dividing the number of articles for each volume by the number of years covered in the volume (or the appropriate fraction, based on months of coverage as noted in the table). It is clear from table A.3 that the number of articles and periodicals indexed in the *Readers' Guide* increased substantially over the years. Further, the *New York Times* followed a similar pattern, as did the number of congressional hearings (see Ornstein, Mann, and Malbin 1990).

We rejected the idea of standardizing all our measures of agenda access by the totals reported in table A.2 because we believe that the absolute numbers are an important indicator of agenda status. Further, we think that the dramatic increases in overall media coverage shown in the table are important in themselves. American society has progressively become better able to discuss a wide variety of topics at once. Beecher, Lineberry, and Rich (1981) have called this the *issue density* question. Discussions of government overload may find some of their roots in the simple fact that the American communications media and governmental institutions are capable now of considering simultaneously many more issues than was the case in earlier decades. This has had important implications for the power of those who are advantaged by a relatively quiet and secretive discussion of public policy questions. For these substantive reasons, we choose not to standardize our indicators of agenda status.

We might add that the rapid changes apparent in levels of attention in either Congress or the media for most of our issues are not consistent with the slower rate of change in overall coverage in these institutions. For example, Weart (1988) presented nuclear power articles as a percentage of all articles in the *Readers' Guide,* and the substantive conclusions that he drew from that are identical to those we draw from the use of unstandardized numbers.

Table A.3 Summary of organization of *Readers' Guide* and *New York Times Index*

Year	*Readers' Guide* Volume No.	Number of Months Covered	Pages in Volume	Pages per Months Covered	No. of Periodicals Indexed in the *Readers' Guide*	Number of Pages in *New York Times Index*[a]
1900	1	60	1,640	27.33	67	164
1901	1	60	1,640	27.33	67	164
1902	1	60	1,640	27.33	67	164
1903	1	60	1,640	27.33	67	164
1904	1	60	1,640	27.33	67	164
1905	2	60	2,491	41.52	111	244
1906	2	60	2,491	41.52	111	244
1907	2	60	2,491	41.52	111	263
1908	2	60	2,491	41.52	111	325
1909	2	60	2,491	41.52	111	346
1910	3	60	2,868	47.80	115	361
1911	3	60	2,868	47.80	115	300
1912	3	60	2,868	47.80	115	368
1913	3	60	2,868	47.80	115	1,524
1914	3	60	2,868	47.80	115	1,856
1915	4	48	2,193	45.69	111	1,722
1916	4	48	2,193	45.69	111	1,801
1917	4	48	2,193	45.69	111	957
1918	4	48	2,193	45.69	111	848
1919	5	36	1,827	50.75	111	855
1920	5	36	1,827	50.75	111	878
1921	5	36	1,827	50.75	111	1,000
1922	6	36	1,906	52.94	—	1,156
1923	6	36	1,906	52.94	—	1,201
1924	6	36	1,906	52.94	—	1,277
1925	7	48	2,809	58.52	126	1,373
1926	7	48	2,809	58.52	126	1,507
1927	7	48	2,809	58.52	126	1,319
1928	7	48	2,809	58.52	126	1,119
1929	8	42	2,834	67.48	129	1,162
1930	8	42	2,834	67.48	129	2,864
1931	8	42	2,834	67.48	129	2,777
1932	8	42	2,834	67.48	129	2,733
1933	9	48	2,506	52.21	113	2,986
1934	9	48	2,506	52.21	113	2,686
1935	9	48	2,506	52.21	113	2,951
1936	10	24	2,038	84.92	119	3,356
1937	10	24	2,038	84.92	119	2,583
1938	11	24	2,040	85.00	117	2,303
1939	11	24	2,040	85.00	117	2,400
1940	12	24	2,259	94.13	129	2,331

Year	Readers' Guide Volume No.	Number of Months Covered	Pages in Volume	Pages per Months Covered	No. of Periodicals Indexed in the Readers' Guide	Number of Pages in New York Times Index[a]
1941	12	24	2,259	94.13	129	2,173
1942	13	24	2,247	93.63	124	2,026
1943	13	24	2,247	93.63	124	1,859
1944	14	22	1,963	89.23	118	1,997
1945	15	22	2,275	103.41	128	2,265
1946	15	24	2,275	94.79	128	2,716
1947	16	24	2,272	94.67	—	2,406
1948	16	24	2,272	94.67	—	1,211
1949	17	23	2,273	98.83	124	1,161
1950	17	23	2,273	98.83	124	1,258
1951	18	24	2,326	96.92	121	1,216
1952	18	24	2,326	96.92	121	1,293
1953	19	22	2,663	121.05	124	1,224
1954	19	22	2,663	121.05	124	1,223
1955	20	24	2,769	115.38	115	1,267
1956	20	24	2,769	115.38	115	1,424
1957	21	24	2,183	90.96	111	1,059
1958	21	24	2,183	90.96	111	1,025
1959	22	24	1,866	77.75	110	1,092
1960	22	24	1,866	77.75	110	1,131
1961	23	24	2,120	88.33	134	1,125
1962	23	24	2,120	88.33	134	1,062
1963	24	24	2,304	96.00	119	911
1964	24	24	2,304	96.00	119	1,189
1965	25	12	1,222	101.83	126	1,157
1966	26	12	1,335	111.25	128	1,396
1967	27	12	1,319	109.92	128	1,440
1968	28	12	1,346	112.17	160	1,710
1969	29	12	1,361	133.42	160	1,949
1970	30	12	1,349	112.42	157	2,304
1971	31	12	1,306	108.83	157	2,029
1972	32	12	1,336	111.33	164	2,564
1973	33	12	1,210	100.83	160	2,811
1974	34	12	1,232	102.67	163	2,828
1975	35	12	1,232	102.67	172	2,777
1976	36	12	1,290	107.50	163	1,901
1977	37	12	1,316	109.67	162	1,526
1978	38	12	1,582	131.83	186	1,198
1979	39	12	1,601	133.42	188	1,521
1980	40	12	1,763	146.92	183	1,640

(continued)

Table A.3 *(continued)*

Year	Readers' Guide Volume No.	Number of Months Covered	Pages in Volume	Pages per Months Covered	No. of Periodicals Indexed in the Readers' Guide	Number of Pages in New York Times Index[a]
1981	41	12	1,893	157.75	184	1,287
1982	42	12	1,801	150.08	185	1,122
1983	43	12	1,873	156.08	189	1,403
1984	44	12	2,080	173.33	197	1,436
1985	45	12	2,182	181.83	190	1,395
1986	46	12	2,192	182.67	188	1,488
1987	47	12	2,200	183.33	182	1,396
1988	48	12	2,130	177.50	203	1,435
1989	49	12	2,117	176.42	205	1,369
1990	50	12	2,108	175.66	194	1,324

Source: Compiled by authors.

Note: Dashes indicate missing values.

a. The *New York Times Index* is annual since 1907. For the years before then, we report standardized figures.

Encyclopedia of Associations **Dataset**

In chapter 9 we report the results of an analysis of the *Encyclopedia of Associations* (Bureh, Kock, and Novallo, annual). The *Encyclopedia* is the most complete reference book on interest groups available, listing associations of all types in the United States. Updated annually, its editions date back to 1961. We began with the first edition, then used the 1970, 1980, and 1990 editions to construct our panel dataset of environmental interest groups. The *Encyclopedia* lists the name, address, membership size, staff size, publications, and a variety of other bits of information about each group listed. We had our coders read through one edition at a time, selecting every group that was described as primarily concerned with environmental matters. (We excluded groups that were primarily supported by industrial organizations, such as environmental research organizations owned by or affiliated with lumber companies, chemical companies, and the like.) For each edition, we noted the group's name, creation date, membership size, membership type (that is, whether its members are individuals, corporations, state chapters, or whether it has no members), staff size, area of activity (overall environmental quality or protection, wildlife protection, conservation, energy, toxins, water quality, or other). In each successive edition, we noted the same information as well as a code for newly created, defunct, or merged groups. In the 1990 edition, budgetary data were listed for some groups. In all, we counted 461 groups in one or more editions of the *Encyclopedia,* as noted in tables 9.2–9.4.

For groups that were listed in each issue of the *Encyclopedia,* our dataset includes the name, creation date, membership type, area of activity, size of its 1990 budget, staff and member size in each of four years (1961, 1970, 1980, and 1990), and merger/name change information for the periods ending 1970, 1980, and 1990.

The editors of the *Encyclopedia* are unclear in one respect that posed a slight problem. For example, where groups have no staff and where the organization did not respond to the question on staff, the listing would simply give no data. In other words, true zeros and missing data are sometimes impossible to distinguish. In our reporting of these data in chapter 9, we have been careful not to report averages or any other statistics that might be inaccurate because of this ambiguity.

Constructing the Investment-Consumption Ratio

In chapter 11 we show an analysis of investment versus consumption expenditures at the state and federal levels. Federal expenditure data were taken from appendices to the *Budget of the U.S. Government* (Office of Management and Budget 1991). State data were taken from tabulations from the Bureau of the Census in its series on state and local finance (Bureau of the Census 1970, 1990). We categorized this information according to the following procedures. State and local expenditure categories were based on an analysis by Jones (1990) which related policy expenditures to subsequent economic growth using a disequilibrium adjustment model. That analysis used the five largest categories of expenditure. The study suggested that all policies to some extent had mixed effects that varied over the time period studied, as work by O'Connor (1973) would lead one to expect. But in broad terms, expenditures for highways, education, and police and fire protection could be classified as investment expenditures, while welfare and health and hospitals were consumption policies. We have added the categories of water and sewer and natural resources to investment expenditures, and parks, general administration, and interest payments to consumption expenditures, to provide an exhaustive categorization of state and local operating expenditures. Work by Dye (1980) supports the classification of highway expenditures as investment. A study by Plaut and Pluta (1983) indirectly supports the categorization of local expenditures (public safety and water and sewer) as investments. These authors found positive effects of property taxes on growth, and property taxes are levied primarily by local governments.

For the federal government we do not have studies comparable to those conducted at the state and local level. However, it seems reasonable to include all transfer-type policies in the consumption domain. These include the Office of Management and Budget classifications of income security, Social Security, and veterans' benefits. Also included in consumption expenditures are interest on the debt and agriculture programs, where the overwhelming majority of funds go for support payments. Unlike state and local governments, whose debts fund capital projects, the federal government funds its ongoing operations through the deficit. Hence it is clearly a consumption expenditure.

Investment expenditures at the federal level are more difficult to classify. Even if they are designed to influence economic growth, they may not do so, and we have no empirical studies to help with the distinction. The state-level studies suggest that transportation and education expenditures would fall in the investment domain; we have also included natural resources, community and regional development (including housing), natural resources (including energy), and science and technology (primarily funding NASA) in the investment category.

There are two caveats concerning this ratio—one of which we can feel reassured about, one where we have little information in either direction. First is the question of the two components of the investment-consumption ratio following different paths over time. We have analyzed inflation-adjusted per capita expenditures in each of the categories over time and are reassured that the simple presentation of the ratio, as we do in figure 11.2, does not obscure any more detailed information that would be of value.

Second, investment expenditures by both levels of government are underestimated. The federal government often pursues its investment objectives through monetary policies and the tax code. States and localities use a separate capital budget for many investment projects, and we have studied only operating budgets. These two factors operate in opposite directions for the ratio, but they are unlikely to offset one another.

Appendix B

Regression Analysis of Agenda Dynamics

In this book we have presented data graphically, although more technical methods of analysis are available. We have chosen this method for two reasons. First, and most importantly, the graphs speak for themselves. There is seldom any ambiguity about the processes we discuss in this book. Since more advanced techniques were not generally necessary to make the points important to our theory, we have opted to keep our analysis as simple as possible, hoping that such a strategy might broaden the appeal and usefulness of this book. Second, there are a number of problems in fitting time-series analytical techniques to agenda models. We have occasionally fit statistical models to our data, and in this appendix we present some of these results. First, however, we note some of the particular problems one encounters in fitting models to agenda time series. None of the following remarks ought to be taken as evidence that more systematic models cannot be developed. We simply want to indicate some of the difficulties that will be encountered in the process, since we expect that we, and others, are likely to spend considerable effort in the future fitting more sophisticated statistical models to series such as those presented here.

The most critical problem is that the theory we have developed in this book, like any theory based on positive feedback and strong interaction effects, offers strong explanatory power but little predictive power. One can model the results of a positive-feedback process, but one often has no idea exactly when that process might begin. Even more problematical is that relationships among variables change during the period of agenda access. We have repeatedly stressed the way in which policy images change at critical points. We have observed this happening to other variables, such as the relationship between indicators of the systemic and formal agendas.

The typical pattern is for agenda data to increase dramatically at points on the series, then decline abruptly. Such a pattern causes the series to be non-stationary (see Box and Jenkins 1976, 26). This will be superimposed on a second source of nonstationarity: the tendency of both the media and governmental institutions such as Congress to deal with more issues than in the past. The latter problem is easy to deal with. In regression models, trends can be incorporated, with agenda dynamics modeled as deviations from trends. In ARIMA models, differencing the time series will correct for such nonstationarity (McCleary and Hay 1980, 43–44), though there may remain severe problems of heteroskedasticity.

The unpredictable surges and declines in agenda dynamics is the fundamental problem for time series modeling. In some cases, surges of issues on the agenda are preceded by slow softening-up periods, but in others it is more sudden. Now a complex intervention model, either using regression or ARIMA techniques, could be developed, but such models would be different for each case, not a single, theoretically based, solution. One never has a strong theoretical reason for expecting an outbreak in one year rather than another. While our understanding of the systems of punctuated equilibrium that we have described are accurate at the systemic level, they cannot be used to provide precise estimates for the behavior of any particular issue. We simply do not know when a critical point will occur, when a Schattschneider mobilization may be successful, when institutions may be redesigned, or when other factors will combine to create a positive feedback leading to rapid change. Now of course one can redescribe the time series through regression equations, but there is no more predictive power in that than in any other means of description.

In dealing with agenda time series, one finds that the variance of the series will not be stationary after taking first differences, which achieves stationarity for series means. So even when the mean for a series is zero, variances are not constant. Indeed, we believe that students of public agenda processes ought to study variances of series as well as intervention components. Variances indicate that the series has become unstable, and that is exactly what the complex interaction processes at critical points cause. While a theory of punctuated equilibrium implies certain periods of great instability (and high variance of the first differences, therefore), the statistical models that are most common in political science and economics tend to assume constant variance.

There is another way of understanding the general point here. Autocorrelation tends to be a problem in time series models plagued with underspecification, that is, the analyst has failed to take into consideration all relevant factors in a regression model. In our cases, with data usually collected on an annual basis, and the possibility of many different sources of instability, many of which are related to each other, we are unlikely ever to have a complete specification statistically combined with a large number of cases before and after any particular point. In any reasonably simple regression model of agenda processes, autocorrelation is likely to be a problem, since relationships among

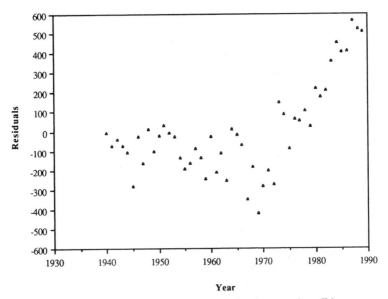

Figure B.1. Regression residuals for grants predicted by hearings on urban affairs.

the component variables differ during periods of low and high agenda status. Figure B.1 presents an example.

In chapter 7 we presented data on the relationship between congressional hearings on urban affairs and grants to states and localities. Figure 7.2 showed the growth in both hearings and grants during the 1960s and 1970s. Figure B.1 graphs the residuals of a regression which simply models grants as a function of hearings, with no lags. The figure shows how severe the autocorrelation problem is: errors are virtually all negative during the early part of the series, then grow steadily during the 1970s and 1980s. The reasons for this are twofold. First, during the late 1960s and early 1970s, the expected grant totals (based on the numbers of hearings) exceeded the actual. This can easily be corrected by lagging the number of hearings, since it takes time to translate hearings into grants. Second, during the 1980s, the actual grant amount exceeded the expected amount based on hearings. Congress lost interest in urban affairs, but a grant legacy continued. One could also correct for this loss of interest easily enough with a simple interaction term or with a new series of lags. We have made these corrections, and we can produce a model which fits much better than the simultaneous one; further, with appropriate interventions and interaction terms, we can do away with the autocorrelation problem altogether. Unfortunately these improvements in the statistical fit each tend to be policy specific; very few of these improvements in the fit of the statistical model can be carried over to the next issue that we might want to study. For example, urban affairs hearings in Congress receded quickly after an initial surge, but in the area of drugs, they continued to be held at a high level after the initial surge onto the public agenda around 1969 (see fig. 8.2). Our point is simple: one can always fit a model to time series on agenda access, but success in one issue-area does not imply generalizability across issues.

Having laid out the pitfalls, and our general feelings that our purposes in this book were best served by a simple graphical illustration of the data, we present below some of the regression models we have employed.

Regression Results and Interpretations

In the case of urban affairs, the equations below are intended only to demonstrate the much superior fit offered by lag models than by simultaneous ones. The tables below present complete regression results for the relationships between congressional hearings and intergovernmental grants, and between media stories indexed in the *Readers' Guide* and hearings. Table B.1 presents regression results for the relationship between *Readers' Guide* citations and congressional hearings, separately for the entire series (1911–89) and for the more recent period (1959–89). The latter results are reported in the text because the complete series are nonstationary (that is, both trend upward), but the more recent series do not share this problem. Figure 7.1 presented the full series which forms the basis for these regressions. The regression coefficients in table B.1 represent the expected increase in annual congressional hearings for each article appearing in the *Readers' Guide*. Both the goodness-of-fit measures and the size and significance levels of the coefficients show the better fit of the lagged model.

Table B.2 reports the results of a similar regression where the dependent

Table B.1 *Readers' Guide* coverage and congressional hearings on urban affairs

	N	Regression Coefficient	Standard Error	R-squared	Durbin-Watson
Entire Series (1911–89)					
Simultaneous	79	0.579	.078	.415	0.354
Lagged (5)	79	0.753	.054	.729	
Recent series (1959–89)					
Simultaneous	31	−0.012	.133	.003	0.391
Lagged (5)	31	0.410	.095	.449	

Notes: Both models use the number of congressional hearings as the dependent variable. Independent variables are the number of articles in the *Readers' Guide* either in the same year or five years previously. The models also included a constant; those values are not reported.

Table B.2   Federal grants to states and localities predicted by number of
congressional hearings, various categories of urban affairs, 1959–1989

Dependent Variable	N	Regression Coefficient	Standard Error	R-squared	Durbin-Watson
Total grants					
Simultaneous	47	1.12	.121	.639	0.388
Lagged (5)	47	1.21	.079	.845	1.17
Social issues					
Simultaneous	47	0.75	.405	.007	0.003
Lagged (6)	47	1.64	.341	.372	0.585
Community development					
Simultaneous	47	0.31	.035	.639	0.912
Lagged (5)	47	0.32	.032	.704	0.915
Infrastructure					
Simultaneous	47	1.02	.277	.231	0.375
Lagged (3)	47	1.27	.247	.386	0.582
Environmental					
Simultaneous	47	0.17	.118	.121	0.566

variable is the inflation-adjusted grants-in-aid going to state and local governments and the independent variable is the number of congressional hearings.
This analysis reports results separately for each of four categories of urban
grants. Within each category, two models are estimated: one with hearings and
grants considered simultaneously; the other with hearings lagged. In the lagged
models, hearings in one year are supposed to be related to grants in a later year.
The regression coefficients indicate the dollars (in millions) in grant funds associated with an increase of one congressional hearing. Our theory does not imply
that each hearing leads to more money being spent; rather increased attention,
as indicated by hearings, could be so hypothesized. We use hearings as an indicator of general levels of congressional attention, not as a simple policy tool.

For every budget category except environmental, the lagged model fits far
better than the simultaneous model. Because we have no reason to expect any
particular lag between hearings and budgets, we have examined all two- to six-
year lags. For all policy areas except environmental, any lag fits better than the
simultaneous model; table B.2 presents the lag which fits the equation best.

Autocorrelation plagues these equations because hearings and grants are not
simply related. The relationship changes over time, often after an issue reaches
the agenda. Hence we are not in a position to pursue more precise modeling of
the relationship between the formal agenda and policy outputs. The reasons for
this autocorrelation are clearly associated with our theories and understandings of agenda-setting, on the other hand. Institutions change abruptly in their
willingness to address certain issues; statistically this implies that errors will
be serially correlated—negative for some period before a shift, as pressure

builds up for change, then positive during a later period, as in figure B.1. While any one of these cases could be fit with an accurate model, our comparisons of a number of them convince us that no single model could fit them all. The various chapters of the book have described our understanding of why these differences exist; we choose not to re-create these descriptions statistically, though we know that a statistical description of these changes might be just as worthwhile as our graphical illustrations of them.

In the study of policy agendas, one might not be interested in levels of variables at all. In particular, one might be interested in comparing slopes between variables over short spans of activity. That is, the increased slope in policy response that occurred in the late 1960s and early 1970s in the case of urban affairs (see fig. 7.3) may be more important than the absolute level of such activity. A similar point can be made for the relationship between media coverage and hearings. Regression and time-series techniques can be useful for showing the changes in such slopes. Table B.3 presents a statistical version of the information contained in figure 8.2.

Table B.3 indicates how a simple statistical analysis can be used to show more systematically the changing nature of the relationship between two variables over time. As drug abuse moved high onto the congressional agenda in the 1970s, an overall increase of approximately one additional hearing per year was actually made up of two contrasting elements: a decrease of about one hearing on education questions, and an increase of about two hearings per year on enforcement questions. Figure 8.2 showed this information graphically; table B.3 tells the same story, relatively accurately.

Table B.3 Determinants of congressional hearings on drug abuse, 1945–1986

	Model 1	Model 2	Model 3
	All Drug Abuse Hearings	Education Focus	Enforcement Focus
Constant	−1.50	−2.41	0.91
	(1.82)	(1.27)	(1.34)
Intervention variable for Nixon's war on drugs (1969)	31.35	25.09	6.26
	(3.50)	(2.45)	(2.57)
Trend, beginning in 1970	0.94	−1.07	2.01
	(0.36)	(0.25)	(0.27)
Moving average of articles on drug abuse in the *Readers' Guide*, previous 5 years	0.34	0.23	0.11
	(0.087)	(0.061)	(0.064)
R^2	.94	.88	0.92
N	42	42	42
Durban-Watson statistic	2.31	1.74	2.06

Notes: Entries are unstandardized regression coefficients; standard errors are in parentheses.

Table B.4 State investment ratios and the impact of
consumption-based federal grants, 1955–1989

	Model I Grant Impact Only	Model II With Federal I-Ratio
Constant	4.036	3.862
	(0.685)	(0.876)
Grant impact	−0.251	−0.246
	(0.0093)	(0.0085)
Federal I-Ratio		0.571
		(0.197)
R-squared	.958	.967
N	34	34
Durbin-Watson	0.991	1.17

Notes: Entries are unstandardized regression coefficients; standard errors are in parentheses.

In chapter 11, we presented graphically the relationship between the state investment ratio and grant impact, defined as the percentage of state and local budgets going to consumption purposes that came from federal grants (estimated by grants going to individuals). The equations presented in table B.4 quantify these relationships.

Table B.4 presents estimates of two models. Model I assumes that state investment ratios vary only because of the impact of federal grants and exogenous factors. Model II includes the federal investment ratio in the equation to see if the federal government's priorities affect the priorities of the state governments in ways not accounted for by the grant structure. These equations suggest that the federal government does indeed influence state priorities in other ways than the grant structure, but that the primary mode of influence operates through the grant structure. (The negative coefficient for grant impact simply means that consumption priorities of the federal government cause state investment priorities to decline, as is to be expected.)

The Durbin-Watson statistic implies autocorrelation problems in both equations. This stems from changes in the relationship between the key variables. As we discussed in chapter 11, federal grants had little effect on state priorities in the 1950s and early 1960s. Then between 1967 and 1978, state investment priorities and grant impact became tightly linked. After that period, the relationship again grew weak.

We can deal with this autocorrelation problem in two ways: either by fitting linear regression estimates separately for the distinct periods or by fitting a curvilinear model. Either is satisfactory, but the curvilinear model has some significant advantages. For example, a cubic polynomial regression on the state investment ratio for grant impact alone yields an R-squared of .965, with all three regressors (x, x-square, and x-cubed) statistically significant, and a

Durbin-Watson statistic of 1.26. This model implies an S-shaped curve for the relationship between grant impact and state investment ratio, with the greatest changes in the investment ratio coming in the middle of the curve. During the early period, when grant levels are low, they have little impact on state behavior. Later, as grants pass a threshold, the relationship becomes strong; finally, a saturation point appears, and the relationship is again weak.

This exercise reinforces the major point of this appendix: that the occurrence of strong interaction effects at irregular periods in politics implies that we can never know in advance when positive feedback will occur. Further, these systems are characterized by strong threshold and saturation effects. We may model the occurrence with nonlinear equations (such as the cubic polynomial regression above) or with interrupted time-series designs, but these are posthoc descriptions of the process rather than rigorous predictors of it. We may expect the relationship to follow such a curvilinear pattern, but we may not be able to offer precise predictions of when the process may begin or when the satuaration point may be reached. Thus, we face the continuing trade-off between prediction and explanation in science. While we can predict the type of change that is likely to occur, we generally cannot predict its precise manifestations or timing in each case, no matter how well we understand it or describe it after the fact. This fundamental principle need not frustrate the science of politics; rather, it should liberate it.

References

Aberbach, Joel D. 1990. *Keeping a Watchful Eye: The Politics of Congressional Oversight.* Washington, D.C.: Brookings Institution.

Aberbach, Joel D., Robert D. Putnam, and Bert A. Rockman. 1981. *Bureaucrats and Politicians in Western Europe.* Cambridge: Harvard University Press.

Aldrich, Howard, and Udo Staber. 1986. The Dynamics of Trade Association Evolution in the United States: Birth, Death, and Transformation. Paper presented at the annual meeting of the American Political Science Association, Washington, D.C.

American Humane Association. 1989. *Highlights of Official Aggregate Child Neglect and Abuse Reporting, 1987.* Denver, Colo.

American Lung Association. Tobacco control. http://slati.lungusa.org/appendixa.asp.

Anton, Thomas. 1989. *American Federalism and Public Policy.* Philadelphia: Temple University Press.

Arthur, W. Brian. 1988. Self-Reinforcing Mechanisms in Economics. In Philip W. Anderson, Kenneth J. Arrow, and David Pines, eds., *The Economy as an Evolving Complex System.* Reading, Mass.: Addison-Wesley.

———. 1989. Competing Technologies, Increasing Returns, and Lock-in by Historical Events. *Economic Journal* 99: 1 16–31.

———. 1990. Positive Feedbacks in the Economy. *Scientific American,* February, 92–99.

Atomic Energy Commission/Nuclear Regulatory Commission. Annual. *Annual Report.* Washington D.C.

Attorney General of the State of California. n.d. Master settlement agreement. http://ag.ca.gov/tobacco/msa.php.

Bach, Stanley, and Steven S. Smith. 1988. *Managing Uncertainty in the House of Representatives.* Washington, D.C.: Brookings Institution.

Bachrach, Peter, and Morton Baratz. 1962. The Two Faces of Power. *American Political Science Review* 56: 947–52.

Barabasi, Albert-Laszlo. 2005. The Origins of Bursts and Heavy Tails in Human Dynamics. *Nature* 435 (12 May): 207–11.

316
References

Barrett, Paul. 1990. Moving On: Though the Drug War Isn't Over, Spotlight Turns to Other Issues. *Wall Street Journal,* 11 November.

Baumgartner, Frank R. 1987. Parliament's Capacity to Expand Political Controversy in France. *Legislative Studies Quarterly* 12: 33–54.

———. 1989. *Conflict and Rhetoric in French Policymaking.* Pittsburgh, Penn.: University of Pittsburgh Press.

Baumgartner, Frank R., Jeffrey M. Berry, Marie Hojnacki, David C. Kimball, and Beth L. Leech. 2009. *Lobbying and Policy Change: Who Wins, Who Loses, and Why.* Chicago: University of Chicago Press.

Baumgartner, Frank R., Suzanna L. De Boef, and Amber E. Boydstun. 2008. *The Decline of the Death Penalty and the Discovery of Innocence.* New York: Cambridge University Press.

Baumgartner, Frank R., and Bryan D. Jones. 1991. Agenda Dynamics and Policy Subsystems. *Journal of Politics* 53: 1044–74.

Baumgartner, Frank R., Christoffer Green-Pedersen, and Bryan D. Jones, eds. 2006. Comparative Studies of Policy Agendas. Special issue of the *Journal of European Public Policy* 13 (7).

Baumgartner, Frank R., and Jack L. Walker, Jr. 1988. Survey Research and Membership in Voluntary Associations. *American Journal of Political Science* 32: 908–28.

———. 1990. Response to Smith's "Trends in Voluntary Group Membership: Comments on Baumgartner and Walker": Measurement Validity and the Continuity of Results in Survey Research. *American Journal of Political Science* 34: 662–70.

Beecher, Janice A., Robert J. Lineberry, and Michael J. Rich. 1981. Political Power, the Urban Agenda, and Crime Policies. *Social Science Quarterly* 62: 630–43.

Beer, Samuel. 1976. The Adoption of General Revenue Sharing: A Case Study of Public Sector Politics. *Public Policy* 24: 127–95.

———. 1977. Political Overload and Federalism. *Polity* 10: 5–17.

———. 1978. Federalism, Nationalism, and Democracy in America. *American Political Science Review* 72: 9–22.

Bennett, Lance. 1990. Toward a Theory of Press-State Relations. *Journal of Communication* 40: 103–25.

Bennett, Linda M., and Stephen Bennett. 1990. *Living with Leviathan.* Lawrence: University Press of Kansas.

Bennett, R. R. and D. J. Kettler. 1978. Dramatic Changes in the Costs of Nuclear and Fossil-Fueled Plants. Monograph, EBASCO Services, Inc.

Bentley, Arthur F. 1908. *The Process of Government.* Chicago: University of Chicago Press.

Berry, Jeffrey M. 1977. *Lobbying for the People.* Princeton, N.J.: Princeton University Press.

———. 1989a. *The Interest Group Society.* 2d ed. Glenview, Ill.: Scott, Foresman.

———. 1989b. Subgovernments, Issue Networks, and Political Conflict. In Richard Harris and Sidney Milkis, eds., *Remaking American Politics,* 239–60. Boulder, Colo.: Westview Press.

Berry, Jeffrey M., Frank R. Baumgartner, Marie Hojnacki, Beth L. Leech, and David C. Kimball. 2007. Washington: The Real No-Spin Zone. Paper presented at the annual meeting of the American Political Science Association, Chicago, IL.

Berry, William. 1979. Utility Regulation in the States: The Policy Effects of Professionalism and Salience to the Consumer. *American Journal of Political Science* 23: 263–77.

———. 1984. An Alternative to the Capture Theory of Regulation: The Case of State Public Utility Commissions. *American Journal of Political Science* 28: 524–58.

Best, Joel. 1990. *Threatened Children: Rhetoric and Concern about Child-Victims.* Chicago: University of Chicago Press.

Boeckelman, Keith A. 1989. Industrial Policy in the American States. Ph.D. dissertation, University of Illinois, Urbana.

Bosso, Christopher J. 1987. *Pesticides and Politics: The Life Cycle of a Public Issue.* Pittsburgh, Penn.: University of Pittsburgh Press.

———. 1989. Setting the Agenda: Mass Media and the Discovery of Famine in Ethiopia. In Michael Margolils and Gary Mauser, eds., *Manipulating Public Opinion.* Pacific Grove, Calif.: Brooks- Cole.

———. 1991. Adaptation and Change in the Environmental Movement. In Allan J. Cigler and Burdett A. Loomis, eds., *Interest Group Politics,* 3d ed., 151–76. Washington, D.C.: Congressional Quarterly Inc.

Box, George E. P., and Gwilym M. Jenkins. 1976. *Time Series Analysis: Forecasting and Control.* San Francisco: Holden-Day.

Brinkley, Joel. 1986. Expedient Drug Law: Politics Plays Role in Bull's Emphasis on Enforcement Instead of Education. *New York Times,* 27 October.

Brown, JoAnne. 1990. The Social Construction of Invisible Danger: Two Historical Examples. In Andrew Kirby, ed., *Nothing to Fear: Risks and Hazards in American Society.* Tucson: University of Arizona Press.

Browne, William P. 1988. *Private Interests, Public Policy, and American Agriculture.* Lawrence: University Press of Kansas.

———. 1990. Organized Interests and Their Issue Niches: A Search for Pluralism in a Policy Domain. *Journal of Politics* 52: 477–509.

Bureau of the Census. 1970. *Historical Statistics of the U.S.: Colonial Times to 1970.* Washington, D.C.: Department of Commerce.

———. 1990. *State Government Finances, 1989–90.* Washington, D.C.: Department of Commerce.

———. 1991. *Statistical Abstract of the United States.* Washington, D.C.: Department of Commerce.

Bureau of Justice Statistics, n.d. *Drug Law Violators, 1980–86.* Washington, D.C.: Department of Justice.

Bureh, Deborah M., Karin E. Kock, and Annette Novallo, eds. Annual. *Encyclopedia of Associations.* Detroit: Gale Research.

Burnham, Walter Dean. 1970. *Critical Elections and the Mainsprings of American Politics.* New York: W. W. Norton.

———. 1999. Constitutional Moments and Punctuated Equilibria: A Political Scientist Confronts Bruce Ackerman's "We The People." *The Yale Law Journal* 188: 2237–77.

Burns, James MacGregor. 1978. *Leadership.* New York: Harper and Row.

Campbell, John C. 1979. The Old People Boom and Japanese Policy Making. *Journal of Japanese Studies* 5: 321–57.

Campbell, John L. 1988. *Collapse of an Industry: Nuclear Power and the Contradictions of U.S. Policy.* Ithaca, N.Y.: Cornell University Press.

318

References

Carmines, Edward G., and James A. Stimson. 1986. On the Structure and Sequence of Issue Evolution. *American Political Science Review* 80: 901–20.

———. 1989. *Issue Evolution: Race and the Transformation of American Politics.* Princeton, N.J.: Princeton University Press.

Carson, Rachel. 1962. *Silent Spring.* Boston: Houghton Mifflin.

Cashore, B., and M. Howlett. 2007. Punctuating Which Equilibrium? Understanding Thermostatic Policy Dynamics in Pacific Northwest Forestry. *American Journal of Political Science* 51: 532–51.

Casstevens, Thomas. 1980. Birth and Death Processes of Governmental Bureaus in the United States. *Behavioral Science* 25: 161–65.

Catanzaro, Michael J. 1998. Republicans Planning to Approve a Tobacco Deal that Massively Increases Federal Power and Taxes. *Human Interest,* 27 March.

Chubb, John E., 1985. The Political Economy of Federalism. *American Political Science Review* 79: 994–1015.

Chubb, John E., and Paul E. Peterson, eds. 1989. *Can the Government Govern?* Washington, D.C.: Brookings Institution.

Clymer, Adam. 1989. Polls Contrast U.S.'s and Public's Views. *New York Times,* 22 May.

Cobb, Roger W., and Charles D. Elder. 1983. *Participation in American Politics: The Dynamics of Agenda-Building.* Baltimore: Johns Hopkins University Press.

Cobb, Roger W., Jeannie-Keith Ross, and Marc Howard Ross. 1976. Agenda Building as a Comparative Political Process. *American Political Science Review* 70: 126–38.

Cohen, Bernard. 1980. Society's Valuation of Life Saving in Radiation Protection and Other Contexts. *Health Physics* 38: 33–51.

———. 1981. Nuclear Journalism: Lies, Damned Lies, and News Reports. *Policy Review,* 70–74.

Cohen, Michael, James G. March, and Johan P. Olsen. 1972. A Garbage Can Theory of Organizational Choice. *Administrative Science Quarterly* 17: 1–25.

Congressional Information Service, Inc. Annual. *CIS/Annual: Abstracts of Congressional Publications and Legislative History Citations.* Washington, D.C.

Conlon, Timothy. 1988. *New Federalism: Intergovernmental Reform from Nixon to Reagan.* Washington, D.C.: Brookings Institution.

Conn, Richard L., Marguerite L. Leng, and Joseph R. Solga. 1983. *Pesticide Regulation Handbook.* New York: Executive Enterprises.

Cook, Fay Lomax, and Wesley G. Skogan. 1989. Agenda Setting: Convergent and Divergent Voice Models of the Rise and Fall of Policy Issues. Paper.

Costain, W. Douglas. 1991. "Up and Down with Ecology" Revisited: Anthony Downs and the Political Evolution of the Environmental Movement. Paper presented at the annual meeting of the Western Political Science Association, Seattle, Washington, 21–23 March.

Crenson, Matthew A. 1971. *The Unpolitics of Air Pollution.* Baltimore: Johns Hopkins University Press.

Dahl, Robert A. 1961. *Who Governs?* New Haven: Yale University Press.

Davidson, Roger H. 1989. Multiple Referral of Legislation in the U.S. Senate. *Legislative Studies Quarterly* 14: 375–92.

Davidson, Roger H., and Walter J. Oleszek. 1977. *Congress against Itself.* Bloomington: Indiana University Press.

Davidson, Roger H., Walter J. Oleszek, and Thomas Kephart. 1988. One Bill, Many Committees: Multiple Referrals in the U.S. House of Representatives. *Legislative Studies Quarterly* 13: 3–28.

Del Sesto, Steven L. 1980. Conflicting Ideologies of Nuclear Power: Congressional Testimony on Nuclear Reactor Safety. *Public Policy* 28: 39–70.

Derthick, Martha. 1979. *Policymaking for Social Security.* Washington, D.C.: Brookings Institution.

Derthick, Martha, and Paul J. Quirk. 1985. *The Politics of Deregulation.* Washington, D.C.: Brookings Institution.

Dodd, Lawrence, and Richard Schott. 1979. *Congress and the Administrative State.* New York: Wiley.

Downs, Anthony. 1972. Up and Down with Ecology: The Issue Attention Cycle. *Public Interest* 28: 38–50.

Duffy, Robert J. 1997. *Nuclear Politics in America.* Lawrence, Kansas: University Press of Kansas.

Dunlap, Thomas. 1981. *DDT: Scientists, Citizens, and Public Policy.* Princeton, N.J.: Princeton University Press.

Dye, Thomas. 1980. Taxing, Spending, and Economic Growth in the States. *Journal of Politics* 42: 1085–1117.

Edelman, Murray. 1964. *The Symbolic Uses of Politics.* Urbana: University of Illinois Press.

————. 1989. *Constructing the Political Spectacle.* Chicago: University of Chicago Press.

Edwards, George C., III. 1989. *At the Margins: Presidential Leadership of Congress.* New Haven: Yale University Press.

Eisinger, Peter K. 1988. *Rise of the Entrepreneurial State.* Madison: University of Wisconsin Press.

Elder, Charles D., and Roger W. Cobb. 1983. *The Political Uses of Symbols.* New York: Longman.

Eldredge, Niles. 1985. *Time Frames.* New York: Simon and Shuster.

Eldredge, Niles, and Stephen Jay Gould. 1972. Punctuated Equilibria: An Alternative to Phyletic Gradualism. In Thomas J. M. Schopf, ed., *Models in Paleobiology.* San Francisco: Freeman Cooper.

Elkin, Stephen. 1987. *City and Regime in the American Republic.* Chicago: University of Chicago Press.

Eyestone, Robert. 1978. *From Social Issues to Public Policy.* New York: Wiley.

Falco, Mathea. 1989. *Winning the Drug War: A National Strategy.* New York: Priority Press.

Fenno, Richard. 1966. *The Power of the Purse.* Boston: Little, Brown.

Fiorina, Morris P. 1989. *Congress: Keystone of the Washington Establishment.* 2d ed. New Haven: Yale University Press.

Fischhoff, Baruch, Paul Slovic, Sarah Lichtenstein, Stephen Read, and Barbara Combs. 1978. How Safe Is Safe Enough? A Psychometric Study of Attitudes towards Technological Risks and Benefits. *Policy Science* 9: 127–52.

Foard, Ashley and Hilbert Fefferman. 1966. Federal Urban Renewal Legislation. In James Q. Wilson, ed., *Urban Renewal: The Record and the Controversy.* Cambridge: MIT Press.

320
References

Foster, Mary Lecron. 1977. Speaking of Energy. Department of Anthropology, University of California, Berkeley. Paper.

Freudenburg, William R., and Eugene A. Rosa, eds. 1984. *Public Reaction to Nuclear Power: Are there Critical Masses?* Boulder, Colo.: Westview Press.

Fritschler, A. Lee. 1989. *Smoking and Politics.* 4th ed. Englewood Cliffs, N.J.: Prentice-Hall.

Frontline. 1998. Inside the Tobacco Deal. Washington, DC: Public Broadcasting Service. http://www.pbs.org/wgbh/pages/frontline/shows/settlement/.

Gais, Thomas L., Mark A. Peterson, and Jack L. Walker. 1984. Interest Groups, Iron Triangles, and Representative Institutions in American National Government. *British Journal of Political Science* 14: 161–85.

Gamson, William. 1990. *The Strategy of Social Protest.* 2d ed. Belmont, Calif.: Wadsworth Publishing Co.

Givel, Michael. 2006a. Punctuated Equilibrium in Limbo: The Tobacco Lobby and U.S. State Policymaking from 1990 to 2003. *Policy Studies Journal* 34: 405–18.

———. 2006b. Change through Multiple Policy Instruments and Venues: The Tobacco Industry Policy Subsystem in the States from 1990 to 2003. *Policy Studies Journal* 34: 453–57.

Glantz, Stanton A., John Slade, Lisa A. Bero, and Peter Hanauer. 1998. *The Cigarette Papers.* San Francisco: University of California Press.

Golay, Michael W. 1980. How Prometheus Came to Be Bound: Nuclear Regulation in America. *Technology Review* 82: 29–39.

Goldberg, Peter. 1980. The Federal Government's Response to Illicit Drugs, 1969–1978. In Drug Abuse Council, *The Facts about Drug Abuse.* New York: Free Press.

Goodman, Marshall R., and Margaret T. Wrightson. 1987. *Managing Regulatory Reform.* New York: Praeger.

Gormley, William T, Jr. 1983. *The Politics of Public Utility Regulation.* Pittsburgh, Penn.: University of Pittsburgh Press.

Gould, Stephen Jay. 1989. *Wonderful Life.* New York: Norton.

Greenberg, George D., Jeffrey A. Miller, Lawrence B. Mohr, and Bruce C. Vladeck. 1977. Developing Public Policy Theory: Perspectives from Empirical Research. *American Political Science Review* 71: 1532–43.

Greenberg, Michael R., David B. Sachsman, Peter M. Sandman, and Kandice L. Salomone. 1989. Risk, Drama and Geography in Coverage of Environmental Risk by Network TV. *Journalism Quarterly* 66: 267–76.

Greenstone, J. David, and Paul Peterson. 1976. *Race and Authority in Urban Politics.* Chicago: University of Chicago Press.

Griffith, Ernest S. 1939. *The Impasse of Democracy.* New York: Harrison-Hilton Books.

———. 1961. *Congress: Its Contemporary Role.* New York: New York University Press.

Grossback, David, David Peterson, and James Stimson. 2006. *Mandate Politics.* Cambridge: Cambridge University Press.

Gusfield, Joseph. 1963. *Symbolic Crusade: Status Politics and the American Temperance Movement.* Urbana, Ill.: University of Illinois Press.

———. 1981. *The Culture of Public Problems: Drinking-Driving and the Symbolic Order.* Chicago: University of Chicago Press.

Hall, Richard L., and Bernard Grofman. 1990. The Committee Assignment Process and the Conditional Nature of Committee Bias. *American Political Science Review* 84: 1149–66.

Hamm, Keith. 1983. Patterns of Influence among Committees, Agencies, and Interest Groups. *Legislative Studies Quarterly* 8: 379–426.

Hansen, John Mark. 1985. The Political Economy of Group Membership. *American Political Science Review* 79: 79–81.

Hayes, Michael T. 1992. *Incrementalism and Public Policy.* New York: Longman.

Heclo, Hugh. 1978. Issue Networks in the Executive Establishment. In Anthony King, ed., *The New American Political System.* Washington, D.C.: American Enterprise Institute.

Hilgartner, Stephen, and Charles L. Bosk, 1988. The Rise and Fall of Social Problems: A Public Arenas Model. *American Journal of Sociology* 94: 53–78.

Huntington, Samuel P. 1981. *American Politics: The Promise of Disharmony.* Cambridge: Harvard University Press.

Hurley, Patricia A., and Rick K. Wilson. 1989. Partisan Voting Patterns in the U.S. Senate, 1877–1986. *Legislative Studies Quarterly* 14: 225–50.

Inglehart, Ronald. 1984. The Fear of Living Dangerously: Public Attitudes toward Nuclear War. *Public Opinion* 7: 41–44.

Information Please Database. Pearson Education, Inc. http://www.infoplease.com/ipa/A0908700.html.

Is Government Dead? 1989. *Time,* 23 October.

Jacob, Hebert. 1988. *Silent Revolution.* Chicago: University of Chicago Press.

Jacobs, James. 1989. *Drunk Driving: An American Dilemma.* Chicago: University of Chicago Press.

James I. 1604/1869. *Essayes in Poesie, 1585: A Counterblaste to Tobacco, 1604.* Ed. Edward Arber. Transcribed by Risa S. Bear, the University of Oregon Renascence Editions, 2003. http://www.uoregon.edu/~rbear/james1.html.

Jenkins-Smith, Hank C., Gilbert K. St. Clair, and Brian Woods. 1991. Explaining Change in Policy Subsystems: Analysis of Coalition Stability and Defection over Time. *American Journal of Political Science* 35: 851–80.

Johnson, Eric J., and Amos Tversky. 1984. Representations of Perceptions of Risks. *Journal of Experimental Psychology* 113: 55–70.

Jones, Bryan D. 1986. Government and Business: The Automobile Industry and the Public Sector in Michigan. *Political Geography Quarterly* 5: 369–84.

———. 1989. Why Weakness Is a Strength. *Urban Affairs Quarterly* 25: 30–40.

———. 1990. Public Policies and Economic Growth in the American States. *Journal of Politics* 52: 219–33.

———. 1994. *Reconceiving Decision-Making in Democratic Politics.* Chicago: University of Chicago Press.

———. 2001. *Politics and the Architecture of Choice.* Chicago: University of Chicago Press.

Jones, Bryan D., and Lynn W. Bachelor. 1986. *The Sustaining Hand.* Lawrence: University Press of Kansas.

Jones, Bryan D., and Frank R. Baumgartner. 2005. *The Politics of Attention.* Chicago: University of Chicago Press.

Jones, Bryan D., et al. 2007. *A General Empirical Law of Public Budgets: A Comparative Analysis.* Seattle: Center for American Politics and Public Policy.

Jones, Bryan D., and Michelle Wolfe. 2007. Public Policy and the Mass Media: An Information Processing Approach. Paper prepared for the Workshop on Public Policy and the Mass Media: Influences and Interactions, European Consortium for Political Research, Helsinki, Finland, 7–12 May.

Jones, Charles O. 1975. *Clean Air.* Pittsburgh, Penn.: University of Pittsburgh Press.

———. 1979. American Politics and the Organization of Energy Decision Making. *Annual Review of Energy* 4: 99–121.

Jones, Charles O., and Randall Strahan. 1985. The Effect of Energy Politics on Congressional and Executive Organization in the 1970s. *Legislative Studies Quarterly* 10: 151–79.

Kantor, Paul. 1988. *The Dependent City.* Glenview, Ill.: Scott, Foresman.

Kaufman, Herbert. 1976. *Are Government Organizations Immortal?* Washington, D.C.: Brookings Institution.

Kerr, Peter. 1986. Anatomy of an Issue: Drugs, the Evidence, the Reaction. *New York Times,* 17 November.

Kessler, David A. 2001. *A Question of Intent: A Great American Battle With A Deadly Industry.* New York: Public Affairs Press.

King, David C. 1991. Congressional Committee Jurisdictions and the Consequences of Reforms. Paper presented at the annual meeting of the Midwest Political Science Association, Chicago, Ill., 18–20 April.

Kingdon, John W. 1984. *Agendas, Alternatives, and Public Policies.* Boston: Little, Brown.

Kirp, David L. 1982. Professionalization as a Policy Choice. *World Politics* 34: 137–74.

Kitschelt, Herbert B. 1986. Political Opportunity Structures and Political Protest: Anti-Nuclear Movements in Four Democracies. *British Journal of Political Science* 16: 57–85.

Knoke, David. 1990. *Organizing for Collective Action: The Political Economies of Associations.* New York: Aldine de Gruyter.

Komonoff, Charles. 1981. *Power Plant Cost Escalation.* New York: Van Nostrand Reinhold.

Krehbiel, Keith. 1990. Are Congressional Committees Composed of Preference Outliers? *American Political Science Review* 84: 149–63.

———. 1991. *Information and Legislative Organization.* Ann Arbor: University of Michigan Press.

Kuklinski, James, Daniel S. Metlay, and W. D. Kay. 1982. Citizen Knowledge and Choices on the Complex Issue of Nuclear Energy. *American Journal of Political Science* 26: 615–42.

Lanouette, William. 1990. How Atomic Agency Managed the News in Early Years. *Newsletter of the National Association of Science Writers* 38: 1–3.

Larson, Stephanie, and David Grier. 1990. Agenda Setting and AIDS. Paper prepared for presentation at the annual meeting of the American Political Science Association, San Francisco, Calif., August 29–September 2.

Laurence, Michael. 1988. The Legal Context in the United States. In Michael Laurence, John Snortum, and Franklin Zimring, eds., *Social Control of the Drinking Driver.* Chicago: University of Chicago Press.

Lender, Mark, and James Martin. 1987. *Drinking in America.* Rev. ed. New York: Free Press.

Lester, James P., and W. Douglas Costain. 1991. The Evolution of Environmentalism, 1890–1990: From Elitism to Participatory Democracy? Paper presented at the annual meeting of the American Political Science Association, Washington, D.C., August 29–September 1.

Lindblom, Charles E. 1959. The Science of Muddling Through. *Public Administration Review* 19: 79–88.

———. 1977. *Politics and Markets.* New York: Basic Books.

Livingston, William. 1952. A Note on the Nature of Federalism. *Political Science Quarterly* 63: 81–95.

Logan, John, and Harvey Molotch. 1987. *Urban Fortunes.* Berkeley: University of California Press.

Lowe, Philip, and Jane Goyder. 1983. *Environmental Groups in Politics.* London: George Allen and Unwin.

Lowi, Theodore J. 1964. American Business, Public Policy, Case Studies and Political Theory. *World Politics* 16: 677–93.

———. 1979. *The End of Liberalism.* 2d ed. New York: Norton.

Maass, Arthur. 1951. *Muddy Waters: The Army Engineers and the Nation's Rivers.* Cambridge: Harvard University Press.

May, Peter, Joshua Sapotichne, and Samuel Workman. 2006. Policy Coherence and Policy Domains. *Policy Studies Journal* 34: 301–403.

McCleary, Richard, and Richard Hay. 1980. *Applied Time Series Analysis for the Social Sciences.* Beverly Hills, Calif.: Sage.

McCombs, Maxwell E. 1981. The Agenda-Setting Approach. In Dan D. Nimmo and Keith R. Sanders, eds., *Handbook of Political Communication.* Beverly Hills, Calif.: Sage.

McConnell, Grant. 1967. *Private Power and American Democracy.* New York: Alfred A. Knopf.

McCubbins, Matthew, and Thomas Schwartz. 1984. Congressional Oversight Overlooked: Police Patrols versus Fire Alarms. *American Journal of Political Science* 28: 165–79.

McFarland, Andrew S. 1987. Interest Groups and Theories of Power in America. *British Journal of Political Science* 17: 129–47.

———. 1991. Interest Groups and Political Time: Cycles in America. *British Journal of Political Science* 21: 257–84.

Majone, Giandomenico. 1989. *Evidence, Argument, and Persuasion in the Policy Process.* New Haven: Yale University Press.

Marcus, Ruth. 1991. Bush Wants More Drug War Funding. *Houston Chronicle,* 1 February.

Mayhew, David. 1991. *Divided We Govern.* New Haven: Yale University Press.

Mazur, Allan. 1981a. *The Dynamics of Technical Controversy.* Washington, D.C.: Communications Press.

———. 1981b. Media Coverage and Public Opinion on Scientific Controversies. *Journal of Communication* 31: 106–16.

Meier, Kenneth. 1985. *Regulation: Politics, Bureaucracy, and Economics.* New York: St. Martin's.

Milward, H. Brinton, and Wendy Laird. 1990. Where Does Policy Come From? Paper presented at the annual meeting of the Western Political Science Association, Newport Beach, Calif., 23–25 March.

Mitchell, Robert C. 1981. From Elite Quarrel to Mass Movement. *Society* 18: 76–84.

Molotch, Harvey, and Marilyn Lester. 1974. News as Purposive Behavior: On the Strategic Uses of Routine Events, Accidents, and Scandals. *American Sociological Review* 39: 101–12.

Monitoring and Evaluation Program. 2002. Influence of the Tobacco Industry on Wisconsin Tobacco Control Policies. Madison, WI: University of Wisconsin Comprehensive Cancer Center, figure 7.

Montgomery, T. L. and D. J. Rose. 1979. Some Institutional Problems of the U.S. Nuclear Industry. *Technology Review* 81: 53–62.

Mooz, William E. 1979. *A Second Cost Analysis of Light Water Reactor Power Plants.* Santa Monica, Calif.: Rand Corporation.

Morone, Joseph G., and Edward J, Woodhouse. 1989. *The Demise of Nuclear Energy?* New Haven: Yale University Press.

Musto, David. 1987. *The American Disease.* Exp. ed. New York: Oxford University Press.

Myers, John. 1986. A Survey of Child Abuse and Neglect Reporting Statutes. *Journal of Juvenile Law* 10: 1–72.

Nader, Ralph. 1965. *Unsafe at Any Speed.* New York: Grossman.

National Advisory Commission on Civil Disorders. 1968. *Report.* New York: New York Times.

National Center for Health Statistics. 2004. Facts A to Z. http://www.cdc.gov/nchs/fastats/lcod.htm.

National Institute on Drug Abuse. 1989. *Annual Data 1988: Data from the Drug Abuse Warning Network.* Washington, D.C.: U.S. Department of Health and Human Services, Public Health Service.

———. N.d. *Drug Abuse, Drinking, and Smoking: National Survey Results from High School, College, and Young Adult Populations, 1975–1988.* Washington, D.C.: U.S. Department of Health and Human Services, Public Health Service.

Neilson, Lars B., 2002. *American Tobacco Policy in the 20th Century.* Seattle: Center for American Politics and Public Policy, University of Washington.

Nelkin, Dorothy. 1971. *Nuclear Power and Its Critics.* Ithaca, N.Y.: Cornell University Press.

———. 1987. *Selling Science.* New York: W. H. Freeman.

Nelkin, Dorothy, and Susan Fallows. 1978. The Evolution of the Nuclear Debate: The Role of Public Participation. *Annual Review of Energy* 3: 275–312.

Nelson, Barbara J. 1984. *Making an Issue of Child Abuse: Political Agenda Setting for Social Problems.* Chicago: University of Chicago Press.

O'Connor, James 1973. *The Fiscal Crisis of the State.* New York: St. Martin's.

Office of Managment and Budget. 1991. Historical Tables. Budget of the United States Government, Fiscal Year 1992. Washington, D.C.: Government Printing Office.

Olson, Mancur. 1965. *The Logic of Collective Action: Public Goods and the Theory of Groups.* Cambridge: Harvard University Press.

———. 1982. *The Rise and Decline of Nations.* New Haven: Yale University Press.

Olson, Susan M. 1990. Interest Group Litigation in Federal District Court: Beyond the Political Disadvantage Theory. *Journal of Politics* 52: 854–82.

Oreskes, Michael. 1990. Drug War Underlines Fickleness of Public. *New York Times,* 6 September.

Ornstein, Norman J., Thomas E. Mann, and Michael J. Malbin. 1990. *Vital Statistics on Congress, 1989–1990.* Washington, D.C.: Congressional Quarterly Press.

Page, Benjamin. 1983. *Who Gets What from Government.* Berkeley: University of California Press.

Paik, Soon, and William R. Schriver. 1981. The Effect of Increased Regulation on Capital Costs and Manual Labor Requirements of Nuclear Power Plants. *Engineering Economist* 26: 223–44.

Patterson, Samuel C., and Gregory A. Caldeira. 1990. Standing up for Congress: Variations in Public Esteem since the 1960s. *Legislative Studies Quarterly* 15: 25–47.

Pecorella, Robert. 1987. Fiscal Crisis and Regime Change. In Clarence N. Stone and Haywood T. Sanders, eds., *The Politics of Urban Development.* Lawrence: University Press of Kansas.

Peters, B. Guy, and Brian W. Hogwood. 1985. In Search of the Issue-Attention Cycle. *Journal of Politics* 47: 239–53.

Peterson, Mark A. 1990. *Legislating Together.* Cambridge: Harvard University Press.

Peterson, Paul. 1981. *City Limits.* Chicago: University of Chicago Press.

Peterson, Paul, and Mark Rom. 1990. *Welfare Magnets.* Washington, D.C.: Brookings Institution.

Peterson, Paul, and Kenneth Wong. 1986. *When Federalism Works.* Washington, D.C.: Brookings Institution.

Plaut, Thomas, and Joseph Pluta. 1983. Business Climate, Taxes, and Expenditures and State Economic Growth in the United States. *Southern Economic Journal* 50: 99–119.

Plein, L. Christopher. 1991. Popularizing Biotechnology: The Influence of Issue Definition. *Science, Technology, and Human Values* 16: 474–90.

Polsby, Nelson W. 1984. *Policy Innovation in America: The Politics of Policy Initiation.* New Haven: Yale University Press.

Popkin, Samuel L. 1991. *The Reasoning Voter.* Chicago: University of Chicago Press.

Pralle, Sarah. 2006. *Branching Out, Digging In.* Washington, DC: Georgetown University Press.

Prigogine, Ilya, and Isabelle Stengers. 1984. *Order Out of Chaos.* New York: Bantam Books.

Quotations Page, The. Quote from John Adams, "Argument in Defense of the Soldiers in the Boston Massacre Trials," 1770, http://www.quotationspage.com/quotes/John_Adams/.

Rankin, William L., Stanley M. Nealey, and Barbara Desow Melber. 1984. Overview of National Attitudes toward Nuclear Energy: A Longitudinal Analysis. In William R. Freudenburg and Eugene A. Rosa, eds., *Public Reaction to Nuclear Power: Are There Critical Masses?* Boulder, Colo.: Westview Press.

Raver, Ann. 1991. Audobon Society Pursues an Identity beyond Birds. *New York Times,* 9 June.

Redford, Emmette S. 1960. A Case Analysis of Congressional Activity: Civil Aviation, 1957–58. *Journal of Politics* 22: 228–58.

———. 1969. *Democracy in the Administrative State.* New York: Oxford University Press.

Rich, Michael J. 1989. Distributive Politics and the Allocation of Federal Grants. *American Political Science Review* 83: 193–213.

Riker, William H. 1980. Implications from the Disequilibrium of Majority Rule for the Study of Institutions. *American Political Science Review* 74: 432–46.

———. 1982. *Liberalism against Populism.* Prospect Heights, Ill.: Waveland Press.

———. 1983. Political Theory and the Art of Heresthetics. In Ada Finifter, ed., *Political Science: The State of the Discipline.* Washington D.C.: American Political Science Association.

———. 1984. The Heresthetics of Constitution-Making: The Presidency in 1787, with Comments on Determinism and Rational Choice. *American Political Science Review* 78: 1–16.

———. 1986. *The Art of Political Manipulation.* New Haven: Yale University Press.

Ripley, Randall B., and Grace A. Franklin. 1987. *Congress, the Bureaucracy, and Public Policy.* Chicago: Dorsey Press.

———. 1991. *Congress, the Bureaucracy, and Public Policy.* 5th ed. Pacific Grove, Calif.: Brooks-Cole.

Robinson, Michael J. 1981. Three Faces of Congressional Media. In Thomas E. Mann and Norman J. Ornstein, eds., *The New Congress.* Washington, D.C.: American Enterprise Institute.

Robinson, Scott. 2004. Punctuated Equilibrium, Bureaucratization, and Budgeting Changes in Schools. *Policy Studies Journal* 32 (1): 25–39.

Rogers, Everett M., James W. Dearing, and Soonbum Chang. 1991. *AIDS in the 1980s: The Agenda-Setting Process for a Public Issue.* Journalism Monographs no. 126. Lexington, Ken.: Association for Education and Journalism.

Rolph, Elizabeth. 1979. *Nuclear Power and the Public Safety.* Lexington, Mass.: Lexington Books.

Rose, Mark H. 1979. *Interstate: Express Highway Politics, 1941–1956.* Lawrence: University Press of Kansas.

Rosenberg, Gerald N. 1991. *The Hollow Hope: Can the Courts Bring about Social Change?* Chicago: University of Chicago Press.

Rothman, Stanley, and S. Robert Lichter. 1982. The Nuclear Energy Debate: Scientists, the Media, and the Public. *Public Opinion* 5: 47–52.

———. 1987. Elite Ideology and Risk Perception in Nuclear Energy Policy. *American Political Science Review* 81: 383–404.

Sabatier, Paul A. 1987. Knowledge, Policy–Oriented Learning, and Policy Change. *Knowledge: Creation, Diffusion, Utilization* 8: 649–92.

———. 1988. An Advocacy Coalition Framework of Policy Change and the Role of Policy-Oriented Learning Therein. *Policy Sciences* 21: 129–68.

———. 1991. Political Science and Public Policy. *PS: Political Science and Politics* 24: 144–47.

Sabatier, Paul A., and Hank C. Jenkins-Smith. 1993. *Policy Change and Learning: An Advocacy Coalition Approach.* Boulder, CO: Westview.

Salisbury, Robert H. 1984. Interest Representation: The Dominance of Institutions. *American Political Science Review* 78: 64–76.

Sapotichne, Joshua. 2006. *Media Attention and Congressional Hearings Activity: Testing the Baumgartner and Jones Model of Agenda-Setting.* Seattle: Center for American Politics and Public Policy.

Saunders, Peter 1979. *Urban Politics.* London: Hutchinson.

Sayre, Wallace S., and Herbert Kaufman. 1965. *Governing New York City: Politics in the Metropolis.* New York: Norton.

Schattschneider, E. E. 1935. *Politics, Pressures, and the Tariff.* New York: Prentice-Hall.

———. 1960. *The Semi-Sovereign People.* New York: Holt, Rinehart and Winston.

———. 1969. *Two Hundred Million Americans in Search of a Government.* New York: Holt, Rinehart and Winston.

Scheiber, Harry N. 1987. State Law and Industrial Policy in American Development, 1790–1987. *California Law Review* 75: 414–44.

Schlesigner, Arthur M. 1986. *The Cycles of American History.* Boston: Houghton Mifflin.

Schneider, Anne, and Helen Ingram. 1993. Social Construction of Target Populations: Implications for Politics and Policy. *American Political Science Review* 87: 334–49.

Schneider, Judy. 1980. Multiple Referrals and Jurisdictional Overlaps, House of Representatives, 94th and 95th Congress. In U.S. Congress, House Select Committee on Committees, *Final Report.* H. Rept. 96–866. 96th Cong., 2d ses. Washington, D.C.: Government Printing Office.

Schneider, Mark, Paul Teske, and Michael Mintrom. 1995. *Public Entrepreneurs.* Princeton, NJ: Princeton University Press.

Schoenfeld, A. Clay, Robert F. Meier, and Robert J. Griffin. 1979. Constructing a Social Problem: The Press and the Environment. *Social Problems* 27: 38–61.

Sebok, Anthony J. 2004. The Federal Government's RICO Suit Against Big Tobacco. *FindLaw,* 4 October. http://writ.corporate.findlaw.com/sebok/20041004.html.

Shaiko, Ronald G. 1991. More Bang for the Buck: The New Era of Full-Service Public Interest Organizations. In Allan J. Cigler and Burdett A. Loomis, eds., *Interest Group Politics,* 3d ed. Washington, D.C.: Congressional Quarterly.

Sharp, Elaine B. 1991. Interest Groups and Symbolic Policy Formation: The Case of Anti-Drug Policy. Paper presented at the annual meeting of the American Political Science Association, Washington, D.C., 29 August–1 September.

———. N.d. Agenda Setting and Policy Results: Lessons from Three Drug Policy Episodes. Manuscript.

Shefter, Martin. 1985. *Political Crisis/Fiscal Crisis.* New York: Basic.

Shepsle, Kenneth A. 1979. Institutional Arrangements and Equilibrium in Multidimensional Voting Models. *American Journal of Political Science* 23: 27–59.

Simon, Herbert A. 1977. *Models of Discovery.* Boston: D. Reidel.

———. 1983. *Reason in Human Affairs.* Stanford, Calif.: Stanford University Press.

———. 1985. Human Nature in Politics: The Dialogue of Psychology with Political Science. *American Political Science Review* 79: 293–304.

Smith, Tom. 1985. The Polls: America's Most Important Problems, Part I: National and International. *Public Opinion Quarterly* 49: 264–74.

Speth, J. Gustave. 2004. *Red Sky at Morning.* New Haven: Yale University Press.

———. 2006. Foreword to *Punctuated Equilibrium and the Dynamics of U.S. Environmental Policy,* ed. by Robert Ropetto. New Haven: Yale University Press.

Stein, Robert. 1990. Economic Voting for Governor and U.S. Senator: The Electoral Consequences of Federalism. *Journal of Politics* 52: 29–53.

328

References

Stimson, James A. 1991. *Public Opinion in America: Moods, Cycles, and Swings.* Boulder, Colo.: Westview Press.

———. 2004. *Tides of Consent: How Public Opinion Shapes American Politics.* New York: Cambridge University Press.

Stone, Clarence N. 1976. *Economic Growth and Neighborhood Discontent.* Chapel Hill: University of North Carolina Press.

———. 1980. Systemic Power in Community Decision-Making. *American Political Science Review* 74: 978–90.

———. 1989. *Regime Politics.* Lawrence: University Press of Kansas.

Stone, Deborah A. 1988. *Policy Paradox and Political Reason.* Glenview, Ill.: Scott, Foresman.

———. 1989. Causal Stories and the Formation of Policy Agendas. *Political Science Quarterly* 104: 281–300.

Studlar, Donley T. 2002. *Tobacco Control: Comparative Politics in the United States and Canada.* Peterborough, Ontario: Broadview.

Subcommittee on Legislative Branch Appropriations. Annual. *Hearings.* Washington, D.C.: Government Printing Office.

Summary of Comparative Data on the U.S. House of Representatives. 1991. In *Congressional Record, House,* 3 January, pp. 15–18. Washington, D.C.: Government Printing Office.

Sundquist, James. 1969. *Making Federalism Work.* Washington, D.C.: Brookings Institution.

Taylor, Leon. 1991. The Race to Build: Infrastructure Competition among Communities. *Economic Development Quarterly* 5: 60–63.

Thurber, James A. 1991. Dynamics of Policy Subsystems in American Politics. In Allan J. Cigler and Burdett A. Loomis, eds., *Interest Group Politics,* 3d ed. Washington, D.C.: Congressional Quarterly.

Tidmarch, Charles M., and John J. Pitney, Jr. 1985. Covering Congress. *Polity* 17: 463–83.

Tobacco in Virginia. Virginia places, geography of Virginia. http://www.virginiaplaces.org/agriculture/tobacco.html.

Treaster, Joseph. 1991. Cocaine Use Found on the Way Down among U.S. Youths. *New York Times,* 25 January.

True, James L., Bryan D. Jones, and Frank R. Baumgartner. 2007. Punctuated-Equilibrium Theory: Explaining Stability and Change in Public Policymaking. In Paul A. Sabatier, ed., *Theories of the Policy Process, 2nd Edition.* Boulder, CO: Westview.

Truman, David B. 1951. *The Governmental Process: Political Interests and Public Opinion.* New York: Alfred A. Knopf.

US Center for Disease Control and Prevention. 2006. Fact Sheet: Cigarette Smoking-Related Mortality. http://www.cdc.gov/tobacco/data_statistics/Factsheets/.

US Department of Health, Education and Welfare. 1964. *Smoking and Health: Report of the Advisory Committee to the Surgeon General of the Public Health Service.* US Department of Health, Education and Welfare, Publich Health Service Publication No. 1103.

US Department of Health and Human Services. 1986. *The Health Consequences of Involuntary Smoking: A report of the Surgeon General.* Public Health Service, Center for Disease Control, Center for Health Promotion and Education, Office on Smoking and Health.

———. 1988. *The Health Consequences of Smoking: Nicotine addiction.* Public Health Service, Center for Disease Control, Center for Health Promotion and Education, Office on Smoking and Health.

US Nuclear Regulatory Commission. 2004. Fact sheet on the Three Mile Island Accident. http://www.nrc.gov/reading-rm/doc-collections/fact-sheets/3mile-isle.html.

Veblen Eric P. 1981. Liberalism and National Newspaper Coverage of Members of Congress. *Polity* 14: 153–59.

Vogel, David. 1989. *Fluctuating Fortunes: The Political Power of Business in America.* New York: Basic Books.

Walker, Jack L., Jr. 1969. The Diffusion of Innovations among the American States. *American Political Science Review* 63: 880–99.

———. 1977. Setting the Agenda in the U.S. Senate. *British Journal of Political Science* 7: 423–45.

———. 1983. The Origins and Maintenance of Interest Groups in America. *American Political Science Review* 77: 390–406.

———. 1991. *Mobilizing Interest Groups in America.* Ann Arbor: University of Michigan Press.

Waste, Robert. 1990. Of the Things That Policymaking Isn't, Which Is It Most Like? Paper presented at the annual meeting of the American Political Science Association, San Francisco, Calif., 29 August–2 September.

Wayne, Leslie. 1991. Bank Bill Becomes Snagged on Egos and House Politics. *New York Times,* 14 October.

Weart, Spencer. 1988. *Nuclear Fear: A History of Images.* Cambridge: Harvard University Press.

Weingast, Barry R. 1980. Congress, Regulation, and the Decline of Nuclear Power. *Public Policy* 28: 231–55.

———. 1989. Floor Behavior in the U.S. Congress: Committee Power under the Open Rule. *American Political Science Review* 83: 795–815.

Weisberg, Herbert, and Jerrold Rusk. 1970. Dimensions of Candidate Evaluation. *American Political Science Review* 64: 1167–85.

Wessel, David. 1991. The Bond Club: Treasury and the Fed Have Long Caved in to "Primary Dealers." *Wall Street Journal,* 25 September.

Wildavsky, Aaron. 1964. *The Politics of the Budgetary Process.* Boston: Little, Brown.

———. 1984. *The Politics of the Budgetary Process.* 4th ed. Boston: Little, Brown.

Wilsford, David. 1991. *Doctors and the State: The Politics of Health Care in France and the United States.* Durham, N.C.: Duke University Press.

Wilson, James Q. 1973. *Political Organizations.* New York: Basic Books.

Womach, Jasper. 2005. *Tobacco Price Support: A Review of the Program.* Congressional Research Service Report for Congress 95–129.

Wood, B. Dan. 1988. Principals, Bureaucrats, and Responsiveness in Clean Air Enforcements. *American Political Science Review* 82: 213–34.

———. 1991. Federalism and Policy Responsiveness: The Clean Air Case. *Journal of Politics* 53: 851–59.

330
References

Wood, Robert S. 2006a. Tobacco's Tipping Point: The Master Settlement as a Focusing Event. *Policy Studies Journal* 34: 419–36.

———. 2006b. The Dynamics of Incrementalism. *Policy Studies Journal* 34: 1–16.

Worsham, Jeffrey. 1998. Wavering Equilibriums. *American Politics Quarterly* 26: 485–512.

———. 2006. Up in Smoke: Mapping Subsystem Dynamics in Tobacco policy. *Policy Studies Journal* 34: 437–52.

Wright, Deil. 1988. *Understanding Intergovernmental Relations.* Pacific Grove, Calif.: Brooks-Cole.

Index

Aberbach, Joel D., 194–95, 200
Ackerman, Bruce, 287
Adams, John, 289
Agricultural Adjustment Act, 270
agriculture, 45, 183–84, 270–71. *See also* pesticides; smoking and tobacco
AIDS/HIV, 50
air transportation, 45, 120, 210–14, 238
alcohol abuse, 150, 161–64, 171, 194, 238
Aldrich, Howard, 45, 177
American Council on Intergovernmental Relations, 225
American Humane Association, 170
American Lung Association, 279
American Phytopathological Society, 185
Americans for Democratic Action (ADA), 282
Anslinger, Henry J., 153–54, 155
Anti-Saloon League, 154
Anton, Thomas, 143, 217, 218, 226
apathy, 18–21, 238–39
argumentation. *See* debate; rhetoric
Arthur, W. Brian, 16
associations, 177–78, 180–81, 182, 185–89. See also *Encyclopedia of Associations*
Atomic Energy Commission (AEC), 54, 60, 64, 65, 67, 68, 69, 70–73, 238. *See also* Nuclear Regulatory Commission (NRC)
attention spans, xxiii, 250–51
Audubon Society, 188
automobile safety, 121–24, 125. *See also* highways

Bach, Stanley, 199
Bachelor, Lynn W., 227
Bachrach, Peter, 44
Barabasi, Albert-Laszlo, xxii
Baratz, Morton, 44
Baumgartner, Frank R., xxi–xxii, xxiii, xxiv–xxvi, 11, 30, 42, 48, 49, 177, 195, 255–56, 264, 269, 287
Beecher, Janice A., 250, 301
Beer, Samuel, 141, 143, 146
Bennett, Lance, 274
Bennett, Linda M., 142, 145
Bennett, R. R., 71
Bennett, Stephen, 142, 145
Bennett, William, 170
Bentley, Arthur F., 12, 42
Berry, Jeffrey M., xxv, 187
Berry, William, 43, 229
Best, Joel, 168
bias: in Congress, 203–15; and federalism, 234; mobilization of, 11, 12, 16, 85, 117, 175–92, 194, 210, 215, 243, 249
Black, Duncan, 13
Bloomberg Poll, 261
Boeckelman, Keith A., 227
Bosk, Charles L., 106
Bosso, Christopher J., 45, 46, 47, 95, 96, 97, 188, 191
bounded rationality, xxiii–xxvi
Box, George E. P., 308
Boydstun, Amber E., xxiv

Brinkley, Joel, 156
Brown, JoAnne, 67
Brown and Williamson, FDA v., 276
Browne, William P., 6, 43
Burch, Deborah M., 54, 177, 180, 185, 304
Bureau of Drug Abuse Control, 155
Bureau of Justice Statistics, 157
Burnham, Walter Dean, 286–87
Burns, James MacGregor, 22
Bush (G. H. W.) administration, 156, 158,
    160–61, 169, 260, 262, 284
Bush (G. W.) administration, 261, 279, 280

Caldeira, Gregory A., 50, 295
Campbell, John C., 47
Campbell, John L., 35, 45, 60, 66, 67–68,
    77, 229
capital punishment, xxiv–xxv
Carmines, Edward G., 22, 47, 127, 146
Carson, Rachel, *Silent Spring,* 97, 98, 129,
    190, 194, 242
Carter administration, 72n, 142, 148, 159,
    213, 260, 261, 284
Cashore, B., xxi
Casstevens, Thomas, 17
Catanzaro, Michael J., 274
Centers for Disease Control, 272
Chang, Soonbum, 50, 296
Cheney, Dick, 261
child abuse, 46, 150, 164–70, 171, 194,
    230–31, 241, 247
Child Abuse Prevention and Treatment Act
    (CAPTA), 168
Child Abuse Prevention and Treatment and
    Adoption Reform Act (CAPARTA), 168
Children's Health Bureau, 231
Chubb, John, 218, 235
cities. *See* urban affairs
citizens' groups, 176–77, 180, 182–84
Civil Aeronautics Board (CAB), 211, 212,
    213, 238
civil disorders, 127–30, 134, 242
class interest, 249–50
climate change, 260–64
Clinton administration, 260, 271, 279, 284
Clymer, Adam, 118
coalition theories, 271–72
Cobb, Roger W., xviii, 11, 30, 36, 42, 48, 52,
    67, 89, 93, 129, 131, 239
cognitive friction, 264
Cohen, Bernard, 119–20, 121
Cohen, Michael, 88

Commonwealth Edison, 77
comparative case analysis, 47–48
Comprehensive Alcohol Abuse and Alcohol-
    ism Prevention, Treatment, and Rehabilita-
    tion Act, 163
Concordet, Marquis de, 13
Congress and congressional hearings: and air
    transportation, 210–14; and alcohol abuse,
    161–64, 171, 194; and automobile safety,
    122–23; and bias, 203–15; and child
    abuse, 167–68, 171, 194; congressional
    hearings data, 297–300; and drug abuse,
    153, 158–60, 163, 194, 196, 206, 207–9;
    and federalism, 219; increase in staff and
    resources, 196–201; and issue definition,
    243, 244; and nuclear power, 72–75, 100,
    195, 196, 201, 257–59; and pesticides,
    97–98, 100, 196, 203–7; reforms, 45, 55,
    75, 193–215; and smoking and tobacco,
    209–10, 274; and urban affairs, 128,
    129–44, 147, 194, 196, 219
*Congressional Information Service Abstracts
    (CIS),* 52, 90, 130, 204, 297
Congressional Record, 90
Congressional Research Service, 197
Conlon, Timothy, 141, 142, 143, 147, 219
Conn, Richard L., 231, 232
Consolidated Edison, 77
Cook, Fay Lomax, 107, 170
Costain, Douglas, 191
Council of State Governments, 231
countermobilization, 4–5, 9–10, 147, 251.
    See also mobilization
Crenson, Matthew A., 44
criticism. *See* mobilization
cross-sectional comparisons, 41–46
cycles, 243–46

Dahl, Robert A., 15
data sources, 291–306
Davidson, Roger H., 199, 200, 212–13
DDT, 94, 97, 98, 111. *See also* pesticides
Dearing, James W., 50, 296
debate, 35–36, 107–9. *See also* rhetoric
De Boef, Suzanna L., xxiv
defense policy, 33
Delaney, James, 96, 201
Del Sesto, Steven, 201
democracy, xviii
Derthick, Martha, 45, 47, 178
diffusion, policy. *See* policy diffusion
disruptive dynamics, 253, 285–89

Dodd, Lawrence, 45
Dow Chemical, 76
Dow Jones Industrials, 77
Dow-Jones Utility Index, 77–78
Downs, Anthony, 10, 46, 47, 86–89, 96, 97,
   98–99, 100–101, 151, 161, 170, 179,
   191, 239
drug abuse, 150–64; and apathy, 238;
   congressional hearings on, 153, 158–60,
   163, 171, 194, 206, 207–9, 247; education, treatment, and enforcement, 33–34,
   153–56, 158–61, 169, 207–9; media
   coverage of, 152–60, 169, 247; and policy
   venues, 207–9; statistics on, 156–58, 170
drunk driving, 163, 231. *See also* alcohol
   abuse; highways
Duffy, Robert, 259
Duke Power, 77
Dye, Thomas, 305

Edelman, Murray, 10, 44, 152
education policy, 32–33
Edwards, George C., 169
Eisenhower administration, 259, 284
Eisinger, Peter K., 222
Elder, Charles D., xviii, 11, 30, 36, 42, 48, 52,
   67, 93, 129
elderly and crime, 107–8
Eldredge, Niles, 17, 19n
elite privilege, 3, 24, 44
Encyclopedia of Associations, 54, 177, 179,
   180–81, 185–89, 304–5
Energy Research and Development Agency
   (ERDA), 69
enthusiasm. *See* mobilization
environmentalism: growth of, 179, 184–91,
   214, 249; and media coverage, 106; and
   nuclear power, 75–76, 229–30, 261; and
   pesticides, 96–99, 231–32, 242; and the
   urban initiative, 139
Environmental Protection Agency (EPA), 38,
   191, 232, 272
Europe, punctuated equilibrium in, xxvi,
   255–56
experts, 42–43, 67, 236. *See also* policy
   monopolies
Eyestone, Robert, 37

Fair Trade and Equitable Tobacco Reform
   Act, 271
Falco, Mathea, 161
Fallows, Susan, 76

Farm Act, 271
FDA v. Brown and Williamson, 276
Federal Agriculture Improvement and Reform
   Act, 271
Federal Bureau of Narcotics, 153
Federal Environmental Pesticides Control
   Act, 97
federal grants, 132–33, 138–42, 143, 147,
   216, 218, 224–27, 228, 230, 241, 247
Federal Insecticide, Fungicide, and Rodenti-
   cide Act (FIFRA), 95, 231
federalism: and bias, 234; congressional
   interest in, 219; vs. local control, 34–35;
   and nationalization, 217, 219–20, 228–34,
   244; and policy specialization, 220–27;
   and policy venues, 216–34, 239–40,
   244; and positive and negative feedback,
   227–28; and smoking and tobacco,
   276–78
Fefferman, Hilbert, 134
Fenno, Richard, xxiv
financial markets, 45–46, 53, 76–79
Fiorina, Morris P., 193
Fischhoff, Baruch, 121
Foard, Ashley, 134
Food Additive Amendment, 96
Food and Drug Administration, 94, 96, 272,
   274, 276
Ford administration, 159, 169, 213, 259, 284
Foreign Affairs Committee, 208
France, 30, 48, 49
Franklin, Grace A., 41, 43, 92
Freudenberg, William R., 64
Fritschler, A. Lee, 43, 45, 92
Frontline, 274

Gais, Thomas L., 43
Gallup Polls, 87, 144–45
Gamson, William, 44
Gardner, Mary, 262n
General Motors, 76
Givel, Michael, xxi, 279
Glantz, Stanton A., 266
Golay, Michael W., 77
Goldberg, Peter, 160
Goodman, Marshall R., 77
Gormley, William, 41, 229
Gould, Stephen Jay, 17, 19n
Goyder, Jane, 185
grants, federal. *See* federal grants
Greenberg, Michael R., 39, 44, 120
Greenpeace, 188

Green-Pedersen, Christoffer, 255
Greenstone, J. David, 141
Grier, David, 90
Griffin, Robert J., 106
Griffith, Ernest S., 7, 43
Grofman, Bernard, 203
Grossback, David, xvii, 287
group theory, 14–15
Gusfield, Joseph, 162

Hall, Richard L., 203
Hamm, Keith, 43, 60
Hansen, John Mark, 11, 45, 177
Hay, Richard, 308
Hayes, Michael T., 9
health care policy, 178, 249
Heclo, Hugh, 8, 43
highways, 137, 160, 163, 225, 231. *See also*
     automobile safety
Hilgartner, Stephen, 106–7
HIV/AIDS, 50
Hogwood, Brian W., 87, 191
Hojnacki, Marie, xxv
House Commerce Committee, 200
House Rules Committee, 199
housing, 134–37
Housing Act, 134–37
Houston Industries, 77
Howlett, M., xxi
Hunt, Valerie, 277n
Huntington, Samuel, 244
Hurley, Patricia A., 130

image, policy. *See* policy image
income security, 284
incrementalism, 5, 9–10, 16–18, 83, 235–36,
     250–51, 255
Information Please Database, 281
information processing, 287–89
Inglehart, Ronald, 61
Ingram, Helen, 270
Insecticide Act, 94
institutionally induced equilibria, 19
institutions: and bias, 12; and change, xx, 14,
     16, 37, 54–55, 83, 89, 173, 193–215; and
     mobilization, 87–89; and policy venues,
     31–38
interest groups, 175–92; agriculture, 183–84;
     citizens' groups, 176–77, 180, 182–84;
     consumers' groups, 45; environmental-
     ism (*see* environmentalism); growth in,

54, 171, 176–89, 196, 214, 243, 244;
     and policy venues, 276–77; profit-sector,
     176–77, 180, 182–84; trade associations,
     177–78, 182; urban affairs, 126
intergovernmental grants. *See* federal grants
Interstate Highway Act, 123, 137
investment-consumption ratio, 222–27,
     305–6
issue assignment. *See* policy venues
issue definition, 16, 20, 22–24, 29, 31, 202,
     243–46, 271
issue density, 300–305
issue expansion, 17–18, 25, 35–37, 83–102
issue networks, 42–43. *See also* policy venues

Jacob, Herbert, 47
Jacobs, James, 163, 231
James I, 265–66
Jenkins, Gwilym M., 308
Jenkins-Smith, Hank, 42, 203, 272
Johnson, Eric J., 121
Johnson administration, 72n, 127–28,
     140–42, 143, 146–47, 148, 160, 164, 259,
     268, 281, 284
Joint Committee on Atomic Energy (JCAE),
     60, 68, 69, 195, 201
Jones, Bryan D., xxi–xxii, xxiii, 15, 34, 225,
     227, 255–56, 264, 269, 274, 287
Jones, Charles O., xviii, 17–18, 21, 45, 140,
     191, 194, 202, 211
Journal of European Public Policy, 255
juridicial democracy, xviii

Kahn, Alfred, 213
Kantor, Paul, 222
Kaufman, Herbert, 5, 17
Kay, W. D., 76
Kennedy administration, 141, 259, 284
Kephart, Thomas, 199
Kerr, Peter, 155
Kessler, David, 274, 276, 277
Kettler, D. J., 71
Kimball, David, xxv
King, David C., 33, 37, 200
Kingdon, John, xviii, 5, 7, 11, 29, 30, 47, 48,
     49, 88, 99, 124, 154, 155, 160, 164, 169,
     210–11, 242, 248, 265
Kirp, David, 31
Kitschelt, Herbert B., 76
Knoke, David, 185
Kock, Karin E., 54, 177, 180, 185, 304

Komonoff, Charles, 77
Koop, C. Everett, 270, 272, 277
Krehbiel, Keith, 14, 197, 203
Kuklinski, James, 76

Labor and Human Resources Committee, 208
Laird, Wendy, 11
Lanouette, William, 65, 66
Larson, Stephanie, 90
Laurence, Michael, 163
Leech, Beth, xxv
Legislative Reorganization Act, 200
Lender, Mark, 163
Leng, Marguerite L., 231, 232
Lester, James, 191
Lester, Marilyn, 106
Lewis, Michael, 277
liberalism, 246–47
Lichter, S. Robert, 65–66, 120
Lilienthal, David, 67
Lindblom, Charles E., 9, 15
Lineberry, Robert J., 250, 301
Livingston, William, 217
local government. See state and local government activities
Logan, John, 222
longitudinal studies, 46–47
Lowe, Philip, 185
Lowi, Theodore, xviii, 5, 21, 41

Maass, Arthur, 8, 119
macropolitics, 21–22
Madison, James, 4, 8
Majone, Giandomenico, 27–28, 36
Malbin, Michael J., 197–98, 301
mandate elections, xvii, xix
Mann, Thomas E., 197–98, 301
March, James G., 88
Marcus, Ruth, 161
Martin, James, 163
mass transit, 29
Master Settlement Agreement, 278, 279
May, Peter, 281
Mayhew, David, 243
Mazur, Allan, 50, 61–64
McCain, John, 274, 278, 280
McCombs, Maxwell E., 105
McConnell, Grant, xviii, 5
McCubbins, Matthew, 20
McFarland, Andrew S., 43, 244, 245, 251
McLeary, Richard, 308

McMahon Atomic Energy Act, 64, 66
media coverage, 49; of alcohol abuse, 161–64; of automobile safety, 121–24, 125; of child abuse, 164–68, 247; choosing a single focus, 104–7; coding of, 291–95; comparing indices, 295–97; of drug abuse, 152–60, 169, 247; dynamics of, 20, 103–25; and noncontradictory arguments, 107–9; of nuclear power, 50, 51, 61–70, 100, 108, 119, 120–21, 129, 247, 262–64; of pesticides, 95, 97–99, 100, 109–13, 119, 129, 238, 247; and risk and conflict, 118–24; of smoking and tobacco, 90–93, 109–10, 114–17, 247, 266–69, 274; tone, 51, 61–70, 89–90, 99, 103, 108–10, 111–13, 114–17, 125, 266; of urban affairs, 129–32, 142, 147, 247, 282–84
Medicaid program, 143, 147, 225
Medicare program, 277–78
Meier, Kenneth, 6, 176
Meier, Robert F., 106
Melber, Barbara Desow, 80
metaphors, 105
Metlay, Daniel S., 76
Milward, H. Brinton, 11
Mintrom, Michael, 278
Mitchell, Robert C., 68
mobilization: of bias, 11, 12, 16, 85, 117, 175–92, 194, 210, 215, 243, 249; and countermobilization, 4, 9–11; of criticism / Schattschneider, 35–36, 84–90, 92–93, 97, 98–99, 100–101, 110, 117, 170, 179, 189–90, 191, 202, 239, 257; of enthusiasm / Downsian, 84–90, 95–96, 97, 98–99, 100–101, 110, 151, 170, 178–79, 189–90, 191, 239, 257; and issue content, 41–46
Molotch, Harvey, 106, 222
Monitoring and Evaluation Program, 279
Montgomery, T. L., 77
Moore, Michael, 277–78
Mooz, William E., 68
Morone, Joseph G., 60, 66, 68
Mothers against Drunk Driving, 123
Mulford v. Smith, 270
Musto, David, 152, 154, 155, 160
Myers, John, 230

Nader, Ralph, 68, 122
National Center for Health Statistics, 266
National Commission on Civil Disorders, 127–28

National Environmental Policy Act, 69, 97
National Environmental Protection Act
(NEPA), 38, 232
National Highway Safety Act, 163, 231
National Highway Safety Bureau, 163, 231
National Institute of Drug Abuse, 157, 158
National Institute on Alcohol Abuse and
Alcoholism (NIAAA), 163
nationalization, 217, 219–20, 228–34
national mood. *See* public opinion
Nealy, Stanley M., 80
negative feedback, 6; and federalism, 217,
227–28; and incrementalism, 9–10,
16–18, 236; and smoking and tobacco,
281; and stability, 256, 288; tension with
positive feedback, 271–72
Nelkin, Dorothy, 76, 105
Nelson, Barbara J., 46, 47, 150, 164, 167,
168, 230
New Deal, 137, 141, 230, 286
New Federalism, 147, 219
New York Times, 120, 191, 268, 282
New York Times-CBS poll, 261
New York Times Index, 50–51, 89, 92,
114–15, 164–65, 291–97, 301–4
Nielson, Lars B., 267, 268, 269
9/11, 261
Nixon administration, 30, 72n, 138, 142–43,
146, 147, 148, 152, 155, 156, 158, 160,
161, 164, 169, 213, 219, 241, 261, 284
Novallo, Annette, 54, 177, 180, 185, 304
nuclear power: and apathy, 238; change in
1970s, 45; and climate change, 260–64;
and Congress, 72–75, 100–101, 195, 196,
201, 227, 247, 257–59; and environmentalism, 75–76, 184, 189, 229–30, 261; and
financial markets, 76–79; media coverage
of, 50, 51, 61–70, 100, 108, 119, 120–21,
129, 247, 262–64; and mobilization theories, 88–89; and nationalization, 229–30;
and policy image, 26, 59, 60–70, 79–82,
230; and policy monopolies, 59–60,
81–82; and policy venues, 35, 59, 69–70,
80–82, 217, 229–30; regulation of, 69,
70–73; in State of the Union speeches,
257, 259–60; Three Mile Island (TMI),
79–80, 129, 242, 259; as a valence issue,
151
Nuclear Regulatory Commission (NRC), 69,
70–73, 259. *See also* Atomic Energy Commission (AEC)

O'Connor, James, 228, 305
Office of Management and Budget (OMB),
131, 132, 223, 225, 284
Oleszek, Walter J., 199, 200, 213
Olsen, Johan P., 88
Olson, Mancur, 11, 221
OPEC, 259
Ornstein, Norman J., 197–98, 301
overhead democracy, xviii, xix

Paik, Soon, 77
Pareto, Wilfred, xxii
partial equilibrium, 18–21
Patterson, Samuel C., 50, 295
Pecorella, Robert, 244
Pepper, Claude, 155
pesticides: congressional hearings, 97–98,
100, 196, 201, 203–7, 227, 247; and
environmentalism, 96–99, 190, 242;
longitudinal studies, 46–47; media
coverage of, 95, 97–99, 100, 109–13,
119, 129, 238, 247; and policy image, 85,
95–99, 110, 184, 189, 239; and policy
venues, 96, 184, 203–7; regulation of,
94–97, 231–32
Peters, B. Guy, 87, 191
Peterson, David, xvii, 287
Peterson, Mark A., 43, 196
Peterson, Paul, 34, 141, 221, 221n, 223, 227,
235
Philip Morris USA Inc, US v., 279
Pitney, John J., 295
Plaut, Thomas, 305
Plein, Christopher, 26–27
pluralism, 14–15
Pluta, Joseph, 305
police policy, 33
Policy Agendas Project, xx, xxi, 257, 259,
272, 282, 287
policy diffusion, 6, 16–18, 230–32, 240–42,
288
policy entrepreneurs, 11, 23, 29–30, 42, 48,
85–86, 105, 106, 107, 218, 222, 239,
265, 278
policy image: and focus, 109; and mobilization, 184, 239, 265; and nuclear power, 26,
59, 60–70, 79–82, 230; and pesticides,
96, 110, 239; and policy monopolies, 7–9,
15, 20; and policy venues, 25–38, 86, 196,
201, 239, 240; and smoking and tobacco,
114, 266–70

policy monopolies, 4, 5–9, 15, 20–22, 26, 59–60, 81–82, 83, 85–86, 89, 240, 248
policy outputs, 54, 132–34, 264
policy specialization, 220–27
policy venues: and drug abuse, 207–9; and federalism, 216–34, 239–41, 244; as indicators, 52–53; and media coverage, 104, 106–7; and mobilization, 184, 239; and nuclear power, 35, 59, 69–70, 80–82, 217, 229–30; and pesticides, 96, 203–7; and policy image, 25–38, 86, 196, 201, 239, 240; smoking and tobacco, 272, 276–78
political parties, 21–22, 126–27, 144–49, 271, 282–84, 286–87
polls: Bloomberg Poll, 261; Gallup Polls, 87, 144–45; *New York Times*-CBS poll, 261
pollution, 45, 138, 232
Polsby, Nelson W., 47
Popkin, Samuel, 242
positive feedback: and capital punishment, xxiv–xxv; and Congress, 193, 202; and environmentalism, 190, 230, 232; and federalism, 217, 227–28; image-venue interaction, 37; and the media, 106, 125; and nuclear power, 72; and policy change, xix, xxii, 236, 256; and policy diffusion, 6, 16–18, 240–42, 288; and public opinion, 248; and smoking and tobacco, 274, 280, 281; tension with negative feedback, 271–72; and urban affairs, 128, 148
Pralle, Sarah, 276–77
Price-Anderson Nuclear Industries Indemnity Act, 257
Prigogine, Ilya, 19n
problems, 27–29, 241–42
Prohibition, 150, 153–54, 161
public opinion, 53, 246–48, 261. *See also* Gallup Polls
punctuated equilibrium, xviii–xxvii, 3–24, 37–38, 57, 83–84, 89, 101–2, 125, 235–51, 253–54, 255–56, 281, 285–89
Putnam, Robert D., 195

Quirk, Paul J., 45

race relations, 127, 134, 139, 146, 148–49, 249
Rankin, William, 79, 80
rationality, bounded. *See* bounded rationality
Raver, Ann, 188
Readers' Guide to Periodical Literature,

50–51, 64, 89, 91–92, 111, 114, 121, 129, 142, 153, 158, 163, 164, 266–67, 274, 291–97, 301–4
Reagan administration, 33, 72n, 126, 133, 140, 143, 147–49, 155, 156, 160, 169, 186, 213, 219, 225, 247, 260, 262, 272, 282, 284
Redford, Emmette S., xviii, 7, 8, 19, 21–22, 34, 43, 211
regression analysis, 307–14
regulation: of financial markets, 45–46; of nuclear power, 69, 70–73; of pesticides, 94–97, 231–32
rhetoric, 29–30, 44. *See also* debate
Rich, Michael J., 218, 250, 301
Riker, William H., 5, 12, 13–14, 15, 19, 22, 29–30, 47–48, 89
riots. *See* civil disorders
Ripley, Randall B., 41, 43, 92
Robinson, Michael J., 295
Robinson, Scott, 256
Rockman, Bert A., 195
Rogers, Everett M., 50, 296
Rolph, Elizabeth, 68, 69
Rom, Mark, 227
Roosevelt administration, 144, 146
Rosa, Eugene A., 64
Rose, D. J., 77
Rose, Mark H., 123
Rosenberg, Gerald, 242
Ross, Jeannie-Keith, 89, 131, 239
Ross, Marc Howard, 89, 131, 239
Rothman, Stanley, 65–66, 120
Rusk, Jerrold, 145

Sabatier, Paul A., 43, 272
Salisbury, Robert, 177
Sapotichne, Joshua, 281, 282
Saunders, Peter, 34
Sayre, Wallace S., 5
Schattschneider, E. E., xviii, 11, 15–16, 35–36, 48, 67, 80, 89, 92–93, 97, 98–99, 100–101, 170, 179, 189–90, 191, 202, 239, 248–49
Scheiber, Harry N., 222
Schlesinger, Arthur, 244
Schneider, Anne, 270
Schneider, Judy, 199
Schneider, Mark, 278
Schoenfeld, A. Clay, 106
Schott, Richard, 45
Schriver, William R., 77

Schwartz, Thomas, 20
Sebok, Anthony J., 279
Shaiko, Ronald, 177, 187
Sharp, Elaine B., 155, 158, 160, 161, 209
Shefter, Martin, 244
Shepsle, Kenneth A., 5, 14, 19, 37
Sierra Club, 185, 191
Simon, Herbert, 10, 19–20, 104–5, 250
Skogan, Wesley G., 107, 170
Smith, Mulford v., 270
Smith, Steven S., 199
Smith, Tom, 144
Smoking and Health, 268
smoking and tobacco, 84–85, 264–81;
    coalition theories, 271–72; and Congress,
    170–71, 196, 202, 209–10, 247, 274; criti-
    cism of, 93, 100, 117, 184; and federalism,
    276–78; and the Food and Drug Admin-
    istration, 274, 276; and health, 265–70;
    Master Settlement Agreement, 278, 279;
    media coverage of, 90–93, 109–10,
    114–17, 247, 266–69, 274; and policy im-
    age, 114, 266–70; and policy venues, 272,
    276–78; promotion of, 270–71; regulation
    of, 272–75; secondhand smoke, 265, 268,
    270, 272, 274, 279
social choice theory, 13–14
social programs, 137–40
Social Security, 47, 147, 148, 178
Solga, Joseph R., 231, 232
Southern California Edison, 77
space policy, 33
Speth, James Gustave, xix
Staber, Udo, 45, 177
stability, xix–xx, xxi, xxiii–xxiv, xxvi, 256
Standard and Poor, 77–78
state and local government activities, xviii, 53,
    75–76, 216–34, 279
State of the Union speeches, 257, 259–60
Statistical Abstract of the United States, 119
St. Clair, Gilbert K., 203
Stein, Robert, 223
Stengers, Isabelle, 19n
Stimson, James A., xvii, 22, 47, 127, 146,
    246–47, 247n, 287
Stone, Clarence N., 34, 222
Stone, Deborah A., 11, 27, 28, 29, 153, 164
Strahan, Randall, 21, 140, 194, 202, 211
structure-induced equilibrium, 83, 238, 244
Studlar, Donley T., 270, 272
study design, 39–55

Subcommittee Bill of Rights, 199
Substance Abuse and Mental Health Services
    Administration, 272
Sundquist, James, 218
Supreme Court, 242, 270
symbols, 44, 66, 105

Taylor, Leon, 227
telecommunications, 45
Terry, Luther L., 268
Teske, Paul, 278
Texas Poll, 61–63
Three Mile Island (TMI), 79–80, 129,
    242, 259
Thurber, James A., 6, 176
Tidmarch, Charles M., 295
tobacco. *See* smoking and tobacco
tone, 51, 61–70, 73–75, 84, 89–90, 99–101,
    103, 108–17, 125, 204, 266
trade associations, 45, 177–78, 180–81, 182
Treaster, Joseph, 157
trucking, 45
True, James L., xxiii, 255
Truman, David B., 4, 11
Truman administration, 259, 284
Tversky, Amos, 121

Uniform Crime Reports, 157
Union of Concerned Scientists, 68, 69
urban affairs, 126–49, 241, 242, 281–84;
    civil disorders, 127–30, 134, 242; congres-
    sional hearings on, 128, 129–44, 147, 219,
    247; highways, 137; housing, 134–37;
    income security, 284; mass transit, 29;
    media coverage of, 129–32, 142, 147, 247,
    282–84; policy coherence, 281–82; social
    programs and community development,
    137–40, 225
U.S. Bureau of the Census, 223, 305
U.S. Center for Disease Control and Preven-
    tion, 266
US v. Philip Morris USA Inc, 279

valence issues, 150–51. *See also* alcohol
    abuse; child abuse; drug abuse
Veblen, Eric P., 295
Vogel, David, 15, 119, 177

Walker, Jack L., 17, 37, 42, 43, 44, 45, 46, 54,
    123, 177, 179, 180, 182–84, 185, 186, 195
War on Poverty, 141

Waste, Robert, 50, 90
Wayne, Leslie, 200
Weart, Spencer, 47, 50, 51, 60–61, 64, 66,
  69–70, 108, 262, 263, 291, 301
Weingast, Barry R., 77, 199
Weisberg, Herbert, 145
welfare programs, 225, 284
Wessel, David, 245
Wildavsky, Aaron, xxiv, 9
Wilderness Society, 188
Wilsford, David, 178
Wilson, James Q., 41, 44
Wilson, Rick K., 130

Wolfe, Michelle, 274
Womach, Jasper, 271
Women's Christian Temperance Union
  (WCTU), 154
Wong, Kenneth, 34, 221, 221n, 223
Wood, B. Dan, 72n, 218
Wood, Robert S., xxi, 256, 274, 278, 279
Woodhouse, Edward J., 60, 66, 68
Woods, Brian, 203
Workman, Samuel, 281
Worsham, Jeffrey, 270, 271–72, 281
Wright, Deil, 143
Wrightson, Margaret T., 77